Patrick Crowhurst is Honorary Visiting Fellow at Leicester University. He is regularly published by the Central European Studies Journal Kosmas and taught for many years at Slezska Univerzitá in the Czech Republic. An expert on Czech and Central European History, he has also written widely on British and French trade in the nineteenth century.

HITLER AND CZECHOSLOVAKIA IN WWII

Domination and Retaliation

PATRICK CROWHURST

I.B. TAURIS

LONDON · NEW YORK

Published in 2013 by I.B.Tauris & Co Ltd
6 Salem Road, London W2 4BU
175 Fifth Avenue, New York NY 10010
www.ibtauris.com

Distributed in the United States and Canada
Exclusively by Palgrave Macmillan
175 Fifth Avenue, New York NY 10010

International Library of Twentieth Century History 52

ISBN 978 1 78076 110 7

A full CIP record for this book is available from the British Library
A full CIP record for this book is available from the Library of Congress

Library of Congress catalog card: available

Typeset by Newgen Publishers, Chennai
Printed and bound by CPI Group (UK) Ltd, Croydon, CR0 4YY

CONTENTS

ACKNOWLEDGEMENTS

It gives me great pleasure to be able to thank the many individuals and institutions who have helped to make this research possible. The support of the British Academy over a number of years has enabled me to visit many record offices in Britain, Germany and the Czech Republic. Without this support the research would not have been possible. Encouragement and help has come from many people and it is impossible to give due credit to them all. However, Phil Cottrell has given great encouragement and shared his extensive knowledge of modern Czech economic history. On at least one occasion he directed me to sources I would not have known about otherwise. Understanding the history and cultural background of German-Czechoslovak relations has been a formidable task for an Englishman. Without the help and encouragement of Miroslav and Libuše Chleboun and the many other Czech and Slovak friends, especially colleagues and students at the Obchodný Fakulta of Slezska Univerzità in Karviná in the Czech Republic and the Akademia Vzdelavania in Bratislava, the task would have been impossible. I am grateful to them all. Polish friends, especially Zigmunt Rakowski, have helped me to understand the history of Czech–Polish relations in the politically sensitive part of Northern Moravia and the continued (fortunately muted) tensions there. The other area in which individuals have been crucial to this research has been in archives and museums in the three countries. Many people have been very helpful and have gone out of their way to obtain important documents. In Britain I am particularly grateful to Stephen Walton at the Imperial War Museum Archives at Duxford. In the Czech Republic, Dr Štěrbová at the Zemský archiv in Opava provided invaluable help. I am also grateful to Dr Jiři Novotny at the National Bank archives in Prague. Tomasz Hoskins at I.B. Tauris has also given great encouragement. My thanks are finally to my long-suffering wife, Helen, for her understanding and continued support.

TABLES

MAP

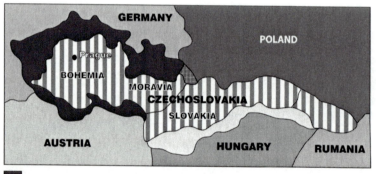

 SUDETENLAND Czech Territory ceded to Germany at Munich, September 30th 1938

Czech Territory given to Hungary by Germany and Italy at Vienna, October 2nd 1938

Czech Territory annexed by Poland November 1, 1938

INTRODUCTION

Czechoslovakia lost the Sudeten German borderlands to Germany after the Munich Agreement in September 1938. Approximately six months later German troops occupied the remaining part of Bohemia and Moravia and declared it a German protectorate. Czechoslovakia had existed for little more than 20 years. For many Germans, it was a state that should never have been created. In some ways it was the product of unforeseen circumstances rather than a gradual and inevitable political process. Earlier, in the second half of the nineteenth century, there had been a rise in Czech nationalism, which reflected growing Czech financial power as industry developed. The Czechs built a national theatre, created savings banks and other financial institutions, established large cultural and social societies and demanded a greater share in the government of Bohemia, where Czechs were in a majority. But Czech politicians were not united and the Germans were able to deny them any significant increase in political power. During the First World War, contrary to later Czech claims, Czechs generally served loyally as soldiers in the Austrian army. There were no mass desertions and when Czech prisoners in Russia asked to fight against the Austrians, their request was refused. It was only later, when Tomáš Masaryk visited Russia, that the Czech Legion was formed, but it did not see service in the First World War. However, there were Czechs who fought with distinction in the French and Italian forces and these had helped to raise the political profile of Czechs by the time the war ended.

Emergence of the Czech state

Within the traditional Czech lands of Bohemia and Moravia, Czech politicians demanded autonomy, not independence, during the First World War. It was the decision by US President Wilson to create nation states – the right to self-determination – that significantly changed the situation, though Britain did not want the Austro-Hungarian Empire to collapse. The Emperor of Austria Franz Joseph offered the Czechs autonomy, but he was too late. The first step towards the creation of a Czech and Slovak republic was taken by Czech politicians independently in Prague. When the fighting was coming to an end in October 1918, the Romanian military garrison in Prague returned home. On the 28th the Prague National Council, consisting of representatives of all political parties, proclaimed itself to be the new government. The following day the Slovak representative, Dr V. Šrobár, was appointed a member of the Council. He was a supporter of Tomáš Masaryk, a former Professor of Philosophy at the Czech University in Prague, who had become the leader of the Czechs in exile during the war. Šrobár declared in Turčanský Sv. Martin that 'the Slovak nation is both by language and history a part of a united Czechoslovak nation'. This laid the basis for a single Czech and Slovak state. The Council elected Masaryk as the first President of the democratic Czechoslovak Republic. He returned to Prague on 21 December 1918. But the new state had to wait for official recognition from the Allies and the boundaries had to be decided at Versailles. There, the Czech and Slovak delegations were invited to present their case for defining the new state and the frontiers were established by the treaties of St Germain with Austria (September 1919) and Trianon with Hungary (June 1920).

These treaties created the First Czechoslovak Republic and guaranteed the rights of all citizens, including the minority Germans, Hungarians, Poles and Ruthenes (Ukrainians or Little Russians). But the creation of this new, Czech-dominated state roused fierce antagonism among the German population. Not only did they lose their former dominant status, but many felt that they were being unjustly denied the right to self-determination that had been given to others. They thought little of Czechs in general and even less of Slovaks.

German opposition ranged from sadness to indignation. The picture of Emperor Franz Josef that had hung in every school and public office and was a familiar sight to all Germans was replaced by one of Masaryk, who was virtually unknown to them. Many Germans felt so strongly that they tried to join their areas to the adjoining German or Austrian provinces. But this attempt to break away and ignore the treaty of St Germain was crushed by former members of the Czech Legion, who had fought in France and Italy. Many Germans fled and there was some loss of life. The result was that Czechs regarded Germans as politically unreliable and never gave them the full legal rights enjoyed by Czechs and Slovaks. This remained a source of discontent throughout the short history of the First Czechoslovak Republic. It reflected anger on both sides. Austrians demonstrated in Vienna against 'Czech tyranny' in 1919.[1] The feeling was mutual. The Czech attitude towards Germans was reported by Michael Spencer-Smith, sent to Prague as representative of the Bank of England to negotiate the transfer of the assets of the Anglo-Austrian bank. He wrote: 'The hatred of the Czechs for the Austrians is intense and colours every thought and action. The Austrians are treated like dirt ...'[2] German politicians, reflecting this mood among their compatriots, initially refused to take any part in the political process of creating the new Czechoslovak Republic.

The industrial development of the new state

Although the Republic was riven by deep political divisions, in theory the new state had many economic advantages. It had been given the major part of the industries of the former Austro-Hungarian Empire and had a well-educated and experienced population to exploit them. What proportion of these were German and Czech it is impossible to state with any certainty, for many ambitious Czechs had learnt German and became assimilated into German society as a means of gaining economic and social advantages. There were similar problems over ethnicity in the Slovak lands, where Hungarian had been imposed as the state language and the Slovak language and culture suppressed. What is clear, however, is that in the Sudeten area along the German and Austrian frontiers, there was a wide variety of successful industries: coal mining and quarrying, chemical, textile, glass and porcelain, civil and mechanical engineering and musical instrument making. In reality, many of these faced serious difficulties in the new state. In the textile industry, for example, some spinning and weaving mills were now separated because they were in different countries. Some manufacturers had to import raw materials instead of buying them within the former Empire. All faced the difficulty that they could produce more than the new Czechoslovak Republic could consume, and the surplus had to be sold abroad across tariff barriers, which reduced their competitiveness. The new successor states (Austria, Hungary, Romania and Yugoslavia) were anxious to establish their own industries and used tariffs as a way of excluding Czechoslovak competition. The former tariff-free Empire, stretching from West Bohemia to Romania and from southern Poland to the Balkans had disappeared. Many of the workers in these factories facing new competition were Sudeten Germans (Germans living in the western border area of the new state). Unemployment, or the fear of it, increased their antipathy towards the new Czech-dominated government, which appeared to have little interest in their problem.

The creation of the new Czechoslovak currency

The first priority for Alois Rašín, the new finance minister, and the government was to establish Czechoslovak control over the state's assets. A census of the population and their property was carried out to see what these consisted of. The next step was to isolate the country from the economic uncertainty and inflation in the neighbouring states. The frontier was officially closed to prevent the movement of currency into or out of Czechoslovakia and all banknotes in the country were overprinted. These became the only form of legal money in Czechoslovakia. The next step was to replace these overprinted notes with new ones and fix the exchange rate of the new Czechoslovak crown in relation to other currencies. All this was carried out smoothly and efficiently, though the initial exchange rate was too high. The new currency created economic stability and Sudeten German businessmen and workers were able to see the benefits of belonging to the new state in comparison to the uncertainty elsewhere. As a result, the attitude of the Sudeten German population began to change and their politicians became more willing to take part in Czechoslovak politics.

The transfer of industrial control

The Czechoslovak government also wanted to establish control over the state's assets, especially its industries. Originally these had been financed by Austrian and Hungarian capital and, until the First World War, Vienna had been the centre of Central European finance. As a result, Viennese banks were major shareholders in Czechoslovak companies, whose head offices were situated in Vienna. Rašín ordered that all head offices of Czechoslovak companies should be moved to Prague and this was followed by the transfer of shares from Vienna to Prague. This was only possible because foreign capital was invested in Czechoslovak companies and banks. The difficulty facing Czechoslovakia was that the Czech banks were not as large as the Viennese. Before the war Prague had been no more than a provincial capital. There were large Czech investments, but they were mainly in savings institutions and not in commercial banks.

The largest Czech bank, the Živnostenská banka, was a major investor in Czech industry.[3] The second, the Agrární banka, attracted the funds of small agricultural, financial institutions, especially local agricultural companies and credit cooperatives. Others, formed before the First World War, specialised in different areas of business and had been helped by a wave of nationalism in 1903, which had led many Czechs to transfer their investments from German to Czech banks. The Czechoslovak government solved the problem of national control by ordering that branches of Austrian banks in the new Republic should become Czechoslovak institutions and sever their links with the parent banks. The result was that Czechoslovak banking in the interwar period consisted of Czech banks, led by the powerful Živnostenská banka, several Czech-German banks, some German banks and one Anglo-Czech, the Anglo-Czechoslovak Bank (formerly the Czech branches of the Anglo-Austrian Bank).[4]

Foreign investment in industry

The replacement of Viennese by Czechoslovak capital was only possible with large American, French and British investments, some of which were in banks (which owned companies' shares) and companies. Before the war, Britain, France and Germany had been the major creditor nations in the world, but after 1918 Germany was replaced by France.[5] Britain was still the largest investor, but most of British capital went to the British Empire. Comparatively little British finance (8 per cent) went into Europe. On the other hand, more than half of all French investment (60 per cent) was in European business. The USA, also a major financial power after the First World War, also invested considerable sums in Europe – much more than France – but these only amounted to 30 per cent of American overseas investments.

But this only tells part of the story. Foreign investment in Czechoslovak business was by no means evenly spread. Some industries were more important economically and strategically. One was mining and metallurgy – coal, iron and steel – and Britain invested far more in this (61 per cent of foreign investments) than any other foreign country (second was France with 15 per cent).[6] Closely linked to the iron and steel industry was Škoda, which had been the main armaments industry in the Austro-Hungarian Empire. One of the main Allied concerns at the Versailles peace negotiations was that this should not be owned by Germany or Austria. Immediately after the Versailles Treaty had been signed, the French company Schneider et Cie bought 73 per cent of the shares.[7] Thereafter, when more were issued, Schneider bought some of them. Although the French majority holding was never in doubt, it was not clear what proportion the French company owned. French ownership of the majority of the shares did not However, mean that the French dictated commercial policy. The French were content that their control of Škoda, as in other French investments, had prevented it remaining in German hands.

This French interest in strategically important industries was not confined to Škoda. One of the other important French investments was in the oil industry, which was becoming more important with the development of motor transport after the First World War.

The French bought control of Apollo, an important company that refined Romanian oil.[8] Founded in 1895 in Bratislava, the company was Hungarian, with headquarters in Budapest. Apollo bought Romanian oil, transported it by barge via the Danube, refined it at its own refinery in Bratislava and produced paraffin and lubricating oil. These were carried by rail to markets in the main cities and manufacturing centres in the Empire. But by the end of the First World War the company was also beginning to produce petrol. In 1924 the headquarters were moved from Budapest to Prague and the company was registered as Czechoslovak, with a share capital of 7 million Czechoslovak crowns. Finance for this transfer came from France: the Societé Français des Pétroles de Malopolska and the Crédit Générales des Pétroles. Motoring developed in the 1920s in Czechoslovakia: cars were made by Laurin and Klement (later bought by Škoda), ČKD (Českomoravské Kolben Daněk) and Tatra. These companies also made commercial vehicles. Besides these there were smaller firms such as Aero which made lightweight two-seaters, and others which manufactured rudimentary canvas covered vehicles (cyclocars). Motorcycles were made by Jawa and other small firms. All helped to create a market for petrol and Apollo decided to have its own petrol stations. The firm increased its capital in 1925 to 12 million crowns (60,00 shares) and used the additional shares to merge with a Czechoslovak company which owned petrol stations. French control of Apollo thus gave it an important stake in the Czechoslovak industrial economy.

The rest of Czechoslovak industry was dominated by three companies: Vítkovice Mining and Foundry Works in Ostrava, the Mining and Metallurgic Company in Třinec and the Prague Iron company in Kladno. These produced virtually all pig iron, and almost three-quarters of steel and rolled products. All were very large conglomerates, owning coal mines, coking plants and related industries. Like other companies in the Austro-Hungarian Empire, they had formed a cartel before the war and continued to dominate the industry during the First Republic, gradually absorbing most of the smaller producers. Their evolution from Austrian to Czechoslovak companies shows how the change took place.

Vítkovice had originally been founded jointly by the Viennese branch of the Rothschilds and the Guttmann brothers, Viennese financiers. After the war, although the shares were still in the same hands, all accounting was done in Paris and the company's representative was Eugène Rothschild.[9] The Viennese branch of the Rothschilds had transferred much of its capital to Paris and it was the Rothschilds rather than the Guttmanns who set the pace of modernisation and increased the company's efficiency and output. The second firm was the Mining and Metallurgic Company of Třinec. This was also situated in the North Moravian coalfield, east of Ostrava. It was an area with a mixed Czech, German and Polish population, in which it was widely believed that Poles formed a majority and which Poland claimed, unsuccessfully, after the First World War.[10] It was also an area in which the workers were increasingly attracted to Marxism, and strikes had broken out in 1920. The result was that the value of the shares had declined and German and Austrian shareholders had decided to sell. But because of the size of the company, even the Živnostenská banka had insufficient capital to buy the majority of these shares. In 1920 after lengthy negotiations it was left to the important French iron and steel company, Schneider et Cie-Creusot, to buy a controlling interest.[11] The third company in this group, the Prague Iron Company, had originally been the major steel producer before the First World War and was the principal shareholder in the Österreichische Alpina Gesellschaft. In the spring of 1919 the Niederösterreichische Escomte Gesellschaft, the main shareholder, bought the shares of the Alpina company and later, in 1926, transferred a major part (57 per cent) to the German Vereinigte Stahlwerke. Czech control of the company was maintained through directors who represented the Czech Escomte Bank and Credit Institute in Prague, which before nostrification (Czech control) had been part of the Niederösterreichische Escomte Gesellschaft in Vienna, and which retained an important presence on the board.

Major Czechoslovak companies

This industrial expansion was typical of Czechoslovak companies in the 1920s. Škoda was the outstanding example of a company that changed from being an armaments manufacturer to a company with a wide variety of industrial interests.[12] The Austrian owner, Karel Škoda, was replaced by Josef Šimonek, who linked the company to the large and influential Czechoslovak Agrarian Party. Many of the managers were also members of this party and the Živnostenská banka was an important shareholder. Schneider Creusot provided financial stability and management expertise to help with reorganisation to reduce the very high production costs. From 1919 Škoda began to design and manufacture locomotives, diesel engines, brewery and sugar refining equipment, agricultural implements and buses (many for relatively undeveloped countries such as Afghanistan, Indonesia and China) and equipment for breweries and sugar refineries. Repayment was spread over a number of years, but financed by foreign (mainly British) loans negotiated by the finance director, Karel Loevenstein, in 1923. In the opinion of one Dutch rating firm, this loan established Škoda as the largest European engineering company. Three years later Loevenstein negotiated an even larger loan – £22.5 million.

The second half of the 1920s was a period of intense rivalry between Škoda and ČKD, which produced a similar range of products. There was a serious clash in the mid 1920s when ČKD claimed that Škoda's monopoly of supplying arms to the Czechoslovak army enabled it to charge unrealistically high prices and discouraged research. However, this did not end Škoda's monopoly. In 1928 it signed a new contract with the Ministry of Defence worth 451 million crowns but also promised to build new armaments factories at Dubnica nad Váhom in Slovakia and Adamov near Brno that would be less vulnerable to German attack. In the second half of the 1920s Škoda's exports rose from just under 690 million crowns in 1926 to 1,638 million crowns in 1930. This reflected a rapid rise in output in 1928–9 which was roughly double that of its rival ČKD.[13] In the 1930s both survived the Depression, mainly by sales of armaments to Romania, Czechoslovakia's ally in the Little Entente, and payments for earlier sales. As the Depression ended and the threat from Germany increased under Hitler, both companies took an active part in equipping the country for possible war. Both produced tanks, guns, weapons of all types, motor vehicles and other forms of military *materiel*.

Another major Czechoslovak company with a European reputation was the boot and shoe manufacturer Bat'a.[14] Whereas Škoda's success was built on scientific knowledge and engineering experience, Bat'a's was based initially on village craftsmanship. From humble beginnings, by the end of the First World War this firm had grown into a major manufacturer of boots and shoes. Tomáš Bat'a, the firm's founder and driving force, had gained first-hand experience of factory production by working in American factories and based his approach to factory production on Taylor's theory of Scientific Management, using the most modern machinery and methods of manufacture. Workers were trained to perform simple tasks efficiently and quickly and output was governed by the speed of the assembly line. Employees worked as teams and it was in their joint interest to maximise production and maintain a high quality. Under Bat'a's control, output rose and prices fell, driving many smaller firms out of business.

The story of the Bat'a company during the First Republic is one of steady progress. The company expanded to cover all aspects of production from the purchase and preparation of leather and other raw materials to manufacturing and sales. Tomáš Bat'a claimed that he wanted to provide simple, cheap, good quality shoes for the whole world. His factory at Zlín became a large industrial complex which included not only the manufacture of boots and shoes but also the machines with which these were made. But Bat'a was not simply a hard-driving taskmaster. He created a factory town in which all the employees, managers and workers alike were well housed in modern buildings. He also provided a school and college for training workers, a hospital, hotel and leisure facilities. When foreign countries threatened to block imports of his shoes in the 1930s, he established factories there which were largely self-supporting, though linked to the head office at Zlín by a common work ethic and methods of business. He was also unique in insisting that all his employees who worked overseas should respect local customs. But above all, Bat'a created a worldwide, commercial empire. Within Czechoslovakia Bat'a made boots and shoes, motor tyres, machinery, socks and stockings. The company also owned quarries, an advertising agency, a film company, an airline, a shipping company, a company savings scheme and made light aircraft. The company also had a subsidiary, Omnopol. This had originally been created to sell Bat'a products overseas. But it also acted as agent for many small companies that wanted to import and export but could not afford to employ their own staff. The basis of this commercial empire was efficient manufacture and carefully planned marketing. Managers of Bat'a shops who achieved sales above the company targets were well rewarded. Those who failed to meet the targets were penalised. It was said that being a manager of a Bat'a shoe shop ended either with making a man rich or driving him to suicide. But Bat'a himself was a driven man who also took considerable personal risks. When sales fell disastrously in 1932 he cut his prices by half and advertised this reduction widely in a big advertising campaign. Sales soared and he was able to clear stocks that would not have been sold if he had followed the traditional policy of making successive small, piecemeal reductions. But he was forced to reduce production. He laid off 5,000 workers and reduced the wages of the others. Thanks to this, his business survived and although Tomáš Bat'a was killed in an air crash in 1932, the company continued to develop in the same way in the second half of the 1930s.

These were the main Czechoslovak companies which were the principal German target for exploitation. None was specifically German or Czech. There was also a wide range of other companies, many medium or small, which represented the range of Czechoslovak industrial strength in the First Republic. They included heavy and light engineering, chemical, glass making and textile companies. The common feature was an ability to innovate and develop beyond their original expertise. They showed a general sense of progress and prosperity, temporarily halted by the Depression, but recovering before the full effect of the Sudeten crisis and the Munich Conference.

Sudeten nationalism

While this is true of Czech companies, it does not reflect the feeling among Sudeten Germans. In the early years of the First Republic they had been involved in an unsuccessful struggle to maintain their independence of Czech control.[15] Although economically life improved after

1923, there remained a strong nationalist sentiment and the Sudeten German firms did not necessarily share in the economic progress. The nationalist sentiment was expressed, for example, in the *Sudetendeutscher Katechismus* published in 1923 and which followed a similar 'catechism' published in 1919. The author was Erwin Volkmann, a pseudonym for Erich Gierach of Reichenberg (Czech Liberec), who taught at the German University in Prague from 1921 to 1936 and then joined the Nazi Party and went to Munich. He claimed that it was the Germans who had the true historical claim to the Sudeten area, and not the Czechs.

The Czechoslovak government was aware of right-wing German attitudes and the danger this posed to the state. In 1927 a law was passed making it a serious crime to do anything that might undermine the unity of the state. Two years later the Nazi Party made its first appearance as the *Volkssport*, or to give it its full name *Verband Volkssport, Nationalsozialistischer Verband für Wandern, Radfahren, Spiel und Sport aller Art.* On the surface, this was no more than a sporting club organised by a minor right-wing political party. It was given official recognition – and approval – in April and was based in Fulnek. In reality it was a Nazi SA (*Sturmabteilung*) organisation that set out to indoctrinate young Sudeten Germans. Among the courses it offered was one on leadership (*Führerkurse*). This was not a course for potential leaders but one intended to teach the need to be disciplined and obey a strong leader: the *Führerprinzip.* *Volkssport* also taught paramilitary subjects: weapons training and map reading as well as a range of physical activities. The sessions were held as *Heimatabende*, stressing the element of German folk culture. The organisation gradually became more confident and its members began wearing a uniform with swastika armbands and jackboots. It was active in Prague among German students and Joseph Goebbels was invited to speak in February 1930. The banner announcing his visit stated: '*Achtung hier* [*ist*] *Deutschland. Der Nationalsozialismus marschiert. Burschen heraus zur N. S. Woche. Alle Mann* [sic] *an die Front.* [Attention. This is Germany. National Socialism is on the march. Contribute to National Socialist week! Everyone must take an active part]

This Nazi activity took place at a time of rising unemployment. Sudeten Germans were alarmed about their economic prospects and there was good reason for this. One example is Josef Kaub's machine construction and foundry company in Domažlice in West Bohemia, which expanded in 1927 but soon had to begin laying off workers. It did not recover until 1944. In September 1930, the Social Democratic Party and the *Gewerkschaftsbund* united and held a congress in Prague to publicise the rising economic hardship. Speakers claimed that unemployment among Sudeten Germans was higher than among Czechs. A speaker claimed that in 61 purely Czech districts there were 27,288 unemployed of a total population of 2.8 million. In 41 purely Sudeten German districts there were 27,042 unemployed out of 1.5 million. For the country as a whole unemployment among Czechs was 9 per 1,000 but 18 among Sudeten Germans. There were similar complaints from workers in the chemical, tobacco and clothing industries. This combination of rising unemployment and increasing Nazi activity led the Czechoslovak government to ban members of *Volkssport* wearing their official uniform. But all that happened was that they began wearing another: blue cap, white shirt and black tie. The cap badge had the monogram VS, which could be reversed to appear as SA. In neighbouring Austria, Nazi activity became more threatening. In 1931 Nazis tried to seize power in Upper Styria and in 1932 a memorial concert was held in Salzburg to commemorate those killed in demonstrations for Sudeten German independence in 1919. Membership of *Volkssport* increased in Czechoslovakia from 5,000 to 40,000 in 1932 and groups openly sang the Nazi song '*Die Fahne hoch*' ['Carry the flag high'].

Czech reaction

Finally the Czechoslovak government reached the limits of its tolerance. In September 1932 a group of Sudeten German Nazis in Brno were charged with organising Nazi storm troop groups under the guise of *Volkssport* and *Jungsturm* organisations. The trial was intended as a warning. Although the movement was intended to destroy the Czechoslovak state – a crime under the 1927 law – the accused were only given jail sentences of one to three years. But this was followed by the arrest and trial of five Sudeten German parliamentary representatives in January 1933 – an action which was criticised by the Communists who were afraid the same might happen to them ('We don't need a trial. Give us bread and work'). This was the start of a concerted attack by the Czechoslovak government on all members of extreme right-wing Sudeten German groups. In June 1932 the government proclaimed a state of emergency with fines of a maximum of 50,000 crowns. Forty-two Sudeten German Nazis from the West Bohemian textile town of Asch – which was suffering extreme hardship in the Depression – were put on trial for attending Nazi meetings in Germany. This was only the beginning. On 19 June the German ambassador in Prague reported to the German Foreign Office that there were 1,300 trials of political activists and 700 were in prison awaiting trial. Sudeten German students at the German University in Prague could not engage in politics. No activity calling for the union of all Germans in one state (*gleichgeschaltet*) was tolerated and another 98 Reich newspapers had been banned.

Official German support for Sudeten Germans

This marks the point at which the German Foreign Office began to become actively involved in the activities of the Sudeten German Nazi Party. The German embassy in Prague learnt of many Sudeten Germans in prison awaiting trial. This caused serious economic hardship for all their dependants. When this was reported to Berlin, funds were made available for their support, on Hitler's orders. But since all participation in this political activity, or even association with it, was illegal, the German diplomats had to be extremely careful to avoid disbursing this money openly and being accused of breaking the law. News of this money began to circulate among the Sudeten German political activists, who appealed to the embassy for help. The correspondence between Koch, the senior German diplomat in Prague, and the Foreign Ministry in Berlin show how the embassy was gradually forced to become the Nazi Party's representative in Czechoslovakia. Koch disbursed money to the dependants of activists, paid back money that had been taken illegally from union funds to pay for legal representation (600,000 crowns for the defence of the union leader Krebs) and eventually became Konrad Henlein's paymaster as the latter moved towards leadership of the apparently more moderate SdP (Sudeten deutsche Partei). He passed on considerable sums of money for Sudeten German (Nazi) newspapers and for election expenses at a time when Germany was very short of foreign exchange. Koch himself was not a Nazi. But he believed in the German superiority over Czechs and considered that the Sudeten Germans had been harshly treated.

This was the situation when Konrad Henlein swept to victory in the 1935 elections with 66 per cent of the Sudeten German votes. He represented apparently moderate Sudeten German opinion and struck a balance between the extreme Nazis and the moderate 'activists' who supported the Czech-led government. In reality, Konrad Henlein had received a great deal of financial help from Germany and from right-wing groups in the Sudeten German community. He was also an experienced organiser of mass community sporting activities. From 1935 Konrad Henlein followed a policy of pressing the Czechoslovak government for greater political power for the Sudeten German population but had to hold a balance between his moderate supporters and the extreme Nazis such as his deputy Hans Frank.

Hitler's plans to invade Czechoslovakia

By July 1936 Hitler had decided that he could start planning his eastward expansion: a continuation and development of Germany's eastern policy in the First World War (*Drang nach Osten*). His Order No. 23 instructed the army to plan an invasion of Czechoslovakia. Hitler realised that Henlein's pressure on the Czechoslovak government would not be enough to cause its collapse. Konrad Henlein was demanding an improvement in Sudeten German rights; but their status as second-class citizens did not change. There was still widespread discontent. Sudeten Germans considered that they had not been supported during the Depression and felt excluded from the renewed prosperity of Czech companies which were benefiting from government defence contracts. However, Henlein's bargaining position was weakened by the continued support given by Sudeten German 'activist' (traditional) parties to the Czechoslovak government. These continued to claim to represent Sudeten German interests and the government was prepared to negotiate with them on this basis. The speech by President Beneš at Reichenberg in August 1937 was conciliatory and seemed to show that the government was prepared to make reasonable concessions.

Unknown to Beneš, German plans to invade Czechoslovakia had been approved in outline in June. By July they had reached an advanced stage; the military garrison at Dresden would make the main attack. Additional military activity to the west would divide Czechoslovak military forces. These advanced preparations for war encouraged Hitler to hold a meeting with senior German diplomats and military leaders in November. The only record of this, the Hossbach memorandum, has been discussed at length because although it seemed to set out a plan of campaign – an attack on Czechoslovakia and Austria – this is not what actually happened. The main purpose of the November meeting was to prepare senior members of the Foreign Ministry and army for war in the near future, though they believed that war would not come before 1942.

The Anschluss and Sudeten crisis

Early the following year Hitler increased the pressure on Austria for a union with Germany. Hitler had already created the Austrian Legion of Austrian Nazis. These were trained in street fighting by members of the Leibstandarte 'Adolf Hitler' and were infiltrated into Austria. The Austrian Chancellor, Schuschnigg, resisted Hitler's demands and was summoned to the Obersalzburg on 12 February. On his return to Vienna he asked Britain for support and organised a plebiscite on the proposed union. Before this could take place, on 12 March Hitler sent German troops into Austria. Seyss Inquart replaced Schuschnigg and on 14 March Hitler entered Vienna.

These events were closely followed by the Sudeten German population. Hitler's success led the Sudeten German activist parties to ally

themselves with Henlein's SdP. This unleashed a wave of popular feeling among Sudeten Germans, who believed that it would quickly lead
to changes in Czechoslovak government policy. The situation is vividly
described in a telegram by Eisenlohr, who had replaced Koch as the
senior German diplomat in Prague:

> Following the merger of the German Activist parties with the SdP
> about 36 meetings of Henlein's movement with some 500,000
> members took place in Sudeten German area on Sunday March
> 27. Demonstrations naturally overshadowed by happenings in
> Austria [the Anschluss] and were characterized by very violent
> outbreaks of enthusiasm on the part of Sudeten German people,
> who expect complete reshaping of their destiny. In this connec-
> tion, understand from reliable agent that, for instance, [Nazi]
> Party flags were hoisted on town hall in Asch, accompanied by
> pealing of all church bells, during armed demonstration. Out
> of 34,000 inhabitants of Eger, 25,000 Germans deployed like-
> wise to accompaniment of church bells. Henlein's movement war
> standard was hoisted on town hall. Out of 18,000 inhabitants of
> Saaz, 15,000 Germans marched shouting "One people, one Reich,
> one Führer." In Görkau, where Government representatives had
> forbidden German salute, speaker commenced his speech with
> "On behalf of you all I salute our Führer and the entire German
> people with upraised hands." In locality where formerly Activist
> or non-party burgomaster went over to Sudeten German Party,
> this even was symbolised by hoisting German Sudeten Party
> flag on town hall to accompaniment of church bells.
>
> On orders from above Czechoslovak police and *gendarmerie*
> showed great restraint. At various places Government represent-
> atives were obliged to render military salute to Sudeten German
> Party flag. Population feel behaviour of police to be helplessness
> and abdication of civil authority. They reckon on complete *volte-
> face* after 10 April [probably a reference to the plebiscite on union
> of Austria with Germany] and possibly even Reich intervention.
>
> ... Party leaders of Sudeten German Party have recognised
> present enthusiastic mood as dangerous.[16]

This was followed by rumours that members of German athletic clubs were being armed and that the former *Ordnerdienst,* a paramilitary organisation that had formerly protected party meetings, was being re-created. Henlein tried to calm the situation by enlarging the SdP membership and enforcing discipline on members. But tension remained high. The Nazi Party, SA and SS in Austria were circulating rumours along the frontier that German troops would invade Bohemia and Moravia after the plebiscite that Hitler had called for 10 April to approve the Anschluss. It appeared that Sudeten Germans were being asked to prepare fighting units as soon as possible. Henlein reported that uniforms were being made in Krumau (Czech Krumlov) in preparation for the entry of German troops. Women's organisations were making swastika flags and importing many more illegally. Henlein felt that he was losing control of the situation and was being criticised by students in Prague who considered his policy too moderate. The Czechs responded by arming Czech civilians in the frontier districts, Sokol clubs, Red Guards and the frontier guards. Heavily armed, motorised Czechoslovak units were also formed. War was expected; the Czech Chief of General Staff, Krejči, had remarked to the departing Austrian military attaché, Longin: "We shall probably come to blows."[17]

Faced with the threat of war, France restated its support for Czechoslovakia, but this failed to calm the situation in the Sudetenland. On 9 April Henlein's, deputy, Frank reported that the situation in northern Bohemia was 'catastrophic and shattering'. Sudeten German opinion was turning against the Czech minority. Dr Eckert, Henlein's agent, reported that a 'single shot for Sudeten Germans would suffice to start a blood bath among Czechs'. At the same time, support for Henlein was being weakened by his willingness to negotiate with the Czechoslovak government. Sudeten Germans thought that he had abandoned his demand for autonomy. All he had achieved was a promise to move the elections, which offered to give the SdP greater power at a local level, forward to June. His failure to present a clear political programme was also damaging his reputation abroad. Hitler reconsidered his plans to invade Czechoslovakia. On 21 April in discussion with Keitel, chief of staff, he decided to abandon *Fall Grün* (Case Green), the planned invasion of Czechoslovakia, because of world opinion. He no longer had any confidence that the army could complete the conquest of Czechoslovakia in four days as originally planned. Instead, he decided to foment political unrest and hoped that this would provide an opportunity for intervention in the Sudetenland.

The next stage in the crisis was Henlein's Karlsbad speech on 24 April. Although if accepted, his demands would have breached the Czechoslovak constitution and undermined Czechoslovak democracy, Hitler expected that, like the Austrian ultimatum that precipitated the First World War, Henlein's demands would be rejected by the Czechoslovak government and provoke war. The German Foreign Ministry was finally informed of the invasion plans and told that mobilisation had already begun. All missions abroad were warned that war could break out. Czechoslovakia also prepared for war. In the May Crisis that followed, Czechoslovakia called up a large part of its army and manned the frontier defences. Mobilisation was carried out swiftly and efficiently. There were also rumours on the 18th and 19th of a German invasion and that four motorised divisions – part of a force of 11 divisions – had been formed north of Bohemia. The British consul in Dresden heard of forces massing in Silesia and northern Austria. There were also stories of Germans being taught Czech and roads from Chemnitz being full of troop convoys.[18] These were denied by the German Foreign Ministry. It is possible that German troops had earlier moved from their barracks in Dresden to take up positions near the frontier as part of the planned attack. Hitler and the German army felt that they had to be prepared for war. When the immediate crisis was past and the Czechoslovak government was persuaded to demobilise its forces, British diplomats were sent to the German–Czechoslovak frontier to check whether the rumours had been true. It was hardly surprising that they found no sign of the soldiers.

The situation in the summer of 1938 was that Europe had apparently come close to war. British Prime Minister Neville Chamberlain tried to discover the causes of the Sudeten complaints by sending Lord

Runciman to Czechoslovakia, but he was unsuited to the task, failed to understand what was happening and spent most of his free time with Sudeten Germans rather than Czechs. Runciman's mission had little or no influence on events. In any case Henlein and other Sudeten Germans had already presented their case to Vansittart and other British diplomats and politicians in London and had been able to create the impression that the whole Sudeten population was on the brink of civil war. This marks the final stage of the Sudeten crisis. Believing that only concessions by the Czechoslovak government could avert war and that Hitler's demands were reasonable, Chamberlain tried to find what concessions Hitler would accept. There followed the two meetings and the Munich Conference, in which Britain and France believed that they had averted war by sacrificing a minor power to a major. So little did Chamberlain really understand about the matter that it was comparatively easy for Hitler to fix the terms of the agreements and set the new frontiers.

This effectively destroyed Czechoslovakia as a viable state because it took away the frontier defences and a large part of Czechoslovak industry. It also encouraged Poland to demand the strip of territory north of Ostrava and the exodus of Czechs and anti-Nazi Germans from the Sudetenland was matched by a smaller flow of refugees from the territory seized by Poland. Public outrage in London, a British loan and public donations to the Lord Mayor of London's appeal to help these refugees marks the end of the First Czechoslovak Republic. It was only a short time before Germany took the remaining part of Bohemia and Moravia, encouraged Slovak demands for independence and began to assimilate the Czech economic and social assets in the preparation for war. The German army already had a good general idea of Czechoslovak industry (major industrial centres and numbers employed) from an earlier report in the 1920s. From the end of March 1939 they were able to seize everything of economic and military importance and the equipment of the Czechoslovak army. The German population of Czechoslovakia, not all of which was in the Sudetenland, expected to be once again in control and were potential allies for Hitler's plans to exploit the country. Czech weakness — their inability in a crisis to obtain help from their allies the USSR,

France and the Little Entente – suggested that it would be simple to exploit them in any way that Hitler and the German army thought necessary to help in the planned eastward expansion. Thus the scene was set for the final preparations for war on Poland and, later, the USSR.

CHAPTER 1

DEEPENING CRISIS,
THE MUNICH CONFERENCE
AND REFUGEES

Reduced to the bare essentials, Hitler's policy in the final Czechoslovak crisis of September 1939 and the subsequent dismemberment of what remained of Czechoslovakia was based on no more than bluff. Conditions in the Sudeten German area were never as bad as he claimed, though there was serious hardship and widespread discontent. Events which he claimed were 'proof' of Czech hostility were exaggerated or deliberately provoked. Nor was there any real risk of civil war in Czechoslovakia. Equally, there had been discontent in the predominantly Polish area around 'Teschen' (Czech Český Těšín, Polish Cieszyn) and 'Freistadt' (Czech Karviná-Fryštát) for a long time, but nothing to suggest that the area was in such ferment that a transfer to Poland would solve the matter. The same could be said about the southern border of Slovakia inhabited by a majority of Hungarian speakers or the Ruthene area in the extreme east occupied by people who were ethnically Ukrainian. Yet within six months of the Munich Conference, Czechoslovakia had lost territory to Germany, Poland and Hungary and the remaining Czech lands in Bohemia and Moravia had been seized and renamed the Protectorate. Czechoslovakia had ceased to exist, but without creating the peace and stability that Hitler and German diplomats had claimed would be the result.

Every move by Hitler was accompanied by violent threats of imminent destruction. He claimed in every case to be acting in the name of peace, trying to find a solution to events that were rapidly falling into chaos. He succeeded partly because he appeared plausible and because he was a unique head of state. Diplomats and politicians had never encountered such a man before in that position. He was the first twentieth-century politician to base his aggressive policy on the simple, Machiavellian thesis that anything was permissible if it was successful. His later policy from March 1939 to the outbreak of the Second World War was no more than a continuation of this. He wanted more living space for Germans. At the same time he was thinking of ways of disposing of (killing) as many of the inhabitants of these lands in Central and Eastern Europe and the USSR that could not be 'Germanised'. In the case of the Czechs, at the centre of this study, this would have resulted in a 'solution' that would have destroyed them as a people, either by starving them or turning them into some form of second-class 'German' people.[1] Fortunately for the Czechs, Hitler never had the time or opportunity to complete these plans and put them into effect, though German control of the former Czechoslovakia from 1938 to 1945 caused immense hardship. It also resulted later in the expulsion of virtually all of the Sudeten Germans in an act of revenge. Only those married to Czechs or who were regarded as pro-Czech were allowed to stay and they changed the spelling of their German family name to make them appear 'Czech'. The German presence in Czechoslovakia disappeared.

Prelude to the Munich Conference

By August 1938 Hitler's plans for invading Czechoslovakia were complete and the army had been persuaded that it could be successful. The Sudeten German political demands had been backed by German writers in Czechoslovakia and Germany, who claimed that the Sudeten Germans had never been treated fairly and that Czechs and Germans had hated each other for centuries. In Berlin, Rudolf Jung's book, *Die Tschechen; Tausend Jahre deutsch-tschechischer Kampf* had appeared in 1937 in a second, enlarged, edition. In 1938, as the crisis deepened, there were attempts to influence British foreign policy and public opinion by articles in *The Times, Observer, Daily Mail* and *Daily Express*. To this were added books such as the apparently reasonable pro-Sudeten German book by 'Diplomaticus', *The Czechs and their Minorities,* published in London. The earlier, measured, Czech response to German claims in Josef Chmelař, *The German Problem in Czechoslovakia*, published in Prague in 1936, had failed to carry equal weight. There were British newspapers that took a pro-Czechoslovak view: *Daily Telegraph, Sunday Times, News Chronicle* and *Daily Herald*, besides the important provincial newspapers *Manchester Guardian* and *Yorkshire Post.*[2] When the Slovak separatists were encouraged to seek independence in 1938, there appeared the strident *Should Britain go to war – for Czechoslovakia?* published by the Slovak Council in Geneva. This opened with a section headed 'Why is Czechoslovakia not worthy of being helped?' which set the tone of the whole book.

The earlier, liberal and pro-Czech views of Wickham Steed, former foreign editor of *The Times,* and Professor Seton-Watson carried no weight because they were out of favour.[3] Nor did the report by a group of British students in *We saw Czechoslovakia,* published in 1938. They declared: 'Is Czechoslovakia worth defending? To those of us who saw something of its achievements in the past 18 years and felt something of the passion of its people for democracy and social justice, only one answer is possible. We say "Yes."' Toynbee, writing in *The Economist* in July 1937, had also warned that if Britain ignored events in Central Europe the British would eventually either have to accept German domination of Europe or would have to fight to keep a balance of power. But there were more powerful influences on Chamberlain. Most Conservatives considered that fascism was somehow 'all right'. The influential Cliveden Set and the 30 peers and 30 MPs in Anglo-German fellowships also influenced him.

It was not merely Chamberlain's ignorance of Czechoslovak affairs and his urgent desire to avoid war that made the crisis from August 1938 so severe. What is clear from the British diplomatic correspondence is that the Foreign Office knew that Hungary and Poland were also pressing demands against Czechoslovakia. This widened the problem by threatening a more general European war. In the case of

Hungary, the Versailles settlement had awarded Czechoslovakia land on its Hungarian frontier that was occupied by a majority of Hungarian speakers. Hungarian hopes of regaining this territory had never disappeared, but had been held in check by the Little Entente. Hungarian relations with Romania and Yugoslavia were also in a state of 'virtually constant tension'.[4] During the August 1938 crisis the Hungarians attended a conference of the Little Entente at Bled and in return for a promise of non-violence were given assurances that the condition of the Hungarian minority would be improved, though this promise was never ratified.[5] There were also German–Hungarian discussions at Kiel, where Hitler promised Upper Slovakia to Hungary if the two countries jointly attacked Czechoslovakia. But Hungary was worried about possible action by the Little Entente in the event of a German–Czechoslovak war.[6] The German view was that Yugoslavia would remain neutral but the Hungarian army was still relatively weak and the government preferred a peaceful solution.

This crisis in August, accompanied by Czechoslovak mobilisation, made the British government anxious to try and find a solution to the problem that was not only about the Sudeten Germans but also the other minorities as well. Liddell Hart, writing to Anthony Eden on 10 September, offered an analysis of a possible German–Czech war to help the government form its policy. He stressed British military weakness (inadequate anti-aircraft defence) and the likelihood that Germany would attack Czechoslovakia from Austria, between Brno and Bratislava.[7] He thought that Germany might initially make rapid progress there. But he felt it would be unable to conquer the whole country quickly. The Czech army was capable of putting up a prolonged resistance, provided the Germans did not have total control of the air. The only help that the French could offer was to tie down German forces on the Maginot Line. Nor could Russia offer any more assistance. Its army was unbelievably slow, though it might invade East Prussia, if given permission by Latvia and Lithuania to enter their territory. The central problem would be how to remove the German forces if the initial stage of the war came to a halt. This might be done by economic pressure, and by demoralising the German troops.

This was a serious attempt to provide the government, via Eden, with a realistic military assessment of the situation. However, it had one serious weakness. It assumed that the German army had a battle plan to invade Czechoslovakia from Austria. This was unlikely. The *Anschluss* had taken place little more than a year earlier. No battle plan would have been made before then unless Hitler was working to a timetable that made the seizure of Austria a first step. There was no evidence for that. Nor was it likely that the German military planners would have had time to make a detailed invasion plan between the *Anschluss* and the August 1938 crisis. A further weakness was that any invasion from that part of Austria would require large numbers of troops and all their equipment, including tanks, to be moved by rail from Germany. The build up and initial manoeuvres to test the battle plan would alert foreign diplomats and the Czech army, which could take defensive measures. There was also a line of bunkers and defence posts to protect the southern frontier. It was much easier for Germany to plan an invasion based on the existing military base at Dresden. Even in that case, however, rumours about the initial troop manoeuvres reached foreign diplomats and the Czechs, who had time to prepare their defence.

A plebiscite seemed to offer a way out of this dangerous situation. It had become Henlein's chief demand, and therefore might solve the problem. But, as the Foreign Office memorandum of 11 September showed, opinions were mixed about whether it might prove a long-term solution.[8] The Foreign Office opinion was that, in any case, Britain had a moral and legal obligation to prevent aggression, especially since Britain would quickly be drawn into any general war. Alternatively, the races could be separated: 'No one wants to compel a person to stay in a state to which they are not loyal'. But if a plebiscite were held to establish popular choice, it needed law and order to guarantee that the results were fair. Also, if Germany were to take the territory after the plebiscite, a four-power conference would be needed to provide stability and give people time to leave. There was also the problem of German treatment of the Jews and the risk that the Czechs would resist and 'go down fighting'. This would be the first stage of dismembering Czechoslovakia. It was a perceptive assessment of the situation and was borne out by results.

Hungarian and Polish demands

Discontent among the Hungarian population of Slovakia also formed part of this crisis. On 14 September, the Hungarian Chargé d'Affaires in Prague asked what the British attitude was towards the treatment of these people.[9] The message was passed to the Foreign Office in London. In reply, Vansittart told the Hungarian ambassador that any concessions offered to the Sudeten Germans should also automatically be given to other minorities.[10] The Hungarian government moved quickly to exploit this. *The Times* had carried an article on 7 September on the possibility of the Sudeten Germans being given a plebiscite. On 15 September the British ambassador in Budapest, Sir G. Knox, was told by the Hungarian foreign minister that if the Sudeten Germans were given a plebiscite, Hungary would demand the same for its minority in Slovakia.[11] The same day, Chamberlain had his first meeting with Hitler at Berchtesgaden. Hitler appeared reasonable. He knew that he would not be able to invade Czechoslovakia before 1 October and in the meantime was concerned to keep up the pressure on the Sudeten German issue. Chamberlain, for his part, made his position as an arbitrator clear: 'In principle I had nothing to say against the separation of the Sudeten Germans from the rest of Czechoslovakia, provided that the practical difficulties could be overcome.'[12] However, far from easing the tension as Chamberlain had hoped, Hitler continued to raise his demands. In Czechoslovakia many expected war to break out. Sudeten Germans had no definite information about what was happening. Czech newspapers were heavily censored, no German newspapers could be imported and German information was regarded, correctly, as propaganda. Radios and telephones had been confiscated and all contact with the outside world was broken. To give one example of conditions in the Sudetenland, the German population of the textile town of Fleissen in West Bohemia were fleeing to Germany, terrified by stories of Germans being hunted and beaten by Czechs.[13] Factories, shops and businesses were closed and the town was deserted. There was a feeling of helplessness and that war was inevitable. The Czechs were equally tense.

Poland used this crisis to press its claim regarding the Polish minority in the Cieszyn–Český Těšín area in north Moravia. The Polish government, like Hitler and the Hungarians, claimed the Poles were being persecuted. On 16 September, Kennard, the British ambassador in Warsaw, reported that the Polish government was considering sending a note to the British, French and Czechoslovak governments demanding self-determination for the Polish minority.[14] The same day he also reported that if any concessions were given to the Sudeten Germans, the Polish government would demand the same for its people. When the Hungarian government learnt of this it demanded the same. Following the large increase in the military budget – which took the army above the limits imposed by the Treaty of Trianon – the Hungarian government was able to back its demands with the threat of military force.[15] But it was initially very cautious and although there was a partial Hungarian mobilisation, this was not announced officially.

While Hungary was cautious, Poland was more aggressive. On 19 September Knox reported from Budapest that the Polish and Hungarian governments were working together. The Poles had announced that if any Sudeten territory was transferred to Germany, Poland would seize 'Teschen' (Český Těšín – the Czech half of the former town of Teschen, divided by the River Olša).[16] The frontier was only lightly defended at this point and lacked the elaborate system of bunkers that had been built elsewhere on the German and Hungarian frontiers.[17] Poland backed this campaign of intimidation with an aggressive anti-Czech press campaign, and increased its forces on the frontier. The reason for this, as Kennard made clear in his report from Warsaw, was that it appeared that Britain and France were about to sacrifice Czechoslovakia. In that case, Poland would seize 'Teschen' and Britain would be faced with a *fait accompli*.[18] The same day, Knox sent a Hungarian note that proposed to unite the Hungarians in Czechoslovakia with 'their mother country' and asked for British support. Meanwhile, Poland continued to raise the political pressure. Kennard reported a rumour that the Poles were considering sending a note to Czechoslovakia demanding a revision of the frontier along ethnographic lines. This had originally been agreed by the Polish and

Czech National Councils on 5 November 1918, but was never carried out. Polish demands were backed by further demonstrations of a build-up of troops in Kraków, though the Poles insisted that force would only be used as a last resort. Similarly, the Hungarians claimed that military reinforcements sent to the Slovak frontier were merely defensive, matching the Czech troops already there. The Czechoslovak government, recognising Hungarian weakness, had not hesitated to strengthen its eastern frontier.

French and British policy

While pressure had been mounting on Czechoslovakia to make concessions to Hungary and Poland, France and Britain had been considering their own policy. Chamberlain believed that the Sudeten Germans should not be offered a plebiscite, because Hungary and Poland would also demand one for their minorities. The Czechoslovak ambassador in London, Jan Masaryk, also opposed giving the Sudeten Germans a plebiscite, though for different reasons.[19] In his view the [Czech] population would not agree to it. He also claimed that 'the areas in question have formed a territorial and economic part of the historical lands of Bohemia for a thousand years. If they, by hook or by crook, were attached to Germany, nothing would stand in the way of German expansion through East and South East Europe.' Ignoring this sound advice, Chamberlain proposed transferring Sudeten German territory to Germany. Some found the proposal deeply offensive. Colin Coote, writing to Eden on 20 September called it:

> ... a squalid scuttle. It is surely analogous in many points to the affair which caused your resignation ... You said there must be a settlement by agreement. This is a sacrifice of the method of negotiation and a surrender to a naked threat. You said ... that there must be no breach of our solidarity with France. This plan means bitter recriminations with France, leading to a dissolution of this solidarity. Already the rubber stamps which exist to supply Mr Chamberlain with a Cabinet are explaining that they were forced to surrender because France would not fight ... there

seems to be no limit whatever to the Nazi policy of blackmail. Personally I was not in the least concerned to keep the Sudetens within Czechoslovakia, but most deeply concerned with the method by which any change in their status was effected.[20]

Not surprisingly, the French initially resisted this proposal to transfer the Sudetenland to Germany. They were unwilling to abandon their Czech allies and were promised support by the USSR. But eventually they bowed to British pressure, on condition that the remaining part of Czechoslovakia would be guaranteed by Britain and France. This was the plan put to Beneš. On 20 September he rejected it, but was forced to accept the following day when it became clear that this was an ultimatum. If he had continued to reject the proposal, Britain and France claimed they would not have been responsible for the outcome. Unwillingly he accepted and the government fell. Chamberlain paid a second visit to Hitler, at Godesberg, to put the plan to him, but Hitler now raised the stakes. He refused to accept the Anglo-French proposal, claimed that Sudeten Germans were being massacred and insisted that German troops should be sent at once to protect them.

This sequence of events is now so well known that it is hard to realise that at the time few ordinary people had much idea of what was really going on. The Western press described events (both fact and fiction) and the public in Britain, France and elsewhere were made aware of the serious nature of the crisis. They also knew that Chamberlain was being forced to make concessions in the interests of what he regarded as world peace. For the ordinary Czech living far away from the Sudetenland, life was no doubt very different. The Sudeten German complaints were not new. Few can have realised how close the country was to being dismembered. The atmosphere is described most vividly in Mark Slouka's novel *The Visible World*, based on the experiences of his Czech parents in Czechoslovakia in this period. Hanuš, a Czech former inmate of the Mauthausen concentration camp, who returned from there a cripple, describes the events after the war to a 12-year-old boy.

"This is what I'm trying to say to you: For a long, long time, nothing happens. And then it does.

In a place called Berchtesgaden, a tall Englishman with a white moustache named Chamberlain unfolds himself from a limousine. Arguments are made. Tea is sipped. Important men stab their fingers at the polished table. *'Sie müssen... Wir werden... Etwas Tee, mein Herr?'* In Bad Godesburg this Englishman smoothes his hair with his right hand and says. 'I take your point, Herr Ribbentrop. And yet, if I may ... we feel that ... in the matter of ... Can I take that as your final position? And it comes to pass."

Mr Hanuš smiled. "Berchtesgaden. Bad Godesberg. Berlin. All those Bs'.

But you look around ... Nothing has happened."[21]

But in Prague a new Czechoslovak government was formed under General Syrovy who ordered mobilisation.[22] The August crisis had severely strained the existing Czechoslovak system of coalitions and the new government was intended to provide a stronger foundation for resisting German pressure. The cabinet consisted of specialists and individuals representing national institutions. They included the Mayor of Prague, Dr Zenkl and Dr Butovsky, head of the patriotic Sokol organisation. Political parties were excluded, minimising the influence of Henlein's SdP and party rivalry. A separate committee was formed to include political representatives, but the members were former ministers who accepted the Anglo-French proposals for the Sudetenland. Their role was purely advisory. Having formed a new government, President Beneš invited the Slovak People's Party for talks. The appointment of the new government calmed Czech fears but demonstrations continued in Hungary and Poland, each of which continued to move troops towards the frontier. Faced with Poland's determination to get 'Teschen' and British and French support for Polish demands, the Czechoslovak government finally agreed to cede 'Teschen' provided assurances of friendly cooperation were given in return.[23] Hungary, on the other hand, was only given British assurances that its claims would 'receive consideration at the appropriate moment'.[24]

Britain and France were more concerned about their reply to Hitler than dealing with Hungary. What ultimately swayed both Britain and

France was the apparent military strength of Germany and their own perceived weakness. Britain had begun to rearm and in at least two ways Czechoslovakia was helping Britain and should in turn have been supported. One was the Anglo-Czech cooperation between the Royal Small Arms Factory at Enfield Lock and Škoda. This was the development of a British version of the Czech Lehky Kulomet [light machine gun] ZB vz30 which became known as the Bren Gun – the standard British infantry light machine gun of the Second World War.[25] The other was armour plate supplied to the Admiralty by the Vítkovice steel works. In April a British technical expert, W. S. Walker of the steel company Firth, Brown & Co., was sent to Vítkovice to supervise a secret Admiralty order.[26] This was followed on 31 May by a report that a British draftsman, C. C. Bachelor, would also be sent there. Following a conference at Vítkovice in April 1938, the Admiralty had expressed an interest in buying about 3,000 tons of plate, which may have been in addition to the earlier secret contract that Walker and Bachelor were supervising.[27] On 28 September Newton sent a telegram from the British Legation in Prague to say that 200 tons of armour plates were ready to be delivered and suggested that they should be sent to Britain via the Polish port of Gdynia.[28] The Czech authorities had agreed to facilitate this export and Newton suggested that Poland be contacted to make the necessary arrangements. Both these items required continued Czech cooperation and should have ensured that Czechoslovakia received fair treatment, at least from Britain.

The Munich Conference

But neither Britain nor France felt that they were prepared to fight for what they considered a distant country that neither knew nor cared much about. France had hoped an alliance with Czechoslovakia would help protect against a resurgent Germany, not the other way round. Chamberlain wanted to avoid the horrors of another major war and had been informed in Cabinet that the British army was still weak, though rearmament had begun. If he had realised that his action in giving way to Hitler would have allowed Hitler to equip another 11 infantry divisions with modern weapons after March 1939, he might have thought twice before accepting Mussolini's suggestion. As it was, the proposal for a conference at Munich on 29 September was accepted and was greeted with relief by public opinion. At Munich Mussolini presented Britain and France with proposals that had been decided by Hitler in advance, but which Hitler pretended he had not seen. He welcomed them as a solution to the Sudeten problem. The discussions, which lasted for a total of 13 hours, resulted in an agreement to transfer areas occupied by a majority of German speakers to Germany in stages. The transfer was to begin on 1 October and be completed by 10 October. The four powers also called on the Czechoslovak government to settle its differences with Hungary and Poland as soon as possible. The negotiations were finally finished early on the morning of 29 September and the Czech representatives received a copy at 2 a.m.

The first official information given to the Czech government was a letter from Hencke, the German Chargé d'Affaires in Prague, to the Czechoslovak Minister of Foreign Affairs at 6.20 a.m. on 30 September.[29] This enclosed the text of the agreement that had been made by the four powers and invited the Czechoslovak government to send a representative and a military expert to a meeting of the International Commission. It assumed that the Czechoslovak government would accept the terms. The first meeting of the International Commission was to be held at 5 p.m. the same day, at the German Foreign Ministry. It provided virtually no opportunity for the International Commission to discuss the arrangements for the transfer, which was to begin the following day. The Czechoslovak government was also given very little time to reply. It was the Italian ambassador who was given the task of seeing the Czechoslovak president or 'some other high Czechoslovak official', urging him to accept the Munich Agreement and avoid any incidents during the transfer of territory.[30] At about noon the principal Italian, French and British diplomats met Krofta, the Czech Foreign Minister, who told them bluntly: 'The President and the Government submit to the conditions of the Munich Agreement which has come into being without Czechoslovakia and against her'.

When the French ambassador tried to offer condolences, he was cut short: 'We have been forced into this situation; now everything is at an end; today it is our turn, tomorrow it will be the turn of others.' When the British representative said, with some difficulty, that Chamberlain had 'done his utmost' he received the same reply. At 12.50 p.m. Hencke was informed that Mastný, the Czechoslovak ambassador in Berlin, and General Husárek of the general staff, would fly to Berlin. They reached the German Foreign Ministry in time to attend the second part of the session. By then the commission, which had begun the meeting at 5.30 p.m., had already agreed to appoint a sub-committee to handle the evacuation of Zone I (which consisted of territory with at least 90 per cent German speakers). The commission had also agreed that the supervision of the Czech evacuation and German occupation would be left to German and Czech liaison officers. This removed the matter from international control and left it in German hands. The other main issue, the defining of the areas in which a plebiscite should be held, was also left to a sub-committee. The Czech representatives were not invited to speak and the meeting lasted less than four hours. At no other time in history has a state been destroyed so quickly.

It is easy to condemn Chamberlain. Immediately after the war there was considerable discussion about the causes of Munich. The French historian Étienne Mantoux, writing in 1946, summed up the general sense of postwar frustration:

> In the dismal days of September 1938, when the best hearts were rent between a sense of honour and a love of peace, the life and liberty of Czechoslovakia weighed very little against the heavy pressure of the 'guilt complex' [of Versailles]. After all, was it not only a question of frontiers? The perils of the future lay not in frontiers or sovereignties, but in food, coal and transport.[31]

That sums up historical opinion after the war. In Prague, after the Munich Conference, Krofta tried to get the Germans to end anti-Czech propaganda and his deputy asked for details of the imprisonment and ill-treatment in Germany of an important Czech Foreign Ministry official. Both Krofta and his deputy stressed that this made it difficult for the Czechoslovak government to carry out the Munich Agreement. It was also the Czech wish that the agreement would herald a new era in Czech–German relations 'now that all points of friction, including, for all practical purposes, the Russian pact, had been removed by the Munich Agreement'. The Czechs wished for coexistence between the 'great [German] and the small Czech people, inspired by mutual respect'.[32] Hencke expressed similar views and asked for all Reich nationals to be released from prison as a gesture of goodwill.

Renewed Polish and Hungarian demands

The Polish government also renewed its pressure. About midnight on 30 September Poland demanded the transfer of the area of Teschen and Freistadt, and a plebiscite in the surrounding area, to be agreed by 2 October.[33] Its tone was peremptory and a summary was sent by the British legation in Prague to the Foreign Office. The language is similar to that used by Hitler and offered ample opportunity for further disputes on points of detail. The main points were:

1. The Czechoslovak [plan] is entirely insufficient and dilatory and [the] Polish Government can no longer have faith in declarations of [the] Czechoslovak Government.
2. [The] Polish Government therefore make[s] [the]following categorical demands:

(a) Evacuation of a certain defined area within 24 hours as from mid-day October 1.
(b) The cession of [the] remainder of [the] districts of Teschen Frysztat within ten days starting from the same date.
(c) Public utilities and communications in evacuated areas to be left intact and defensive works to be disarmed.
(d) [The] Question of plebiscite in other areas to be subsequently agreed between the two Governments with the possible participation of third parties.
(e) Persons of Polish tongue born in [the] districts of Teschen Frysztat to be immediately released from military service and all political prisoners of Polish origin to be released.
(f) A reply accepting or rejecting demands [is] to be given by mid-day October 1. Should [this] reply not be forthcoming or contain

a refusal [the] Polish Government will hold [the] Czechoslovak
Government solely responsible for the consequences.[34]

Beneš had appealed to Britain for support against these Polish demands.
He had pointed out that if the Polish claim was met, it would not only
take important coalmines but would also cut rail communications between the Czech and Slovak lands. But after Munich, such hopes of
support were in vain and on 1 October Beneš accepted the Polish ultimatum.[35] The same day Morton, the British military attaché in Prague,
informed Major General Ismay at the Committee of Imperial Defence
that the Czechs had offered to sell arms to Britain.[36] Although these
were a different calibre to the standard British weapons, Morton warned:
'If the four Power agreement involves the Czechs handing them to the
Germans, it will be necessary to keep a close watch on what happens
to them. If they are not used to strengthen German defence forces, the
Germans may endeavour to sell them to countries already armed with
weapons of a similar type [i.e. Romania, Yugoslavia], obtaining thereby
further political and economic advantages. Or the weapons may be used
in Spain, China, Palestine etc [Palestine was a British mandated terri-
tory].' This perceptive and important comment was apparently ignored,
with disastrous consequences for the subsequent war.

At the same time that Beneš was forced to accept the Anglo-French
terms, the Hungarians made a similar claim for self-determination for
Slovaks and Ruthenes.[37] But for Britain and France, the immediate crisis
was over. The Sudeten question had been settled, the transfer of land would
take place under international supervision and the future of the remainder
of the state was guaranteed. They also assumed that the Hungarian and
Polish problems would also be solved quickly and peacefully.

The four powers had agreed a framework for carrying out the Munich
Agreement that on the surface appeared reasonable. It provided for
international supervision of the handover of territory. Census returns
were available to establish the proportions of German and Czech speakers. Property in these territories was to be handed over intact and no
damage would be done to public utilities. A moratorium was imposed
which prevented companies with branches in the Sudetenland transferring goods from there to the Czech area.[38] The Czechs were to be

allowed to remove weapons, ammunition and artillery from their defensive system, which were in the first two zones.[39] There was to be provision for exchange of individuals and families who might wish to change from one ethnic area to another. Also, the rights of any Sudeten Germans who continued to live outside the new German territory would be protected. Many of the arrangements would take time to put into practice. It was also agreed that soldiers from Britain, France and Italy would supervise the transfer of territory.

But almost immediately questions were raised which invalidated the proposals: should these be regular soldiers or reservists? Should they be armed? What powers would they have? It was suggested that the British contingent would consist of members of the British Legion, but they were not suitable for this role. Instead, the British wanted to send regular troops. Italians proposed to use reservists. It was also difficult to agree whether they should be armed. This was only one problem. Another was the appointment of observers for the plebiscite, for which the Saar plebiscite was to be the model, and which would be held before the end of November.[40] Each issue had to be agreed between the four powers and by the Czechoslovak government. To simplify matters and try to make progress, sub-committees were created to deal with specific matters and these reported back to the main committee, of which the chairman was the German Foreign Minister. On the very first day, 1 October, the commission realised that the Czechs would not have enough time to remove guns and ammunition from the former frontier defences.[41] On 2 October the French agreed with the Czechs that they should be given extra time: 15 days to remove the heavy guns and ammunition.[42] The same day, Hitler told the German members of the commission his plans for plebiscites.[43] The demand for these had always formed part of his strategy for seizing the Sudetenland and he made it clear that he intended to take full advantage of this concession.

Transfer of territory

Where there was a large German majority, the area in which a plebiscite would be held should be enlarged to include surrounding territory. The Germans hoped they would get that as well. Hitler was prepared to exchange small German language enclaves for similar Czech ones. He would insist, however, that the area between Zwittau and Silesia – the whole northern frontier territory – would become German. The result of the proposed plebiscites would leave 300,000 Germans in Czechoslovakia. Of these, 140,000 would be in Slovakia and the Ruthene area, 30,000 of which would be in Pressburg (Slovak Bratislava), 18,000 in the language enclave of Iglau in Moravia, about 40,000 in Prague, 50,000 in Brno and the remainder in other small language islands. The Germans also wanted to have a plebiscite in Mährisch-Ostrau (the Moravian part, south of the River Ostravice, of the industrial city of Ostrava). Hitler believed that the majority of the population were Polish speaking (termed locally Slonzaks) and pro-German, and that there was also many Germans.[44] Success in this plebiscite would give Hitler control of one of the main Czechoslovak steel producers, the important Vítkovice works.

These were important details, but they were ignored by British diplomats. British public opinion had welcomed Chamberlain's claim to have achieved 'peace in our time' and avoid war. They were unaware of the way the agreement had been manipulated by the Germans. One of those who supported the agreement was Sir Roger Lumley, Governor of Bombay, who 'praised the courage of Chamberlain to avoid war'.[45] He believed that it was right that Chamberlain had saved the lives of 10 million or so by sacrificing 'under pressure and threats' the minorities in Czechoslovakia, which would not have been worth a war. He also believed that if Britain did declare war, it would be better to do it when the country was better prepared.

Meanwhile, it appeared that the first stage of the transfer was going smoothly. In the predominantly German areas, the German soldiers were apparently given a warm welcome. Troops marched along streets lined with Nazi banners and crowds lining the streets giving the Nazi salute.[46] It was the same in the countryside, where smiling, relaxed German soldiers were welcomed as liberators from Czech oppression.[47] But these pictures were intended as propaganda. As one Sudeten, Eric Pasold, who had become by then a British citizen, wrote later:

It was with a heavy heart that I followed the advance of the German troops, read about border incidents, and looked at the

photographs of so many familiar places. There was a picture of
the barrier being raised at the frontier at Wildenau to let Hitler's
army enter, of the main street at Asch lined with cheering men,
women and children, of the historic market square at Eger packed
with people giving the Nazi salute, and of swastika flags everywhere. Yet I knew that the hearts of thousands of Sudetenlanders
were as heavy as mine, in spite of the photographs in *The Times*
which told a story of nothing but jubilation and flowers for the
Führer and his soldiers.[48]

Hitler had already made preparations for absorbing the Sudeten territory into the Nazi state. On 1 October Hitler issued an order appointing Henlein as Reichskommissar for the Sudeten territory.[49] His main
responsibility was the full incorporation [*Aufbau*] of the area into
the German Reich. But Henlein did not have supreme power in the
Sudetenland. This was reserved for the military commander of the
occupying forces who held the title *Oberbefehlshaber des Heeresgruppen.*[50]
This person had three tasks: the arrest of named political figures, the
issue of new (German Reich) laws, and the appointment of officials
to enforce the new legal arrangements. Germans quickly put their
own interpretation on the Munich Agreement. It had been agreed at
Munich that the Czechs would be allowed to remove weapons and
equipment from the defences, and they had been given extra time to
do this. But when Czech soldiers began to remove concrete anti-tank
'hedgehogs' on 3 October they were stopped by the Germans.[51]

Hitler had already decided that he would not wait for international
approval of the transfer, as agreed at Munich, but would immediately
incorporate the Sudetenland into Germany. One result was that Ernst
Woermann, Director of the Political Department, refused to accept
a British proposal that there should be international control of the
transfer. On 3 October, the International Commission gave way and
agreed that the neutral zone separating the German and Czech troops
would be supervised by Czech police until German troops arrived. The
commission also noted that a fight had broken out between Germans
after the occupation; Nazis were taking revenge on their opponents.
When Polish troops entered the Teschen area, Hungary demanded

that talks on the Hungarian minority should begin three days later, on 6 October. Henke, reporting from Prague, said that the Hungarians wanted Slovakia to be independent of Prague so that they could take control of that and Ruthene lands, but were opposed by Italy.[52] Poland, with an interest in small Polish minority groups in northern Slovakia, wanted Slovakia to be independent. There were also Slovak demands for independence from Czechoslovakia.

The question of plebiscites – a matter of interest to Hungary and Poland as well as Germany – was taken a stage further on 4 October. Germany proposed that the 1918 statistics should be used and where there was a 51 per cent German majority, the area should go to Germany. The Czechs opposed this very strongly and it was only after several hours' discussion that a French compromise was accepted: that the statistics of 1910 and 1921 were to be compared and an average taken. It was rapidly becoming clear, however, that the four powers were not going to let Czech opposition delay the process. The next day, 5 October, the four powers agreed the line of the new frontier, which German troops would reach by 10 October. Their decision was based on population statistics of 1918, and they agreed the figure of 51 per cent German as forming the majority population.[53] The Czechs argued against this, because it would give Germany control of a much larger area and cut important Czech road and rail communications. It would also leave Czech groups in German territory. To overcome the problem of minority groups, the Germans suggested exchanging populations 'as soon as possible'. The Munich Agreement had specified that people would have the right to move within six months and a German–Czech commission would consider the matter. A memorandum by Weizsäcker, the State Secretary, shows that Germany was using international support to defeat Czech opposition. Referring to Czech territory that he wanted for Germany, Weizsäcker wrote:

> ... it was just at that very point that there could be no tampering with the frontier line on the part of the Germans. Trifling deviations from the strict ethnographical determination of the zones to be transferred without a plebiscite were of course contemplated in the Munich Agreement in certain exceptional cases.

For the place under discussion, however, no amendment could be considered.

The Italian representative then made the following proposal. In order to meet the anxiety of the Czech delegates regarding the cutting of certain railway lines which would be absorbed into German-occupied territory, these railway lines should be crossed as late as possible – but naturally within the time limit fixed for 10 October. The Czech and German authorities should also get in touch with each other at once, to regulate this through traffic, also for the period after German occupation.

The German delegate urged the Czechs to deliver their answer to the proposal of the four powers immediately, if possible in the course of the evening but at the latest by midday on 6 October [the following day]. The difficulties entailed by a delay in this answer were obvious – the entry of the troops on 6 October was imminent. The Czech representatives were then, at a suitable moment, confronted with the protocol of the session of midday on the 5th, which the four powers had already agreed on and were committed to.[54]

The episode demonstrates the way that Hitler was able to take the parts of the Sudetenland that he wanted for strategic or economic reasons. The Germans were able to produce maps that showed, or claimed to show, authentic records of ethnic distribution. Neither Henderson, the British ambassador, nor François-Poncet, the French ambassador, had any idea whether these were accurate when they signed the protocol. By the time the British government realised what had happened and reprimanded Henderson, it was too late. What both ambassadors wanted was a smooth transfer of territory that would restore cordial international relations. Hitler had stated that this was his last territorial demand. When the Czechs pointed to the effects of these proposals on the Czechoslovak economy, Attolico, the Italian ambassador, pretended to play the role of honest broker. The end result was never in doubt. German dominance was emphasised by the peremptory refusal to make any serious concession and by the German demand for immediate agreement. The same day, Hungary renewed its pressure on the Czech government by claiming that Hungarians were

still being persecuted. The Czech reply was to propose starting negotiations on 15 October, by which time the Sudeten transfer would have
been completed.

Encouraged by Czech weakness, Slovak separatists also increased
their demands for independence. The executive committee of the HSL
met on 5 October at Žilina and the Populists and all other Slovak
parties except for the Social Democrats agreed to pursue the Populist
demand for autonomy. This envisaged the transfer of power to a Slovak
autonomous government of five ministers, who were to be appointed by
Tiso, the vice-president of the Populist Party. The Prague government
was forced to give way and Tiso was appointed minister for Slovak administration on 6 October. What had formerly been Czechoslovakia
now became Czecho-slovakia, a federal state.

Resignation of Beneš

These events made it impossible for Beneš to remain as President. His
policy of cooperation with Britain and France and his support for the
League of Nations had totally failed to protect Czechoslovakia. It was
announced on 6 October that he would resign. He no longer represented Czech interests. Czechs regarded the Munich Agreement as a
national disaster and compared it to the Battle of the White Mountain
of 1620, which had resulted in Habsburg domination for almost 300
years.[55] Prague became a city in mourning, with people openly crying
in the streets. There was now a fundamental change in Czech politics.
Munich ended the political diversity that had been a hallmark of the
First Republic. In its place was a desire for national unity and strong,
authoritarian government. Western democratic ideals that had formerly
been the basis for government, were now rejected. In this new, authoritarian political climate the state centralised all institutions. Sokol for
example, the nationalistic gymnastic organisation, took over all youth
activities including the Boy Scouts. Separate legislatures were created
in Slovakia and Ruthenia and there was also a return to religion, including Catholicism. All this contributed to efficient government.

The main emphasis in Czech foreign policy was the desire to ally
closely with Germany. The immediate result was the appointment of

a new Foreign Minister, Chvalkovsky, who epitomised the new Czech subservience to Germany. His first request was that Germany should guarantee the new Czechoslovak state, but he was informed that this would not be done until all outstanding questions had been settled. One concerned the Hungarian minority. Hungary tried to exploit Czechoslovakia's weakness, appealing again for German support and claiming that Hitler had promised Pressburg (Slovak Bratislava) to Hungary. This new Hungarian demand created problems for Hitler. His dream of expansion eastward assumed that both the Czech and Slovak lands would become German puppet states. Hungary had recently announced a large military budget and had designs on the whole of Slovakia and the Ruthene area. If Hungary got these, it would block German eastward expansion. There was also the danger, from Hitler's point of view, that if Hungary gained the Ruthene territory it would have a common frontier with Poland. There had already been signs that these two countries had tried to form a common policy against Czechoslovakia and they might do the same against Germany. The German army expressed a similar fear and recommended that Slovakia should not be separated from the rest of the remaining Czech state. The initial German reply to Hungarian demands on 6 October was therefore evasive. Events in Slovakia had their own momentum, however. On 6 October the Slovak government was created under Tiso and announced an anti-Jewish policy and a willingness to settle outstanding territorial issues.

From the German point of view, these events appeared promising. A memorandum prepared by the Political Department for Hitler on 7 October recommended that Slovakia should be made dependent on the Czech government.[56] It would then be relatively easy to control if Germany dominated the Czech lands. Slovakia would become a puppet state. It was unlikely that Slovakia could become economically independent, but the country did have natural resources of timber and minerals. It also had part of the Czech armaments industry. The memorandum opposed a Hungarian–Slovak or Polish–Slovak union. Poland had been strengthened by seizing Teschen and might try to get Slovakia as well. As to the eastern Ruthene area, it was in Germany's interest that this too should be dependent on Slovakia and the Czech lands. Germany might expand eastwards beyond the Ruthene lands, and could use these as the basis for an enlarged Ukraine, which could include Ukrainians in Poland as well. Germany's policy should therefore be to encourage all people in this region to demand self-determination, since this would keep Hungary and Poland out. As to the German population of Slovakia, Hitler had no intention of moving them. They could form the nucleus for further German expansion eastwards.

German troops had meanwhile advanced to the demarcation line (the new frontier) agreed by Germany and the other powers. Control of the Sudeten territory had begun cautiously: initially Freikorps, SS and police were not allowed to take independent action. Nor were party leaders allowed to enter the new territory on 6 October. But once the transfer was completed Hitler paid a visit. He found that the Czech defences had been much stronger than he had imagined. If the invasion had gone ahead as planned, progress would have been much slower than expected and there would have been considerable loss of life. It would thus have been impossible to defeat Czechoslovakia before France could mobilise. Hitler also realised how valuable the defensive system and armaments were. He therefore decided that the Czechs should not be allowed to remove any guns or ammunition. On 8 October an order was issued to this effect, reinforcing the earlier action by German troops in stopping the Czechs removing anti-tank defences. By 10 October the German advance had been completed. Czechoslovakia had lost 39.7 per cent of its industry and 42.8 per cent of its factory workers.[57]

Refugees were leaving the Sudetenland for the Czech state; a total of 160,000–170,000 Czechs, anti-fascist Germans and Jews fled.[58] In the final stage of the transfer German soldiers were entering territory that was no more than 51 per cent German and contained a great many Czechs. This can be seen very clearly in the case of Opava, where German propaganda photographs showed a sea of German banners and gave the impression that most if not all of the population was Sudeten German. The reality was far different. The total population of the district of Opava was 64,000–66,000.[59] Of these, the Czech population of the town of Opava was 21,518 in 1930 and 9,452 in 1939.

In the district of Opava the figures were 31,765 in 1930 and 26,498 in 1939. To the east, in the adjoining district of Bilovec the figures tell a similar story: 40,025 Czechs in 1930 and 34,132 in 1939. The town of Opava was far from being totally German and Czechs were expelled or fled in large numbers. This example explains why some photographs, taken by inhabitants and not Nazi press photographers, tell a different story. In this case the soldiers received a far less enthusiastic welcome. In the village of Batošovice, about 35 km (20 miles) south-west of Ostrava, very few villagers made the Nazi salute as German troops entered on 10 October.[60] Most people seemed to be looking on in sullen silence. František Klečka, who lived there, said the village had only a small German minority. The official German report in the *Lagebericht* of 19 March spoke of a muted and hostile atmosphere (*Die Stimmung des Volkes ist verbissen und keineswegs freundlich*) in the occupied territory.[61] A military parade by a *panzer* division on the 19th (a Sunday) helped to emphasise German power. This was typical of the final stage of the German occupation.

Some Czech villages lay within the Sudetenland and were incorporated into Germany. One example is the district of Šumvald north of Olomouc.[62] In 1930 it had a Czech population of about 63,500; in 1939 this had fallen to about 47,500. Areas such as this, which had a predominantly Czech population, were more forcibly Germanised than those in the Protectorate. The active discrimination took the form of prohibition of all Czech cultural activities, the use of German instead of Czech in primary schools, the closing of secondary schools, the seizing of Czech farms, the expulsion of farmers and the imposition of forced labour. Czechs were also treated much more harshly by the courts than Sudeten Germans.[63] To complete the process of Germanisation, Volksdeutsch such as Gottfried Terza and his wife, Tyrolean Germans from Bolzano, were brought to take the place of Czechs who were expelled.

The remaining Germans lived in Prague, Brno and some isolated areas. These people had assumed that the Munich settlement would bring them similar benefits to those living in the Sudetenland. Their resentment was matched by that of the Czechs who saw the whole affair as a tragedy for their country. The rights of these German citizens had been guaranteed by the Czechoslovak government and the International Commission had ordered the British Legion to protect them. But there was a risk that they would be persecuted or would at least face opposition from Czechs. This caused Keitel, the supreme army commander, to inform the German Foreign Ministry on 10 October: 'If the situation in Brünn and Iglau assumes a *threatening* character for the Germans living there, it is to be reckoned with that the Führer will order the immediate entry of German troops into those areas.'[64] This was an example of Hitler's aggressive language and did not necessarily represent what was happening elsewhere in the Sudetenland. For example, when Eric Pasold returned to Fleissen he found a town that was quiet and little changed apart from swastika flags and having to drive on the right-hand side of the road. There was a shortage of coins, which were being hoarded, and people used postage stamps instead.[65] In Asch a similar action was taken, except that the stamps were overprinted, and given ten times their nominal value. The exchange rate was changed from 1 crown = 8¾ pfennigs to 1 crown = 10 pfennigs by the army and finally to 1 crown = 12 pfennigs by Göring on 10 October. This made him popular until people realised that they were no better off since costs were higher in Germany. It did, however, make items in the Sudeten shops very cheap for Germans from the Reich and led to a large influx of Germans looking for goods that were not only cheap but more easily found than in Germany.[66]

The completion of the German occupation and the Polish seizure of land had a profound effect on the Czech economy. Not only was a large part of the industrial capacity of the state lost, but so too was a large part of the assets of the major banks. For example, the Böhmische Union Bank (BUB), founded in 1872, had branches throughout the Sudetenland. It kept its German character during the First Czechoslovak Republic and had many Jewish customers. The transfer of the branches in the Sudetenland to German control officially dated from 1 November 1938, but even before then many branches had notices 'Deposits for Deutsche Bank accepted here'. Eventually Deutsche Bank took 23 branches, transferring the assets and liabilities. BUB only kept a few named customers. Separating these branches from the head office in Prague proved very difficult.[67]

The incorporation of the Sudetenland into Germany also had an effect on all road and rail traffic. On 11 October W. Hough wrote to Halifax from the British legation in Prague that the railways through the occupied territories were not working around Bohumin.[68] This had been one of the key railway terminals that originally had linked Vienna with St Petersburg and Prague with the Slovak lands. Hough reported that the railway from Poland had been torn up near the frontier. This line was the only one to Constanzia, the oil terminal in Romania, though the line had been blocked by congestion and there were in any case few trucks. If this report by Hough is correct – Prague is over four hours by train from Bohumin and this may have been no more than an exaggerated rumour – it was probably intended by Czechs or Poles to block railway links between the coal and steel city of Ostrava and Germany. Navigation on the Elbe, which normally carried goods almost to the Czechoslovak frontier, was also temporarily suspended. This was a serious blow to Britain, because the consignment of 200 tons of armour plates for the admiralty had not yet been sent from Vítkovice. Newton confirmed this by telegram on 13 October. Fortunately for the Admiralty, on 15 October Kennard, the British ambassador in Warsaw, was able to report that the Polish Ministry of Foreign affairs had approved arrangements for forwarding the armour plate from Bohumin.

If people in Britain thought that the Munich Agreement would usher in a period of peaceful relations with Germany, they soon found they were mistaken. On 11 October, the day after the Sudetenland had been finally incorporated into Germany, Hitler gave a speech in Saarbrücken.[69] In it he claimed credit for bringing 10 million Germans into Germany and made it clear that he regarded this now as solely a matter of internal German politics. Instead of expressing gratitude to Britain for helping to bring this about, he said that there were English politicians who were a threat to peace. He named Duff Cooper, Eden and Churchill as warmongers (Duff Cooper and Eden had both resigned from the government). He also made it clear that he regarded the threat from these men as very serious. He said there was a serious danger from international Judaism and Bolshevism, but his call for redoubled efforts to strengthen Germany's western defences showed that he regarded the threat as coming from the west, not the east. There was strong reaction in Britain to this, which was reported by Dirksen, the German ambassador in England, to State Secretary Weizsäcker.

> The point of view repeatedly emphasised by our friends in the Conservative Party seems to me to be particularly worthy of attention. It is said that the Führer, by mentioning Churchill, Eden, and above all Duff Cooper,[70] has given these individuals just the opportunity for emerging once more from the eclipse which they had suffered. The mere fact that the Führer actually considered them worthy of mention gives them a platform from which to publicize their views and aims with some hope of a hearing from the public. Chamberlain's position is thought to have been made thereby more difficult...[71]

The real purpose of Hitler's speech was to prepare the German people for war at some point. He had been denied the military conquest of Czechoslovakia. Keitel's earlier threat of war was also reflected in a request to the German ambassador in Tokyo to find out what Japan's reaction would be to a European war.[72] On 12 October Hitler informed the German Foreign Minister that he did not want to hold any more plebiscites and the International Commission should be closed as soon as possible. This would leave all matters to be discussed by German and Czech officials, with the inevitable results. Hitler also wanted to create effective links between Germany and Austria and said that Germany should aim to persuade the Czechs to allow a motorway and rail link to be built from Breslau to Vienna via Brno. He also planned to seize the important Vítkovice steelworks in Ostrava at some time:

> Regarding the Mährisch-Ostrau and Witkowitz area, the State Secretary is to ask the Polish Ambassador to come to see him and to tell him the following: In contrast to Germany's lack of interest in Oderberg[73], she is interested in Mährisch-Ostrau and Witkowitz. Future developments will decide whether Mährisch-Ostrau and Witkowitz are to remain in Czechoslovakia. If the

future of these areas comes up for discussion, we shall demand a plebiscite under international control.

As to the question of Hungary, Hitler's view was that the Hungarians had missed an opportunity to get the territory they wanted earlier:

The Führer invited the Hungarian Prime Minister and Foreign Minister to visit him at Obersalzburg and there advised them both to press their cause somewhat more energetically. In the critical days which followed, the Hungarians did nothing and this explains their present difficult diplomatic situation.

Hitler considered that Hungary should get the area in Slovakia inhabited by Hungarians and that Germany would do nothing to stop this. To reach a decision, discussions were held the following week between Germany, Czechoslovakia and Italy about the Slovak territory that should be given to Hungary. Slovaks and Hungarians both claimed Pressburg (Slovak Bratislava), once the city in which Hungarian kings had been crowned, the industrial city of Kashau (Slovak Košice) and a number of towns of regional importance. Meanwhile, Czech troops were occupying the southern Slovak frontier area and Ruthenia. The frontier had also been strengthened with an efficient system of bunkers that had been built since 1936.[74] Neither side would give way and appealed to Germany and Italy to arbitrate. Germany firmly rejected a Hungarian suggestion that the matter should be decided by a four-power conference (similar to Munich). Finally, on 31 October Hitler and Mussolini reluctantly agreed to act as arbiters and a meeting was held in Vienna on 2 November.[75] Weizsäcker made it quite clear to the major powers that the International Commission set up to settle the Czech–German dispute would not be invited to take part. Poland and Romania, which also had interests in the outcome, were also excluded, though Poland received some small areas of territory on the northern and eastern borders.

The Vienna arbitration finally completed the division of Czechoslovakia into ethnic parts. Czechoslovakia lost 4,760 square miles of territory and 972,092 of its population according to the 1930 census. Just over half – 53.9 per cent – were Hungarian. Hungary's population increased by 11.7 per cent and the territory by 13 per cent. Czechoslovakia kept Bratislava but lost Košice (70,000 inhabitants) and Užhorod (27,000). But this did not mark the end of Hitler's ambition in what remained of Czechoslovakia. On 21 October he ordered the army to be ready at any time:

1. To defend German frontiers and protect Germany against surprise air attacks.
2. To liquidate the remaining Czech state.
3. To occupy Memelland.[76]

Czechoslovakia had now lost about 30 per cent of its territory. The economy had been severely damaged, and it was widely expected that there would be high unemployment in the coming winter. The results for the population of the remaining Czech lands were serious and long lasting.

The consequences of Munich: political terror and the refugee crisis

The transfer of the Sudetenland from Czechoslovakia to Germany had three important results. It fatally undermined the economic viability of the remaining Czech and Slovak lands. After Hitler's threats, many of the Czech inhabitants felt they would not be able to live safely in the Sudetenland and fled to the Czech state, taking as much of their money as possible. This made the economic situation there worse. People who knew they would be victimised by the new regimes – principally Jews and members of German opposition parties who had attacked Nazi Germany – knew they also had to leave. This threw much of the textile trade into confusion, because most of the wholesale merchants were Jewish and they left unpaid bills.[77] The result was a flood of refugees from the Sudetenland. The same was true of the area in north Moravia occupied by Polish forces. Here there were similar reasons – the fear of ethnic persecution and the awareness of Polish anti-Semitism. This drove people from their homes. Hitler's orders to the army (referred to above) make it only too plain that these fears were fully justified.

In the case of Czechs, the statements made by refugees to officials in the regional office in Plzeň are witness to the scale of human distress.[78] The following examples reveal this human disaster.

Rudolf Plešák was born on 27 November 1919 in the village of Litice a few kilometres to the south-west of Plzeň.[79] At the time of Munich he was working for a business preparing cooked meat in the nearby village of Štěnovice, a few kilometres further out from Plzeň. The business was probably a small family-run shop with a kitchen attached, and he lived above it in a furnished flat which he owned that was valued at 120,000 crowns. He was also a member – probably an active member – of the Czech National Party. When the Germans completed their seizure of territory, the new frontier put his village of Štěnovice inside Germany. On 21 October the Gestapo arrested Rudolf – he was on their list of political Czech activists – and threatened to put him in prison. He fled to Plzeň.

Václav Jakuba was born on 21 January 1911 in Dobčany, south-west of Plzeň and was employed at the large Škoda factory in Plzeň.[80] He too found himself within the German Reich and was required to attend German political meetings. As a Czech he felt himself threatened and moved to Plzeň.

Václav Babka was born on 20 September 1891 in Tlučná, west of Plzeň.[81] He worked at the Škoda factory for 24 years. After the German military occupation he was told at the new German administrative office that there would be restrictions imposed in the frontier zone. He thought this would stop him working at the Škoda factory and west to live in Plzeň.

Josefa Kočarová was a widow, born on 18 March 1895, who had been living at Střibo, some distance west of Plzeň.[82] She too found herself living inside Germany. She had a small widow's pension, but this was too small to meet her needs and she depended on money sent by her children. Under new German currency regulations the transfer of money would be forbidden.

Immediately after the occupation, many people were arrested, some because they were on a list of political opponents, others simply at random. By 19 March the army, under orders from Konstantin von Neurath, had arrested 600 Communists. A week later this had risen to 2,500.[83] They were interrogated by the Gestapo and then many, thoroughly frightened, were released.[84] To hold an official post in a town was no protection. In letters of 9 November, it was reported that among the many people arrested in the small town of Kotterbad was the town's *Rechtsanwalt* Dr Singer, who was almost certainly Jewish, together with the tenants of both a lodging house for workers and a meat shop.[85] One person, presumably a Slovak, was expelled and sent to Košice. In another case, a number of citizens of a small village of Igla were arrested and later released with a caution. Scared by this news, another person, a tenant of a small business, also fled to Plzeň.

These brief glimpses of life under German rule in the month following the German occupation throw considerable light on German aims in the new territory. In the case of Rudolf Plešák, the Gestapo crushed political opposition by driving people out of the German territory and into the Czech. The Gestapo were fulfilling the first order that had been given to the army before the occupation had begun, to destroy political parties. It is very unlikely that Rudolf was a major figure in the local Nationalist Party. But to remove a local official from village life made sure that no one else would dare to oppose the new regime. Václav Babka was the victim of regulations intended to stop an extensive smuggling network that had developed, and the widow Josefa Kočarová was penalised by currency regulations concerning the transfer of funds from one country to another. The case of Václav Jakuba shows how Hitler was putting pressure on the big Škoda factory by interfering with the right of its employees to cross the frontier freely when travelling to and from work. The Germans could also cut supplies of coal from the west and north Bohemian coalfields owned by Škoda that were now in Germany. The only remaining important sources of coal were in the Karviná area east of Ostrava, now under Polish control. The German seizure of the Sudetenland and the Polish extension of territory into north Moravia made it much more difficult for Škoda to continue its armaments and industrial production.

These are examples of German attitudes towards Czechs. Sudeten Germans also suffered. The example of Dr Otto Tippmann, a doctor in the chemical town of Aussig (Czech Ústí nad Labem), shows how dangerous pro-Jewish or pro-Social Democrat views could be under the new regime.[86] Dr Tippmann was a doctor working for a chemical company in the town. On 19 October 1938 he was summoned to appear before a Gestapo tribunal to face eight charges. These were:

1. That he was doing the work of the Social Democrat Party [*bei der Sozialdemokratischen Partei organisiert*].
2. He had personal connections with Director Mattl, a Social Democrat, the representative of the chief medical officer in the regional health fund in Aussig.
3. Following a statement by Director Prochaska, he had given information about the health fund to a reporter of a Jewish newspaper.
4. He had opposed the views of Dr Schwertner following the death of General Field Marshall von Hindenburg.
5. He had spoken against the choice of the SdP candidate in the newspaper *Der deutsche Arzt*.
6. He was a freemason.
7. How had he gained the post of factory doctor in a chemical firm?
8. He had treated Jewish patients.

He was summoned to face these charges the following day before Dr Friedrich Tauber, the *Bezirksärzteführer,* and two other judges. It showed how quickly medical services had been brought under political control. Under the Nazi *Führprinzip* the leader at every level had absolute power. None of the acts that Dr Tippmann was charged with had been illegal before the Sudetenland was transferred to Germany. It was only the absolute power of the Nazi state, with its hatred of Jews and of all political opposition, especially on the Left, that had turned what had been normal life into illegal activity. Dr Tippmann was thus facing not only political-criminal charges but accusations that could not only end his career as a doctor but send him to prison or a concentration camp. Dr Tauber pointed out that he could avoid answering these charges by leaving Aussig and moving to Peterswald or Schönwald, industrial towns near Ostrava.

Dr Tippmann had no intention of giving in so easily and made a vigorous defence of his German background. He had been born in Aussig in 1893, the second of seven children. He attended Volkschule and Gymnasium in Aussig and studied medicine at the German university in

Prague between 1912 and 1919, which included a period of military service in the First World War. During this time he served on the front line first as a medical orderly in 1915 and in 1916 as medical lieutenant. He was twice wounded and decorated five times. After qualifying as a doctor he began work in Aussig in November 1922. He had married in May 1922 and at the time of the trial had a 15-year-old son, Paul. His marriage had ended in September 1936 and he had custody of his son. His former wife, Auguste (née Schuma) was from a completely Arian family. In June 1938 he married Margaretha (née Michel), also from a completely Arian family. She and her four sisters had been members of *völkisch* groups for a long time. His son, in the fifth class of the Aussig gymnasium, had been a member of the *Turnerjugend* for a long time. This information established Dr Tippmann as a German patriot, who had spent all his life in a German cultural environment. He had a distinguished war record and his private life had been impeccable. His two marriages were unblemished politically and his second wife and son had shown their German cultural affiliation by membership of German *völkisch* groups. On the more straightforward question of his political affiliation, he denied that he had ever been a member of the Social Democratic Party and was not in sympathy with it. He had stated this to his colleague Dr Hüttl.

However, in this politically charged atmosphere, the information was not enough to clear Dr Tippmann of all charges. He had to show that he had personally been a true German patriot. His explanation of what a patriotic young German was likely to do during the rise of Henlein and the SdP shows the range of German patriotic groups in Sudeten society. Dr Tippmann explained that he came from a family of traditional German nationalists [*national eingestellten Familie*] and had always personally taken part in nationalist activities. While at university he had been in the Germania reading and speaking club and later joined other *völkisch* groups. Since the age of 26 he had been a member of the Ruder- und Eislaufvereines Aussig 1874, from 1922 he had been in the Deutsche Turnverein Schönpreisen, and had been an active competitor. Since 1932 he had also been a member of the Deutsche Turnverein Aussig. This covered his principal cultural activities. While at school he had also been a member of the Bund der Deutschen in Böhmen and for many years had been a member of the

Deutscher Kulturverband. As a public-spirited German he had also been doctor for a volunteer fire brigade, the Freiwillige Feuerwehr Schönpreisen. This participation in German cultural activities was important. So too was his sporting activity in gymnastics and running – he was well aware that Hitler laid great emphasis on physical activity that created strong, healthy German patriots. Finally, Dr Tippmann showed his support for SdP activities by pointing to the example of an unemployed SdP member, Frau Julia Dörfler, whom he had helped. He had also provided medical help for children's holiday activities organised by Frau Richter, the *Frauenschaftsführerin*.

Turning to the specific charges, Dr Tippmann challenged them by pointing out that the charge concerning Dr Mattl could not be proven because he was dead. In any case, he had never had any political connection with him. As to the charge that he had defamed the memory of Hindenburg, he said that when he and others were in a coffee house, a colleague had expressed an opinion based on an article in the Social Democratic newspaper *Volksrecht*. He had merely replied that he had his own opinion of the matter (*Und ich bleibe doch bei meine Meinung*). A colleague, Dr Schwertner, had agreed to support this under oath. As a former front line German soldier in the Austrian army in Russia and Albania he had the highest opinion of Hindenburg. Dr Tippmann also returned to the subject of his social activities by pointing out that he had held important posts in medical administration for a number of years, but none of these had been political.

Dr Tippmann also had to deal with the charge that he was pro-Jewish and had helped to choose a Jewish doctor for the medical fund. This charge concerned the appointment of a Jewish doctor, Dr Heimburg, from Brno. Dr Tippmann's defence was that he was never a member of the panel that made the appointment and he had no influence on its decisions.

He then came to the central issue. He had been offered the post of doctor at a large chemical company in Aussig in January 1938. Knowing that Dr Tauber already held the post, he asked why he was being offered it. The director conducting the interview, Dr Řipa, said that the board had decided to appoint an Aussig doctor and that if he did not accept, the post would be offered to someone else. Also, if the local German doctors created any difficulties the board would appoint a Czech doctor from Prague. Dr Tippmann asked for time to consider this offer, consulted the senior German doctor in Aussig and they agreed that it would be better to have a German doctor than a Czech. After further discussions, he had assumed that Dr Tauber was unable to continue to work full time at the factory. He accepted the offer and began work in November.

There remained one charge: that he was a freemason, but he turned this to his advantage. He admitted being admitted to the Aussig lodge in November 1934 but claimed that he had done this because his former school friends from the Aussig gymnasium were also members. Far from being a secret society with anti-German aims, it turned out in Dr Tippmann's description to have been yet another German patriotic group. The first duty of members, according to Dr Tippmann, was to be loyal to fellow Germans and their homeland [*Volk und Heimat*]. The lodge was also committed to improving the conditions of Germans in the Czech state (which was also Henlein's rallying cry). Members tried to stem the influx of Jews into positions of authority in the Prague lodge. This was also deeply resented by the Czechs and eventually led to violence between the two groups in April 1938, which had to be put down by the police.

At the end of the Gestapo interview Dr Tippmnn was told that he would be hearing further from the *Bezirksärzteführer* (the leading Nazi doctor in the district) Dr Tauber. In two subsequent discussions with him, Dr Tauber said that he had complete confidence in Dr Tippmann's patriotic attitude [*völkische Gesinnung*] and had always regarded him as a good German. He also said that he had not understood the way the Freemasons had worked and had been under a misunderstanding concerning his part in the appointment of the Jewish doctor. Although Dr Tippmann would not be able to continue his work in the medical finance office, Dr Tauber assured him that because he was of true German blood, Dr Tauber would help him find alternative employment and would recommend to the *Gauaerztführer*, Dr Feitenhansl, to have all sanctions against him lifted.

Finally, Dr Tippmann pointed out in his defence to the Gestapo that the charges against him had destroyed his career [*meine wirtschaftliche Existenz*], which he had followed in Aussig for 16 years. He said that all he now wanted was to remain in his home district [*Heimat*] and continue working. He admitted he had made mistakes, but he had never treated any Jews in private practice and was, above all, a completely German patriot.

The case is interesting for a number of reasons. The first was the complete transformation of Sudeten German society by being incorporated into Germany. Attitudes and activities that had been acceptable and legal in the past could be, and often were, transformed into matters of almost life and death importance. A man like Dr Tippmann, a prominent member of the local German society in Aussig, could be dismissed from his post and have to face a Gestapo tribunal that could have sent him to prison or a concentration camp. Local rivalries were emerging and old scores being settled. His acceptance of the job of factory doctor while it was still being held by a local Nazi lay behind the charges against him. He emerges from the detailed report as a distinguished war veteran, active in all aspects of social and cultural life in the German community, a man with a social conscience who was willing to take on onerous duties and was above all a 'good German'. He also shared, or claimed to share, the Nazi hatred of Jews. But he was never a member of the Nazi Party. The picture he gives of Aussig society also reveals the way that everything, including membership of the Freemasons, formed part of this inward-looking German culture, in which Czechs had no place. The suggestion by a Czech director that a Czech doctor from Prague might be appointed to a position was enough to make him want to accept the post. But the result was a lingering suspicion that he had been part of a conspiracy against Dr Tauber, whose position he had taken. When Dr Tauber was given the leading position in the local political-medical Nazi heirachy, it was inevitable that he would try and get his revenge. Only Dr Tippmann's distinguished war record and impeccable German credentials saved him from disgrace. To further emphasise Dr Tauber's power, he made it clear that Dr Tippmann could not be reinstated, even though all charges against him had been proved false, but he would be offered another post through the goodwill of Dr Tauber. Nothing could demonstrate Nazi political power more clearly than this.

Nazi pressure on all opponents, or perceived opponents, of the new regime forced many Czechs to abandon their homes and flee into

Czech territory. It is impossible to know how many became refugees in this way. But in the case of the area occupied by Poland in north Moravia the position is much clearer. The Poles did not expel Czechs, nor did they arrest political opponents, but the new Polish authorities made it clear that they were going to increase the number of Poles living there. The basis of their claim to the land around Český Těšín and Karviná was that the majority of the inhabitants spoke Polish. Under the principle of self-determination this area, in Polish eyes, should have been given to Poland after the First World War. But there were also important economic reasons why Poland wanted this area. One was the coalfield which formed an extension of the larger one in southern Poland and on which the iron and steel industry of Katovice was based. The other was the important iron and steel works at Třinec, which used coal from the Karviná coalmines. The seizure of this land by Poland at the beginning of October 1938 had been preceded by strong anti-Czech propaganda. This alone was enough to persuade many Czechs to flee when Polish troops arrived. Jews were also the subject of anti-Semitic propaganda and there were a number of Germans who also decided to leave. These people left at the rate of 80–100 a day, beginning early in October 1938. The following table shows the total numbers and the proportion of each.

Table 1.1 Number of refugees in Moravská Ostrava

Date	No. applying for refugee status	No. given permission
12.11.1938	9,304	9,043
26.11.1938	11,176	10,569
15.12.1938	13,635	12,669
01.01.1939	15,220	14,013
31.01.1939	18,952	16,887
01.03.1939	22,374	18,514
01.04.1939	23,979	19,473
29.04.1939	24,376	19,553
01.06.1939	24,801	19,897

Source: Aleš Homan, 'Moravská Ostrava jako útočiště uprchlíků z německého a polského záboru na podzim roku 1938' [Moravian Ostrava as a refuge for the people fleeing from German and Polish occupation in the autumn of 1938] in *Ostrava příspěrky k dějinám a současnosti ostravy a ostravska*, 21, (2003), p. 229.

Table 1.2 National structure of refugees

Date	Total	Czechs	Germans	Poles	Jews	Others
12.11.1938	9.043	8,511	123	6	353	50
26.11.1938	10,569	10,085	115	0	324	45
15.12.1939	12,669	12,218	110	0	311	30
01.01.1939	14,013	13,584	108	0	304	17
31.01.1939	16,887	16,437	118	0	308	24
01.03.1939	18,514	18,059	123	0	308	24
01.04.1939	19,437	18,970	157	1	308	37
29.04.1939	19,553	19,029	175	1	309	39
01.06.1939	19,897	19,317	229	1	309	41

Source: ibid.

What is striking about these figures is the relatively small number of Germans among the refugees. The reason is political. Poland was unwilling to alienate Germans because Germany had shown such an aggressive attitude towards seizing the Sudetenland. The small number who were not categorised were a mixture of Slovaks, Ruthenes and Ukrainians who had come west in search of work. On the other hand, there were a number of Jews who took fright and left, many of them small shopkeepers and traders. The large numbers of Czechs posed a serious problem for the Czech authorities. They were temporarily housed by the Red Cross when they first arrived and personal details were registered. The majority were workers and many were already employed in Ostrava, but like those living near Plzeň, found themselves on the wrong side of the frontier. In the case of Ostrava, where the river formed the new frontier, the city was divided. Workers who were driven out of the Třinec iron and steel works could be employed by the larger Vítkovice company. There were also similar, though smaller, steel works in the surrounding area and from that point of view, it was not impossible to find employment for many of the refugees. The cost of supporting those who had no work was high.

These were not the only areas which changed hands. The Vienna arbitration had given a large part of southern Slovakia to Hungary. Pressburg (Bratislava) remained in Slovak hands but the industrial city of Kashau (Košice) was given to Hungary, and Slovakia kept the cathedral city of Nitra. Details of the actual transfer of territory and the final frontier were to be agreed by a Hungarian–Czechoslovak commission. Transfer of the territory began on 5 November and ended on 10 November. On 2 November a report reached the government in Bratislava that terrorists were being trained in Hungary who would be used to occupy Czechoslovak territory.[87] Whether or not this was true, it soon emerged that the Hungarian soldiers who were sent to occupy the land were terrifying the Slovak inhabitants. This ensured that they left and became refugees like the Czechs in the Sudetenland. Official complaints by the Slovak autonomous government such as that of 7 November had little or no effect.

On 8 November, for example, there was a report concerning three people. These were police officer Michal M. and carpenter Emil S. in the village of Král'ovský Chlmec and Martin T. in the village of Mierovo, all of whom were forced to leave their homes. Some Czechs and Slovaks deeply resented this transfer of land to Hungary and the Minister of Education M. Černak appealed to the intelligentsia not to leave.[88] Violence by Hungarian soldiers continued across the ceded territory and in some cases the local Hungarian population joined in, looting Slovak property. As the occupation continued, Hungarian police also expelled Slovaks. The Hungarian threats were intended to be taken seriously. Those Slovaks who left, such as Jozef K., his wife Eliška and Katerina M. from the village of Blahová-Bellova Ves, did so because they felt their lives were in danger.[89] They left behind property and possessions worth 6,000 crowns. Others suffered greater losses. Jozef N. of the village of Lúč na Ostrove left behind property valued at 25,000 crowns.[90] Many of those seized had been taken by Hungarian soldiers to the local police station, told to give their nationality and were then put on a bus and sent across the new frontier into Czechoslovakia. To make it appear that the Slovaks were leaving of their own free will, they were forced to sign documents to that effect. An alternative was to accuse them of having arms. They were then arrested, briefly imprisoned, their possessions and property were confiscated and they were expelled. In some cases, such as in the village of Nová Vieska, the local Hungarians were so confident that they did not wait for soldiers to arrive before expelling Slovak inhabitants.[91] In the village of Gbelce, treatment of Slovaks was even worse. The Central Office of the Slovak League reported to the Czechoslovak Red Cross that villagers there were being killed by terrorists.[92]

By 20 November it had become clear that the Hungarians had decided to expel as many Slovaks as possible from the ceded territory. Official complaints by the Slovak autonomous government had no effect. The result was that the Slovak police decided to retaliate by expelling Hungarians, and anyone with a home in Hungary.[93] The next day, 21 November, Hungary announced that it would send all remaining Slovak citizens out of the occupied territory.[94] On 22 November the government in Prague passed a law granting autonomy to Slovakia and the Ruthene area.[95] Two days later there was a report that all Czechoslovak nationals would be expelled from Hungary. Attacks on Czechoslovak citizens continued. On 25 November, three weeks after the signing of the arbitration award and the beginning of the Hungarian occupation, there was a report from Nové Zámky that houses and shops belonging to Czechs, Slovaks and Jews had been looted and destroyed and 450 Jews expelled. The Slovak government requested compensation and proposed to seize Hungarian property of the same value. By the end of November, Hungarian hatred of Czechoslovak property had resulted in the desecration of a monument to Czechoslovak soldiers in Lučenec. Life in general became even more difficult. Prices of food and household goods increased by up to 100 per cent and the exchange rate between the Hungarian pengö and Czechoslovak crown changed to Hungary's advantage. The Slovak school became Hungarian – forcing any remaining Slovaks to have their children educated in Hungarian – and the local branch of Baťa was taken over by the Hungarian firm Ika.[96] Finally, there were attempts by Hungarian soldiers in some areas to force Slovaks to sign a petition asking for their villages to be annexed to Hungary. At the beginning of December the Slovak authorities finally retaliated and also began negotiations for the transfer of the remaining Slovaks to Slovakia, though offering to stop the expulsion of Hungarians if the Hungarian authorities stopped harassing Slovaks.[97] In spite of all complaints by the Slovak government attacks, harassment, arrest, torture and beating of Slovak citizens in the occupied territory continued at least to the end of March. By then many Slovaks had left and the administration and all aspects of social life had become Hungarian.

The theme which runs through this chapter is Hitler's success in destroying Czechoslovakia. He persuaded Chamberlain, through Henlein's propaganda, that the Sudetenland was on the brink of civil war. He posed as the popular hero of the Germans there. He claimed that the settlement of this matter would bring lasting peace and that it would be his last claim to territory. But Hitler knew that Poland and Hungary also wanted to seize parts of Czechoslovakia and that he could present the crisis as likely to lead to a European war. No one challenged this. His stage management of the Munich Conference was masterly. He pretended that he had not seen Mussolini's proposals and said he considered that they would bring lasting peace. It needed comparatively little time to persuade Chamberlain to accept them, because he knew that many British conservatives thought that Czechoslovakia was worth sacrificing for the sake of peace. Once the agreement had been signed, the safeguards were not worth the paper they were written on. For example, the German advance into the Sudetenland was so rapid – only ten days – that decisions on which troops should be used for international supervision were overtaken by events. Germany supplied all the important maps showing the population statistics. These were not challenged. Germany's refusal to give way on any important matter, whether it concerned the proportion of Germans in an area or the economic effect of land allocation, left the Czechs little choice but to accept. Leaving disputes to be decided by German and Czech officials merely put more power into German hands. The transfer of land to Germany, Poland and Hungary resulted in forms of ethnic cleansing. The entry of German troops between lines of cheering, flag waving Sudetens was a carefully staged propaganda event. The reality was different, as Eric Pasold made clear. Many Sudetens had not wanted to become German citizens, subject to oppressive Nazi control. The Czechs, abandoned by their former allies, were powerless to resist and even before the creation of the Protectorate in March 1939, the remainder of Bohemia and Moravia had become in effect a German client state that was barely economic. This was the legacy of Munich.

CHAPTER 2

THE DESTRUCTION OF CZECHOSLOVAKIA

The Munich Conference marked the beginning of the end of the Second Czechoslovak Republic. Not only did it remove an increasingly troublesome racial minority, but it also took away a large and important part of the Czechoslovak economy: coal mining in West Bohemia, the chemical industry of Aussig (Ústí nad Labem), the West Bohemia textile industry around Asch (Aš) and the Bohemian glass and porcelain industry. Elsewhere in the Sudeten territory there were medium and small engineering companies as well as distilleries and food factories that met the basic needs of the Czechoslovak population. Put simply, it was difficult to see how the rump of the Czech state could survive economically without considerable foreign assistance. It was also defenceless, having lost the elaborate defensive system that had been constructed since the mid 1930s. So the crisis over Czechoslovakia did not end with the Munich Agreement. Not only were Germans left outside the area incorporated into Germany but the seizure of the Sudetenland only marked a stage in Hitler's creation of *Lebensraum*. In itself it was no more than part of the foundation for Hitler's dream of a new German empire, since there were still many Czechs and Slovaks living in the remains of Czechoslovakia who had not yet been reduced to the status of second-class citizens in their own state.

But Hitler never worked to any detailed campaign of aggrandisement. He created situations to be exploited by swift and brutal action.

As a result, in the months following Munich, Hitler ordered the army to be able to seize Czech territory very rapidly if an opportunity arose. At the same time he made the Hungarians believe that they might also get Slovak land. Hitler also encouraged Slovak elements who wanted to be completely independent of the Czechs to claim autonomy. Hitler expected that both Hungarians and Slovaks would foment discontent that he could 'solve' by appropriate action 'in the name of restoring peace and harmony'. In the meantime, Hitler made sure that the Czechs recognised German power and followed a subservient policy. To ensure that they never regained influence he worked to limit their military and defensive strength and isolated them from their former allies and Britain. At times the Czechs showed surprising resilience in resisting German pressure, but they were worn down. Conditions that made the Protectorate possible and apparently justifiable came about gradually. Later, Slovakia became officially independent and placed itself under the 'protection' of Germany. When it was finally created, the (Czech) Protectorate was initially important as a demonstration of Hitler's contempt for international agreements. Then, from March until June, Neurath, the *Reichsprotektor*, followed a moderate and generally fair-minded policy. Czechs began to favour national unity and firm, autocratic government. Rising Czech–German tension in the summer led to a much harsher German policy from June until the outbreak of war in September.

In the late autumn of 1938 the stage had been set for the next part of Hitler's policy. In his army order of 21 October, the key passage, which set the tone for his policy, was:

It must be possible to smash at any time the remainder of the Czech State, should it pursue an anti-German policy. The preparations to be made by the Wehrmacht for this eventuality will be considerably less in extent than those for Operation *Fall Grün* (Case Green); on the other hand, as planned mobilisation measures will have to be dispensed with, they must guarantee a continuous and considerably higher state of preparedness. The organisation, order of battle, and degree of preparedness of the units earmarked for that purpose are to be prearranged in peace time for a surprise assault so that Czechoslovakia herself will be deprived of all possibility of organised resistance. The aim is the speedy occupation of Bohemia and Moravia and the cutting off of Slovakia. The preparations must be made so that the defence of the western frontier [*Grenzsicherung West*] can be carried out simultaneously.[1]

This plan assumed, among other things, that the Czech air force would be eliminated to remove any threat to German forces. Hitler's readiness to use military force to crush any Czech policy that he considered 'anti-German' gave him considerable leeway in deciding when and how to act. It had only one disadvantage. It was impossible, as Hitler knew, to keep troops at instant readiness for very long. What Hitler therefore stressed to Keitel, head of the armed forces, and the army was that plans must exist that could easily and rapidly be put into effect.

One example of the potential for causing trouble in the future is shown in a German Foreign Ministry memorandum of 4 November about Germans in what remained of Czechoslovakia.[2] Hitler and Mussolini had forced the Czechs to grant territory to Hungary at Vienna. This had settled the issue of Hungarian claims. But it raised more clearly the problem of the status of the Germans such as those in Brno, Prague and the enclave of Iglau. Kundt, a Sudeten German deputy in the Czechoslovak parliament, proposed that these Germans should enjoy a privileged status in the remaining Czech state. But the Foreign Ministry did not want to sign a treaty with the Czechs about the protection of minorities. This would give the many Czechs living in German areas equal rights. Instead, it was proposed that a transfer of population could be discussed with the Czechs and that all matters relating to Germans would be referred to Kundt. This ensured that any dispute would be settled in Germany's favour.

Establishing the new Czechoslovak frontiers

Another matter that Germany deliberately left vague was the final frontiers of the Czechoslovak state. On 1 November the currency in the Sudetenland was switched from the Czechoslovak crown to the German Reichsmark, with an exchange rate that favoured Germany.[3] The German–Czechoslovak frontier was also established and this should have been the signal for an official recognition of all the new frontiers, including that with Hungary. The new Czech Foreign Minister, Chvalkovský, obsequiously thanked Henke, the German Chargé d'Affaires for what he claimed were fair results in ending the Czechoslovak–Hungarian dispute.[4] He then '... hoped ... to be able to discuss the guarantee of new frontiers by the Axis Powers as visualised in the Munich Agreement. In consideration of the situation in the Carpatho–Ukraine and in Slovakia, the guarantee had now become particularly vital for Czechoslovakia from the viewpoint of external and internal politics.' Henke replied evasively that '... the guarantee question would probably only become acute after having been individually determined by appropriate committees'.

Henkle also made it clear that the Czechs should not take steps to try and defend themselves: 'In view of certain unchecked rumours, according to which some Czechoslovak General Staff officers were playing with the idea of new frontier fortifications, I warned the Foreign Minister urgently against such attempts.' It is striking that although the frontier had been effectively decided since the German advance halted on 10 October, no final decision on the frontier had been agreed. Moreover, the Sudetenland had, in effect, been incorporated into Germany from the first day with the appointment of Henlein as Gauleiter for the Sudetenland and the introduction of German law. The official German policy was made clear on 8 November in a report to the Foreign Minister. Hitler had decided that virtually no territory would be returned to the Czechs, even though some of the occupied area had a completely Czech population. Any small, local changes would only be made if there was at least a 90 per cent Czech population. Some concessions might be made to Czechs concerning railways, but these would amount to no more than transit facilities. This refusal to make any serious concessions would, as before, be accompanied by a statement that Germany had only made modest demands! As a further threat, it was stated at a meeting of the German–Czechoslovak Frontier Committee on 10 November that the International Commission had agreed on 13 October that the occupation line was only to be taken as a basis for the work of final demarcation.[5] There remained the possibility of further deviations from the purely ethnographic frontier, where the army required more Czech territory for strategic reasons.

This meeting also revealed another problem that should have been debated. The German claims were based on a census of 1910 but as Heidrich, the Czech delegate, pointed out this only registered the person's language. This led to a short exchange between Heidrich and von Richthofen about the current numbers of each nationality in areas claimed by the Germans. The minutes reveal how the latter treated this serious issue:

M. Heidrich pointed out the large numbers of Czechoslovak nationals [i.e. Czechs] remaining in German territory.

Baron von Richthofen emphasised that these numbers had already altered enormously. Considerable evacuation of Czechs from places inside the German-occupation line had already taken place. Population figures would alter quickly. The great influx of Czechs had only taken place after 1918.

M. Heidrich replied that quotation of the 1910 figures did not give a correct picture of national conditions either but only which language was used. He asked further whether the map, etc., given him was to be considered as the proposal of the Reich Government.

Herr von Richthofen referred him to the text which had been read and added that the Reich Government had to bring forward these *claims* [italics in the original].

M. Heidrich remarked that therefore the map handed in represented the claims of the Reich Government within the meaning of article 6 of the Munich Agreement. He enquired whether the map contained the reaction to the Czech requests.

Herr von Richthofen answered in the affirmative.[6]

The Czech delegate, Heidrich, was making a great effort to get justice for the Czech position, but it was a vain hope. All he could do was point out discrepancies and weaknesses in the German case. The language issue was particularly important because before the First World War many well-educated Czechs had adopted German as their first language to get state posts or work in German industry and commerce. It was also the language often used in mixed (German–Czech) marriages. A far more accurate basis for nationality in 1938 would have been a postwar census, in which Czechs, conscious of having their own state, would have been using their own language. But this would have weakened the German case. The minutes also refer to the many Czechs who had fled from the occupied areas. But no one had precise figures for these, though it was clear that this represented a major disaster for the people involved. Heidrich's final point, that he might not be able to give his government's reply before the following Sunday, was a final attempt to assert his own authority. The Germans had earlier asked for a reply as soon as possible – by Saturday. The Germans also emphasised their dominance in the address by the German chairman of the Frontier Demarcation Committee:

> As is known, the basis of the final determination of the frontier was laid down according to the ethnographic point of view by the decision of the International Commission of October 5 and 13, [the Czechs had accepted this]. It is therefore a question of decisions reached on the lines laid down at the time which awarded certain territory to Germany once and for all.
>
> Yet comprehensive requests have come from its Government which would lead to a complete alteration of the line of October 5 and 13. I must inform the Czechoslovak delegation that the presentation of these requests has caused the greatest surprise to the Reich Government. The Reich Government is determined to settle this matter in the shortest time possible and takes the following standpoint:
>
> 1. The Reich Government does not intend in any circumstances to give up any part of the occupied areas.
> 2. On the other hand, the Reich Government for its part still has certain claims to put forward.

.....These German claims are based on compelling considerations. They have been reduced to a minimum. It means a great sacrifice for the Reich Government not to extend them further in view of the large German-language areas of Brünn and surroundings, Olmütz, Iglau, Budweis, etc., which lie adjacent to the German frontier. It was solely in order to speed up appeasement between Germany and Czechoslovakia that the putting forward of further claims has been abandoned.

3. The final frontier demarcation must be carried out as soon as possible. Recent experiences render it necessary to take the still outstanding final decision at once. The Reich Government therefore requests the Czechoslovak delegation to let it have in a day or two its assent to the projected frontier demarcation.[7]

Nothing could demonstrate the German dominance more clearly. The demands to the Czech government were, as before, peremptory. The claim that the German government was being modest and reasonable was in flat contradiction to the reality and the forceful language used was Hitler's, not normal diplomacy. There was little time for the Czech delegation to fly back to Prague, for the Czech government to meet and discuss the issues and for the Czech delegates to return. The German object was always to act with the greatest possible speed to deny its opponents any opportunity to resist or get help from other powers.

The completion of arrangements for the transfer of territory led to a further important act. On 14 October senior officers in the German army were told that preparations for war would be intensified. Göring spoke of a gigantic programme being developed in the following months that would make previous efforts appear trivial. The cost of this would be met partly from the Czech money that had been seized and also from a greatly increased export drive. At present, Göring explained, there were no funds available for this increased output, but brutal methods would be used to achieve this aim. Jewish funds in Austria would also be used. The military need was so great that sacrifices would have to be made in the production of consumer goods (guns not butter).

Sub-Carpathian Russia – the Ruthene area

Another issue in German–Czechoslovak relations was the question of the Ruthene area that formed the eastern end of Czechoslovakia. This had a population that was considered Ukrainian. Hitler had decided that it would be used as the basis for a future Ukrainian state, though whether he was thinking about the total Ukrainian population or merely the Ruthenes and Ukrainians living in Poland is not clear. Hitler's policy was therefore to try and foster Ukrainian nationalism among the Ruthene people and proposed that they might be given self-determination. This would produce a small, economically weak state that would be dependent on Slovakia and ultimately Germany.

At the same time that the German delegation was establishing the frontier of the new German–Czechoslovak state, Göring was setting out German aims to Durčansky, the Ruthene minister. He explained that Slovak and Ukrainian (Ruthene) matters would be dealt with as part of Czechoslovakia but that Germany's aim was an independent Slovakia and an autonomous Ukraine 'orientated towards this independent Slovakia'. Göring referred to possible help that the Czechoslovak government could provide under pressure from Germany. There was also a brief discussion about the future of a small German enclave close to Bratislava. Its German name was Theben (Slovak Devin) and it lay at the confluence of the Danube and March (Morava) rivers. The Slovak deputy at the meeting, Karmasin, explained that the castle there was 'Slovakia's sole historic monument and that "all Slovak history books would have to be burned" if the castle were lost'. He claimed that German military requirements could be met by special agreements without the cession of territory. Not surprisingly, this request received little sympathy from Göring and the Germans decided to occupy the town.[8]

The Czechoslovak government's complete collapse in the face of German pressure is also shown in their reply concerning the German–Czechoslovak frontier. Heidrich had said that he might not be able to give his government's reply to the Germans before Sunday (12 November). In fact, the Czech government capitulated on the 11th and at midnight the German chargé d'affaires sent a telegram to Berlin to this effect. In a faint hope that the German government might still have some consideration for Czechoslovak interests, the Czechoslovak government:

> ... has taken cognisance that the Reich Government has renounced the intention of making further demands. The Czechoslovak Government expresses the hope that the Reich Government will not turn down certain modifications of its demands where consideration for Czechoslovak national feeling appears possible without disadvantage to German ethnic interests.
>
> True to the principle of its new policy to bring about loyal *rapprochement* and close collaboration with Germany, the Czechoslovak Government has met the German demands on the assumption that henceforth nothing stands in the way of a German guarantee of the new and final frontiers of the Czechoslovak State. [9]

The more the Czechoslovak government bowed to German pressure, the less popular it was at home. Henke, reporting from the German legation in Prague on 12 November, explained the position. The German demands had caused consternation and the Foreign Minister, 'who feels personally hurt', only submitted the German demands to Cabinet in the evening, after discussions about a presidential election, dissolution of parties and a new constitution had taken place. The Cabinet spent hours in difficult and impassioned debate before accepting German demands. Beran, the new leader of the Unity Party that was being formed, was not told of the decision. But he had already said that he thought that the Foreign Minister, Chvalkovský, had lost public support because he had done no more than Beneš to protect Czechoslovak interests. Henke thought that it was unlikely that Chvalkovský would be elected president, as had been widely expected. Beran also said he thought that the government should appeal to a four-power conference on the matter of Germany's final demands, the so-called '6th zone'. Henke also asked that Germany should support Chvalkovský by giving him 'a certain prestige success in order to strengthen with people and parties his personal position, which is at present shaken'. Henke evidently did not realise that any German action to raise Chvalkovský's prestige would have the opposite effect. The more he was seen as Germany's puppet, the less popular he would be with Czechs.

Hungary and the Ruthene area

Germany's claim to be moderate and reasonable in its demands was not helping to solve the problem of the Ruthene area, which Hungary wanted. It had a large Hungarian minority in a mixed population consisting of Ruthenes, Hungarians, Jews, Germans and Romanians. According to a census of 1930 the relative figures for the different nationalities and religious affiliations were as shown in Table 2.1.

These figures show the attraction for Hungary – approximately 100,000 Hungarians. That they were not the majority was hardly important. Hungary had lost so much land and so many of the people it regarded as 'Hungarian' after the First World War that any success in reclaiming Hungarians of any sort would be popular at home. But

Table 2.1 Population of the Ruthene area (Sub-Carpathian Russia), 1930

Population		Nationality		
Total	Increase since 1921		Total	Increase since 1921
725,357	+19.94%	Ruthene	446,916	+20.67%
		Hungarian	109,457	+5.46%
		Jewish	91,255	+14.47%
		Czechoslovak	33,961	+55.56%

N.B. There were also 49,636 others, including 12,641 Romanians and 13,249 Germans.
Religious affiliation

	Roman Catholic	359,167
	Evangelical (Lutheran)	74,173
	Jewish	103,542
	Orthodox	112,034

Source: Jaromír Nečas, 'Politická situace na Podkarpatské Ruse; Národnosní mapa republiky Československé' (The political situation in Sub Carpathian Russia; Czechoslovak nationality map) in F. B. Škorpil, Zeměpisný atlas (Geographical atlas) (Prague 1934), quoted in Kárník, České země v éře První republiky, vol. 2, p. 236.

the Ruthene area had little economic value and was extremely poor. The standard of living was the lowest in Czechoslovakia, which was indicated by the lack of public utilities (electricity and water) and comparatively few schools.

The fact that the area would be an economic liability hardly mattered. Economic concerns seldom carry much weight when matched by demands for uniting people of the same nationality.[10] This explains the nature of Hungarian policy towards the Ruthene area. In many ways it matched the German policy towards the Sudeten German area before the Munich Conference. If the reports were accurate, Henlein's success in the Sudetenland had encouraged Hungarians in the Ruthene area to demand similar treatment – union with Hungary. This is shown by the report by the German ambassador to Hungary of 15 November:

> The Regent ... mentioned that he was worried over the problem of Carpatho-Ukraine. The Hungarian Government was being besieged with requests to put an end to the untenable conditions there .... Because of the course of the rivers the needy population of the mountainous remainder of Carpatho-Ukraine was entirely dependent on Hungary as a market. Troops with a leaning toward Bolshevism, who had previously been driven out of the Ukraine and incorporated into the Czech Army, were terrorizing the population .... There is the possibility that, in the event of an explosion in Carpatho-Ukraine, Hungarian troops would march in and remain there until the population was guaranteed the right of self-determination, perhaps through the sending of international troops for the duration of the plebiscite. The mountainous country of Carpatho-Ukraine, intersected by deep valleys running north and south, was moreover ill suited as a line of communication for the German activity to be expected in the future in the Ukraine, which must be brought about in conjunction with similar action by Italy and Japan to stem the Bolshevik danger.

Nothing was better calculated to try and win German support than the threat of Bolshevism from across the eastern frontier of the Ruthene area. The Hungarians claimed that they would be able to check this. They also believed that although the Hungarians were not the largest single group, they would obtain the most votes in a plebiscite. But the Ruthenes were also trying to win German support for self-determination with the help of Slovak political allies. The Ruthene leader Durčansky, and Karmasin, leader of the *Volksgruppe* in Slovakia, arranged for Durčansky to visit Berlin in mid November to try and present his case personally to the German Foreign Ministry. This brought a complaint by Druffel, the German consul in Bratislava, who realised that he was being bypassed and had lost control of German–Slovak relations.

> In my present sphere of activity the various elements have up till now been to some extent coordinated...Last week this cooperation suffered a severe blow as a result of Karmasin's not only arranging Durčansky's visit to Berlin without consulting me but also adopting an attitude of particular secrecy towards me.
>
> I do not know the reasons for this; they are probably to be sought not here on the spot but in some unpleasant experiences with the machinery of the Foreign Ministry's so-called 'diplomacy'.[11]

There were too many people and groups trying to gain influence in this confused situation. It was Hitler and not the Foreign Ministry who was directing German diplomacy. In addition, German groups with an interest in the *Volksdeutsch* (Germans living outside Germany in the German diaspora) were also trying to gain influence. Druffel's complaint shows his confusion:

> With regard to this incident I should like to raise the question whether it would not be in the interests both of the Foreign Ministry and of the foreign policy of the Reich if the leaders of the *Volksgruppe*, and incidentally the *Volksdeutsche Mittelstelle*, too, were to confine themselves to the affairs of the *Volksgruppe*, leaving political relations with Slovakia, in so far as they are not conducted through Prague, to the Foreign Ministry and its machinery.

Matters proved less serious than Druffel had feared. He was assured by Under State Secretary Woermann that Durčansky's visit had been arranged at short notice. But it was clear that Hitler's policy of allowing different groups to compete for power and influence tended to cause confusion.

Much clearer was the information given to Hitler on 17 November about the relative numbers of *Volksdeutsch* in Czechoslovakia and Czechs in Germany and Austria. These figures, based on 1930 statistics for Czechoslovakia and 1934 for Czechs in Germany, reveal the unequal population distribution in the final frontier arrangements. A total of 676,478 Czechs would be transferred to Germany and 478,589 *Volksdeutsch* would remain in Czechoslovakia. This figure included not only the Germans in Brno, Prague and the language enclaves but also others in Slovakia, most of whom lived in Bratislava and the rest in some of the Špis former mining towns.[12] There were also Germans in the land transferred to Hungary and Poland and 263 in small areas of land that formed the final transfer area that the Czechs were allowed to retain. There were 32,274 Czechs living in Germany and Austria. These official figures did not take any account of the large numbers of Czechs who had fled from the Sudeten areas. The treaty of 20 November which followed was, in theory, an official attempt to resolve the problem of nationality by the so-called option scheme. This allowed people who had been Czechoslovak citizens on 10 October 1938 to choose German nationality if they fulfilled certain criteria. But it did not necessarily allow them to move. Hitler was reluctant to allow *Volksdeutsch* to leave the rump Czechoslovak state. The treaty was followed a day later by a plebiscite in which 98.90 per cent approved of the *Heim ins Reich* transfer to Germany.[13]

Germany signed a protocol for building an Oder-Danube Canal on 19 November to consolidate the incorporation of the Sudetenland into the Reich and bring the Czech lands into the German economic sphere of influence. The diplomatic records give details of how the cost was to be divided between the two countries and arrangements for tolls. On the surface it appeared to be a sensible arrangement that would benefit both countries. But the real reason for constructing the canal was to provide an inland waterway linking Germany and Austria that was safe from British or French attack in wartime. The canal could also be used to transfer Romanian oil cheaply and easily from the Danube to north-east Germany. The River Oder was already navigable as far as the German–Czechoslovak frontier. The proposed canal would complement the Main-Danube canal linking the Danube to the Rhine, as well as the canals linking Berlin to the Oder in the east and to a network of other rivers crossing north Germany in the west. Under the terms of the protocol, Germany would pay for the land. But it would pay with money seized in the Sudetenland, thus making Czechoslovakia meet the whole cost.

While progress was being made on this point, the problem over the Ruthene area continued. On 19 November the German ambassador in Hungary reported that the Hungarian Foreign Minister had said that the 'overwhelming majority of the Carpatho-Ukraine population' had demanded union with Hungary. As a result, the matter had assumed national importance for the Hungarians. The Foreign Minister continued: 'As this movement has the backing of very influential people here, he did not know whether the efforts of the Hungarian Government to prevent a union by force would be successful. He had suggested to the Czechoslovak Minister [Miloš Kobr], who had complained about propaganda here, that more serious possible developments might be prevented by a plebiscite under international control'.[14] The German reply was cautious, saying that the action was inopportune and Germany would not support Hungary if the latter's action caused an international crisis. This was misinterpreted by Hungary to mean that Germany did not disapprove but was only anxious about Hungary. Emboldened by this, the following day the Hungarian military attaché in Rome told Mussolini that the situation in the Carpatho-Ukraine was becoming increasingly untenable and the Hungarian army would therefore occupy it within 24 hours.

Hungary had to be stopped. Hitler was consulted and the Italian ambassador to Germany, Attolico, was told to send the following message to Mussolini, who would inform the Hungarian government:

1. The German Government was extremely surprised at the interpretation of its reply. Furthermore, the Hungarian

Government had even given a written assurance that it would take no steps without informing the German Government.

2. The Führer was of the opinion that a Hungarian occupation of the Carpatho-Ukraine would discredit the Axis Powers, whose award Hungary had unconditionally accepted three weeks ago. Hungary was playing a frivolous game if she intervened by force now, and she would bear the full responsibility for all eventual consequences. The outcome of a Czechoslovak–Hungarian conflict, which would inevitably result, could not be foreseen; possibly Germany too would be forced to intervene.[15]

Further correspondence in the following days showed that Hitler's message stopped the Hungarians.

Having checked Hungarian ambitions concerning the Ruthene territory, Hitler could now return to the matter of Czechoslovakia. He had succeeded in forcing the Czechoslovak government to accept all the frontier changes and it was following a pro-German policy. Hitler was able to maintain pressure on the Czechs by attacking anything that he did not like and claimed that it represented a return to Beneš' policies which, he claimed, had caused the original crisis. But Hitler also had to be sure that the Western powers would not intervene when he took his next step. Germany had already referred to Czechoslovak affairs as being within its own sphere of interest, but the International Commission, established by the Munich Conference, still met from time to time and had the power to intervene. Germany tried to end the work of this committee, but the heavy-handed attempt by Ritter, a Foreign Office official, failed. On 3 December, Ritter summoned the French, British, Italian and Czech representatives to see him, nominally to discuss the agenda for the next International Committee meeting. When he suggested that the commission should be 'finally buried' he was opposed by all the other diplomats. His harsh treatment of the Czech, in front of the others, appears to have alienated them:

At first the Czechoslovak Minister tried to uphold a dissenting view – especially with reference to the third supplementary declaration to the Munich Agreement. I [Ritter] told him that any attempt to maintain his dissenting view at the meeting would be interpreted by Germany as meaning that Czechoslovakia wanted to rely upon the help of the other powers represented on the Commission against Germany. Such an impression would certainly not be in Czechoslovakia's interest. Thereupon the Czechoslovak Minister said that he would not dissent at the meeting.

The Italian Ambassador was unable to come and had sent Signor Magistrati. He too referred to the third supplementary declaration of the Munich agreement and thought it would be premature to fix a time now for the winding up of the International Commission. The British and French Chargés d'Affaires said that a decision of this kind at the forthcoming meeting would embarrass them. They were not prepared for it and therefore had no instructions. They must therefore, in any case, reserve their opinion in order to obtain instructions from their Governments.[16]

The matter was dropped, since any open rejection at the International Commission's meeting would have hindered German plans later. On 21 November the commission agreed that all boundary matters had been agreed and two days later a similar letter from the German chargé d'affaires in Prague reported that all similar matters relating to the Polish–Czechoslovak and Hungarian–Czechoslovak frontiers had also been settled.

The Czechoslovak army

Germany's next step was to reduce the size and effectiveness of the Czechoslovak armed forces to make it easier to invade the rump state. Keitel suggested that the best approach was to ask the Czechoslovak Foreign Minister how his government was proposing to reconstitute its armed forces and reject all proposals until something acceptable was proposed.[17] The Wehrmacht preferred a more direct approach and on 21 November made their own suggestions:

1. No fortifications or barriers on the Czech–German frontier and no preparations for such.

2. Czech armed forces of minimum size must look towards Germany and break off their connections with other countries (German Military mission). Proposals as to strength, organisation, and armament must be submitted to the German Government for approval.

3. Standardisation on German pattern of the types of arms and ammunition manufactured by the Czech armaments industry and retooling of the Czech armaments industry for use by Germany.

4. No intelligence service against Germany and no toleration on Czech territory of intelligence services by third powers against Germany.

5. The right of Germany to transport troops by rail and road, in war and peace, between Silesia and Austria through Czech territory subject to previous notification.

6. Special regulations for military service for German minority remaining in the Rump Czech State.

7. The roads leading from Dresden, Glatz, or Ratibor through Czech territory to the Ostmark [Austria] must be completely available for military movements. Also in time of war.[18]

Acceptance of these would have not only left the Czech state defence-less, it would also have provided the Wehrmacht with weapons that were compatible with their own and factories that could continue to supply them. As to the Czech air force, on 10 November Göring had already suggested that there should be a close relationship between the Germans and Czechs. He also said that he would like to see General Fajfr appointed as the air force commander. He repeated this demand in a letter on 29 November.

It is against this background of mounting political pressure and German refusal to make any concessions on territory of Czech national importance that the new Czechoslovak president was elected. Beneš had resigned on 5 October and, according to the constitution, a new president should have been elected within 14 days. But the transfer of the Sudetenland and other Czechoslovak territory had made it impossible to have an election before 30 November, 55 days after Beneš' resignation. Until it was known which parts of Czechoslovakia would be lost, no one knew which members of the Senate and Chamber of Deputies would still have the right to take part in the election. The final result was that 69 deputies and 33 senators were removed and lost their votes.[19] There was also considerable political manoeuvring within parliament. The new Party of National Unity wanted an election. Members of the previous parliament, including General Syrový, did not. They wanted to block the new, younger generation. Eventually there was a compromise. The Party of National Unity gradually absorbed all other parties except the Communists, and a new president was elected. The first choice had originally been the Foreign Minister, Chvalkovský, but as it became clear that he was pro-German his popularity waned. There was also a whispering campaign against him, claiming that he and his wife were partly Jewish. Although this was not true, it was enough to make Chvalkovský withdraw from the election.

Election of Hácha as President

Instead, Hácha was elected. He was the former president of the Supreme Administrative Court, but largely unknown to the general public. Hácha was 66 and had enjoyed a blameless reputation as a judge. He was in no sense a politician and even claimed he knew nothing about politics. His main advantage in German eyes was that he had consistently supported Sudeten German ethnic claims. He was without independent means and was dependent on his small income. He was also modest and self-effacing, fond of music and art and deeply religious. The summons to be president seemed to him to be a call of fate which he could not refuse. His comment when taking leave of his old cabinet and welcoming the new was that, like St Wenceslas, his highest aim was to achieve a true German–Czech understanding by overcoming psychological obstacles. This was the man chosen to oppose Hitler's gradual destruction of Czechoslovakia.

The election of this mild-mannered and modest man ensured that Germany could pursue its interests in the rump state unopposed. The first step was the signing of an economic agreement between the government of the Ruthene area and the German Gesellschaft für Praktische Lagerstättenforschung on 7 December. This gave the German company a monopoly for prospecting rights for minerals and exploiting any that were found. The company could also transfer these rights to German companies. Although the agreement stated that these minerals should be used to meet Ruthene needs first, in practice it would be the Germans who would benefit. The real reason for the agreement was the hope of finding oil, which would be sent to Germany. To compensate the Ruthene provincial government, the agreement stated: 'in the production of mineral oil, provided a net profit is made, the German side will make over 2 per cent of the gross output to the Provincial Government of the Carpatho-Ukraine'.[20] In addition, to ensure that the new German rights were respected, the agreement also stated: 'The Provincial Government of the Carpatho-Ukraine will, as soon as possible, amend its legislation so as to ensure that free lots and mining rights lapse immediately if the owner of such rights has not met his production obligations in a satisfactory manner.' This ensured German control. The area was too poor and backward to engage in extensive prospecting and exploitation of any minerals. Prospecting for oil, which was the main attraction, needed considerable funds.

While Germany was beginning to take an interest in the possible exploitation of Ruthene minerals, the condition of the remaining Germans in Czechoslovakia was worsening. Rumours reached Germany that they were being ill-treated. But, as Henke, the German chargé d'affaires in Prague reported, these stories were often exaggerated and sometimes invented. These Germans wanted their areas to be included in the German Reich. Their main complaint was that they were losing their jobs and unemployment was rising: Czech and Jewish companies were taking their revenge by dismissing their German employees. Under the new economic conditions, trade was becoming more difficult because companies were separated from their sources of raw materials and their markets in much the same way as they had been when the First Republic was created. Unemployment under these conditions was inevitable and these Germans were being made the scapegoat. To make matters worse, Czechs were boycotting German business and foreign markets were being closed to German companies because of reaction against Nazi treatment of Jews. Conditions for some Germans were becoming extreme. For example, lecturers and junior doctors in Prague clinics had not been paid for weeks. Consequently they would not be able to pay rent and taxes and their property would fall into Czech hands. Czech officials were also making life difficult for Germans and Hungarians.

This German remnant had also lost faith in Henlein because they believed he had lost interest in them and had failed to represent their interests properly. Hitler wanted to keep them in the Czech state, but many wished to go to Germany. Many believed that Kundt, the parliamentary deputy whose job was to keep them in the Czech lands, was trying to build up his own power and ignore his fellow Germans. Henke closed his report with the comment:

> Only when our Germans here realise, as a result of the firm and visible establishment of Czechoslovakia's role of dependence on the Reich, the responsible and at the same time advantageous mission which they have to fulfil here as co-guarantors of this dependence, and when, further, there is no longer any doubt among the mass of the Czech population that unconditional recognition of the full equality of their German fellow citizens is a vital question of their nation, can a real contentment of the remaining German element be expected in the course of time.[21]

This was not a realistic assessment of the situation. Every effort by the Germans to assert their power over the Czechs and encourage the Germans to stay led to greater Czech resentment. In turn that made life more difficult for the German minority. The only solution was for Hitler to seize what was left of the Czechoslovak state. The first step was the treaty of 9 December creating a customs union between the two countries. The Wehrmacht had complained that when they imported weapons and ammunition from Czechoslovakia they had to pay import duty. There was also a more general problem for Sudeten companies which had formerly traded within Czechoslovakia and which also had to pay more for imports from the rump Czechoslovak state. Their business had also been hit by the increased official value of their factory production costs. They had also been incorporated into the German state planning system of business associations which controlled supplies of raw materials and markets. The customs union was thus a step towards the complete integration of the whole of Bohemia and Moravia into Germany. This was to be Hitler's next move and by 17 December he had decided to act. He ordered the army to prepare to invade Czechoslovakia, assuming that it would be virtually unopposed. Only a relatively small force would be needed and no advance warning of the move should be given. No troops would leave their barracks until the night before and no motorised units would approach the frontier without Hitler's express permission.[22]

Unaware of this, the Czech government introduced a new pro-German policy. On Christmas Eve the Cabinet decided to ban the Communist Party. In another attempt to curry favour with Germany, it announced that all Jewish teachers in German educational institutes (colleges and schools) would be suspended or pensioned from 1 January 1939. However, Jewish teachers elsewhere and Jewish businesses were not attacked, though this acted as an advance warning. At the same time, Germany was making it clear to foreign diplomats that the rump Czechoslovakia was now a German client state. The Italian Foreign minister, Count Ciano, had asked about Germany's plans to guarantee the integrity of Czechoslovakia. Weizsäcker repeated a comment he had made to the French ambassador: 'Czechoslovakia was dependent on Germany alone. A guarantee by any other power was worthless.'[23] This ended any hope that a British and French guarantee, which had been part of the Munich Agreement, would have any value.

Increase of German economic influence

The new Czechoslovak government recognised this. It also became worried about the economic situation facing the country after the loss of a large part of the human and economic resources in the Sudetenland. On 7 January the government called a meeting which agreed that much of the foreign investment would have to be transferred to German banks.[24] The result was that the Dresdener Bank took a major share in the Zivnostenská banka and the Böhmische Eskomptebank und Creditanstalt (Bebca).[25] The Deutsche Bank controlled the Böhmische Industrielbank, the Böhmische Eskomptebank und Creditanstalt and the Böhmische Union Bank und Deutsche Agrar- und Indistriebank. The Kreditanstalt Wiener Bank took shares in the Mährische Bank in Brno. German credit institutions and savings banks also took control of the equivalent Czech. The financing of German–Slovak trade had already come under German control and Jewish influence driven out.[26] Foreign companies had become alarmed by the aggressive German behaviour. One example is the Apollo Oil Company, which had its head office in Prague, a refinery in Bratislava and a national network of distributors. It was owned by a French consortium. The Board of Directors decided in December 1938 that an entirely new board had to be created; some of the members were Jewish and had to be excluded.

In Czechoslovakia the first step towards Arianisation had already been taken. A law of 3 December 1938 gave the state the authority to take over Jewish companies, many of which were owned by American or British Jewish institutions or in which Jewish interests held a major share. Banks were treated in the same way and came under joint German–Czech control. There were similar transfers to Germany of railway locomotives and rolling stock, industrial output and agricultural land. In total the loss of industrial assets accounted for about 40 per cent of Czechoslovakia's exports.

British and French companies could see that they would be penalised by this new German influence and sold their shares to Czech banks. The main example was Schneider-Creusot, who owned Škoda and held a minority share in the armaments company Škodovka-Zbrojovka-Explosia – the remaining 77 per cent was owned by the government. Another was the Anglo-Prague Bank.[27] Shares in the Vítkovice steel works, owned by the Austrian Rothschilds and the Gutmann Brothers, were transferred to the Alliance Assurance Co. in London. This was owned by the British branch of the Rothschild family and the Vítkovice steel works became nominally British.[28] Ownership of the important Třinec steel works east of Ostrava also passed out of Czech hands, though in this case to Poland, following the Polish acquisition of the area.

The new Czech government tried in this way to cooperate with Germany's plans for the remaining Czech lands and did all it could to win favour. In a letter of 12 January Henke reported that the Czech government had promised to deliver armaments and any other things the Germans wanted. The government was extremely worried by rumours that Germany was about to invade. Henke said that these stories originated from Sudeten sources but the Czechoslovak government also had copies of correspondence between Dr Lokscha, a German official in Brno, and Prince Franz Joseph of Liechtenstein in Vienna. These letters confirmed the rumours. When challenged by the Czech government, Henke denied any knowledge of German plans to invade Bohemia and Moravia. He also claimed that the statements had been either invented or were being inaccurately reported.

This probably did little to calm Czech fears. Chvalkovský's meeting with Hitler on 21 January did little to reassure the Czechs either. Hitler claimed that Germany and its allies were invincible and said that Czechoslovakia should reduce its army to a mere 10,000 or 20,000. He said that the Czech army still had 20,000 more soldiers than the German. The Czechs did not need an army of this size, which was useless against the Germans and a heavy financial burden. He also complained about a Jewish matter. He said Britain had promised to take 2,000 Jewish refugees and to allow them to emigrate to Australia and New Zealand, but had done nothing. These Jews were still in a concentration camp. Chvalkovský agreed, complaining that although Britain had made a loan of £10 million, there were also precise instructions about how this money was to be used to help Jews.

In a meeting the same day between Chvalkovský and Ribbentrop, further pressure was put on the Czechs to dismiss government officials who had been appointed by Beneš. Ribbentrop also repeated the earlier complaints about Czech boycotts of German business, the difficulties facing *Reichsdeutsche* who applied for residence permits and the dismissal of Germans from Czech war factories. Ribbentrop commented ominously: 'The impression ... still remained that in Czechoslovakia itself conditions lacked stability, and Germany must wait to see whether the course of reason would prevail.' He also wanted stricter press censorship and the removal of Jews from the media and administration.

British loan – help for refugees

This reference to the help offered to Jewish refugees reflects serious British concern after Munich and a widespread sense of national shame. It was widely appreciated that the condition of Jews in Czechoslovakia had deteriorated. The Lord Mayor of London had launched an appeal to try and provide help. Britain and France also agreed a £10 million loan to the Czechoslovak National Bank. Of this, £4 million was a gift, but the loan carried a 1 per cent interest charge on the full £10 million.[29] The main purpose was to pay for the maintenance and settlement or emigration of refugees 'regardless of their religion, political opinions or racial origin'. No refugees were to be forced to leave Czechoslovakia if this would endanger their health, liberty or life. The Bank of England would keep £8 million, which would not be exchanged for other currencies. Any changes to the terms of the loan would have to be agreed between the Czechoslovak government and the British liaison officer with the government, the commercial secretary at the British Legation or the French Legation in Prague. The refugees were defined as:

1. People normally resident in Czechoslovakia but either not quali-fied for Czechoslovak citizenship or qualified for it but unable to support themselves.
2. Germans or Austrians temporarily living in Czechoslovakia.
3. Any others of a status agreed by Britain and France.

The sum of £4 million was to cover the cost of emigration. Each indi-vidual or family who qualified for help but was destitute would receive £200 and the cost of transport to the person's or family's destination. The individual or family would also receive £200, in exchange for Czechoslovak crowns, in the country the person or family was going to. Any extra funds could also be exchanged for sterling or the currency of the country to which the person was going. Any dividends, interests, rents etc. were to be transferred as soon as possible and were to be guar-anteed by the Czechoslovak National Bank. In addition, the cost of providing reconstruction and other public work as employment could also be met from this loan. This was a comprehensive arrangement that was intended to cover all Jews, refugees from Austria and Germany (especially Social Democrats and Communists) and Czechoslovak citizens who could not continue to live in Czechoslovakia. Official Czech recognition of British help took the form of the award of the Order of the White Lion to British Ambassador Sir Ronald Macleaye.[30] Important work was also done by Nicholas Winton who saved 669 Jewish Czech children. Winton was a stockbroker at the London Stock Exchange who visited Prague late in 1938 at the invitation of a friend in the British Embassy. He found that nothing was being done for the children in the refugee camps. He began to organise help in early 1939 in Prague and on his return to London persuaded the Home Office to allow children to enter Britain, but he had to find a family and a £50 guarantee for each one as well as funds to help pay for the transport. In nine months, with the help of the British Committee for Refugees from Czechoslovakia and Čedok, the Czech travel agency, he organised eight trains (*Kindertransport*) from Prague to London. Another 15 boys were flown out via Sweden. But the largest train, the ninth, with 250 children, was caught in Berlin by the outbreak of war on 3 September. It is no surprise that Chvalkovský complained to Hitler about arrangements to help Jews.

The problem was that the administrative arrangements to meet the refugees' needs took time to organise and nothing could be done quickly to allow Jews to emigrate to Britain, the Commonwealth or America. Some idea of the scale of the problem can be seen in a report written in Brno (which had a large Jewish population) in January 1939. An organisation, the Emigration Movement for Moravian and Silesian Jewish Refugees, had been set up to try and help Jews escape to Palestine. One problem they faced was *Kapitalistenzertifikaten* (establishing their financial assets). For people who had assets in gold, silver or jewellery, it was hard to establish a current market value. The organisation had 2,237 members, formed of 602 families. But there were a great many young, old or ill people, who had presumably rushed to join the organisation which offered them the only chance of escape. There were few Jews from the professions – they were able to make their own arrangements and in any case were not destitute. There were 1,676 people in this category, ranging from the very young to teenage. Roughly three-quarters of the total – 73.87 per cent – were small traders. A majority of these (62 per cent) were handcraft workers, with another 11.71 per cent employed in agriculture. There were very few with any qualification: only 2.01 per cent had some form of technical training, 0.93 per cent were qualified engineers, 0.58 per cent worked in the textile industry, 1.52 per cent were doctors or worked in the medical profession. The organisation was not short of funds: it had 45 million crowns and the Czechoslovak National Bank had arranged to transfer funds for setting up business in Palestine. There was also the possibility of exporting goods there. The report shows what the problem was for many Jews. Few had the means to move elsewhere, most were small traders with their roots in Brno's Jewish society, few had any technical or professional qualification and most probably only spoke Yiddish, Czech and German. There is no suggestion in the report that this was a Zionist organisation, merely one that set out to try and help the Jews escape from potential danger. But given the problems of organising this transfer of so many people it is not surprising that few managed to leave Brno before the establishment of the Protectorate.

But this was not the only problem facing those living in the Czech lands. It was estimated that 20,000 workers had lost their jobs. Roughly one-third of these – 6,000 – were Slovak, and these returned to Slovakia.[31] But great efforts were made to try and provide work for the remainder. At the end of October 1938 a number of work camps had been established in Prague (on the Ruzyně airfield), Český Budějovice, Zlín, Brno, Klatovy and other towns. By the middle of February 1939 there were 19, consisting of 72 workshops and employing 12,000. This greatly eased the problem of unemployment.

In early February, hoping to match political with economic stability, Britain and France made another attempt to get the new Czechoslovak frontier officially recognised. But any recognition had to include a settlement of Hungarian claims as well as German. To help agree these quickly and assist Britain and France, Hungary suggested that Germany should support Hungary's demands. But Germany was in no hurry to help Hungary or any other power: 'It was a considerable time since the British had declared themselves for a frontier guarantee for Czechoslovakia ... these British views are of no interest to us. The only frontier guarantee that could be effective or of consequence for her was a German one. We had however postponed it as conditions in Czechoslovakia had not yet sufficiently calmed down.'[32] But neither Britain nor France knew of this example of Germany's intransigence and hoped to get a more positive response. In their *Notes Verbales* of 8 February, they made it clear that they were standing by their offer of a guarantee for the new frontiers in accordance with the Munich Agreement and expected Germany to do the same. They knew from Anglo-Italian talks of 12 January that before the guarantee could be signed, three conditions had to be met:

1. The internal constitution of Czechoslovakia had to be settled.
2. Czechoslovakia had to be declared neutral.
3. The new frontiers had to be precisely defined. Previously they had only been shown on maps.

The British government note ended on what was clearly intended to be a firm and decisive tone: 'His Majesty's Government would now be glad to learn the views of the German Government as to the best way of giving effect to the understanding reached at Munich in regard to the guarantee of Czechoslovakia.' Neither the British nor the French notes had any effect on German policy.

Hitler continued to cause trouble. He encouraged Slovaks to demand independence, so that when this led to open disagreement between Slovaks and Czechs, he was able to intervene. There were several rival Slovak politicians and on 12 February Hitler had a meeting with one of them, Professor Tuka.[33] Tuka was a radical Slovak separatist, who had been sentenced to a long term of imprisonment for spying and high treason in 1929. Like other Czechs and Slovaks who met Hitler, Tuka was anxious to create the right impression and addressed him as 'My Führer'. He also claimed to represent all Slovak people. Hitler's reply was to make a characteristic tirade against Czechs, repeating that they had to accept 'their natural destiny' and inferring that he favoured a situation which would enable Slovaks to have a separate existence. However, his comments were so vague that Tuka could interpret them in any way he chose. Tuka was suitably impressed and spoke of the meeting as 'the greatest day in my life'.

The Czechoslovak government also recognised Hitler's power and cut its army estimates later in February to a level that left the country virtually defenceless. Not everyone agreed that this should be done. There were opposition voices saying that Germany was leaving Czechoslovakia to her fate and that it was pointless to make concessions. Their proof was that Germany had not given the promised guarantee. What the Czechoslovak government wanted was for Czechoslovakia to be neutral, to abolish its army and to end the alliances with France and Russia. This was no more than a demonstration of Czechoslovak weakness. It was further exploited by Germany the following day, 18 February, by Göring's demand that part of the gold reserves of the Czechoslovak National Bank should be transferred to Germany.[34] Göring claimed the right to the gold on the grounds that it represented the bullion reserve covering the Czechoslovak currency that had been in the Sudetenland when that was transferred to Germany and which the Germans withdrew from circulation. The claim was valued at 391.2 million Czech crowns. The Foreign Minister, Chvalkovský, suggested that in return, the German government should take responsibility for part of the Czech national debt, but it is unlikely that this was accepted. Göring needed the gold to support the increase in arms production and prevent inflation. The transfer of the gold, held by the Bank of International Settlement at Basel, was finally agreed on 13 March.[35]

In spite of this growing German pressure, or perhaps as a desperate last attempt to restore independence, the Czech government sent notes to Britain, France, Italy and Germany simultaneously. In these the government stated that it was asking for a guarantee for its frontiers to be linked to neutrality and a promise of non-intervention in Czech affairs. The German reply was characteristically cool: '... it must strike me [Weizsäcker] as strange that in such a matter the Czechoslovak Government should approach all four Munich Powers simultaneously, without entering into an exchange of views on the subject with us alone'.

At the beginning of March the Czechoslovak government took further steps to appease Hitler. It offered to have a German minister in the Cabinet, to be nominated by Berlin, and the government would reorganise the army to suit German wishes. Minority ethnic groups would be protected and there would be cooperation on economic and currency policy. In return the Czechs asked once again for a guarantee, but without success. Pressure soon mounted from Slovakia as well. On 7 March a group of Slovak ministers demanded a reduction in the Slovak share of the financial burden in the budget, far-reaching concessions in managing departments with joint membership and responsibilities, the dismissal of General Syrový from his post of Minister of Defence in Slovakia, and for all government decrees to require the countersignature of Slovak ministers. If these demands had been met in full, they would have given Slovaks a large measure of equality with Czechs but without the same financial burden. But the real reason for these demands was to provoke a breakdown in Czech–Slovak relations. The Slovaks believed that the Czechs could not accept these demands in full. This would give them an excuse to declare independence. However, the group making these demands only represented a minority. When the Prague government told them that they were free to declare independence, the majority of Slovaks said they would prefer to remain in Czechoslovakia.

Hitler's aim, as noted already, was that Slovakia should be a puppet state under German control. Hitler's meeting with Tuka had been intended as part of that strategy. In early March rumours began reaching the Czechoslovak government that Germany was planning to grant economic assistance to Slovakia if the latter would proclaim independence. When asked about this Henke, as usual, claimed that he had no knowledge of it. But these were not the only rumours that suggested that Germany was about to take action against Czechoslovakia. The same day, 9 March, Councillor Schubert of the Czechoslovak Legation in Berlin reported:

1. The Landrat of Landskron was issuing passports to Sudeten Germans who wanted to visit Czechoslovakia for six months only. He had commented that after that Czechoslovakia would be occupied.
2. A financial official at Eisenbrodt in North Moravia had said that Germany would occupy Czechoslovakia in four weeks.

3. A treasury official at Wimberg (Böhmerwald) had also said that German troops would soon occupy Czechoslovakia.
4. There was information from a French source that troop movements were taking place on the German–Czech frontier and that presumably Czechoslovakia would be occupied.
5. Diplomats in Berlin were openly expecting Slovakia and the Ruthene area to declare their independence and be given to Hungary in return for the latter's help in any war against Romania.

What these rumours suggest was that German troops were moving into position close to the frontier, as Hitler had ordered earlier. It was impossible to hide this from the local populations, and the soldiers themselves were bound to draw some conclusions from what was happening. The diplomats were also correct in thinking that events in Slovakia were moving towards a crisis. On 10 March Altenburg, Head of Political Division IVb, reported that talks between the Prague government and the Slovak ministers Tiso and Sidor had broken down. The Slovaks would not promise not to declare Slovak independence. President Hácha dismissed the Slovak Prime Minister Tiso and two other ministers, Durčansky and Pružinsky, and had them arrested. Under the constitution he had the power to do this and was preparing to form a new Slovak government under Sidor. This was an unexpectedly firm move by the Czech President, who hoped to bring the situation in Slovakia under control.

But it provoked the crisis that Hitler had been waiting for. The following day, 11 March, Keitel drafted an ultimatum which would be given to the Czech President. The terms were:

1. No resistance by the army or police. The army to stay in barracks.
2. All aircraft, military, transport and civil to be grounded.
3. All anti-aircraft guns and machine guns to be stored in barracks.
4. No alterations to be made to airfields.
5. All officials to remain at their posts ready to hand over to Germans.
6. All business and commercial life to continue as normal.
7. No anti-German public statements.

The tension was heightened by reports of Polish and Hungarian troop movements on Czechoslovak frontiers. Fighting broke out in Brno on 13 March between groups of Czechs and Germans. The same day, the Hungarian Regent told Hitler that he was planning a frontier incident on the 16th, which would be followed by an attack (on the Ruthene area).

Hitler was forced to take action. He had talks with Tiso the same day in which he again attacked what he termed the 'Beneš spirit' and claimed that Germans had suffered intolerable losses through mass dismissal from jobs.[36] In terms that were reminiscent of the pre-Munich crisis he said that there was turmoil in Czechoslovakia and he could not tolerate this. As in other situations, Hitler said he wanted to resolve the matter very quickly: 'It was not a question of days but of hours'. To further emphasise this he said that Slovakia should declare independence or be abandoned. He also told Tiso that Hungarian troops were reported to be on the Slovak frontier. Later that day Henke reported on further disturbances in Prague in which the Czech fascists had sided with Nazis in anti-Semitic activities, though he considered that the fascist leader Gajda was anti-German.

The German government now made the final preparations for seizing the rest of Bohemia and Moravia. The German Legation in Prague was ordered not to receive any communications from the Czechoslovak government for the next few days. The Italian ambassador in Berlin was told that the Czech government had acted high-handedly in a number of ways: in the Ruthene area, in appointing a Czech general as minister in Slovakia and in dismissing Tiso and setting up a new government under Sidor. Germany also claimed that there had been disturbances in which Germans were ill-treated and claimed that this showed the emergence of the old Beneš spirit. Events in Slovakia were brought to a head by a telegram declaring Slovak independence. This had apparently been drawn up by Tiso and Kepler, a German Foreign Office official. The telegram called for German protection for an independent Slovakia.

The stage was now set for the seizure of the rest of the Czech lands. At 9.30 p.m. the Abwehr reported that the Czechoslovak government had called up reservists and troops were moving towards Slovakia.

Polish forces were moving towards the Ruthene area and reservists had been called up in Hungary. But there was no military activity in France or Britain. The British government had been warned that something of this sort might happen. Henderson, the British ambassador in Berlin, had written to Halifax on 9 March about Hitler's possible plans for eastward expansion.[37] He had questioned whether Britain could continue to rely on Hitler's promises. The same day Henderson had a long talk with State Secretary Weizsäcker about the crisis. Henderson was particularly anxious that the visit by Stanley, President of the Board of Trade, should not coincide with any violent German action against Czechoslovakia. When asked whether Germany was planning either to destroy or preserve Czechoslovakia, Weizsäcker claimed that all Germany wanted was order, though this was being undermined by Czech attacks on Germans. Henderson ended the conversation by saying that Britain recognised that German interests were paramount in the Czech area. At midday came the first definite news from the German consul at Chust. He reported that four regiments of Hungarian soldiers had invaded the Ruthene area. Czech troops and the Sitsch militia (who had been armed by the Czechs) were likely to resist and fighting had broken out. The Hungarian government sent an ultimatum to Prague demanding the withdrawal of Czech forces from the Ruthene area and an end to ill-treatment of Hungarians there.

However, in London the German ambassador tried to calm British fears. He told Sir Horace Wilson that newspaper reports of the imminent entry of German troops into Moravia were untrue and that the situation was relatively calm. But he presumably knew that Germany was planning to invade Slovakia as well as the Czech lands. Weizsäcker warned the German consul in Bratislava by telephone that German troops would enter Slovakia, bypass Bratislava and advance as far as the valley of the River Vah. The consul was to inform the Slovak government at once because the troops would begin their advance at 6.00 a.m. The Hungarians had decided to invade the Ruthene area. First there would be small-scale preliminary raids on 14–16 March and invasion would follow on the 18th. Hungarian troops would advance to the Polish frontier and occupy the whole area. This would prevent

Poland, which also had an interest there, seizing any Ruthene territory. This gave Hitler the chance of encouraging rival Polish–Hungarian claims in the future if he so wanted.

The situation in Czechoslovakia had now reached a critical stage. Hácha must have realised that rumours of German, Hungarian and Polish military activity, as well as stories of civil unrest, originated in Germany. Whatever Hitler was planning was also influencing Czechoslovakia's diplomatic opponents Poland and Hungary. Faced with threats from so many quarters and aware of Czech military weakness, Hácha decided to go to Berlin and appeal to Hitler. This was a brave move by a modest, man of 66 in poor health (he had a weak heart). He was advised by his doctors not to fly and arranged instead to travel to Berlin by Pullman train.[38] Hácha left Prague at 4.15 p.m. but did not reach Berlin until 10.40 p.m. He was given a short time to rest and at 11.30 was called to an interview with Ribbentrop. The meeting with Hitler did not begin until 1.15 a.m. The records show that Hitler was taking no chances. He had already drafted the ultimatum and German troops were about to invade Czechoslovakia. Hácha appeared to be open to German pressure, but his bold move earlier in sacking and imprisoning Tiso – who had Hitler's support – and two other Slovaks showed that he was very determined and courageous. His spirit had to be broken if Hitler was to succeed.

Hitler had already prepared the Italians for his next move. Weizsäcker had made the case for German intervention to the Italian ambassador. His claims about events in the Czech lands are worth quoting in detail:

> The Czechoslovak state is breaking up. The Hungarians have invaded the Carpatho-Ukraine. Slovakia has declared her independence. The rump territories of Bohemia and Moravia are in a desperate state. Chaotic conditions prevail in the German-language enclaves. Incidents have been reported from the north. There German troops are about to occupy certain areas. The fate of our fellow Germans in Bohemia and Moravia is causing us great concern. The Prague President, Hácha, and Foreign Minister Chvalkovský, who undertook this [visit to Berlin] on

their own initiative, are expected this evening in Berlin. The Führer is absolutely determined to establish peace in Bohemia and Moravia. The future fate and the political structure of Bohemia and Moravia will be discussed today with Hácha. This territory must never again be a military power. The Beneš spirit has again shown its head; our patience is exhausted. Intrigues have been spun with our enemies in the west. [Beneš was now living in London.][39]

Weizsäcker concluded by saying that the crisis concerned Italy as well as Germany and was 'a useful preparation for a contest in another direction which will be necessary sooner or later' and which would involve both Axis powers.

Hácha knew nothing of this. While he was travelling to Berlin the first part of the German invasion began. At 5.30 p.m. German troops entered the southern part of the city of Ostrava (south of the River Morava). There was no Czech resistance and the Leibstandarte (SS) occupied the city at 6.40. The German defence of this illegal act was that Czechoslovakia had descended into chaos and Germany was forced to restore order. This was the situation when Hácha finally met Hitler early on the morning of 15 March. Hitler was anxious that Hácha should see this as a confrontation between an all-powerful Germany and a weak Czechoslovakia. On the German side were Ribbentrop, Foreign Minister Göring, Keitel, head of the armed forces, Weizsäcker and three senior state officials. Hácha had only the obsequious Chvalkovský to support him. After Hácha had tried to win Hitler's favour, Hitler replied with his usual mixture of false ingenuousness and open threats. He claimed that he had never been anti-Czech and had tried to minimise the damage done to the state. He then announced to a no doubt astonished Hácha that German troops had already begun to invade Czechoslovakia to ensure the safety of the German people. The main part of the invasion would begin at 6 a.m. Any resistance would be faced with overwhelming force and would be broken with great brutality. The choice for the Czech people was either to fight and be crushed or to accept German control, which would continue to guarantee that the Czechs had their own head of state and a degree of autonomy. On the positive side, Hitler claimed that German control would invigorate the Czech economy, which would flourish. At one point Hácha collapsed and had to be revived. Eventually he accepted the inevitable and a joint German–Czech statement was issued stating that Hácha had 'placed the fate of the Czech people and country in the hands of the Führer of the German Reich. The Führer accepted this declaration and expressed his intention of taking the Czech people under the protection of the German Reich and of guaranteeing them an autonomous development of their ethnic life as suited to their character.[40] Hácha had accepted the ultimatum. On hearing this news, the Czechoslovak government resigned.

German invasion of Czechoslovakia

To the Czechs this news came as a profound shock. This is graphically described by František Fajtl, at that time a young air force lieutenant.[41] He woke early on the morning of 15 March and heard the news on the radio. He felt overwhelmed, humiliated and insulted. He woke others in the air force barracks and they all felt equally powerless, having heard on the radio that they were under orders to hand over the aerodrome and aircraft intact to the Germans. It was impossible to do anything else. Snow was falling and no one could have taken off and flown the aircraft abroad. They soon learnt that the air force barracks at Olomouc had been occupied at 7 a.m. and later that morning a German officer arrived to check the aircraft and place the airfield under armed guard. Fajtl's description of the German occupation makes it clear that many Germans felt that they were superior to the Czechs and provided this was recognised, the Czechs would be treated fairly. For the Czechs, this was not acceptable and Fajtl was one of many who subsequently escaped to Poland.

The occupation first of Ostrava and then of the rest of Bohemia and Moravia came as a profound shock to the Czechs. No one had expected it and they were stunned. Mark Slouka's novel provides a graphic account of the reaction of ordinary Czechs to the German motorcade on Národní Avenue carrying Hitler to Hradčany Castle on that day.

The speaker is Hanuš, the crippled survivor of the Mauthausen concentration camp, remembering the scene years later:

> And suddenly they're there, like a thunderclap out of a March blizzard, the Mercedes limousines with their horsehair-stuffed seats moving down Národní Avenue past the statues and the frozen saints to the river. The city is quiet. No people, no trams. The tracks are still, the cobbles are marbled with snow like that cake your mother gets in that deli on Queens Boulevard. Gargoyles with long tongues stare from their niches under the pediment. You watch from inside your apartment, looking through cracks in the curtains, like everyone else. As they pass, far below, you can hear the snap and crack of banners.
>
> There's nothing to be done. Nothing at all. The motorcade passes over the Vltava. The walls of Hradčany Castle are barely visible; the archers' clefts are empty. In the woods of Petřín, which are also deserted, there is only the slicing sound of the snow, seeping up through the orchards. The government, the newspaper says, has been dissolved. Bohemia and Moravia – the woods, the fields, the towns, the paths you knew, the ponds you swam in – are now called the 'Protektorat Böhmen und Mähren' ... And still, even now, inside of you, it doesn't feel as if anything has changed. Things go on.[42]

This description in a novel catches the Czech sense of shock and betrayal. In reality the streets of Prague did have people welcoming Hitler when he visited the city and spoke from the balcony of the Hradčany Castle. The banners were Nazi banners, put there by members of the Nazi Party. The streets were certainly not silent; there was a large German population in Prague who turned out to welcome Hitler. But for the Czechs, whose country was being seized in this dramatic way, the silent observation through gaps in drawn curtains was real, or very close to it.

As for France and Britain, trying to solve a European problem in Czechoslovakia, their initial reaction was predictable but ineffective. The French ambassador in Berlin visited Weizsäcker on the afternoon of 15 March and read him the instructions that he had received from Paris. These included the following:

> The Munich Agreement had been regarded in France as a factor contributing to peace, as a definite stage in Franco–German relations, and as a beginning of Franco–German cooperation. The instruction then touched upon the guarantee annex to the Munich Agreement, then passed on to the agreement for consultation of December 6, 1938, and compared with that Germany's action against Czechoslovakia (namely the invasion of Moravia near Mährisch-Ostrau on the afternoon of March 14). From this the instruction concluded that serious anxiety regarding Germany's attitude toward the rest of Europe was justified.[43]

The French ambassador was deeply shocked by Germany's action, which had broken the Munich Agreement. Weizsäcker's reply probably disturbed him even more, for he justified Germany's action in terms of what he claimed were Czech mistakes and said that Germany had been forced to intervene. France, in Weizsäcker's view, should do well to forget the Munich Agreement, not lecture Germany, and turn eyes westward.

The British reaction was more muted. Henderson, the British ambassador in Berlin, merely said:

> His Majesty's Government have no desire to interfere unnecessarily in a matter with which other Governments may be more directly concerned than His Majesty's Government in the United Kingdom. They are, however, as the German Government will surely appreciate, deeply concerned for the success of all efforts to restore confidence and a relaxation of tension in Europe.[44]

The remainder of the statement was concerned with improving economic relations and the effect of Germany's actions on general European confidence. Churchill's comment the previous day had been more perceptive: 'In the destruction of Czechoslovakia the entire balance of Europe was changed. Many people at the time of the September Crisis thought they were only giving away the interests of Czechoslovakia, but with every month that passes you will see that they were giving away the interests of Britain and the interests of peace and justice.'[45] Dirksen, the German ambassador in London, tried to justify the action by claiming that it was forced upon Germany. The Japanese sent their congratulations. German troops had entered Prague on 15 March. An English journalist, G. E. R. Gedye, sent a graphic account of the Czech shock and sadness. On 16 March Weizsäcker sent a note to all foreign embassies informing them that Tiso had asked Hitler to take Slovakia under German protection and Hitler had agreed to accept this. Karmasin, leader of the German minority in Slovakia, used this opportunity to ask Henlein, now Gauleiter for the Sudetenland, for funds to support the Germans there.

While this was happening Hungarian troops invaded the Ruthene area. Germany made it clear that it had no interest in the area and Hungary could continue its military advance. Germany would not make it a protectorate. Hungary, Poland and Romania, which all had interests there, were left to settle the matter among themselves. Finally, Hitler issued a proclamation setting out the form of the new administration of the Czech lands, emphasising Germany's absolute control over the state which they now called Czechia. The official establishment of the new Protectorate followed on 16 March.[46]

The Protectorate

The creation of the Protectorate was more than just the seizure of territory. It was the first time that Hitler had taken control of land that was populated predominantly by people who were not German. Though linked to a Germanic culture by trade and industry by their Habsburg past, Czechs were believers in the virtues of parliamentary democracy and liberal institutions. If Hitler was to control and exploit these people, he had to have their tacit support, at least initially. The man he chose to act as the supreme political figure, the *Reichsprotektor*, was not a rabid Nazi. Baron Konstantin von Neurath was a conservative Württemberg aristocrat. Some regarded the appointment of Neurath as a reward by Hitler for past favours. Neurath had helped to resolve the Munich crisis the previous September. But a more likely reason was the fact that, for all his ideas of German superiority over Czechs, Neurath could be relied on to treat the Czechs with courtesy and emphasise the rule of law rather than political opportunism. In the same way, nothing was done to disturb the economy, which had already suffered severe blows from the transfer of the Sudetenland. Nor was there any immediate action against the Jews. In the same way the general commanding the German troops in the Protectorate, Johannes Blaskowitz, maintained discipline among his troops. He also treated the Czech forces with respect, ordering German soldiers to salute Czech officers and used German troops to stop looting of Czech homes by Slovaks in the Slovak territory under his control.

This was the appearance of normality that Hitler wanted to create to ensure that the Czechs would continue to administer the Protectorate. Without this, it would have been impossible to continue normal government. There were nowhere near enough Sudeten Germans who could speak Czech to do the work otherwise. But hidden behind this facade was the political reality that was established by Hitler's decree, published on 16 March. This gave Neurath total power. Under him, the Czechs had their own president, government and legal system, and were in theory autonomous. In reality, though, the Czech legal system continued to be the basis for the state, Neurath had the power to cancel any action by the Czech government if he considered it to be against the interests of the Reich. The Reich could also issue regulations. Neurath could dismiss members of the government and Hitler could dismiss the president, though Hitler never found it necessary to do so. The Protectorate was made part of an enlarged Reich – *Grossdeutsches Reich* – though it did not enjoy the same status as the Reich *Gaue* and *Länder*. Germany controlled all the normal important functions of government – defence, foreign policy, the army, customs, monetary policy and even post and telecommunications, thus ensuring effective censorship.[47] The Czech population, unable to oppose this, tried to unite and make the best of the situation. The result was a sense of national unity, reflected in the coalescing of political parties into one from which only the Communists were excluded. Czechs found it easier to accept these new, straightened political circumstances because they had rejected the old, liberal views after being abandoned by France. Thus Czechs came to accept the more authoritarian stance of the German-controlled Czech government.

For Hitler there remained the lingering fear of a Czech revival. He prevented this by disbanding the army and replacing it with a token military unit of 280 officers and 7,000 men in the summer of 1939. It was not popular among Czechs and few wished to serve in it. Hitler argued that the Czechs no longer needed an army because they would become a neutral state. When the army and air force were demobilised in the spring, most found work in industry and commerce. The majority were employed in the Protectorate but later some went to Germany, attracted by offers of higher pay. Initially they were reasonably well treated, though they never had the same status as German workers. Some decided that they had to escape abroad and join foreign armies that might eventually drive out the Germans. Many of these escaped to Poland, joined the French Foreign Legion at French consulates or the French embassy and were taken to France, where they served in the battle of 1940. After Dunkirk they went to England, where they were formed into a Czech unit in the British army. The pilots fought in the Battle of Britain. František Fajtl was one of these.

The story of these pilots was the basis for a recent film *Tmavo modrý svět* [Dark blue world] directed by Jan Svěrák. Though they never formed a large part of the RAF they made an important contribution as fighter and bomber pilots and air crew. The highest-scoring pilot in the Battle of Britain was a Czech fighter pilot in a Polish squadron. Others, such as Josef Beneš, were soldiers.[48] Beneš received his demobilisation papers from the Czechoslovak army in April and initially joined an illegal group in Brno, one of many that were created in March 1939. When it became clear that these groups had no effective role their members escaped abroad. Beneš, like Fajtl, went to Poland. From there he went to Sweden and eventually reached London. When there were sufficient numbers of Czech soldiers in England, they were formed into a Czech Legion. Others who joined the French Foreign Legion in Poland later served in North Africa as part of the Czech army. Still more went east, some joining the Slovak forces who fought as German allies in Russia; others to Russia, where they eventually formed part of the Ukrainian army that invaded eastern Slovakia via the Dukla Pass in 1944.[49] Less fortunate were those who reached Spain and were interned in a concentration camp.

These were the men from the Czechoslovak army and air force. There remained the question of what would happen to their weapons and equipment. Earlier, in September 1938 during the Runciman mission, Czech military leaders had realised that whatever the outcome of the crisis, they would no longer need all the stocks of weapons and ammunition. They offered to sell these to Britain, hoping in this way that they would not fall into German hands, but the offer was rejected.[50] The official British reason was that Czech weapons were of a different calibre. The British attitude towards Czech weapons had been summed up in a secret letter from Morton, an official at the Foreign Office, to General Ismay in September 1938. Morton had no idea of the likely quantity or quality of the Czechoslovak weapons and equipment. His only concern was that they might be sold to Hitler's allies. He commented: 'It is necessary to keep a close watch on what happens to them [the arms]. If they are not used to strengthen German defence forces, the Germans may endeavour to sell them to countries already armed with weapons of a similar type, obtaining thereby further political and economic advantages. Or the weapons may be used in Spain, China, Palestine etc. wars [sic].' Morton was a diplomat, not a military expert. A similar view has been expressed more recently by Richard Evans: 'All of this [the very large number of aircraft, artillery etc.] amounted to only a tiny fraction of Germany's military requirements; some was sold abroad in any case to earn much-needed foreign currency.'[51] Both Morton and Evans have taken Hitler's claims concerning German military strength at face value.

Hitler had claimed that his army was immensely powerful and was fully equipped with the most modern weapons. Military parades and exercises appeared to confirm this boast. It was only when many military vehicles broke down during the entry of German troops into Austria that more perceptive observers could have seen the reality. Many items were of excellent quality but there were nowhere near enough for the major war that Hitler expected to have to fight at some time. Nor had all the equipment been tested rigorously under battle conditions. Hitler had recognised the importance of Czech military equipment and factories as early as 1937 when he commented on the plan to invade Czechoslovakia. He recognised that it might be necessary to destroy Czech factories during the planned advance but he wanted to ensure that the short war would inflict as little damage as possible, especially to factories such as Škoda which were major armaments producers. In the same way, after Munich, Hitler began to use these resources by making the Czech government agree to change military production to meet German needs and begin supplying the Wehrmacht with weapons and military equipment.

Above all, it was the quality of Czech armaments that counted for so much. This is borne out by General Major Hellmuth Rheinhardt, who was questioned about captured war material in 1952.[52] Rheinhardt was scathing in his comments on most Austrian military equipment taken after the *Anschluss* and which was sold to Hungary. He said that most of the equipment was old and only the mountain artillery was useful. By contrast the Czech equipment was of excellent quality and played an important part in Germany's battles in the first year of the war.[53] Some idea of the scale of this booty can be seen from the fact that there was enough to equip 11 infantry divisions. And although Germany won the battle in France by superior military strategy rather than larger numbers, these additional 11 divisions were an important element in the German victories.

The Wehrmacht was well aware of the value of these items. A preliminary inspection of the Protectorate had been made on the day that Germany invaded Czechoslovakia. Special units had been given the task of locating and inspecting the Czech military equipment. Fajtl's account of the arrival of the German officer at his airfield near Olomouc and the immediate posting of German sentries showed that the Wehrmacht did not want to lose any of the aircraft, ammunition or other equipment.[54] The Wehrmacht made a preliminary report of their survey of all military bases on 16 March and on the 22nd reported on the transfer of military equipment to Germany. There was a total of eight Czech military depots (Tábor, Písek, Klattau, Taus, Příbram, Rokitzan, Plzeň and Budweis (Czech Budějovice)). There were also three camps in Brno and five tank depots.[55] The contents of all these were very quickly sent to Germany. Two-thirds – 19,000 wagon loads – had arrived there by 22 March.[56] By 24 March, 24 trains had been sent to Berlin and it was expected that the rest of the equipment would reach Germany by mid May. These figures show the huge quantities of military equipment that fell into German hands. In total it amounted to 2.6 million weapons, 180,849 rounds of ammunition, 1,838 3.7 cm anti-tank guns and large quantities of artillery shells: 2,000 8 cm., 1,609 10 cm., 1,005 15 cm. There were also 3,270 mines, 4,338 artillery guns, 2,274 revolvers, 6,601 grenades, 22.6 million rounds of Czech and 2.7 million rounds of Russian machine-gun ammunition as well as 3,903 lorries. There were also 1,951 gun barrels as well as gas masks, uniforms, horses and saddles. But this was not the total amount because other military depots were found later and Škoda was manufacturing items under government contracts.

One outstanding Czech weapon was the 4.7 cm anti-tank gun, which Rheinhardt considered the most important self-propelled weapon in the first year of the war. There were also two types of tank: the Škoda type 35 and the ČKD type 38. The Škoda was the main battle tank in the Czech army in 1939 and 424 had been made between 1935 and 1938. It was technically advanced, with pneumatically operated transmission and more than adequate armour and fire power. But it proved unreliable in service. When the Germans seized the Czech military equipment, only about half of these tanks were ready for action. The Germans recognised the tank's potential and systematically rebuilt it. This solved the technical problems, and it remained in service in the German army for three years.[57] The other type, the ČKD 38, was a newer design, first built as a prototype in 1937. It was the outright winner of competitive tests in 1938 and as a result an order for 150 had been placed immediately.[58] But production was slowed by the Munich Agreement and none had been delivered before March 1939. The Germans placed an order for these 150 tanks to be completed and production was continued until 1942. By then 1,168 had been made. The tank later served in most theatres of the war except Africa.[59] When it became outclassed by the new Russian T34, the chassis was used as the basis for a variety of military vehicles, including a tank destroyer. Production of this, the *Hetzer,* continued until the end of the war. This huge quantity of captured equipment was not the only benefit that Germany gained. The Škoda type 35 tank design was later sold to Hungary and ČKD tanks were bought by Sweden and Romania. In both cases these enabled Germany's allies, Hungary and Romania, to assist in the invasion of Russia in 1941.

Less important, though still significant, were more than 1,000 aircraft that fell into German hands. These were a variety of Czech, French and Russian designs, built under licence. There were six fighter squadrons at airfields at Prague, Olomouc, Piešťany and Hradec Králové and two bomber squadrons at Prague and Milovice.[60] At the Olomouc airfield, for example, there were eight different types, but most were biplanes, some intended as front-line fighters and others for training and transport. The best fighter was the Avia B35, designed originally as a fast biplane in the mid 1930s, but by the time of the Protectorate it had been redesigned as a fast monoplane.[61] In March 1939 there were 450 of these in the Czech air force, of which half were the latest Mk IV version. When it had been designed as a high-speed fighter in the mid 1930s, it was one of the best ever produced. However, even in monoplane version, it could not match the main German fighters such as the Messerschmitt Bf-109. Also, because it had been designed for speed, visibility from the cockpit was very poor. Many of these were sold to Germany's allies to raise money and during the war were used in Bulgarian, German, Greek and Slovak air forces. The two squadrons of Czechoslovak bombers consisted of French MB-200 and Russian B-71, built under licence. Of these, only the Russian bomber could be considered a modern aircraft. The Czech air force, recognising the need for a more advanced fighter, had tried to buy the Hawker Hurricane, but the British were reluctant to divert any from the Royal Air Force.

Another important item, normally overlooked, is the large number of army horses: 15,000, of which 13,000 were sent to Germany. The Second World War may appear in hindsight to have been a mechanised war. But throughout the conflict, and especially on the eastern front in winter and spring or when the roads were largely impassable for mechanised vehicles, supplies were moved from rail depots to the front line by horse and cart. As the fuel shortage became more serious, horse-drawn transport became even more important. One can see this in the example of three young men in the Schindler family from a village in Silesia. Their father was one of three village blacksmiths and two of his sons were used to working with horses. They served in the army on the eastern front, two bringing supplies by horse and cart to the front line and the third was a motor mechanic. One died after being shot by partisans in July 1941. Another suffered from severe frostbite and spent a year in hospital. The third, Kurt, survived the war. He was transferred from the Russian front, first to Austria, then to Germany and in 1944 was in Normandy at the time of the D-Day landings, still doing the same work. He was wounded, taken prisoner and ended the war in a British military hospital in Birmingham. In view of the significant part that horses played in the war, to gain 15,000 and all their equipment was a major advantage, especially since in Germany by 1939 there was a growing shortage of leather for saddles and harness.

These were the military gains that Germany made. Away from the army depots and railways, civilian life continued much as before. Neurath initially wanted to control the population rather than exploit them. Representatives of the Four Year Plan and the Reich Economic Ministry came to Prague in March but did not introduce any radical changes in the Czech economy. Czechs adapted as best they could to the new circumstances. Companies found it more difficult to do business because of the transfer of the Sudetenland and the new German frontiers. One result was that the two largest Czechoslovak chemical and metallurgical production factories of the Aussiger Verein and Falkenau, which were in Aussig, were now in Germany. The technical and sales management was predominantly Czech and Jewish and the firms were given German managing directors.[62] Aussig was an important chemical and metallurgical town. There were already foreign investments there, including the Alpine Edelstahl Ges m.b.H., which was owned completely by the Austrian Montangesellschaft of Vienna.[63]

Some firms reacted to the economic crisis by forming cartels to try and regulate trade. In Plzeň and the surrounding Czech area, for example, companies felt threatened by the new frontier which had been established a short distance away. One group formed a cartel headed by two brickmakers: E. Škoda akc., Em. Klotz a spol. and a building company Cihelna stavitelů plzeňských s.r.o., who contributed 3.1 million crowns, 2.4 million crowns and 1.2 million crowns respectively.[64] A legal firm, JU Dr Jaroslav Lobkowitz, gave 1.8 million crowns. Three others contributed 1 million or 1.5 million crowns and the remainder between 100,000 and 700,000 crowns. The cartel remained in existence until 1949, when it was wound up after the Communist seizure of power. In the case of Jewish firms, Neurath to begin with acted cautiously. In the Sudetenland Jewish business had been seized soon after the transfer of the land to Germany. Eric Pasold, for example, on a visit to Fleissen (now in Germany) in the summer of 1939 from his factory in England, was offered the chance to buy former Jewish companies cheaply, but refused the offer. In the Protectorate, it was not until June that the Czech administration passed a law making it possible to seize Jewish property.[65]

In the case of large companies that were of interest to Germany, Germans were quickly appointed to senior positions. In the case of Škoda, Gen. Barckhausen joined the company on 19 March as the Wehrmacht's official representative – a move that had clearly been planned in advance. The Dresdener Bank had gained an interest in Škoda earlier through its control of the Česká escomptní banka and German influence in the company continued to grow with the appointment of Albert Göring, Hermann's little known brother, as Export Director in the summer of 1939. Companies looked for opportunities to cooperate with German or Austrian firms. Škoda held secret negotiations with the Austrian firm Steyr in April. Steyr manufactured small-calibre weapons, cars and motorcycles and would have gained a great deal from working closely with an industrial giant like Škoda. However, it seems that the talks did not progress beyond preliminary discussions.[66] Elsewhere, as in the coal-mining industry in Ostrava, Germans imposed their control by appointing a German to run the company and sending staff for intensive German classes for three months. Then, everything was conducted in German.

By the summer, the German authorities felt strong enough to make further demands. They persuaded the Bank of England to allow

800,000 ounces of gold belonging to the Czechoslovak National Bank to be transferred to Prague. Although the British government was unhappy about this transfer, officials at the Bank of England argued that they could not prevent it because it was a legal transaction and in accordance with normal banking practice. By June, Czechs had begun to recover their confidence and mounted a boycott of German business. As tensions rose, a German policeman was murdered in Kladno and the Gestapo arrested the whole town council. They were all beaten and some died. This growing tension provided Karl Frank, the Sudeten German who controlled the police and SS, to persuade Neurath to introduce harsh measures to control the Czech population, and one result was the introduction of the regulations directed against the Jews. This did not crush the Czechs, however. It was followed by a warning in August that any act of sabotage against any state property, including railways and public utilities, would be very severely punished. Not only would the culprit suffer, but the whole Czech population would also be held responsible. This was the situation when Germany invaded Poland and the Second World War broke out. It was followed by student demonstrations in October and an increasingly harsh regime by Karl Frank.

In conclusion, it is clear from the German diplomatic correspondence that the Munich Conference was never intended as a final solution but only a stage in bringing Bohemia, Moravia and Slovakia under German control. The manipulation of rivalry between different nationalities led inevitably to the same ethnic tensions that had existed earlier and to the same claims of ill-treatment of ethnic Germans. Hitler was well aware of differences between Slovaks who wanted complete independence and others who wished to remain in Czechoslovakia. His attempts to foster discord by encouraging Tiso failed initially and he had to wait for rivalries to become more pronounced. But although many Czechoslovak politicians were prepared to follow a pro-German line, others understood only too well what was happening. They were in a minority and it was clear that the Czech government lacked military power. There was little that could be done in the face of German threats. It is therefore all the more surprising that at times Czechs took bold steps to assert their own authority and challenge Hitler.

Such a situation was when Hácha dismissed and imprisoned Tiso and two other Slovak politicians and appointed a new government. But the failure of Britain and France to support Hácha or create an effective guarantee of the rump state shows their own weakness. The main characteristics of Hitler's policy were the speed and decisiveness with which he acted, while at the same time appearing reasonable. It was only when Hitler had blatantly broken the Munich Agreement by invading Bohemia and Moravia that politicians in Britain and France finally recognised the type of man they were dealing with. By then it was too late to save Czechoslovakia. The creation of the Protectorate in March 1939 initially had little effect on the rump Czechoslovak state. Neurath's moderation and the German army policy of appearing to support Czech authority persuaded many Czechs to accept the inevitable and make the best they could of the new situation. The new sense of national solidarity was the one positive result. But by the summer, Czech confidence had begun to return and the murder of a German policeman led inevitably to much stronger measures, including seizure of Jewish businesses and imprisonment of Czech students in a concentration camp. The outbreak of war led inevitably to complete German takeover and exploitation of the Czech economic resources and people.

CHAPTER 3

THE PROTECTORATE GOVERNMENT

It is difficult to assess the impact of German administration of the Protectorate in any fair and dispassionate way. On the one hand there is the view of apologists for the German regime that argued that Germany brought greater efficiency to the business sector, providing jobs and improving the social welfare of the workers – Czech as well as German. There was cooperation between German and Czech firms as the Czechs helped fulfil armaments contracts. Germans might argue, as one German official did after working in the Netherlands, that:

> In the war there was the chance to modernise one's own [i e. Dutch] industry, extend lines, gain modern technical procedures at no cost, develop one's ideas further, keep people in work, and not least to make reasonable profits, which enabled the national budget to fulfil its duties through taxation.[1]

This assumes, among other things, that German industry was better managed and more efficient than that in the countries that Germany conquered. It also assumes that Germans were willing to share their knowledge with those under their control. Neither is necessarily true. What is true of the Czech lands is that in the beginning Hitler appointed a man as *Reichsprotektor*, Neurath, who tried to make his rule, in his own eyes, firm but fair. This changed when he was replaced by Reinhard Heydrich, a ruthless and committed Nazi. But under Neurath there was a degree of economic cooperation as businessmen looked for ways of keeping their firms profitable. From this point of view, with most Czechs passive, life might have continued largely unchanged, though under a harsher regime, had it not been for the assassination of Heydrich in 1942. There followed a regime of terror, after which came Albert Speer's drive to mobilise the Protectorate's economy for total war. This created much greater hardship: more workers were sent to Germany and in the Protectorate everyone worked much longer hours under an increasingly strict regime. Anyone opposing it in any way was likely to be sent to a concentration camp. But meanwhile there was a Czech government in Prague and much of the administration remained in Czech hands, as in other occupied countries. Was this benign but hard rule appropriate for wartime, or harsh exploitation? This chapter will seek to explain the reality of German rule from the entry of German troops in 1939 to the end of the war.

On 16 March 1939 the Czech Parliament passed a law placing the Czech lands under the protection of Germany. The Czech President, Hácha, had been forced to agree to this at his meeting with Hitler the previous day and the law merely confirmed the decision. On the surface the 11 clauses made little change to the condition of life in the Czech lands.[2] The Protectorate was guaranteed independence and its government could follow policies that were appropriate to the Czech people. Its foreign policy would be in harmony with that of Germany. This bland statement was far from the reality. Hitler, speaking from the balcony of Prague castle on the 16th, had told the Czechs the blunt truth that their country no longer existed and the Protectorate was under Germany's protection. He also announced that he would appoint a *Reichsprotektor,* a State Secretary and the Head of the Administration. The following day Hitler left, taking with him the castle's tapestries.[3] The looting of Czech cultural treasures followed, though Neurath was able to protect those in his own official residence. The position of Czechs as second-class citizens had already been emphasised: Hácha had been taken to the servants' entrance of his official residence, Prague castle, when he returned from Germany.[4]

New announcements were soon made that revealed German plans. On 18 March the German government announced that the official exchange rate would be 1 Reichsmark to 10 Protectorate crowns (a ratio of 1:5 would have been more realistic). On 21 March General von Blaskowitz, commander of the German troops in the Protectorate, announced that German and Czech would be the official languages. In an initial conciliatory gesture, on 26 March he laid a wreath on the Tomb of the Unknown Soldier in Prague, accompanied by the Czech Defence Minister, General Syrový. Exploitation followed. At Germany's request, £6 million held in London for the Bank of International Settlements at Basel on behalf of the Czechoslovak government was transferred to the Reichsbank's account. Within a week Hitler appointed the *Reichsprotektor* and on the 22nd the Czech parliament passed a law confirming this.[5] Everything was proceeding in a legal manner. There followed a short period of German military government until the civilian rule of the *Reichsprotektor*, which began on 16 April.

Neurath as *Reichsprotektor*

At first the Czechs' worst fears were not realised. Baron Konstantin von Neurath, the new *Reichsprotektor*, was not a committed Nazi. He was a career diplomat, who had been appointed Foreign Minister by Hindenburg in 1933. He had shown hostility to the Italian fascist government and had represented Germany at a League of Nations conference later that year. Hitler had dismissed him from his post as Foreign Minister because he considered him too conservative. However, Neurath had continued to influence political events, restraining Hitler, holding discussions with the British ambassador, Henderson, during the Sudeten crisis and had helped to draft the subsequent Munich Agreement. His appointment encouraged Czechs to believe that German 'protection' might not be too severe. Once appointed *Reichsprotektor*, Neurath wanted Germans and Czechs to live harmoniously together – there were still a number of Germans living in the Czech lands.[6] Neurath realised that the Czechs did not consider themselves inferior to Germans and he decided that they had to be treated, politically and culturally, in an appropriate way. He therefore favoured autonomy, which would give the Czechs their own way of life, though this would have to be kept under control. The Czech press continued to exist, though censored by the German former press attaché in the Prague legation, who acted under instructions from Berlin. On the surface this gave Czechs freedom of expression, which suited Neurath's policy of official cooperation. The Germans had a similar diet of newspapers, which included national (*Deutsche Allgemeine Zeitung, Der Neue Tag*) and local (*Mährische Schlesische Zeitung*) and magazines (*Sudetendeutsch Monatsheft, Freude in Arbeit*).[7]

Neurath's position was undermined by Hitler's appointment of the Sudeten Hans Frank as Head of the Administration. The Under Secretary of State was a German civil servant, Kurt von Burgsdorff. Frank was a committed Nazi who wanted to follow a much harsher policy towards the Czechs. There was a struggle between Neurath and Frank for control of the important sections of state administration, which mirrored the Czech. Frank used this to encroach on Czech decision making. A number of German administrative offices were established, but in the summer of 1939 they were replaced by 19 regional governors (*Oberlandräte*). German control of the Protectorate was completed by the Gestapo, SS and SD. These were not under Neurath's control and were able to act independently. As a result, however much Neurath might have wanted to be 'firm but fair' to the Czechs, under Frank, the Gestapo, SS and the SD, German administration was extremely harsh. The warning of the reality of German rule had come in September 1938 when German troops had occupied the Sudetenland. German–Czech tension had been high at that time and there had been a flood of Czech and émigré German refugees out of the Sudetenland. The summary arrest of many of those who remained there and who were considered hostile to Nazism showed the regime in its true light. There was also action against Germans who fled abroad. If they remained longer than three months, they were considered potentially hostile and full details were taken for future reference in case they returned.[8] Equally suspect in German eyes were all former Czech and German soldiers who had fought in the Spanish Civil War, who were also arrested.

However, at first the new regime did not appear hostile to most Czechs. Although the entire stock of weapons of the former Czechoslovak army and air force was sent to Germany and 'Technical Emergency' officers took control of power stations and gas works to prevent sabotage, this was not something that the average Czech was necessarily fully aware of. General Georg Thomas, head of the German War Economy and Armaments Board, then sent his officers to collect data on the potential use of factories for war production.[9] Together with information possibly gained from detailed questionnaires, the Germans also gained a great deal of technical information including more than 2,000 technical designs and patents. Much of this was extremely valuable. But this investigation was not necessarily conducted in a hostile way. It is likely that the men who were sent did their work in a friendly and courteous manner. In this respect the Germans will have acted in the same way as those who had visited the Sudeten factories earlier. For example, Eric Pasold, on a visit from his new factory in England to the family firm in Fleissen in West Bohemia (in the Sudetenland), found the German officers courteous, apparently helpful and cooperative and offering financial help to those firms that needed it. Established in his new factory near London and now a British citizen, Pasold was able to reject these offers in a similarly courteous way. Subsequently he learnt of new business opportunities in the Sudetenland: the possibility of buying Jewish businesses cheaply and the good economic prospects for firms prepared to accept the new regime. All this applied to the Protectorate as well and the appointment of Germans to senior positions in firms ensured cooperation with the new regime. It also guaranteed workers their jobs.

This ensured that the first months of the Protectorate were quiet and Neurath must have thought that his policy was likely to succeed. Much of Czech business had been with German firms and there was already a degree of mutual understanding. The first important change had come with the seizure of Czech gold and the subsequent priority in allocating foreign exchange to firms producing armaments for Germany. But this had little impact on Czech society at large. What did affect them was the unequal exchange rate of one Reichsmark to ten Czech Protectorate crowns, which allowed Germans – soldiers in the occupying forces as well as officials and companies – to buy Czech goods at a discount. This made Czechs feel that their state was being plundered. Business leaders became worried in April 1939 when they heard of German plans to incorporate the Protectorate into Germany. The governor of the Prague National Bank, Ladislav Dvořák, warned that this would make it more difficult for Protectorate industry to earn foreign exchange.[10] He argued that the abolition of the tariff barrier between the Protectorate and Germany would force prices up to the German level and make Czech industry uncompetitive. This would damage industry and lead to unemployment and social unrest. Germany would be damaged as well as the Protectorate. Neurath and Frank also opposed the union. Germans in Berlin agreed and in May the customs union was postponed. All Germans wanted to moderate their political control and ensure smooth business cooperation, a point emphasised by General Thomas, head of war economy and armaments and General Udet, Göring's assistant responsible for aircraft production. The subsequent flood of military orders satisfied Czech managers and workers and helped provide work for the former members of the Czechoslovak army and air force, who had become unemployed after demobilisation. This emphasised to an even greater extent the mutual interests of Czech and German firms. Czech exports to the Balkans also increased. It also made up for the decline in trade with the USA and Britain when those countries introduced trade restrictions in the summer.

This mood of commercial optimism encouraged entrepreneurs to try and exploit what appeared to be German support for Czech business. One example is Alois Berger, a man with business experience in the Middle East. He suggested to the Czech Commercial Ministry that profitable trade could be developed with Egypt. Berger was one of the men whose drive and business expertise had created prosperity in the First Republic and it was this type of businessman that the Germans wanted to have working for them. In April 1939 Berger was 31, Roman Catholic and, recognising the prejudices of the new regime, he stated that he was Aryan.[11] He had a good education, spoke and wrote German, Czech, English, French and some Arabic. His initial business experience had been at Renault in Paris, where he had worked for a year. After that he had spent six years working for Bat'a in Alexandria, Beirut and Baghdad. Then he had opened an export business to Egypt, Iraq and Persia. He claimed that his proposal for trade with Egypt would benefit Germany by importing more valuable raw materials that could be used both in Germany and the Protectorate. He would compete effectively with British trade and would produce an annual revenue of £200,000 in foreign currency. His proposal was undoubtedly treated seriously – it was sent to the German Foreign Ministry – but may not have been put into effect. It does show, however, that Czech businessmen could see benefits from the German occupation and were prepared to cooperate with the new regime.

This ensured calm among the civilian population, which was further encouraged by the state support of the poor and needy in the countryside. Although the information concerns Sudeten villages, it is likely that this social support was extended to the Protectorate, where there were still many Germans. In any case, it was difficult at this stage to know who was German and who was Czech. In April 1939 social support took the form of food vouchers. There was additional state help with clothing, food, household goods and heating for the very young, the infirm and elderly.[12] The state also provided help for the unemployed who were travelling and looking for employment as well as those who were injured at work. For example, industrial compensation at the uranium mines in Joachimstal included three days' pay for a miner who was injured and in hospital and 100 Reichsmarks to a widow if her husband was killed, together with the cost of burial. There was also the payment of 50 Reichsmarks for marriage or the birth of a child.[13] Vitamin tablets were given to miners, mines were improved and there was training for miners. These were for Sudeten workers but there were similar efforts to win support among Czechs.

As a result of the questionnaires sent out by the new German administration, by the summer of 1939 Germany had details of all the potential economic assets in the Protectorate. The new regime also needed to establish the official nationality of the people under German control. The first steps had already been taken in the Sudetenland to establish which people were Aryan. There was already a clear distinction in Germany between German-speaking people who were citizens of the Reich (*Reichsdeutsch*) and other Germans (*Volksdeutsch*), and the status of Aryan was clearly defined. The German race laws of 1935 'for the protection of German blood' had seen to that. But nothing had been done in the Sudetenland. The archivist at Olomouc, Julius Röder, explained the problem in January 1939 in a letter to the Regierungs Präsident.[14] The Sippen law (presumably an order by the Sipo security police) required details of relatives for the previous five years, but it was only in October 1938 that people in the Sudetenland had been asked whether they were *Reichsdeutsch* or *Volksdeutsch*. Nor had there been any reference to '*Gültig nur zum Nachweis der arischen Abstimmung*', which stated that the person was Aryan.[15] As a result, it was impossible to define the race of one in five *Sudetendeutsch*, one in five *Ostmärker* (Germans originating in the eastern lands of Romania and the Ukraine) and one in five of those in the Altreich (Germany). To achieve this aim a law was passed in December 1938 introducing *Grossdeutsche Eherecht* (the right to be considered German from one's parents' nationality). This was followed by a preliminary census in January 1939 that asked for details of every person's status as of November 1938. This recorded people in terms of their name, address, occupation, place of birth, knowledge of languages and the names of two referees (*Stellvertreter*).

The July 1939 census

As a result, the census of July 1939 required everyone to complete a detailed questionnaire by 15 August giving full personal details: age, occupation and whether they were *Reichsdeutsch*, *Volksdeutsch*, Czech or foreign. This was no ordinary census. It formed the basis not only of deciding whether or not a person was German but also whether they were wholly or part Jewish. The details of a pensioner, Anton Fejfrlik, shows how this worked. He had been born in Leditz near Plzeň on 17 October 1877. His father was Josef Fejfrlik and his mother was Mosalie (née Tessová). His grandfather on his father's side was Vavřinec and his grandmother Maria (née Košišková). On his mother's side his grandfather had been Martin Fess, his grandmother Fessová (née Nosková).

His wife Maria (née Nosek) had been born at Miroschau in the area of Rokitsan on 14 April 1880. Fejfrlik lived in Kuttowenka in the district of Bilin, which was incorporated into Germany on 20 November 1938. He had been given the option to choose whether to be Czechoslovak or German by a regulation dated 1 March 1939 and had chosen German. This is surprising in view of the lack of German names among any of his family members, but he must have decided he had good grounds for this and would receive better treatment than if he was Czech.

All this information was needed by the German authorities because each name would be checked against the synagogue records which had been seized when the Germans entered the Sudetenland and the Protectorate. In this way they would be able to check who had been born Jewish and had later been baptised. In Nazi eyes, conversion to Christianity made no difference. The person remained Jewish. For the moment, all that the German authorities wanted were the full details of all inhabitants. In the case of those claiming German citizenship, if they were of military age they could be conscripted into the German armed forces. The census also showed the number of Poles, other nationalities and their occupations. For example, in Ústi nad Labem (Aussig), there were 13 Poles, 4 Ukrainians, 1 Yugoslav and 1 Slovak. Poles were already marked out as different, along with Jews. In November 1938 a police order had stated that Poles had to wear a violet star on a yellow background. Failure to do this resulted in a fine of 150 Reichsmarks or six weeks in prison. In April 1940 there were restrictions on where they could go. Poles were forbidden to leave their homes at night, to go anywhere other than directly to and from work and to attend German cultural activities or churches. The penalty was a maximum fine of 150 Reichsmarks or three weeks in prison. Poles with German wives could not live in German areas. However, although the punishments were draconian, people who committed minor offices were normally given a small fine: Josefa Rosmus and Marianna Kulka were fined 3.60 Reichsmarks for failing to register and Wojciech Chamutka was fined the same amount for not having his identity card with him. Of the Ukrainians listed in the census, one had been born in the Sudetenland, spoke German as his first language and had attended a German school. He had absorbed German culture, though he could not claim to be German. The census provided an estimate of the military potential of its citizens as soldiers as well as workers. None of this upset the relatively quiet life in the Protectorate from the spring to the autumn of 1939. The Sudetenland, with its remaining Czech citizens, was now part of Germany.

In this way, Germany was gradually assessing the value of the human as well as material resources in the lands seized after September 1938. What the Protectorate needed next, as far as Neurath was concerned, was a united Czech political movement in place of the existing parties and a single body to replace trade unions. Hácha, hoping to forestall Neurath and strengthen Czech independence, founded a new mass organisation, the National Partnership (Národní souručenství), believing that this would be able to protect the national interest. Other political parties were abolished. The trade unions had already been amalgamated into a single body, the National Union of Employees (NÓUZ), in December 1938. Hácha's action in creating the new national party ended all connection that had previously existed between organised labour and political parties. NÓUZ was organised into sections according to the type of industry and was dominated by right-wing Social Democrats. It looked as if the Protectorate was becoming a corporate state like Italy, in which the economy was organised along functional lines. Hácha hoped that this would keep the Czech economy strong, so that it could resist German pressure. He further strengthened his control over organised labour by outlawing strikes, following disputes in June 1939 in south-east Moravia. But the NÓUZ remained independent of state control until 1940 and was able to negotiate collective contracts for its members. Firms were already organised into chambers of commerce and associations such as the Union of Manufacturers.

Anything that encouraged Czechs was likely to be challenged by Germany. In general, Germany welcomed the plan to concentrate economic power, which made it easier to control with a centralised administration. To prevent this being used by Czechs, Germans were put into senior positions in the associations. They controlled marketing and decided how to allocate government contracts, the distribution of raw materials and the allocation of production quotas. Bernard Adolf, a Sudeten German businessman from Liberec, was put in the key position of chairman of the Central Association of Industry which controlled all other associations.[16] NÓUZ was also brought under German control by Frank, who first appointed an important German member of the German Labour Front, Wilhelm Köstler, to be his intermediary. Then, having bypassed Hácha, Frank dealt directly with NÓUZ. Germany thus brought industry and labour under its control.

While these events were taking place, there was still an official Protectorate government. The Prime Minister, Beran, had resigned on 14 March, after the German troops had seized Bohemia and Moravia. But since there was no system for appointing a new government, Beran had remained in office. The Ministry of Defence, headed by General Syrový, was abolished and the Foreign Minister, František Chvalkovský, was appointed envoy to the German government. A new government was created under General Eliáš, who had met Neurath at disarmament conferences and it was hoped might be able to work closely with him. Other members of the new government were Jiří Havelka (Eliáš' deputy and Minister of Transport), Dr Jaroslav Krejčí (Minister of Justice), Ladislav Feierabend (Minister of Agriculture) and Dr Jan Kapras (Minister of Education). The government was officially sworn in on 28 April and appointed representatives to all other groups that were willing to cooperate with it. There was further pressure from Czech fascists to introduce the German anti-Semitic laws but Neurath rejected this. There was already a degree of anti-Semitism: all Jews had been dismissed from the civil service as part of the general anti-Semitic policy of the previous government. This did not apply to the assimilated, and often baptised, Jews and those of mixed race who the Germans termed 'Mischlinge'. Most of these did not think of themselves as Jews and had often been baptised.[17]

The Protectorate Government

The new government's immediate task was to find employment for about 120,000 people who had become unemployed after 15 March. Most were former members of the Czechoslovak army. There were too many to be absorbed into the new government corps (Vládní voysko) created in August 1939, which was largely ceremonial and only had 280 officers and 7,000 men.[18] Many of the unemployed were given civil service jobs; others remained on full pay until they found work. Some had gone to work in Germany in the spring when German firms began recruiting labour in the Protectorate. Not all Germans welcomed this. A long letter from a German official in Lübeck in February 1940 warned that in view of the Czech–German hatred it would be unwise to employ Czechs in the armaments industry because of the risk of sabotage.[19] However, this was ignored. A notice from the labour office in the mining town of Příbram near Plzeň gives details of the work and rates of pay that were being offered to Czechs.[20] Similar notices were displayed elsewhere and they attracted many young Czech men and women. By August 80,000 were working in Germany. Most of the remainder soon found work in Czech industry. Unemployment, which had been almost 93,000 in March, fell to 57,000 in May and was less than 17,000 in June. In July there was even a shortage of workers. The announcement on 25 July of one year's labour service was based on the similar scheme in Germany, which allowed the state to direct workers to jobs. It was the first step towards the introduction of forced labour for Czech workers in Germany that came later.

This completed the first task of the new government. But there remained a threat to public order from the Czech fascists. They had hoped to play an important role in the new state as allies of the Nazis. But the official Nazi policy was that it could never share power, even with an organisation with similar views. The Nazi Party was the only valid political party and in any case the Czech fascist movement had shown that it was not united in its attitude to Germany. During the Munich crisis the main fascist leader, General Gajda, a hero of the First World War who had commanded the Czech Legion in Siberia and had been war minister until 1926, was one of the strongest supporters of national defence. He returned his French and British decorations to show his disdain for their failure to support Czechoslovakia. He founded the Czech National Committee (Český narodní výbor) and it seemed that he might become head of a new government. To stop this, Hácha had dissolved parliament on 21 March and abolished all political parties. When the Protectorate was established,

Gajda resigned from his fascist organisation, joined Hácha's National Partnership and urged fellow fascists to do the same. Few did. The National Partnership, headed by a 50-member committee, grew to more than 3 million members (98 per cent of all adult voters) by May. It included all political parties except the Communists (whose party had been dissolved in 1938). Most of the leading members were from the Agrarian, Social Democrat and Catholic People's Party and the National Union. There was also a small group of fascists led by Gajda. The National Partnership's programme, representing so many diverse interests, was inevitably vague, expressed in general terms and lacked unity. When the fascists called for a stronger anti-Semitic programme, Hácha dissolved the assembly on 17 May and appointed a new one that still included all parties. Gajda and his fascists resigned three days later. On 27 June the fascist movement received official recognition, following pressure from Neurath, and seven fascists were appointed to the assembly. Gajda's separate group was dissolved.

However, official recognition of the fascists did not create unity among them. There were too many diverse personalities and aims. The movement gradually split into 39 organisations, ranging from the National Fascist Rally (Národní tabor fašistický) and Svatopluk Guards (Svatoplukovy gardy) to groups with only a few dozen members.[21] They became social as well as political organisations, setting up sporting and social events, concerts, summer camps for young people and mass rallies. The best-known group was Vlajka (Flag) (with approximately 13,000 members). The most aggressive was the Nazi Green Swastika (Zelené hákové kříže) with about 3,000. Some of the latter were given German citizenship and became members of the armed police forces. Other groups followed radically different policies and at times fought each other, though in general they collaborated with the Germans.

Neurath and Frank held different views with regard to the largest group, Vlajka. Both recognised that its members wanted German–Czech collaboration and expected to be favoured as a result, but Neurath did not want to encourage them. The party attacked and slandered Hácha, with whom Neurath had to work. Frank, on the other hand, favoured them and wanted to support them as a way of suppressing the majority of Czechs. After the fascists had been officially recognised on 27 June, Vlajka was encouraged to play a more active and aggressive role in local politics. Documents seized in the summer by the police in Přibram near Plzeň showed it to be a violent movement, producing crude anti-Semitic drawings that it intended for mass distribution.[22] The Germans decided that this was likely to cause trouble. The Vlajka members were prosecuted for attempting to disturb the peace and the branch was closed. This showed that Neurath's policy was to preserve peace and try to establish some form of German–Czech harmony. He repeated this when questioned at Nuremberg after the end of the war and claimed that 'the Czech people were the only ones in Central and Eastern Europe who could retain their national, cultural and economic entity almost to its full extent'. He was, of course, trying to defend himself as best he could. The official action concerning the Přibram branch of Vlajka shows that this was also official police policy as well. But Neurath always faced the possibility that Frank, the Gestapo, the SS and the SD would take more violent action against Czechs whom they considered to be enemies of the state. The first time that this happened was in September 1939. The consequences were to change German–Czech relations.

War had broken out between Germany, Poland, Britain and France at the beginning of September and from that point there was always the possibility that the Czechs, who up to this point had not been treated harshly, would demonstrate their support for the Western powers. Czechs hoped that Germany would be defeated, but when that did not happen, they took some satisfaction that their long-term rival, Poland, had been crushed in the autumn of 1939. Czechs began to realise that their best option was to follow a policy of passive resistance and some members of the government joined the Political Centre (Politické ústředí) of the resistance movement. The population had already shown a more openly patriotic and anti-German attitude, boycotting trams on 21 August (St Laurentius Day), the anniversary of the defeat in 1431 of German crusaders by Czech Hussites. Encouraged by the lack of any severe German reaction, there were further demonstrations in many cities and towns on 28 October to mark the anniversary of the founding of the First Republic. These began quietly when crowds paraded with Czechoslovak flags but then they became more openly anti-German: Frank was derisively whistled at and German street signs were torn down. This time the Germans ordered more decisive action. The German police fired on demonstrators, killing one worker and wounding Jan Opletal, a medical student.

The events that followed ushered in a much harsher regime. On 4 November, the German University in Prague was declared a Reich University (i.e. a national German institution). On 12 November Jan Opletal died, raising emotions which Neurath and Hácha tried to calm. Frank wanted a stronger reaction. He got his opportunity after the funeral of Opletal, which passed off quietly. Some students sang the national anthem 'Kde domov můj?' [Where is my home?] and demonstrated against the German police on their way home. The following day Neurath and Frank were summoned to Berlin. On the night of 16–17 November four student residences were occupied and over 1,900 students were arrested. Sokol, the national patriotic sporting and patriotic association, had many members (650,000 in 2,500 local organisations in 1938) and owned student hostels. Frank apparently seized them.[23] He also made an example of nine students whom he claimed were the ringleaders. He arrested them and, on Himmler's orders, they were shot. They included Josef Matoušek, the chairman of academic youth in the National Assembly. Action against Sokol continued as more members were arrested and the Germans tried to destroy the organisation. Neurath issued a public warning – a large red poster – which stated that a group of Czech intellectuals, in conjunction with Czech émigrés abroad, had caused civil unrest. Many had been arrested.[24]

German attack on Czech culture

Having acted in this brutal and decisive way, Frank ordered the release of some students the next day, but over 1,000 were taken into 'protective custody' and sent to the Oranienburg concentration camp. Neurath considered this too severe and put pressure on Frank to have them released. This was gradually done. However, this was only the start of the repression. On 17 November Hitler ordered that all Czech universities and colleges be closed for three years and handed over to the Germans. He claimed that they were centres of anti-German activity and in league with Beneš in London. Subsequently, at Hácha's request, Neurath often appealed to Hitler to allow them to be reopened, but each time he was opposed by Himmler. The result of Hitler's action was that the law faculty at Prague University became an SS barracks, all professors except those in the medical faculty were suspended (they were only allowed to continue their clinics), other university lecturers were sent to teach in secondary schools and students had to do manual work. The entire Czech intelligentsia was expelled from the Sudeten area. Many secondary schools were also closed (70 per cent by the end of 1942) and, by September 1942, 60 per cent of Czech elementary schools had also been closed, reducing the number of pupils by half. By the end of 1942 all girls had been excluded from education, and nursery education for three- to six- year-olds was staffed entirely by Germans. As a result, 6,000 of the 20,000 Czech teachers lost their jobs. Only technical education was expanded. This reinforced the earlier restrictions on Czech intellectual life that had already suffered from persecution. As a result, Czechs believed that they were being turned into a mass of workers with no intellectual elite – a claim that Neurath strongly denied when questioned about it after the war. There was also an attempt by Communists to make a public protest, but this too was dealt with harshly. Following Communist agitation in the spring of 1940, 60 workers were arrested and killed by the Gestapo.[25]

This action against Czech intellectual life was only a more violent form of the anti-Czech attacks which had already begun. For example, on 1 September a German military report had stated that Borovička, the managing director of the Böhmische Waffenwerke, had been arrested by the Gestapo and taken into 'protective custody' by the *Oberlandrat* in Klatau.[26] Borovička was not the only important figure to be treated in this way. Stary, a director of Škoda and the brother-in-law of Vambersky, the managing director, was also arrested. Borovička was lucky. Three days later, after being interviewed by Stahlecke, a senior SS officer, he was released and sent to work in Germany. These were important people, and their public humiliation was intended to cow the rest of the Czech population. Directors and warehouse managers were told that they would be shot if there was a strike and they had to sign a declaration to say they knew this. Teachers were made responsible for their students' loyalty (not writing anti-German slogans or reading banned books). Frank announced in 1940 in a speech to leaders of the National Unity Party that 2,000 Czechs held in internment camps would be shot if prominent Czech statesmen refused to sign a declaration of loyalty. There were also others who suffered.

An example of how the regime targeted intelligent and well-educated Czechs is the case of Josef Fried.[27] Born in 1913 in Plzeň, Fried had attended junior school there from 1919 to 1924 and had then gone to the Masaryk gymnasium from 1924 to 1932. Hard-working and intelligent, he then studied law at Charles University in Prague from 1932 and graduated in 1936 as Ju.Dr. (doctorate in law). In 1939 he was a sales representative in Plzeň, probably for Škoda. He was arrested on 1 September and was sent to Buchenwald concentration camp. He survived the war and was released on 18 May 1945. There is no record of the charge against him. He was presumably a patriotic Czech who represented type of potential anti-German leader. He probably made an ill-judged remark about the Germans, was overheard by an informer and was punished severely as an example to others.

Not everyone was treated as harshly as this and minor figures were dealt with more leniently. Wilhelm Weihs, a miner in Neu Modlan near Aussig, was arrested in February 1939 for saying *'Wir sind immer noch für Heil Moskau'* [We're still supporters of Moscow]. He was a German, Roman Catholic, with Czech grandparents and like many other miners, supported Communism. He was aged 42 and had done military service as *unteroffizier* in a Feldjäger battalion in the Tirol. From the Sudeten point of view, his background was impeccable and there must have been considerable local sympathy for him. His excuse was that he had first gone to the Fortuna *gasthaus* where he got drunk and then went to the dance hall. Later he came out, sat chatting at a table for about 10 minutes and then stood up and made his remark. He denied that he had ever been a member of the Communist Party. He was let off with a warning. Weihs was a German. Czechs were regarded with much more suspicion and were likely to be treated more harshly. Communists continued to try and maintain support among miners in

Příbram, for example, by distributing pamphlets at night showing a worker smashing a swastika with a hammer.[28] The Gestapo arrested those they thought responsible. The Gestapo also seized anyone showing pro-Soviet attitudes. When Czechs working in the north Bohemia coalfields wore Russian clothes (the distinctive loose blouse and baggy trousers) or a Soviet star, they were sent to the Gestapo. This did not deter some of the young Communists. Three were arrested in August 1941 for wearing Russian shirts. Two were Sudeten German clerks and the other was a Czech worker. All were aged about 20. There is no information on their punishment.

Neurath claimed in 1945 that he had done what he could to ease the tense situation. Apart from getting the university students released he said he had also tried to maintain good relations with the Church. He had allowed pilgrimages to continue, though when they had become anti-German they were stopped by the police. To try and minimise further Church–State problems he had remained in contact with the Archbishop of Prague until the latter's death.[29] This was the picture painted by Neurath after the war. The reality was very different. The churches were persecuted. Czech orthodox parishes had to leave the jurisdiction of Belgrade and Constantinople and join the German Orthodox Church in Berlin. A Czech bishop, Gorazd, was executed, together with two priests. The Czech national church was persecuted and in Slovakia in 1940 its property was confiscated. In the Protestant Church certain hymns (praising God for liberation) were banned, together with the preaching of the Gospel, the idea of a universal church, the Jewish origin of the Gospels and all references to Czech national figures such as Huss and Masaryk. Ministers, including the General Secretary of the Czech Student Christian Movement, were sent to concentration camps. On the outbreak of war, 437 Catholic priests had also been arrested and sent to concentration camps as hostages. In September 1942, as Neurath was being replaced by Heydrich, the Serbian Orthodox Church was dissolved.

Neurath made some concessions to Czechs. The Czech majority in Prague was recognised by the appointment of a Czech as mayor, with a German as his assistant. This was not popular with Sudeten Germans. Josef Pfitzner, a former history professor at the German

University, argued that there should be two mayors, a German and a Czech.[30] Neurath also tried to delay Himmler's plans for the forced 'Germanisation' of the Protectorate. This stated that the population of Bohemia and Moravia was to be entirely German. But there were 7.2 million Czechs, approximately half of whom (3.2 million) lived in towns and villages. The most radical proposal was to evacuate them all and send in Germans to replace them, but Heydrich and Hitler soon realised that there were not enough Germans, even including those from further east in Romania and the Ukraine. Another proposal was to introduce selective breeding of some Czechs (Himmler as a former chicken farmer favoured this) and expel the rest. This policy aimed to destroy the 'carriers of culture and tradition' (teachers, writers and singers). It was also considered possible to change the nationality of 'suitable' Czechs. Above all, Hitler considered it essential to destroy the idea of Czech history that covered the previous 1,000 years from St Wenceslas. The German language would be imposed, the Collegium Bohemicum at the German University would be used for a time for higher education and all Czechs would do two years of compulsory labour service. German centres would be linked to impose a cultural unity and the Czech language would become no more than a dialect, as in the seventeenth and eighteenth centuries. Marriages would only be allowed after a racial examination.[31] All this would be strictly carried out by the police, who could send suspects into exile or use 'special treatment' (i.e. torture). In a secret memo of 5 October, Gürtner, the Minister of Justice, said that Czech members of the resistance movement should be brought before the people's court. Hitler wanted all those found guilty to be executed immediately so that there could not be any martyrs. He also wanted to end the equal treatment of Czechs and Germans. Neurath opposed this, which in any case was largely unrealistic.

Neurath was accused by Czechs of increasing German influence by appointing Germans to the higher area councils (*Oberlandräte*). But he was able to show that these had been appointed by decree on Hitler's orders. Neurath also tried to lessen the influence of these councils by using Czech rather than German methods of administration, because he claimed Czech was better. This was part of his policy of trying to keep the Czechs quiet during the war. He was well aware that a decree had been passed on 16 March 1939, which had given Hitler the power to incorporate parts of the Protectorate into Germany. This had raised Czech fears of persecution.

Where Neurath was less successful in his conduct of German–Czech relations was over former members of the Czech Legion. A Czech minister, Havelka, claimed that they were being persecuted when they held public office. The Czech Legion had played an important part in the founding of the First Republic when they had established Czech military control in the Sudetenland. They were consequently rewarded by being given positions in the civil service and were unpopular in the Sudetenland. In general they were fiercely patriotic and the term 'Legionnaire mentality' was a phrase in common use in Bohemia to describe Czech chauvinism. It was clear to Neurath that if there was any public unrest, these legionnaires were a potential danger. Later, in February 1941, it was decided to make a register of them and, in April, a census of civil servants was arranged to identify them more precisely.[32] But before then there was some Czech criticism of legionnaires as a favoured minority. Frank was therefore able to remove some from office in extreme cases, but only when they had joined the Legion as volunteers and not as deserters from the Austro-Hungarian army.

In the following period, until the arrest of General Eliáš in September 1941, both Hitler and Neurath tried to calm Czech fears. The absence of open Czech resistance made it easier to integrate the Czech economy more closely with the German. After the rapid defeat of Britain and France forces, Hitler began planning the expulsion of the Czechs. On the Czech side, a number of important events took place. In January 1940 Ladislav Feierabend, the Minister of Agriculture, and Jaromír Nečas, head of the main price control office, escaped to Britain, helped by Prime Minister General Eliáš. They were members of the main resistance movement and the Gestapo had learnt of their activities. There followed no more than an official brief announcement of government changes. Both Germans and Czechs wanted to maintain peace. In the same way the decision to incorporate the Protectorate in the German customs union was delayed from 1 April to 1 October 1940. A third action was Neurath's success in preventing the arrest of

General Eliáš when the Germans discovered information on his links with Beneš. In the same way, the trial of members of the resistance group Obrana Národa (Defence of the Nation) was postponed. When they were finally sent for trial Hitler ordered that they were not to be sentenced to death.

Parallel with this cautious approach, there was initially no serious anti-Semitic action, though steps were being taken to identify not only Jews but also those who were partly Jewish (*Mischlinge*). The census form that all had to complete declared them to be either Jewish or non-Jewish and if a *Mischling*, of the first or second grade (depending on whether there were one or two Jews among the parents or grand-parents). The form ended with the severe warning against providing any false information: '*Ich bin mir voll aller Straffolgen bewusst, die mir wegen einer Unterrichtigkeit dieser Erklärung treffen werden*'. [I accept that any misleading information will make me liable to severe punish-ment.] However, restrictions on Jews continued. They were allowed to attend synagogues and no synagogues were destroyed. Many of the restrictions seem petty and spiteful. For instance, the Präsidium in Prague decided on 28 June that because large numbers of Jews had been spectators at sporting events, they should be excluded. A notice was to be displayed at the entrances to sports grounds saying that they were not allowed to enter. In August they were only allowed to buy from shops between 11 and 12 a.m.[33] In October they were forbidden to enter public parks and to stop them mixing with the rest of the population they were only allowed to enter shops between 8 and 9 in the morning. The penalty was a fine of between 10 and 5,000 crowns or imprisonment of 12 to 14 days.[34] In November they had to hand in their bicycles. The following February, Jews were ordered to give in their fishing licences and stop fishing or face a fine of between 10 and 5,000 crowns or imprisonment of 12 to 14 days.

The role of Sudeten Germans

In the Sudetenland, Aryan Germans were more closely integrated with the Nazi state by forced entry into state organisations, of which the principal groups were the Hitler Youth (HJ) and the German Women's

Organisation (BDM).[35] From the Nazi point of view, it was essential to indoctrinate young Germans with Nazi ideals – a process that generally worked very well, not least because of the oath of allegiance that all had to swear to Hitler personally.[36] One of the strongest opponents of this policy was the Catholic Church. In retaliation the state closed Catholic organisations. One example was in February 1939, when a Young Catholic group in the village of Freudenthal near Opava in northern Moravia was closed.[37] The main reason in this case was that an anti-Nazi priest led the group. Attempts to exclude him had failed. He refused to sign a document stating that he would not join the group if it was reopened. Later this was seen as part of an attempt to integrate the Sudetenland more closely with Germany. In the same way, it was difficult for Germans to become civil servants unless they were married to Germans. This was because of the belief in the need to maintain 'the purity of German blood'. For this reason, in February 1941 the regulations concerning qualifications for the title of *Beamter* became more rigorous. This was a prestigious title and referred to a recognised office holder. There was an official association, *Reichsbund für Deutschen Beamten,* which provided courses on political indoctrination (*Staatsrechliche und Verwaltungsrechliche Frage*), published books such as a study of Frederick the Great (*Staatsmann und Feldherr; 200 Aussprüche Friedrich der Grosse*) and calendars. The association also organised concerts, talks and exhibitions on German culture. It raised money for presents for soldiers (chocolates and cigarettes) and advised on house purchase. Earlier, the title of *Beamter* had been given to former army officers as a reward for service, but in April 1940 this service was no longer considered sufficient. One of the most important qualifications was a good knowledge of German, which ensured that only those with a high level of education could be appointed.[38] Anyone without this had to do a course of study, since German was the language used in all communications with official bodies. But all costs had to be met by the individual – there was no state help.

The lack of knowledge of good German was clearly a problem. In a state where bureaucratic communication was so important, anyone lacking a good knowledge of German was a liability. Communications – orders, reports and letters – were generally written in a long-winded style that bureaucrats believed reflected their own importance. But to be effective, these had to be written in language that was grammatically correct and used appropriate vocabulary. This is where many *Beamter* failed to meet the normal rigorous German standards. *Sudetendeutsch* was not necessarily standard *Hochdeutsch* – the Sudetenland had been part of the Austro-Hungarian Empire and many people spoke a regional dialect, much like the German-speaking Swiss. The German educational system in the Sudetenland was not necessarily going to produce a good German speaker in the German *Reichsdeutsch* sense.

A further problem was that there were regional dialects and accents. One of the most obvious was in the area of the Silesian coalfield (Ostrava, Karviná and Český Těšín in northern Moravia). Here the coalmines had attracted Germans, Czechs and Poles in large numbers and there were also Slovaks and Ukrainians. For example, a census taken at Darkov, a district of the coalmining town of Karviná, east of Ostrava, showed 1,098 Germans, 214 Czechs, 2 Russians and 1,482 Poles.[39] As a consequence, the local dialect contained many loan words from these languages. Every member of the prominent local language group spoke their own language fluently but was far less accurate or competent in the others. They could 'get by' for all ordinary purposes because everyone lived in their own separate community. But this did not necessarily produce good candidates for the German civil service. In cases where individuals claimed German citizenship under the racial laws the situation was potentially even more complicated. Because of the ludicrous concept of 'German blood' anyone could claim German (*Volksdeutsch*) citizenship if both or either parents or grandparents were German. In extreme cases this could mean that a person was, in Hitler's eyes *Volksdeutsch*. A person only needed one out of six close relatives to be considered German. The person might not even speak German as his or her first language, though an application for German citizenship was far more likely to succeed if the candidate was able to claim that he or she had received a German education and was therefore steeped in German culture. There was the same situation elsewhere in the Protectorate, and it is small wonder that the same demand for officials to speak good German had to be repeated a year later.

Gradually restrictions were introduced which limited Czech cultural activity. One of the most important events in the Czech calendar had been the anniversary of Masaryk's birth. The 90th anniversary was on 7 March 1940 and the day was also commemorated by remembering the dead from the First World War. In 1939 this had been marked by General von Blaskowitz laying a wreath on the tomb of the unknown soldier, but after the student unrest in November 1939, steps were taken to prevent any show of national feeling the following year. The national assembly announced that strong measures would be taken against anyone who used this day as an excuse for anti-German behaviour and emphasised that the same would apply to the anniversary of the founding of the Czechoslovak Republic.[40] By now it was impossible for Czechs to make any active protest, but it was still possible to show anti-German feeling by boycotting German goods. One such action was in May 1940 when Czechs refused to use German shops, encouraged by the slogan 'Češi Kupujte jen české zboží a jen u Čechů' [Czechs! Buy only Czech goods from Czech shops]. Action such as this was difficult to stop and it was hard to find the ringleaders and punish them. In June, Germany tried to crush any Czech hopes in an Allied victory. This followed the German victory in Western Europe and the entry of German troops into Paris. Hitler ordered three days of celebration. Everyone, including churches but excluding Jews, were to hang out German flags, or if they did not have these, flags of the Protectorate. This proved an opportunity for the police to check on political attitudes: a list of those who did not obey this order was made on the 27th.

Anti-German activities such as this encouraged Frank to increase pressure on Czechs. In June the Präsidium took steps to remove all traces of the former Czechoslovak Republic from public life. The order was vaguely worded and allowed far-reaching actions. Street names had already been changed and to this was added the Czech names of buildings, Czech club rooms and their contents, museum displays, tourist signs and anything else that the Sudeten Germans could think of. All memorials to Masaryk and pictures of him at schools, which Frank had wanted to be destroyed, were on Neurath's orders sent to archives. But the drive to remove traces of notable figures in Czech history went even further. Efforts were even made to deface inscriptions on gravestones where the person had played a significant role in founding the First Republic. One example was the defamation of the memorial to Josef Soukup, who had served as a Legionnaire in France during the First World War. His grave was in the Protestant cemetery at Borotice, a village east of Příbram.

Steps were also taken to exclude all non-German influence. One of the most significant was the banning of a wide range of books. The orders show what influences the Germans were trying to stamp out. In July the Präsidium issued a list of 37 books that were banned. Several were by Communists or Bolsheviks: John Reed, *Ve víru mexické revoluce* [At the heart of the Mexican revolution], Ilja Ehrenburg, *Jedním dechem* [In a single breath] and Leonid Sobotov, *Generální oprava* [General repairs] and two books by Upton Sinclair published by a Communist publisher. Others were anti-fascist, such as Jaroslav Koudelka, *Potřebujeme fašismus?* [Do we need fascism?]. Most books were by authors who are unknown today. The same month Karel Čapek's *Válka s mloky* [War against the newts] was added; Čapek had been a close friend of Masaryk. The Germans also wanted popular fiction such as the books by Adolf Zeman removed, and the popular British books by Sapper, *Bulldog Drummond*, were also added.[41]

But the drive to remove banned books from public life did not end there. A notice in the archive in Příbram from the Ministry of the Interior, dated 31 December 1940, specified the books to be used in schools and stated that all forbidden books had to be stamped and handed in to the police. People did not want to part with them. There was also a list of booksellers and of banned books. Other forbidden books included those by popular Czech writers such as Jaroslav Hašek, *Dobrý voják Svejk* [The good soldier Svejk] and Jaroslav Foglar's books of boys' adventure stories. Also banned was the anti-war novel by Erich Remarque, *Na zapadní frontě klid* [All quiet on the western front] and novels by the German exiled writer Thomas Mann, *Buddenbrooks*. Other forbidden authors included Jack London, Martin Eden, H. G. Wells, all Jewish writers and books published by Jewish publishers. This is not to say that all books by Czech authors were banned. Neurath claimed at Nuremberg that many Czech books were published, but they had to meet with the approval of the German censor. The willingness to allow Czechs to continue some form of normal life was extended to include the cinema, theatre and sport, and the Czech Philharmonic Orchestra played mainly Czech music. The Germans were given a similar diet of propaganda and light entertainment in films on subjects that included Bismarck, 'Nordische Land', 'Herz oder Heimat', and 'Magda singt für Europa'.[42] Elsewhere, as in Ostrava, during the war the resident orchestras played a mixture of classical music that included Czech (Dvořak, Smetana), German (Mozart, Beethoven, Wagner, Weber), Italian (Verdi, Rossini) and Polish (Chopin). But towards the end of 1940 Czech cultural activities were further limited. For example, the Junák scout club in the village of Velké Junátka near Přibram was closed down in November 1940.[43] In March 1941 the police even took large dogs from their owners: Airedale terriers, German Schaferhunde, Riesenschmauzer, German boxers, Rottweilers and mongrels that included these breeds and were at least one year old.

It is possible that this first period of the history of the Protectorate to September 1941 showed Germany's pragmatic approach rather than any clear policy. It is certainly true that Hitler had no clear idea how he wanted the Protectorate to be governed after it had been created in March 1939. The administration had been carefully prepared to put Germans in all positions of authority so that they held a monopoly on all real power. But beyond that, Neurath was given no clear guidance. This was not because Hitler had any higher regard for the Czechs than for other Slav races such as the Poles. At one point he wanted to begin planning to remove virtually all Czechs from the Protectorate, but had to shelve these proposals as the war continued. However, when one looks at the German plans for using the Protectorate as an important arms manufacturer it becomes clear that Neurath's main aim was to enable this arms production to take place as smoothly as possible. This explains the care with which he tried to foster German–Czech relations and his efforts to check Frank, Pfitzner and other leading Sudeten Germans who wanted a much tougher attitude towards the Czechs. It also explains the importance of the Gestapo, SS and SD, whose presence, openly and in secret, in arms factories was intended to cow any Czech resistance. The arrest of leading Czech industrialists and possible intellectual leaders points to the same conclusion. It would thus be wrong to see Neurath's rule as *Reichsprotektor* as benign in view of this and the increasing restrictions on Czech life.

Heydrich

By September 1941 Hitler had decided that Neurath was too mild. Hitler wanted a much more severe regime to crush Czech resistance. Nazi leaders were concerned about the increase of this after the beginning of the attack on Russia in June.[44] The same month there was a Czech boycott of the German-controlled press that was encouraged by the BBC. On 27 September Prague radio reported that Neurath was going on leave for health reasons and he retired to his estates until October 1943. He was replaced by the much more committed Nazi, Heydrich.[45] By then part of the power of *Reichsprotektor* had been given to the so-called German State Minister in Bohemia and Moravia, who was under Hitler's direct control.

Heydrich was an interesting choice for a key economic and political position of this type. In many ways he was gifted and intelligent.[46] The son of a well-known tenor and director of a conservatory of music in Halle, Heydrich had himself shown early musical talent and was a promising athlete in running, swimming and fencing. Brought up in a strict Catholic family under a regime of cleanliness, order and discipline, he was expected to develop his considerable talents. But he was held back by shyness and made few friends. When rumours began to circulate at school and later in the navy that his father was Jewish, he countered with arrogant behaviour. The result was a gifted but also twisted personality, ambiguous about his identity and seeking approval and recognition. In short, Heydrich was a torn and insecure man. Tall and blond, he appeared to be the ideal Aryan. Early in his career he had been sacked from the German navy for 'conduct unbecoming an officer', when his harsh treatment of a lady had given her a nervous breakdown. After being appointed to Himmler's staff in 1931 he gradually became his right-hand man. He also proved completely amoral, unrestrained by law or social convention and a brutal psychopath. He was entirely suitable for this next stage in Hitler's policy towards the Czechs.

One of Heydrich's first acts was to create a reign of terror. Czechs were to be forced to obey orders without question. He first had a census made of Jews and ordered that Terezín (Theresienstadt) should be turned into a ghetto by the beginning of October.[47] Jews were excluded from all professions and forms of work. Heydrich, appointed Deputy *Reichsprotektor* in September 1941, proclaimed a state of emergency on 25 September, first in the *Oberlandrat* in Prague and later in the rest of the Protectorate. This established a *Standgerichte* that created 770 capital offences and 1,000 in which the punishment would be imprisonment in a concentration camp. None of the judges in this court had any knowledge of criminal law or experience in criminal trials. Their only qualification was that they were Nazis. Trials were always held in secret, which increased Czech feelings of insecurity. The only sentences they could pass were the death penalty or for the accused to be handed over to the Gestapo. All death sentences were carried out immediately; the victims were shot or hanged.

The official result of the trials up to 20 January 1942 was that at least 486 were executed and another 2,242 sent to concentration camps.[48] Some were sent to Mauthausen to be killed, which avoided reporting even more executions in the familiar red notices at street corners, put up to terrify Czechs. Czech nationalists and Communists were often sent to Berlin to be tried by the People's Court there. Heydrich also had General Eliáš tried by this court, condemned and executed. The Germans had known for some time about his treasonable connections with London but had not wanted to disturb the relatively calm atmosphere. Under Heydrich all this changed. Hácha and his government were also cowed. They were urged by London to resign but did not do so.

To balance this harshness, Heydrich increased some rations of food and shoes and received delegates of workers and farm labourers. He even provided soup in factory canteens, which Hitler thought unwise, since it was not up to the standard of normal Czech soup. While this was happening, Heydrich was considering ending Czech autonomy. But the German failure to defeat the USSR by the end of 1941 helped to persuade him instead to change the status of the Protectorate to an 'administration authorised by the Reich'.[49] He abolished the Council of Ministers and only allowed the government to decide how to carry out orders issued by the *Reichsprotektor*. Heydrich also brought the administration under his personal control by appointing his own nominees. These included the Czech fascist Emanuel Moravec, who was hated more than the Germans. He also ensured that he controlled the government by appointing a German, Walter Bertsch, as Minister of the Economy and Employment. Since Bertsch could only speak German, all official discussions had to be in that language and not Czech. Even the lower ranks of bureaucracy were brought under control by the appointment of Germans to key posts in Czech offices.

This ensured that all aspects of Czech government and administration were under German supervision. As to the Czechs, Heydrich planned to divide them into four categories, according to racial and political criteria. The first consisted of those who could be considered 'racially sound and holding sound views'. These amounted to about one-third of the population and were to be given German nationality 'as an act of charity'. The second 'unsound' group would be sent to the east. This amounted to about another one-third. The third group 'with sound views but racially unsound' would be sent to Germany and sterilised so that they could not produce children. Finally, the fourth group, the 'racially sound, but with unsound views' were the intellectuals who were potentially the leaders of Czech society and therefore, in his view, the most dangerous. If they could not be controlled, then it would be necessary to 'solve the problem once and for all by sending them to the firing squad, for I cannot have them moved out of the country because there in the East they would form a leading social group directed against us'. In all of this, Heydrich was in no doubt about Czech attitudes. In a letter to Martin Bormann of 9 October 1941 he had written of Czech hatred of Germans and how the threat of mass arrests kept Czechs quiet.[50]

In view of Heydrich's reign of terror against Czechs, it is hardly surprising that Beneš should have ordered his assassination. Heydrich represented all that the Czechs hated most about Germans. Even without knowing anything of his and Hitler's plans for the destruction of the whole Czech people, the killing of a major Nazi figure might have been considered a major coup by Beneš and his government in exile in London. But it was to have dramatic and tragic consequences that were out of all proportion to the legitimate warlike act. For this reason it is important to consider why Beneš decided to approve this dramatic gesture. No explanation has ever been given but there are two possible reasons. One is that Beneš frequently heard of the acts of sabotage carried out by members of the Free French resistance and realised that he had to do something similar in the Protectorate. It had proved difficult to get the USA and Britain to recognise his government in exile and the small number of Czech soldiers and airmen could not make any major contribution to the war. In this explanation the decision was therefore forced on him, only the choice of victim remained. The other and more persuasive argument is that Beneš knew from information sent from the Protectorate about the effectiveness of Heydrich's policy. But it was difficult to know in London whether the draconian laws and presence of the Gestapo, SS and SD were more effective in cowing Czechs or whether Heydrich's policy of raising food and clothing rations and his apparent willingness to meet Czech groups was winning Czech hearts and minds. If the latter were true, Beneš had to ensure that any anti-German act would provoke such strong reaction that the Germans would be hated even more. This also matched the decisions that the government in exile were considering to expel all Germans from the country after the war. If this is the true explanation for Beneš' decision, it acted only too well.

The assassination of Heydrich and its consequences

Heydrich was assassinated on 27 May 1942 by Jan Kubiš, a Czech, and Josef Gabčík, a Slovak, two members of a Czechoslovak military group who had been parachuted into the Protectorate in December 1941.[51] They were not the only ones to have been sent into the Protectorate. An earlier group had come from Moscow but had immediately gone over to the Germans and became double agents; others had been captured.[52] This later group received crucial help from the Czech resistance movement inside the Protectorate. Heydrich was not killed directly but died later of his wounds.[53] When Hitler heard of this his first reaction was to order that large numbers of Czechs should be killed. This was impractical, as even Frank realised, but retaliation came swiftly. Police Col.-Gen. Kurt Daluege was appointed deputy *Reichsprotektor* and martial law was proclaimed. This lasted until 3 July. Everyone with knowledge of or 'having approved of' the assassination was brought before Heydrich's people's court, condemned to death and summarily executed. Himmler ordered that 10,000 hostages should be taken. Frank's first step was to offer a reward of 10 million crowns and impose a curfew from 9 p.m. on the 27th to 6 a.m. on the following day.[54] All pubs, theatres and cinemas were closed; anyone ignoring the order would be shot. During the night there were raids by 4,500 police, SS, SA, NSKK and other paramilitary units as well as 2,500 soldiers; 541 people were arrested. Himmler ordered Frank to take 10,000 hostages and another 2,714 police were sent from Germany. There followed a systematic search of Prague, accompanied by a series of executions of hostages. Table 3.1 shows the scale and relentless destruction of what, in the end, was a cross-section of the Czech population.

The arrest and execution of the first six Czechs was only the beginning. A huge manhunt was ordered the following day, using almost 7,000 police and another 2,940 men including soldiers and the Gestapo.[55] These were used for a succession of raids from 28 May to 20 June in virtually the whole of the Protectorate. During this time they arrested a total of 1,148 people and captured 313 weapons of all sorts as well as ammunition and explosives, uniforms, radios and other forbidden items. As a result, 657 were executed. In addition, in Prague and Brno 448 were shot (381 men, 67 women), probably as reprisals. The special court in Brno, one of the people's courts set up by Heydrich in September 1941, condemned 247 people to death (208 men, 39 women). There was no appeal from these courts and sentences were carried out very quickly.

These figures make chilling reading. But even these do not include the destruction of two villages, Lidice and Ležáky.[56] Lidice was chosen because of a note referring to it that was found on a captured British agent. Ležáky was destroyed because a radio transmitter was found there. In Lidice, the larger and better known, 192 males above the age of 15

Table 3.1 Hostages shot or condemned to death 28 May – 3 July 1942

Thursday 28 May	6	Sunday 31 May	18	Sunday 7 June	0
Friday 29 May	12	Monday 1 June	10	Monday 8 June	22
Saturday 30 May	43	Tuesday 2 June	22	Tuesday 9 June	34
		Wednesday 3 June	16	Wednesday 10 June**	31
		Thursday 4 June	24	Thursday 11 June	33**
		Friday 5 June	28	Friday 12 June	18
		Saturday 6 June	13	Saturday 13 June	23
Weekly totals	61		131		161
Sunday 14 June	21	Sunday 21 June	21	Sunday 28 June*	19
Monday 15 June	8	Monday 22 June	28	Monday 29 June*	70
Tuesday 16 June*	25	Tuesday 25 June*	30	Tuesday 30 June	115
Wednesday 17 June	0	Wednesday 24 June	30	Wednesday 1 July	141
Thursday 18 June	0	Thursday 25 June	28	Thursday 2 July	123
Friday 19 June***	76	Friday 26 June	18	Friday 3 July*	86
Saturday 20 June*	108	Saturday 27 June	29		
Weekly totals	238		184		554

Total condemned to death or shot 1,329

* Public demonstrations in support of the Reich

** Destruction of the village of Lidice. The total excludes the men who were shot there.

*** Includes General Eliáš.

Source: Zdeněk Plachý, *Protektorát proti Londýnu – 38 dní heydrichiády* (The Protectorate against London – 38 days of revenge for Heydrich's death) (Nové Sedlo u Lokte, Czech Republic, 2006), passim.

were killed, 196 women were sent to Ravensbrück concentration camp and 105 children were sent to Chełmno, where 88 were gassed. The rest were sent for 're-education' in Germany, probably because they appeared to be Aryan, i.e. fair-haired and blue-eyed. Václav Zelenka was one of the few to survive and be able eventually to return.[57] In Ležáky, 43 adults were killed. Of the 105 children sent to Chełmno, only 14 survived and returned to Czechoslovakia after the war. It should be remembered, however, that no matter how terrible the destruction of these villages was to contemporaries in the Protectorate and elsewhere in the world, it is nothing compared to the destruction of villages in Poland and Russia that lay in the path of the German advance in 1939 and 1941. The difference was that the Germans admitted committing the acts in the Protectorate.

The first executions, on the 28th, set the pattern for the others. All six were from the same district: Rokycan, a suburb of Prague. The notice that went up on street corners – red to attract attention – was intended as a warning to all who may have known the victims and to all the rest of the population in that district. From that point, as the raids by police, army and Gestapo spread across the whole of the Protectorate, the executions set their own pattern. The thorough searches of homes and all public buildings caught many Czechs unawares. Although there were already restrictions on Czech lives, there had been nothing like this before. Former soldiers still had their uniforms and many their weapons from when they had been demobilised. There was also a resistance movement and this had received some supplies from London. The searches found all, or most of, these. The people found in the same house as these forbidden items were arrested and they were probably executed as a matter of course. This served one of the German aims: to discover who was planning armed insurrection or sabotage and kill them. Notice of their execution also served as a warning to others. Many of these were the type of people most feared by the Germans: the well-educated potential leaders. But the Germans' initial policy on founding the Protectorate had identified other potential enemies as well. Managers and those in charge of warehouses had been seen as the ones most likely to sabotage Czech arms production and delivery to the German armed forces. They had been declared hostages. They had been forced to sign a declaration stating that if there was a strike at their firm, they would be executed. This was meant to ensure that no one interrupted the steady flow of war materiel.

The Germans also took the opportunity offered by the assassination to attack other leading members of Czech society and strike terror throughout the Protectorate. A foundation was also established to carry on Heydrich's plans for Germanising the Czech lands.[58] The daily record of executions that followed sometimes reported the victims as two groups. The first recorded the people's titles, indicating their status in society. These were, in German eyes, the intellectuals. The second group consisted of ordinary people. Their place of residence was also reported. This gave a clear indication of the way the system of retaliation worked. There was no daily or weekly quota of deaths. Instead, as people were arrested, groups were formed and sent to Prague to be shot. This created an uneven flow of victims. This can be seen from the second day, Friday 29 May, when four were from Ostrava, the major coal, iron and steel-producing city in the north-east of the Protectorate and the rest were from Brno. Ostrava was chosen as the first provincial city for revenge because of the large number of Communists. Brno was the second city in the Protectorate and an important industrial centre, mainly for textiles. There are no personal details other than names. The victims were workers or ordinary members of society. Gradually the searches widened: executions on the 30th included two from Bat'a's factory town of Zlín in eastern Moravia, four from the nearby town of Valašské Meziříčí, five from Brno, a large group from Prague and five from Tyn nad Vltavou in southern Moravia, close to the Austrian frontier. At 7 p.m. on the same day, Saturday 30 May, Hácha made a broadcast attacking Beneš and claiming that the assassination was the work of British and Russian agents.

On Sunday 31st a renewed appeal for information was made and the reward was raised from 10 to 20 million crowns. Moravec, one of the leading Czech fascist collaborators, also made a radio appeal attacking Moscow and London. The BBC replied criticising Hácha and saying that Heydrich had not been merely a Nazi. As deputy head of the SS he had one of the worst records of any Nazi leader. He was therefore the enemy of all in German occupied territory. That evening another 18 hostages were shot. The German attitude was that this was necessary because of the 'political obstinacy of certain sections of the Czech people'.[59] As in other cases, they were taken from communities across the Protectorate, spreading fear throughout the country. Another raid was made during the following night, in which 2,900 were interviewed and 110 arrested. By now it was becoming clear that the raids were being carried out in many different parts of the country. They were probably no longer attempts to catch the assassins, whom the authorities believed were British and Russian agents. These were widely spaced raids, striking terror into parts of the country which until then had enjoyed a quiet and relatively peaceful life with little German interference.

At this point it became clear that Beneš' government in exile in London had planned the attack and the British had trained the men and dropped them by parachute into the Protectorate. This, and the failure to gain any information about the agents, led the Germans to continue to widen their attack on Czechs. This was not a set of random reprisals against a hated racial minority. The fundamental German attitude towards the Czechs had been expressed by General Federici in July 1939: *'Die tschechische Intelligenz ist der unversönliche Feind Deutschlands, nicht so der Arbeiter und Bauer'* [The Czech intellectuals are the irreconcilable enemy of Germany rather than the workers and peasants].[60] The most important victims were probably the directors of BMM (formerly the heavy engineering company ČKD in Prague).[61] Why these men, whose company was a major armaments manufacturer, should have been chosen is unclear. But it sent a clear message to Czechs that no one was safe. On 1 June the first intellectuals appear among the list of people executed. The list began with a group of people who are identified by their title or profession. They include a doctor and writer Vladislav Vančura, a high-school professor Viktor Felber, a secretary Julius Felber, two members of the council of the agricultural ministry, Jan Mazanec and Bohumír Hanosek, a director of the Kooperativa, ing. Karel Ludvík and a professor of natural science at a former high school, which had been closed. This is not a large number, but it is significant. All were from Prague and all were important people in their profession. This represents the first blow that the Germans struck against the elite of Czech society.

As far as the Germans were concerned, none of these measures had produced any concrete results. No assassins had been betrayed or arrested. The following day, 2 June, they tried a new approach. In an attempt to split Czech society, a number of industrial workers were given favoured treatment. A group of 232 workers and 21 women were sent to the spa at Luhačovice, where they were able to take part in a wide range of sporting activities besides enjoying a holiday. The same day the population of Prague was summoned to a public demonstration in the Staroměsto Square in Prague to demonstrate their support for Germany. According to the official record, 65,000 attended the demonstration in the evening. Not to have done so would have risked being included in the next group of victims, which included dr. advokát (academic lawyer) Vladimír Svoboda and the director of an agricultural savings association, Jaroslav Toninger, both from České Budějovice, an important town in South Bohemia. The others were from Suchol nad Lužnici, a nearby town.[62] What is striking about these lists is that they contain very few Jews. This retaliation was directed against urban Czechs from most walks of life and all parts of society. They were the intellectual elite referred to by General Federici, who had specifically excluded peasants and workers, though with the implied exception of Communists.

Each day more were executed, some from towns, others from nearby villages, many from Prague and others taken almost at random from towns or villages scattered across the Protectorate. The arrests, which may have appeared or even been random, was followed by the inevitable red notice about the execution, which struck terror in every community in the Protectorate.[63] Germans claimed that this was intended to force anyone who knew about the assassins to betray them. After that, there would be no further justification for the terror. The search for the assassins ended in the early morning of 18 June. At 4.15 a.m. a detachment of 700 Waffen SS surrounded the orthodox church of sv Cyril and Metoděj in Resslova Street in Prague. Inside, in the crypt, were seven members of the group that had been sent to assassinate Heydrich. They could not escape. In the ensuing battle, the Germans even used explosives, but could not force the Czechs to surrender. Finally the Germans flooded the crypt, and rather than surrender, all the members of the group committed suicide.

The reason that the SS had been able to find them was that the other member of the group, Karel Čurda, had betrayed them. Whether he did this for the reward or because his nerve broke is impossible to say. It would be easy to condemn his action in betraying his fellow Czechs. But one needs to see his actions in the light of all that the Germans had begun to do: killing Czechs from all walks of life and from all over the Protectorate. Nowhere was safe. He may even have believed that because no one could escape from the Protectorate, they would all be discovered at some point. Germans were also claiming that the majority of Czechs were pro-German and the President had also made an appeal to Czechs for support. Nor had everyone suffered equally. Some workers had been given favoured treatment at the very time that others were being executed, often apparently for legitimate reasons: possession of forbidden material. One might thus argue that the man who betrayed the others suffered a complete loss of nerve in a situation that no one had prepared him for during his training in England.

But the discovery and killing of the Czech agents did not end the executions, which had by now taken on a momentum of their own. Far from ending this, the suicide of the seven agents unleashed another wave of executions: 76 on the 19th and 108 the following day. Then the scale of daily executions remained at about the level it had been before the 18th. Finally at the end of June and the beginning of July there was a final, horrific bloodshed: over 500 were killed. Of these over 300 were shot in three days, 30 June to 2 July. At the same time the scale of the pro-German demonstrations was increased: 60,000 people assembled in Moravské Ostrava on the day before the killing reached new heights. Then, finally it was over. A concert was performed in Wenceslas Square (Václavské náměsti) attended by 200,000 people. The German action had become much more than a hunt for enemy agents. It was an attempt to destroy the Czech elite and cow the rest into total submission through the combination of executions and massed pro-German demonstrations. No one knows how many died. One estimate is more than 1,000 in the whole Protectorate, but it is impossible to verify this. Many Czechs were also arrested for trivial offences and held in German prisons.[64] By the end of March 1943 there were 12,656 Czechs in German penal institutions, mostly in Germany.

Few ever returned home because they were often rearrested by the Gestapo on their release and sent to concentration camps. Nothing could have shown the power of Germany to a greater extent.

One event that showed how the Germans continued their ruthless policy towards Czechs is the prison escape at Rovensko. In March 1943 the inmates tried to escape and killed a German guard and one German official. All prisoners were recaptured and shot. Later, in November 1943, a German district judge was murdered. As a reprisal, 350 prisoners, who had been brought there after March, were also shot. One small detail remains to be told, which throws considerable light on the situation of the average person. A Czech, Skacel, who was a former officer in the Czechoslovak army, made a remark after the assassination that showed he was glad it had happened. This remark was heard by someone who reported it to the Gestapo. Fortunately for Skacel he was warned of impending arrest and disappeared. Every day from then until the end of the German occupation the Gestapo came to his home in the hope of finding him. His son Josef was branded as the son of an enemy of the state and it is likely that he never saw his father again until the arrival of the Russians in April 1945, almost three years later. As a small boy, it would have been unsafe for him to know where his father was. Part of the time he had been able to hide in the house and in the summer he was hidden in the countryside, but he was lucky to survive. Skacel's wife and son had to share their meagre rations with him. They could not appeal for help to anyone else for fear of betrayal. Not surprisingly, after the war Josef, the son, was pro-Russian, became a Russian teacher and a member of the Communist party. Others with a similar wartime experience also welcomed the Russians as liberators.

End of the war

The remaining part of the Protectorate's history was, fortunately for the Czechs, relatively undisturbed until the closing stages of the war. Wilhelm Frick, the Reich Interior Minister, was appointed *Reichsprotektor* in August 1943 – Neurath had been officially on leave until then. He failed to treat the Czech ministers and officials politely as

Neurath had done. Frank was appointed minister of state for Bohemia and Moravia. This made him responsible for administration in the Protectorate. Frick became a figurehead, but with special authority to grant a reprieve from any sentence given by a local (Czech) court. This ensured that no Sudeten German would be punished without very good reason. Martial law was ended on 3 July and the political situation was 'normalised'. In June 1942, during the repression following Heydrich's assassination, events in the war in Russia forced Hitler to demand more Germans for the army to replace the mounting losses. Czechs were recruited as factory workers to replace them. Among other measures was the appointment of new (German) *Oberlandräte-Inspekteure* for the major towns and cities and the reorganisation of German administration in the Protectorate. This was simplified to release as many men as possible and the Czech administration continued to function under German control. This streamlining of the administration also helped Frank to supply more workers when Speer demanded more support for his armaments drive that led, in 1943, to total war. Frank made one effort to please the Czechs. In June 1944, at about the time of the Allied invasion of France, he created the order of the 'Eagle of Duke Venceslas' in three classes for citizens who had 'distinguished themselves by their attitude, fulfilment of duty, and preparedness'. Since this also coincided with growing Czech awareness that Germany was gradually being defeated, it caused nothing but (secret) contempt and derision among the Czechs.

The Protectorate remained quiet. Beneš sent more agents into the Protectorate, and the SOE (Special Operations Executive) planned more operations, but their duty was only to gain information.[65] Whether they served any useful purpose is debatable, since a great deal of information was supplied by František Moravec, the former head of Czechoslovak intelligence, who continued to send valuable information to Britain during the war, No more acts of sabotage were attempted. In the last winter of the war Communists established partisan bands in the Moravian hills and some escaped British prisoners of war joined them. But they did not have the equipment or training to take any effective action. There was an uprising in Slovakia, which received Allied help from the airfield at Bari in southern Italy. But in

August 1944 German troops occupied western Slovakia and the uprising became centred on the Slovak attempt to hold Banská Bystrica in central Slovakia. The Allies and Russians sent military supplies and personnel but the Slovaks, including part of the Slovak army and some escaped French prisoners of war, were outnumbered. The Soviet army, including Czechs and Slovaks, was unable to reach them before they were overwhelmed and forced to surrender. Later, in Košice in eastern Slovakia, a new Czechoslovak government was established under Feierlinger. This later became the first postwar government in Prague. In the Protectorate, all remained quiet until the final days of the war, when the population of Prague rose in revolt on 5 May 1945. In five days of bitter fighting, almost 2,000 Czechs were killed, a significant proportion of a city of 900,000. The outcome of the battle was decided by a group of Red Army soldiers who had previously fought for the Germans. These changed sides. The arrival of Russian tanks on the 9th completed the mopping up of the last German resistance.

There was one unexpected result of this final stage of the war. Because Czechs had remained passive, the Czech birth rate increased. As a result, although the Jews suffered very heavy losses, the Czech population had increased more than the Sudeten German by the end of the war.

CHAPTER 4

FORCED LABOUR

One of the important features of the history of the Protectorate is the contribution made by Czech workers in Germany as well as in Czech factories working for the German armed forces. The movement of these to Germany predates the creation of the Protectorate and has its origins in the German Four Year Plan that began in 1936. In that year the German rearmament programme demanded very heavy investment in expanding iron foundries, chemical factories and other strategically important industries. As a result, German unemployment, which had been half a million men in December 1938, fell to 140,000 in the following spring. At the same time, mobilisation absorbed many others. There was a risk that factories would run out of labour. This had been foreseen as early as 1935 and a system of workbooks was introduced that tied workers to particular jobs. In 1938 this was further reinforced by laws and directives that emphasised labour obligations.

This was not enough to provide all the labour that German industry required and in January 1939 Germany and Czechoslovakia signed an agreement under which 40,000 workers would be sent from Czechoslovakia to work in Germany. Roughly half of these would be railway workers, miners and labourers from Bohemia and Moravia. The rest would be agricultural workers. The creation of the Protectorate, marking the end of Czechoslovakia, was unlikely to hinder this process since there were about 100,000 unemployed Czechs. The first steps towards fulfilling these plans were taken three days after the

Table 4.1 Czech workers in Germany, May
1939 – January 1942

25.5.1939	36,000
31.8.1939	70,000
31.12.1939	91,500
31.12.1940	134,000
25.9.1941	140,000
21.1.1942	141,000

Source: Jana Havlíková, Martin Hořák, Viola
Jakschová, Zdeňka Kokošková, Sanislav Kokoška,
Petr Koura, Jaroslav Pažout, Monika Sedláková,
Museli pracovat pro Říši (They were forced to work for
the Reich) (Prague 2004), p. 14.

entry of the German troops. Two senior officials from the German
Ministry of Labour were appointed to work under the occupation
forces. Thirty-four employment offices were established in six groups
in Prague, Plzeň, Kolín, Moravská Ostrava, Olomouc and Brno. They
were able to use the lists of unemployed that were already available.
These new employment offices supplied labour to all but the largest
firms, which recruited their own. The figures in Table 4.1 show how
the numbers steadily increased.

The first to go were the unemployed and young workers without formal qualifications. These left at the end of March. They were attracted to
what they imagined were better-paid jobs, lower cost of living, cheaper
food and longer holidays. As a result of these expectations, 50,000 men
and women had left the Protectorate by the summer of 1939. They
soon found that conditions were much worse than they had expected:
hard manual work and harsh treatment by the employers. This did not
match the promises made by the recruiting agents and news of these
conditions rapidly reached other workers in the Protectorate, often from
returning seasonal workers. With this news came a growing nationalism among Czech workers, many of whom were now unwilling to work
in Germany. The first leaflets urging people to boycott German companies were found by the Gestapo in April 1939.

German companies still needed foreign workers and the first steps
were taken towards creating a system of forced labour. In April 1939

the regional employment office (*Landesarbeitsamt*) announced that unemployed Czechs who refused to work in Germany would lose their social support. This included large numbers of former soldiers in the Czechoslovak army and the unemployed who had been put in special work camps as well as the so-called disciplinary camps (*Disziplinlagern*). The work camps had been created during the Second Republic to help Czech refugees from the Sudetenland and had been wholly or partly financed from the £10 million loan provided by the British government in January 1939 and money raised in London by the Lord Mayor's appeal.[1] This helped to support people financially but could not protect them from German demands for labour. Other examples of people being forced to go to Germany were as punishment for petty offences or as acts of revenge by the German authorities.

Closely linked with this was a gradual reduction in personal freedom through the series of orders and regulations that were passed in 1939–41 to regulate the Protectorate's economy. The first were issued on 25 July and 24 August. These established the duty of all men aged between 16 and 25 to work for the state. Initially the length of service was one year but in certain cases this could be extended for a second year. On 25 November this was followed by a further order giving the Oberlandräte exceptional powers to direct labour for '*die Sicherstellung von Aufgaben mit besonderer staatspolitischer Bedeutung*' (the safeguarding of firms with particular importance for the state). This order applied to all men aged between 15 and 70. The result was that the following year 10,000 young Czechs were assigned extremely dangerous work in organisations such as *Luftschutz* (anti-aircraft defence) and *Technische Nothilfe* (emergency help following air raids). A further order of December 1939 gave the minister for social and health affairs control of training workers through the employment offices. There were also similar regulations for agricultural workers. These were general powers. To these were added the workbooks in January 1941. These were a record of each person's employment and formed part of the regulations concerning the duty of all men aged 15–50 to work as directed by the state. To complete this control of the workforce, women and mothers with young children were also added, though they could only be made to work in the Protectorate. The result of these regulations was that in 1941 almost 140,000 Czechs were working in German-controlled territory (including Austria), the majority against their will.

Employment of Czech workers in Germany and Austria

The first group of Czech workers had been sent in the spring of 1939 mainly to Brandenburg, Lower Saxony, the north German ports and the former Austria. The principal destinations were Berlin, Hannover, Hamburg, Linz, Halle, Stettin, Elbing (Polish Elblag) and Königsberg (Kalingrad). Between 17 April and 4 May, for example, 24 trains left different Czech towns and cities for Berlin, Braunschweig, Eisenach, Erfurt, Görlitz, Celle, Kreinsen, Hamburg, Bücksburg, Königsberg and Stendal.[2] Most carried about 700 workers. Czechs worked in the construction industry, building roads, railways, gas and electricity lines and in mining. Others worked for major firms such as Mercedes, where one-third of the foreign workers were from the Soviet Union.[3] Many found the conditions intolerable: 79 per cent of the Czech and 70 per cent of the Slovak workers left their work at the Grossbaustelle Espenheim in Leipzig early in 1941.[4] Elsewhere they were employed in the docks or in dredging rivers and canals. Many of the large firms were under the control of Speer or were large state concerns such as I. G. Farben, AEG or the Hermann-Göring Werke. But it was not only men who were employed; the first women had also been sent to work in food processing factories in Stendal, Hannover, Hamburg, Mainz and Braunschweig. But there were very few: 4 per cent of the work-force in 1939 were women and the number did not increase much in the following two years.

To begin with, the workers found that there were financial advantages in living in a camp provided by the large firms, though some lived in guest houses, schools, factories that had closed or in cheap rooms in private houses. This was not satisfactory from the German point of view because it was more difficult to control the workers. The alternative was to construct large numbers of wooden barracks. Germany quickly became a *Land der Lager* (a country of camps): in Berlin alone the number increased from 35 in September 1940 to 400 in April 1941. The harsh life in these camps and the companies soon shattered any illusion that work in Germany would provide valuable training, easier work and a good wage. The problem for the Czechs was that, whatever their qualifications, they were given unskilled labouring jobs, which meant hard physical work and low wages, often allied with poor living conditions and food. This tended to cause disaffection among the workers, but when they complained they were threatened with prison.

Their legal position in Germany and Austria was in any case not clearly defined. The Protectorate formed part of the German lands and the Czechs were in theory in the beginning 'besondere Inlände' (special inhabitants). Gradually discrimination was introduced. In the summer of 1939 the Gestapo head office in Berlin issued instructions that any unwillingness to work, unacceptable political opinions or hostile attitudes would be dealt with harshly. This was to include 'protective custody' – being sent to a concentration camp. From the end of 1939 Czechs were categorised as foreign workers, which also defined their living and working conditions. These gradually deteriorated; they were not allowed to return home at the end of their contracts and were no longer allowed to live outside the camps. Work discipline became harsher and any suggestion of sabotage resulted in transfer to a concentration camp. Morale among the workers declined and many tried to escape to return home. This resulted in the building of special punishment camps near large firms. These included Hallendorf bei Watenstedt, Liebenau bei Hannover, Farge in Bremen and Wuhlheide in Berlin. Here they were housed in unheated wooden barracks without proper sanitation or warm water and had to do very hard physical work without proper clothing. Punishment was brutal and there was a higher death rate than in some concentration camps. The result of this increase in the number of punishment camps was that in May 1941 Himmler defined them as a special category. These regulations gradually spread to the whole of the German-controlled territory.

In 1941, with the invasion of Russia, more and more Germans were recruited into the army. This caused problems in the engineering and electrical industries as skilled workers were taken for military service. Firms tried to retain their workers. The archives contain many letters claiming that a person was indispensable and could not be spared for military service or that they were unfit for duty.[5] For example, there was a struggle in January 1942 between the management of the Zeiss-Ikon factory in Berlin and the Gestapo over 400 Jewish workers. Initially the factory won the right to keep them all because they were indispensable and almost impossible to replace. There was even a chance that other Jewish workers would be transferred there. But the final result, however, was that 250 were taken by the Gestapo and sent to concentration camps and no other Jews were sent to the factory to replace them.[6] However, in the case of Czechs, their value as skilled workers was recognised. To develop their skills and make them more useful workers many young men were sent back to the Protectorate, where technical schools were reopened.

Employment offices

All these workers were recruited through employment offices in the Protectorate. The first had been opened in 1903 and gradually a dense network was established in Bohemia and Moravia. These were taken over by the Germans who, on 5 September 1939, laid the legal foundation for 16 offices in České Budějovice (Budweis), Hradec Králové (Königgrätz), Jičín (Jitschin), Kladno (Kladno), Klatovy (Klattau), Kolín (Kolin), Mladá Boleslav (Jungbunzlau), Německý Brod (Deutsch Brod), Pardubice (Pardubitz), Plzeň (Pilsen), Praha (Prague), Příbram (Pibrans), Strakonice (Strakonitz) and Tábor (Tabor). There were an additional seven in Moravia: Brno (Brünn), Jihlava (Iglau), Kroměříž (Kremsier), Moravská Ostrava (Mährische Ostrau), Olomouc (Olmütz), Prostějov (Proßnitz) and Zlín. This was extended in January 1940 and at the end of the year there was a reorganisation and relocation of some of these offices to include Benešov (Beneschau) and Humpolec (Gumpolds). Each office was given directions about the information required for each person: marital status, whether the person was available because of shortage of work, if he or she was a student, whether they had served in the Czechoslovak army, capacity for work, experience, amount of normal wage and whether they had taken part in any passive resistance.[7] As the number of Czechs recruited increased, further administrative offices were created to control this large network.

Table 4.2 Workers who left the Reich glassworks in 1941 to work in Germany

Name	Born	Work	Date left Reich glassworks	Employed by German firm
Hlaváček, Gustav	1912	Helper	1941	Spiegelau, Bavaria
Juriček, Franz	1906	Helper	1941	Spiegelau, Bavaria
Štefanik, Alois	1910	Glassmaker	1942	Spiegelau, Bavaria
Důjka, Friedrich	1911	Mould maker	1941	Spiegelau, Bavaria
Vrána, Adolf	1922	Mould maker	1941	Spiegalau, Bavaria
Venglář, Josef	1923	Mould maker	1941	Spiegelau, Bavaria
Pavica, Ladislaus	1918	Mould maker	1941	Spiegelau, Bavaria
Eliášová, Josefina	1900	Glass sorter	1942	Spiegelau, Bavaria
Eliášová, Božena	1924	Glass sorter	1942	Spiegelau, Bavaria

Source: Zemský archiv, Opava, Reich company records, Verzeichnis, Charlottenhütte, 13 Nov. 1943.

To begin with, these were concerned with recruiting volunteers for work in Germany. By no means all those who went in 1941 were unemployed. Many were attracted by the prospect of higher wages. Table 4.2 gives details of men who left the Reich glassworks in Krásna to work at a similar factory in Germany.

All the above workers went to work in Germany willingly because they believed they would earn more money and probably have equal or better working conditions. They ranged in age from 18 to 42 and left the Reich factory between March and December 1941 and in January and August 1942. In one case, two women, apparently mother and daughter, left together in August 1942, apparently encouraged by what they heard from those who had already gone to work at the Spiegelau glassworks. They were by no means the only ones to go. The list contains many other names of people with similar, probably low-level skills who went to work at German glass companies in 1942, before the period of forced labour began. Most worked for companies in Thuringia and Bavaria, but there were exceptions. Karl Martinák, a 19-year-old mould maker, was sent in 1943 to work at an armaments factory at the harbour in Kapfenberg; Karl Orság, aged 19 and similarly employed, went in 1941 to work at an iron ore mine in Steiermark, Austria. Emma Hanláková, a 23-year-old glass sorter, found work in the Nordland fish processing company in Kiel.

Details of these workers show that it was not only the unemployed who willingly took jobs in Germany. Many in poorly paid, relatively unskilled work, saw what seemed to be an opportunity to improve their prospects. These were more fortunate than the ones who were sent later. They went to companies where their skills were recognised and where they were able to fill places left by men who had been called up to serve in the German armed forces. Later, as regulations defining work obligations were introduced, the offices handled a growing number of people who were being forced to work in Germany because there was no other work in the Protectorate. The example of Reich shows that this began in November 1942. From this point all workers sent to Germany and Austria were employed in the armaments industry, which included iron ore mines. November 1942 is also the start of the disappearance of young men who wanted to avoid forced labour. Franz Plánka and Ladislaus Kretík, workers at the Reich company, were listed as unknown in a company return dated November 1943.[8] They were presumably chosen by the employment office and Reich was told to send them to Germany, but they left the company and disappeared, hoping to start work in another area where they were not known.

As the demand for skilled workers grew in 1942, the employment offices took on further responsibilities: they were told to send only fit young men. There was also a further political consideration. They had to be careful when choosing staff to work in their own offices. In September 1939 they had been forbidden to appoint 'unreliable people' to responsible positions. 'Unreliable' included former officers in the Czechoslovak army, former members of the Czechoslovak Legion, Freemasons and Jews. Germans were in charge, as elsewhere. The elaborate bureaucracy needed many people to do the work efficiently: 2,633 in April 1943, of whom 581 were German (39 men, 262 women) and the rest Czech (1,510 men, 542 women).[9] The largest office was in Prague, which employed approximately one-fifth (512). Second was Brno with 232. The other cities and towns employed far fewer. One surprising feature is the relatively small staff at Plzeň – 138. Although this was a large industrial city, the large Škoda works (the main employer) was fully engaged in armaments production and the number of workers who could be taken to Germany was therefore limited.

There remained one other aspect of the work of the employment offices. After the initial period of recruiting volunteers, the offices became centres that handled those who were forced to work in Germany. There was to be a change from the selection of labour for construction work. The need now was for young, skilled men. Each economic group (*Wirtschaftgruppe*) in Germany was allocated a number of workers. The group could also specify the type of worker by level of skill, age and sex. This request was then sent to the appropriate employment office in the Protectorate. For example, the *Wirtschaftsgruppe Glasindustrie* demanded workers from the Vsetin office, because there were glass factories in the area under its jurisdiction. In addition, the employment office was told that all workers should be medically fit and able to live in camps, that they should have the skills needed by the German companies (the offices were not allowed to send unskilled workers) and that they should not be too old. Under certain circumstances, when the number requested was very large, women could be sent as part of the quota. In addition, Fritz Saukel, the Thuringer *Gauleiter*, decided that if this system was to work effectively, it needed a more senior official in charge of each office. Each office *Leiter* was therefore replaced by a *Beauftrager*, whose status was higher.

In 1943, in the period of Speer's 'Total War', the Protectorate became an important source of workers, both skilled and unskilled. Each office was given a quota of workers to be recruited. One example is from Vsetin, which in March 1943 was given a list of 413 workers that it had to find. This was divided into men and women, workers and office staff and, additionally, men in four age categories, ranging from under 18 to over 46. Any failure to provide these resulted in severe punishment. The offices recruited their quota by using the wide powers to direct labour that the regime had provided in May 1942. They had card indexes of all the young men in the appropriate age groups and could have chosen the ones to send. But instead the offices delegated the selection to Protectorate companies. When the choice had been made, the office issued an order directing the person to be at a named railway station on a particular day at a certain time. One example is the order given to Josef Pavelka in January 1943. Pavelka, a 22-year-old metal worker, who was employed in the area of Waldenburg (Valašské Meřičí), was told to report to the local railway station on 12 January. Failure to obey this would result in a fine of up to 100,000 crowns or six months in prison or both. He would be employed (in Germany) until the end of the war. To many this must have seemed like a sentence of death. This arbitrary power to send people to places where they knew they would be badly treated and poorly paid, and where they would have to stay until the war ended, made the employment offices one of the most feared and hated symbols of the Nazi regime.

Mobilisation of skilled workers

The German army suffered very heavy losses on the eastern front in 1941 and the high command was forced to mobilise its reserves. In December 1941 Hitler issued his army directive 39 which, among other things, allowed prisoners of war and Russian workers to replace these young men who were called up. In March 1942 Fritz Saukel was appointed to organise the recruitment of labour from the occupied countries – the Saukel Programme. This established a new and more precise method of recruitment.[10] Heydrich saw this as an opportunity to remove Czechs from the Protectorate and offered Speer 16,000 young Czech workers for construction work. In March 1942 the *Gauleiter* of Lower Saxony, Karl Hanke, signed an agreement for 25,000 Czech workers to be sent to his area. As the numbers of workers increased, an Economic and Labour Ministry was created to organise this labour supply. It could also reduce the size of Protectorate companies or close them to provide labour for use elsewhere. In May 1942 Hitler ordered that armaments production in the Protectorate should be increased and that only the surplus of skilled labour should be sent to work in Germany. But this left German industry with a pressing need for more workers. In September the German high command became anxious that there might not be enough workers for the armaments industry and that police raids in public places (*Massnahmen*) would not produce the numbers required.[11] The army's report stated that there were 212,030 workers in the Protectorate, of whom 52,986 were in engineering companies. The survey also estimated the total number of skilled workers and considered introducing a two-shift system to help meet production targets in the Protectorate. But in view of the needs of the armaments industry in Germany, it would be necessary to take more Czech workers aged 20 and 21. This was still not enough and in April 1943 a request was made for another 100,000.

To try and supply these workers, in September 1942 Saukel ordered the German authorities in the Protectorate to register all single men born in 1921 and 1922. From this group agricultural workers, miners, workers in the armaments industry, police, soldiers and post and railway officials should be made available to work in Germany. Major firms protested against this potential threat to their production, but had limited success. To widen the scope of this labour pool, the age range was increased in mid November to those born between 1918 and 1920. It was hoped in this way to be able to take workers from smaller commercial as well as manufacturing companies. Special trains left for Vienna, Dresden, Breslau, Linz and other cities. By spring 1943 these trains had taken almost 70,000 young men to Germany. A total of 135,158 workers were sent to Germany in 1942, most of whom went to work in the armaments industry. By 1943 the demand from both German and Czech industries for skilled men was causing serious problems. When more workers were demanded, the glass company Reich at Krásna in northern Moravia pointed out that it had already sent workers to Germany and in January 1943 apologised that the only 15 men it could send to meet its quota were untrained.[12] The company pointed out that if more were demanded, it would disrupt the current production programme and make it difficult to meet production targets. These not only supplied articles for the armed forces but also articles that played a significant role in German exports. This claim was supported by German ministries. By the autumn there was still a serious shortage of workers in Germany. On 11 September the closure of the Sollmann ball-bearing factory was announced, which would provide 123 workers: 30 skilled men, 65 women and 28 labourers.[13] To try and obtain more workers the military Rüstungskommission and the Erkundungsamt considered closing firms. They had the power to do this as head of the Zentralverband der Industrie. The records of the employment offices also contain lists of companies in the different Wirtschaftsgruppe, and these lists formed the basis of the proposed company closures. It was hoped in this way to get 889 workers in December 1943, 937 in January 1944 and 386 in February 1944. There was further scope for closing five more firms that would give another 993 workers, but deciding which firms to close was a delicate matter in the light of the Wehrmacht's own needs.

Thousands of young men also worked in the Todt Organisation (military construction, mainly of defences) in Norway and France, emergency help, anti-aircraft duty or the army's work units.[14] Speer reorganised this in June 1944 to provide labour for all the planned construction work. He created eight groups, one of which, the Gruppe Deutschland VII, was based in Prague.[15] Many railway and postal workers were also sent to Germany to replace Germans who were called up. The recruitment of so many young men for work in Germany gave rise to a fear among Czechs that this was intended to reduce the population, especially since it was widely known that the work and working conditions were bad. It gave rise to a very large number of marriages in the Protectorate as young men tried to avoid being sent to Germany. Many women became pregnant as a way of avoiding a similar fate. This helps to explain the rise in the Czech population by the end of the war.

Workers born in 1924

The selection of workers as an age group was the key to Speer's plan for work substitution (*Arbeiteinsatz*). By choosing this age (18), Speer could be certain that a young man had had sufficient time to complete an apprenticeship, if he was capable of doing one. He would be able to work as a skilled man (*Facharbeiter*) on a range of machines (turning, milling, boring etc). He would also be young, strong, fit and single. Later, Speer extended the group to cover a larger age range (18–21) who shared the same characteristics. This scheme allowed a company in Germany which was about to lose workers to the army to specify the type of person needed to replace them. In addition, since everyone was issued with a workbook that recorded all the training and work, it would always be possible to know which category a person was in (skilled worker or labourer). Everyone had to carry his or her workbook for identification. Failure to do this was a serious offence and it was possible to stop a person in the street and check their identity and age. In this way anyone who tried to escape forced labour and moved to another job in another place could be found in a large-scale search. The result of this was to make it possible to close firms that were not doing armament work and relocate the workers.

After Speer had declared a state of total war in February 1943, there was a further reduction in the number of commercial and small industrial firms. In February 1943 it was announced in a Sudeten German paper, the *Aussiger Tagblatt,* that men aged 16 to 65 and women of 17 to 45 would be liable for *Kriegseinsatz* (taking the place of German workers who had been called up for military service).[16] They would be summoned in a series of groups from the week of 15–22 February 1943 to 15–21 March. Those targeted were single men and women, widows and widowers, married couples with no children, those working less than 48 hours a week, those working in small businesses or self-employed and women with children over 14, except for agricultural workers, teachers, those in the army or police and foreigners. This shows that Speer's policy of mobilising people for armaments production applied equally to Germans as well as Czechs. This should have made another 10,000 workers available. But it was becoming clear that if any more large groups of workers were sent to Germany, industry in the Protectorate would suffer. In August 1943 Karl Frank, the German Staatsminister for Bohemia and Moravia, noted that the Protectorate's labour reserves were almost exhausted and any further reduction would have serious social consequences. For this reason the numbers leaving the Protectorate were reduced: in the spring they had only amounted to 3,000. However, at the same time, Speer demanded 60,000 workers for the aircraft industry. A compromise was reached in September 1943 under which young workers would do a ten-month apprenticeship in aircraft companies. After this they would be returned to similar industries in the Protectorate as fully qualified workers. The employment offices identified 110,559 young men and women from this age group, but it proved more difficult to send them to Germany. Many were already working there or in important armaments industries in the Protectorate or in mining. To try and avoid service in Germany, with the added danger from Allied air raids, many resorted to self-mutilation or deliberately injured themselves. In some desperation, the employment offices decided that those who were married after 1 September would be regarded as single. In spite of all the efforts of the employment offices, only 33,051 young workers had been found when the list was closed in mid November. The first group of those born in 1924 should have been sent to Berlin in October 1943, but because of transport and other problems, the first train did not leave until 18 January 1944.

Nor was this the only problem. Many young men and women ignored the order to join the train and the police in the Pardubice and Kolín areas had to look for them. There were violent scenes at the railway station before the train finally left in the evening. Subsequent Allied air raids on aircraft factories increased the general sense of panic and the office of the president intervened to prevent any more women being sent. There were further difficulties in recruiting workers and it proved impossible to meet the quota for March. At the beginning of May almost 27,000 young men and women were sent to Germany, where they faced even worse conditions in the aircraft industry: harsh conditions in the barracks, worse food, a 12-hour working day and the constant fear of Allied bombing. For the Germans, the problem was the lack of a well-educated and technically trained workforce for the aircraft industry. To try and meet this need, it was decided to reopen Czech technical schools and send young workers back to the Protectorate to be given a suitable technical education. The first arrived back in September 1944 and by the end of the year almost all those born in 1924 had been sent home.[17] Some German firms complained that they would not be able to replace these workers if they returned to the Protectorate and those at the Junkers factory in Sachsen-Anhalt remained there until the factory was destroyed in a raid. Then they were transferred to the underground Nordhausen factory and joined prisoners of war and concentration camp inmates working in appalling conditions. In spite of appeals by Protectorate officials, around 400 young Czechs remained there until the end of the war.

There was also a serious lack of labour, especially skilled labour, in the Protectorate and Germany in 1944, as increasing numbers of Germans were killed on the eastern front and factories were drained of workers to fill their places. In many cases this produced serious problems for companies engaged in armaments production. The Reich glass company, faced in April 1944 with yet another demand for workers, said that it could not send any more because it was fully occupied in producing glass for lighting. Moreover, it was the only glassworks in the Protectorate that was doing this, which was essential for traffic.[18] It is not known whether this appeal was successful. What is clear is that the demand for labour was unrelenting: in August 1944, in an effort to get more workers for the coal mines, firms were told that they would have to give up a percentage of their workers. This ranged from 1.5 per cent of firms employing fewer than 100 workers, to 3 per cent of those employing over 1,000. To get these, the authorities considered making another raid on communities.

Czech workers in Germany 1942–5

All Czech workers were regarded as foreigners under the general heading of *'dienstverpflichtet'* (forced labour) and were treated in the same way as workers from other parts of Europe. In May 1944, in the former *Gau* of Saxony, there were about 350,000 foreign workers and prisoners of war of a total of 1.78 million. The majority were Russian, Polish, French, Belgian, Italian and Dutch and the longer the war continued, the greater the number employed. There was no attempt to provide them with proper training or guards on dangerous machinery and there were frequent serious accidents, including scalping or amputation. At the beginning of the war the standard working day was 10 hours, but during the war this increased to 12. There were two 15-minute breaks for breakfast and coffee and a half-hour midday break for food. If a worker exceeded this by more than 25 per cent he was punished with a loss of wages or was sent to a disciplinary camp. The first holiday was only given after several months' work but it was difficult to get permission to travel to the Protectorate.[19] Firms often held back some of the wages due in order to encourage the worker to return. Czech workers were paid according to a German tariff of between 50 and 70 pfennigs an hour. Qualified workers were paid 70–100 pfennigs. An unqualified worker therefore received on average 30–40 marks a week; a qualified, married man received 50–60. Czech workers could officially claim state benefits such as family support, but in practice this proved difficult. Some firms paid it, others did not. The workers also had to pay income tax of up to 10 per cent as well as accident and health insurance and dues to the Deutsche Arbeiterfront (DAF). Some also found they had to make a payment to the Winterhilfe fund. On the other hand, living costs in the camp were low – 1–2 marks per day and about 2.50 marks in private accommodation. Most Czechs lived in barrack accommodation which was very basic and vermin-infested. The heating was inefficient and there was a danger of an accumulation of poisonous fumes. Those living in buildings such as schools often had communal dining rooms but everywhere there was a lack of privacy.

These camps were often the unintended targets for bombing raids, because they were close to factories. Until 1942 there were few of these but in 1943–5 Germany and Austria were attacked. Stanislava Zvěřinová was sent to work in the Daimler-Puch factory at Steyr in February 1944.[20] This was bombed and many workers–Germans, Poles, French and some Czech – were killed. When the factory was destroyed she was sent to work in a factory in a tunnel at Libřice on the River Vltava south of Prague, and it was there that the workers were finally freed by the Red Army. There was inadequate air-raid protection in these camps and they became overcrowded when some were destroyed. Ration cards provided food, but Czechs grumbled at the dull and inadequate diet: one warm meal per day, consisting of a stew made from potatoes, cabbage, peas and noodles, normally without any meat. This was an inadequate diet, though better than the Ostarbeiters (Poles and Russians) received, and workers had to supplement it with meals in guesthouses or prepare food themselves. As the war continued the ration was reduced. In the spring of 1942 the weekly rations consisted of 200 grams of bread, 350 grams of meat and a small amount of sugar, margarine, cheese, jam, skimmed milk and ersatz coffee. To supplement this, prisoners depended on food parcels from family and friends. The only concession to personal hygiene was the weekly supply of warm water and a pair of basins without running water for every 100 men. The workers tried to lighten this harsh regime with music, chess and football as well as films and plays. The music ranged from small groups to large jazz and brass bands. In some of the large cities, cultural activities were provided for foreign workers, which for Czech workers included some cultural activities that were begun by Emanuel Moravec in 1942. Sunday, the only rest day, was reserved for sport and a competition was organised in September 1943 by the DAF, in which the Czech team came second to the Dutch. The other Czech national activity, hiking, was impossible during the war. The Germans also tried to influence the Czech workers through a newspaper, *Der Tschechischer Arbeiter,* but the only part that was read was the sports page. Attempts to influence Czech workers by providing libraries of propaganda also failed. To meet the sexual needs of the workers, each camp had a *Freudenhaus für Ausländische Arbeiter* (a brothel). All the Czech workers dreamed of their eventual return home. This dominated their lives and correspondence with family and friends and was the subject of camp songs. For some the strain proved too much and they sank into alcoholism or gambling. Anything that could help workers forget the boredom and harsh conditions of camp life was a welcome relief.

Two lists of workers from the Reich glass company (Böhmisch-Mährisch Glasfabrik A.G. during the war) show how this system worked. When recruited for this work they were all skilled men in a specialised industry that was doing important work for Germany. Their work in Germany was totally different as is demonstrated in Table 4.3.

Table 4.3 Workers from the Reich glass factory sent to work in Germany and Austria, 1943

Krásna factory	Address in Germany or Austria
Grygar, Josef, cutter, born 1916	Markstadt III bei Breslau, Wohnlager 2 M. B.20A
Jaroň, Anton, mould maker,[1] born 1922	Markstadt II, Bezirk Breslau, Wohnlager 2, Baracke 39/16 A
Žitník, Josef, cutter, born 1922	Markstadt bei Breslau, Schliessfach 63
Čáň, Miroslav, apprentice glass maker, born 1915	Markstadt bei Breslau, Wohnlager II/b 15/96
Palát, Franz, cutter, born 1900	Kruppsches Arbeiterheim, Pionier Kaserne, Mühlheim-Ruhr bei Essen
Bochníček, Wenzel, mould maker, born 1923	Kruppsches Arbheiterheim, Pionier Kaserne, Mühlheim-Ruhr bei Essen
Polášek, Gottlieb, cutter, born 1922	Kruppsches Arbeiterheim, Pionier Kaserne, Mühlheim-Ruhr bei Essen
Karban, Stanislaus, mould maker, born 1922	Eisenerz, Lager 65, St. 49
Pšenica, Josef, glass maker,[2] born 1921	Eisenerz, Lager 65, St.49
Kroupa, Anton, mould maker, born 1922	Arbeitslager Ausflug, Plauen i. Vogtl. Färberstr. 1
Holub, Josef, cutter, born 1922	Arbeitslager Ausflug, Plauen i. Vogtl. Färberstr. 1
Konvičný, Josef, cutter, born 1921	Arbeitslager Ausflug, Plauen i. Vogtl. Färberstr. 1
Šedlbauer, Josef, shaper,[3] born 1921	Magnesitwerke, Lagerführerkanzlei, Radentheim, Kärnten
Vrábl, Josef, glass maker, born 1918	Lager Hofland, Hartmansdorf bei Chemnitz in Sa.
Vsetin factory	
Tomášek, Emil, glass worker,[4]	Gemeinschaftslager, Schwarzenberg i. Sa.
Kříž, Josef, mould maker, born 1921	Arbeiterbtl. 3/6, K1 Munheim a/M Str. K5 Schule
Macl, Wénzl, glass maker, born 1921	Philips A. G., Prague IX, Podébrader Str. 183
Studeník, Viktor, heating engineer, born 1908	Bruno Becher, Schwarzenberg i. Sa.

Source: Zemský archiv, Opava, Reich company records, Unersetzbare, seitens der Arbeitsämter abdisponierte Glasfacharbeiter der Firme Böhmisch-Mährische Glasfabriken A.G. vorm. S. Reich & Comp., Prag II, Stephansgasse 65, undated but probably 1943.

[1] *Kölbelmacher*

[2] *Anhefter*, a glass worker who joins pieces of glass together

[3] *Formenmacher*

[4] *Abspränger*, a glass worker who removes glass from moulds

A second list, in a letter from the Reich company to the main Aussig employment office in Prague in May 1943, gives some further information about the work the former Reich employees did when they were sent to Germany and Austria.

Daniel Bedřich, works as a helper at the Karl Mittelbach glass-works, Langeswiesen-Thuringia

Tomašek, Emil, supervisor of making replacement parts for machines from tin at Walter Wiedlich, Metallwarenfabrik, Wildenau-Schwarzenberg, Saxony

Kříž, Josef employed clearing up after air raids at the Arb. Batl.13/6,K 1. Strasse K 5 Schule, Mannheim a/Rhine

Macl, Václav, employed as a glass blower at Philips, Prague

Studeník, Viktor, supervisor of auxiliary work at Bruno Becher, power saw, Schwarzenberg

Románek, Josef, works as maker of glass jars at the Otto Lange glassworks, Ilmenau

Source: Zemský archiv, Opava, Českomoravské company records, letter to Ředitelství Prague (employment office), Vsetin, 25 May 1943.

The lists above and in Table 4.3 show how skilled glassworkers from an important Protectorate company were sent to different parts of Germany and Austria, and how at least some of them were employed. The most fortunate were probably Václav Macl, Josef Románek and Josef Šedlbauer. The first was able to continue work in the glass industry at Philips in Prague. Románek was employed by the German glass manufacturer Otto Lange. Šedlbauer, perhaps helped by his German name, had a job in the office of the camp leader at the Magnesite company. Of the rest, some were used to help clear rubble after air raids – a particularly dangerous task because of falling masonry and unexploded bombs. Others worked for Krupp, and the remainder did a variety of work in different firms. All had badges that showed their nationality and the factory they worked in.[21] Most lived in camps – some described as barracks – and a few were fortunate enough to live in private houses in small towns.

Uniformed services

Thousands of young men found themselves doing another form of labour service in uniformed organisations, which were subject to much stricter discipline and where punishments were decided in military or police courts. The first of these was the Todt Organisation. This had the status of a separate body that did not recruit workers through the employment offices but used its own agents. Its function was to construct military defences and roads. It claimed to offer young men work in romantic places such as the Aegean, Norwegian fjords or the Atlantic coast. In January 1942 Fritz Todt asked Heydrich for 4,000 workers to build a synthetic fuel factory at Záluží (Maltheuern) near Most (Brüx). Later, workers were transferred to other firms within the Todt Organisation and it is impossible to know the total number employed. One so-called privilege that the workers enjoyed was that they were treated the same as Germans, but this was accompanied by a strict work discipline and they were sent to work in harsh climatic conditions.

Other Czechs were classed as Germans because they had a German parent or grandparent and served in the German armed forces and work units.[22] The latter were not sent to Germany with the October and November 1942 groups but instead were ordered to report at a military post in the Saarland, where they were formed into companies. Their task was to repair bomb damage. The Czechs were put in work battalions L12 and L13 and were sent to Saarbrücken, Ludwigshafen, Kassel, Essen, Zeitz and other German cities. They worked under military discipline, were paid at normal German rates in money that could be exchanged at a bank and had free food and accommodation. But the work was arduous and extremely dangerous – accidents were common – and they had to work in all weather conditions. Very often they had to work outside for a whole day with only half a loaf of bread and a piece of sausage. In the evening they had a warm meal (normally a potato or turnip stew). About 3,000 Czechs were sent to the Todt Organisation, the majority unwillingly, and they remained there from the spring of 1942 to the end of the war. It was a similar situation for those in the Technisches Nothilfe (TN), whose job was to repair bomb damage. Most of the approximately 1,600 who were sent were students at technical schools. As the Allied bombing raids intensified, Emanuel Moravec, the Education Minister, decided that young men should get their practical experience in one of the TN units. The first wave, of third-and fourth-year students, was sent from November 1942 to summer 1943.[23] The work was counted as work experience. They were sent first to a military training ground at Brdy and later to Škoda in Plzeň. The second wave consisted of third-year students from engineering courses and were at least 17. Between August 1943 and January 1944 about 2,000 young men, some of them under 17, were sent to Berlin, Duisburg and other badly damaged cities. After a group of 15 students were killed in an air raid in Berlin, the remainder were sent home.

In 1942 and 1943 another 1,000 young Czechs were sent to the Brandenburg town of Beeskow following the decision in the summer of 1942 to reorganise the police. These were formed into a mobile Feuerschutzpolizei (fire defence police) regiment and sent to Lübeck. Besides these, two battalions of Protectorate police were also sent to Germany. One, the Bohemia, was in Bremen, Hamburg, Lübeck and Kiel from June 1943 to January 1944. Their duty was to guard bombed buildings and help with freeing those trapped inside. The other battalion did similar work in the Ruhr. Both units consisted of young men who hoped to be able to transfer to German police units. Finally, about 1,500 young men were sent for anti-aircraft duty in Germany. They were first sent for a month's training to Kiel and Dortmund and from there served in units in north German ports and the Ruhr. They were sent in two groups, the first in October 1942 and the second in June 1943. Six months later Hitler decided not to use them for this any more, partly because of the growing threat to Germany and partly because Germans were becoming increasingly fearful of the growing number of foreign workers in Germany. Czechs in the TN and anti-aircraft units were sent home.

Punishment of offences against forced labour

The introduction of this system of forced labour created a new form of repression and punishment. Soon after Heydrich's appointment at

Reichsprotektor, he decreed that anyone accused of sabotage or interference in war production would be brought before a military tribunal or a special court in Prague or Brno. Heydrich considered the wartime legislation was too lenient. In his view it had failed, for example, to properly punish those responsible for the Avia aircraft factory strike. A month later the first *Arbeitserziehungslager* (work education camp) was established, similar to those which had first been set up in Germany in 1941. These were in fact punishment camps for those who had failed to do their work correctly or had tried to escape from forced labour. In the summer of 1942 there were police raids in towns, swimming pools, restaurants and other popular places. This resulted in the seizure of large numbers of people who had tried to escape forced labour. Another way of catching these people was to issue ration cards only to those with workbooks.

There was a growing number of people who used a doctor's certificate to try and escape forced labour. If the claims were found to be false, the doctors who had issued the certificates were sent to concentration camps and their patients to punishment camps. Anyone convicted of inflicting self-mutilation to escape work duty was sentenced to death. The number accused of trying to escape forced labour continued to climb and reached 9,000 in September 1943, when further raids by police, Gestapo and other units were again carried out in a variety of public places. As a result 786,313 people had their identities checked, of whom 3,004 were arrested. Another 25,176 had to provide evidence that they had performed their work duty. But finding enough workers still proved difficult; in January and February 1944, 6,000 people left their work in Germany.

This increase in the number of people trying to escape work duty led to the forming of two special Gestapo units, the anti-Sabotage IV 2 and another, IV 3, that were directed against all who tried to protect the people trying to escape this work. But these failed to raise the productivity in armaments factories. Work discipline was therefore tightened; lack of punctuality, illness, sleeping and smoking at work were all classed as sabotage. The Gestapo punished these either with a warning or the person had to work an extra shift on Sunday. Anyone who tried to lower workers' morale was sent to a punishment camp. Those accused of deliberate sabotage (damage to machines, poor quality work) were sent before a German court and sent to prison for a long time. This amounted to a death sentence. The extraordinarily large number of people who tried to escape work attracted the attention of the Gestapo. In June 1944, 33,047 workmen claimed they were ill; over half were immediately sent back to work. Another 103 were imprisoned in police cells in Terezín, 355 were given a warning and 188 had to work an extra Sunday shift. In November the management at the Vítkovice iron and steel works were told by an engineering company in Wamberg in the Sudetenland that two former employees, Johann Kolc and Eduard Čamr, had been arrested by the Gestapo.[24] The first was a welder and the other a smith. Both had apparently tried to escape from their forced labour.

Punishment camps

A number of these *Arbeitserziehungslager* (AEL – 'work education' camps) were built in the Protectorate following an order of 7 December 1942. These were similar to camps already established in Germany and were under the control of the Gestapo. Those who were sent to the camps had been accused of lowering workers' morale by refusing to work overtime or failing to meet their production targets. Others were people such as Stanislav Šimak, who had escaped from work camps and had been recaptured. Šimak was arrested by the Gestapo when he returned home to Petrovice and was taken to a camp at Tábor.[25] There were also men who were part Jewish: Ladislav Rychman's mother was Jewish, but he had tried to hide the fact.[26] Until 1943 these people were imprisoned in Germany but from the end of 1943 there were seven camps in the Protectorate as well, with a total capacity of 5,000. These were at Panenské Břežany (Jungfernbreschau), Mirošov (Miroschov), Plzeň (Pilsen), Planá nad Lužnicí (Plan an der Lainsitz), Moravská Ostrava-Vítkovice (Mährisch Ostrau-Witkowitz), Moravská Ostrava-Kunčice (Mährisch Ostrau-Kuntschitz) and Mladkov (Wichstadtl). These held almost 3,000 Czech prisoners. Other nationalities were held at Terezín. These camps were surrounded by barbed wire, so that they could also be used to hold political prisoners and were under the control of either the German police or the SS. The camp guards were members of the Protectorate police. In the beginning the camp regime was not particularly strict but as time passed the amount of hard physical work was increased and the food ration reduced. Within each camp there were two sections. New prisoners spent 10 days in the first before being transferred to the second. Those who had tried to escape from work camps in Germany received the harshest treatment. Prisoners spent between two weeks and 84 days in these camps, working as miners or forestry workers for a daily wage of five crowns. In extreme cases such as a death in the family a prisoner could be given three days' holiday, though this was not deducted from the term of punishment. In spite of the harsh treatment, many prisoners preferred to stay there rather than return to work in German factories, which were being destroyed by Allied bombing. In one case, a Czech who had escaped from a factory in Germany was sent to work in the talcum powder industry in Moravská Ostrava. He wrote to his friends about his happiness that he was closer to home and better fed. Women and girls between 15 and 55 were sent to a punishment camp in Plzeň-Karlov (Pilsen-Karlshof) that had been built near the Škoda works. There they had to work at tidying up and cleaning. Another camp was built in December 1943 at Mladkov (Wichstadl) for boys of 14 to 18. The harshest conditions of all were in camps run by the SS in the Benešov (Beneschau) district, especially the one at Hradišťko pod Medníkem (Hradischko) and Březany (Jungfernbreschau), into which prisoners from the first were sent at the end of 1943. This was similar to Flossenbürg. Prisoners had to do very heavy work in quarries and on the land. For example, in December 1943, 600 prisoners worked on average 1,802,320 hours. A further so-called assembly camp was built at Prague-Ruzyně (Prag-Rusin) in November 1943 into which prisoners from other camps were collected for transport back to Germany. Prisoners spent a maximum of eight days there. Finally, early in 1945 some camps were used for other purposes. For example, the camp at Mirošov (Miroschov) held political prisoners who were later evacuated to a prison in Brno. Shortly before the end of the war the Germans in charge of these camps fled and the prisoners were free to return home.

Slave labour

The first people sent to concentration camps worked, unpaid, in the construction industry. Buchenwald, Mauthausen, Flossenbürg and Groß-Rosen were near Steinbrüchen, Sachsenhausen, Neugamme and Stutthof and produced bricks and other building materials. The work was very heavy and intended to kill the prisoners, who were fed inadequate rations. In the spring of 1942 Hitler decided to locate the camps close to armaments factories. One example is the Deutsche Ausrüstungswerke G.m.b.H. that was built close to the Buchenwald camp. By the spring of 1944 about 250,000 prisoners were working on war production and at least 170,000 more were living and working in inhuman conditions in underground aircraft factories. In December 1944 there were 11,881 citizens of the Protectorate in Buchenwald, Dachau, Flossenbürg, Mauthausen and other camps. These people were paid a small daily wage. Qualified workers received a maximum of six Reichsmarks, but this was after deductions had been made for clothing and food, which amounted to more than 80 per cent of wages. In Bohemia, especially in the former frontier zone (Sudetenland), over a dozen concentration camps were established, similar to Flossenbürg and Groß-Rosen. The worst was at Litoměřice (Leitmeritz), built on a former artillery barracks to hold up to 5,000 prisoners. Most were Poles and Russians, who worked in the underground Richard factory. The first transports arrived in March 1944.[27] There were about 18,000 people, of whom about 770 were women. There were almost 9,000 Poles and 3,500 Russians. The remainder were Germans, Czech, French, Hungarians and Yugoslav.

The slave labour prisoners lived under very harsh conditions. The barrack blocks were overcrowded and had no sanitation or heating. To begin with the daily ration of food consisted of half a litre of ersatz coffee or tea, a litre of watery soup and 200 grams of bread. Later this was reduced. In December 1944 the lack of food and overwork contributed to an epidemic of dysentery in the Litoměřice camp, which caused the death of 701 prisoners. The death rate of 12.9 per cent was the highest of all camps. A crematorium was built to dispose of the bodies; 18,000 bodies were burned. The Jews suffered in a similar way. In

1939 they were excluded from the professions and from 1941 most were used for seasonal agricultural and building work. After Terezín had been made into a ghetto this work ceased and they were sent to concentration camps. In the Sudetenland, however, a network of forced labour camps were created for Jews by the police president of Breslau, SS Oberführer Albrecht Schmelt. These served as a source of cheap labour for Speer. Two years later there were 160 camps, 16 of which were in the Sudetenland. This network, named Organisation Schmelt, had over 50,000 men and women, living in conditions that were little different from the concentration camps. In 1943 Himmler decided to close these and transfer the prisoners to Auschwitz. However, those who were working for the armaments industry remained in nine camps, which served as outposts of Groß-Rosen.

From the autumn of 1944, 90 per cent of all prisoners were in camps close to armaments factories. Of the total of almost 200,000, 14,000 were Czech. These included over 100 prisoners who had been sent to Terezín and who were transferred to work at the underground Richard factory. Another 150 remained in Terezín and made propellers for the Albis Werke in a factory in the cellar of the Litoměřice brewery. They worked up to 12 hours a day and had to march to and from the factory. The hourly rate was 55 pfennigs, but this was paid into the account of the head of the Ordnungspolizei in Prague. In March 1945 this amounted to 1,305,000 crowns.

Digging trenches

As the Russians advanced, Hitler ordered a network of defences to be built. In the summer of 1944 plans were drawn up and the following October the work was begun on the eastern frontier of Austria. This was the so-called South East Wall. The *Gauleiter* of Lower Austria, Hugo Jury, who was made responsible for this work, asked for Hungarian Jews, Russian workers and people from Bavaria and the Protectorate. The German authorities in Prague acted quickly and in December 1944 sent agricultural workers who were not employed in armaments production. The aim was to send 10,000 men from the 1921 to 1923 age group. The economics minister, Adolf Hrubý, tried to prevent this and was supported by officials in the agricultural and forestry organisations. Between 10 and 17 December, Czech agricultural workers were sent to the *Gau Niederdonau* (Lower Austria). In spite of the threat of heavy fines of up to 10,000 crowns and six months in prison, a large number of the workers failed to arrive and police had to search for them. The Czechs were sent to the Neusiedler Lake to dig a 35-km-long anti-tank ditch, and formed part of a large group that included members of Nazi and military organisations.

The living conditions were appalling. The Czechs were housed in unheated barns with no sanitation and minimal medical care. They were forbidden to enter guesthouses or have any contact with the local villagers, who in any case were generally hostile because the ditches were destroying their property. The Czechs also lacked suitable protective clothing in the severe weather and collections of shoes, shawls and other clothing were made for them in the Protectorate. The working day began at 7 a.m. and continued until the day's quota had been completed, which often took until the evening. The daily food ration was inadequate: a cup of coffee in the morning, a piece of sausage and margarine and in the evening vegetable soup. The workers suffered from frostbite, pneumonia and other medical complaints, and conditions became so bad that in the middle of January 1945 a total of 785 seriously ill workers had to be sent back to the Protectorate. A further ten died and some committed suicide. Even many of the seriously ill had to work. Almost 300 tried to escape, in spite of the threat of imprisonment in a punishment camp. The work finally ended in February 1945 and the last forced labourer returned home at the beginning of March.

This was only part of the new defensive system. In December 1944 another set of defensive ditches was planned, this time in Moravia, which included Olomouc and Brno, which the Germans wanted to turn into fortresses.[28] This work was to be the responsibility of Karl Frank, who wanted 50,000 – later raised to 65,000 – workers. Factory managers, who realised that they would lose their workers, opposed this and finally only 37,000 were sent. The work was directed by local Nazi organisations and overseen by members of the SA, Volkssturm and soldiers. After eight weeks it was clear that more workers would be needed and men from the age group born in 1927 and 1928 were included. Finally, in March 1945, boys were sent from secondary schools and remained at work until the Russian forces arrived. On 7 April 1945, 11 boys died.

Homecoming

The final months of the war were the worst. Allied bombing reduced many factories to rubble and foreign workers had to clear this or were sent to help dig defensive ditches. The railway system also suffered and food supplies were reduced to a minimum. At this critical time thousands of Czechs were still doing forced labour in Germany. As the Russians advanced, many workers tried to get home, but it was impossible to travel by train. The only way was on foot. At the end of the war millions were travelling in this way, including many who had been forced westwards by the Russian advance and who became Displaced Persons (DP). UNRRA (United Nations Relief and Rehabilitation Administration) had been set up in November 1943 to provide help for people displaced by war. Czech organisations in London worked for a similar purpose from early in 1943, working with UNRRA to return Czechs to their homes. This was followed by an agreement in the spring of 1944 with the military leaders of SHAEF (Supreme Headquarters Allied Expeditionary Force) to repatriate Czech citizens. When the war ended, displaced persons in the areas liberated by the Allies were collected in camps according to their nationality. Personal details were recorded and repatriation visas given, after which people were returned in large groups. This was carried out very quickly; in the summer of 1945 most were able to return home. In the area liberated by the Red Army in Eastern and Central Europe, including most of Czechoslovakia, the position was very different. UNRRA and other Western organisations were not allowed to work and it was only in Berlin that a Czechoslovak commission was established to deal with Czechs and Slovaks in that city. Within Czechoslovakia the reception centre at Plzeň played an important role. Established by the Americans, who had liberated the city, it acted as a transfer point between the Western and Russian zones. In only seven weeks it registered 45,650 people. Help was given them by the Czechoslovak government and a newspaper, *Služba repatriantům* (Service for the repatriated), first published in May 1945, gave considerable help to workers returning from forced labour in Germany. Many carried with them emotional trauma as well as physical marks of suffering. It had been their first confrontation with one of the most brutal political systems of the twentieth century.

Industry in the Protectorate

In many ways, Czech industry worked under similar conditions to those described in Germany. There was a tight control of discipline and any attempt to undermine morale in any public manner was quickly discovered by the SD, SS or Gestapo who were present in every factory. Nevertheless, when conditions became very bad, it became impossible to hide it, as the following example from the Tatra company shows. In 1940 workers at the Nesseldorf (Kopřivnice) factory complained about the lack of food and poor wages.[29] The German and Czech workers complained that food prices were rising faster than their wages, and they had to work eight- or ten-hour shifts on an inadequate diet. Their rations consisted of dry bread; it was proving virtually impossible to get any meat or fat. No one seemed to know when the butcher's shop would be open. There was no trade union to take up the workers' grievances; the DAF was a political organisation that supported the state rather than the workers. The *Werkschutz*, which was concerned with maintaining a high level of output, was anxious that this would damage productivity. It sent the report to the German military *Rüstungsinspektion*, saying that the complaint was fully justified and warned that this was causing unrest and creating a sharp division between the factory workers and office staff. Although the outcome of this is not known, it was bound to be taken seriously, since it could not be controlled merely by arresting and imprisoning the supposed ringleaders.

Propaganda played an important part in Germany's industrial policy in the Protectorate. The aim was not merely to terrorise the Czechs but to persuade them that Germany was powerful, would win the war and that it was worth supporting. Factory workshops and canteens had Nazi slogans such as *'Gute Stimmung in der Morgenstunde ist der Anfang ein verheissungsvollen Tages'* (a good mood in the morning is the beginning of a day full of promise) as a constant reminder and Hitler's birthday was turned into a carnival.[30] For example, in the case of the Vítkovice iron and steel works, the opportunity was taken to hold a procession of decorated floats that represented the different parts of the company. Speeches were made by senior Nazi Party officials and all was done to make the Germans proud of the company and to persuade the Czechs, Poles and other workers to take a similar view. Social activities were organised with a similar purpose. There were Christmas festivities in 1943 at Vítkovice which were used for a similar purpose and there was unusual latitude in the choice of entertainment.[31] The programme opened at 3 p. m. with jazz and tap dancing – normally regarded as 'American' and therefore anti-German. This was followed by recitation and popular songs. Lively Hungarian czardas rounded off the entertainment. In the long report on the evening, there was great emphasis on lively and popular entertainment, including at one point a short anti-Semitic monologue. As a further piece of encouragement to the workers and staff, each was given 30 cigarettes, which the company had to pay for. The company magazine was used for a similar purpose. Early in the war, the picture on the front cover was of the steelworks working at full capacity. Towards the end of the war, as it became clear that Germany was losing, the picture was an idealised view of peasant life in the countryside, a reflection of the different mood among the workers.

It is hard to know what effect, if any, this had on the workers. Under normal circumstances, a young man would leave school or university and start work for a company and hope to stay there for a long time. During the war all that changed. The Czech universities and colleges were closed and young men aged 18 to 21 were, wherever possible, sent to work in Germany. During the war there was therefore no influx of young men into Czech companies, and the ones who were working for firms were gradually removed to work elsewhere. In some cases, large firms such as Vítkovice received a number of these young men, with the result that its workforce consisted of a mixture of experienced, older workers and office staff who were paid normal wages and salaries, and young, inexperienced men who were paid very little. In Vítkovice in December 1942, for example, there were 2,171 wage earners, 508 monthly paid staff and 969 forced labourers. It is likely that there was considerable friction between those paid a fair wage or salary and those who received very little.

This was only part of the problem. As more and more men and women were sent to work in Germany to replace those taken into the army, Speer realised that further replacements could be found among the prisoners of war. The Geneva Convention stated that soldiers who were taken prisoner could be made to work, provided this was not of strategic importance. Non-commissioned officers could supervise their work but officers did not have to do any, which explains why wartime stories of escaping British prisoners of war are always about officers. From the beginning of the war, British, French and Belgian prisoners of war were being put to work in factories. One of the first questions asked of the prisoner was 'What work did you do before the war?' to which the more astute said 'deep sea diving' or something similar. These prisoners worked in factories, doing much the same work as they had done before the war. But as the war continued, more were needed. The answer was to use Russians. A great many had been captured in the early stages of the attack on Russia, but because Germans regarded them as subhuman, they had been collected into open-air encloses and either starved to death or were given so little food that the result was the same. In 1942, Speer realised that those who were still alive – 455,054 at the end of September – could be put to work.[32] Many were sent to factories and mines in Germany, some were sent to the Protectorate. Two examples will show what was done. One group was sent to the artificial fuel refinery near Most, another to the uranium mine at Joachimstal. In the latter case, in May 1942 there were 62 Russians and 33 French.[33] They were paid a little money in the form of camp currency (*Lagergeld*) that could only be spent in the camp shop on items such as paper and pencils. All were unskilled and underfed, but the work was not necessarily considered at the time to be dangerous to health. Very little was known at this stage of the effects of radiation. The biggest problem of using these Russians as workers was the difficulty of communication, since none spoke any language but Russian.

These workers could easily get to work, since they were put in camps near the factories and mines. For the ordinary workers, transport became a major problem in 1942. Germany had failed to win the war against Russia by the end of 1941 and the increasingly bitter fighting in Russia was placing heavy demands on the railway to keep the armies on the eastern front properly supplied. Added to this was the demand to keep supply routes open to German garrison troops spread across Europe. There were also delays in getting rolling stock back once they had gone to the single-track railways in the Balkans. In addition there was a shortage of locomotives for the trains supplying factories with raw materials and manufactured items in Germany and the occupied countries. The result was that in December it was becoming very difficult to continue to supply adequate transport for the workers in the Protectorate. In fact, overcrowding on the trains became so bad for workers in Brno that General Major Hernekamp, the *Rüstungsamtinspekteur* in Prague, asked for the help of President Hácha. Before long it became generally known that this was a problem that affected other industrial towns and cities as well. As a result employment offices across the Protectorate asked companies to draw up maps showing what forms of transport the workers used to get to work and how far they had to travel. It was hoped in this way to be able to simplify the transport network. The archives contain a large number of maps showing that workers sometimes had to travel first by bicycle or on foot to reach a bus or train that could take them to work. Firms added the numbers who came by each route, so that a reasonable estimate could be made of the capacity needed for each. Travelling in this way, when added to shifts that before long were increased to 10 hours per day for six days a week, put a considerable strain on workers and transport.

This was only part of the burden that workers had to carry. Their wages and the prices they paid for food were all fixed by the Germans and there were also heavy fines for any infringement. Even the weekly and annual markets were strictly controlled, as the example of Aussig (Ústi nad Labem) shows.[34] The charge for bringing a lorry with green vegetables to market was between 1.20 and 2.40 Reichsmarks, depending on the size of the lorry. For a large cart the charge was 60 pfennigs and 36 for a small. A handcart was 12 pfennigs. Local stallholders paid 2 crowns or 24 pfennigs, foreigners (Czechs and Poles since Aussig had become part of Germany) paid 3 crowns or 36 pfennigs. The market prices for items were pasted in an official handbook and ranged from a goose at 6 pfennigs to a stag at 48 pfennigs. There was inevitably a black market and in country districts, where people could grow their own fruit and vegetables and keep poultry, conditions were probably not as bad.

There was a great emphasis on political indoctrination of German youth in the Protectorate and Sudetenland during the war, as in Germany. Boys and girls who, before the war, would have been members of scouts or similar groups now had to attend meetings of the Hitler Youth (HJ) and the similar League of German Girls (BDM). When coming to the first meeting at the age of ten they had to bring their birth certificates to ensure that no Jews or part Jews (*Mischlinge*) were enrolled. All meetings were held in Nazi rooms, which formed part of the indoctrination. This included slogans such as '*Dein Leben ist gebunden und das Leben deines ganzen Volkes. Das ist nicht nur die Wurzel für dein Kraft, sondern auch die Wurzel für dein Leben Adolf Hitler* [Your life is united with the life of your whole people. That is not only the source of your strength but the source of your life is Adolf Hitler]. To be a member of one of these organisations was not the only duty of young Germans. When the Allied bombing began in earnest, young men were enrolled into anti-aircraft units. There was already provision for this in laws of 1935 and 1937 and training was compulsory. Not everyone attended these courses, and punishment was recorded in an official book, the *Reichstrafgesetzbuch*. Anna Bartsch was summoned to a course in the burgomaster's office in March 1943 in Grossprisen. But she failed to attend and her punishment was duly recorded. Older members of the German population joined official bodies such as the Wach- und Schliessgesellschaft, which were a form of local police. All wore a distinctive uniform that gave them status in civilian society. The Wach- und Schliessgesellschaft Argus members in Schreckenstein wore black or dark blue uniforms that were similar to those worn by German Reichsbahn workers. In another district they had a uniform that made them look like Czech police.

It was later decided to change this to bring them in line with the German style of uniforms.

The state also wanted to make foreigners conspicuous. It was not only Jews who had to wear a special badge. In 1940 Poles were ordered to wear a violet star on a yellow background. Anyone failing to do so would be fined up to 150 Reichsmarks or six months in prison. It was in all respects a highly regulated state, governed very strictly according to Nazi Party theory. However, the number of Germans in the Protectorate was relatively small and the German authorities relied on Czech and local German officials to carry out instructions. Apart from the manhunt that followed the assassination of Heydrich and the widespread search for young men who had fled to avoid forced labour in Germany, life in the Protectorate was hard but largely uneventful. *Volksdeutsch* Germans living further east realised that Germany was unlikely to win the war and tried to join companies in the Protectorate to escape the coming invasion. One example is Ivan Minkowsky, a Bulgarian with a German (*Reichsdeutsch*) mother and Bulgarian father, who was a merchant. He claimed to be German rather than Bulgarian. He had attended Realschule in Sofia and then Hochschule in Munich, graduating with a diploma in mechanical engineering in 1927. He had followed this with work at Hanomag in Hannover and Schwarzkopf in Berlin before returning to Bulgaria during the Depression. He had ten years' experience of working on railway wagon repair and wrote to the DAF central office in the hope that he could get a job as *Betriebschef* in a medium-sized company at a salary of 1,200 Reichsmarks per month. His letter was sent to the railway wagon section of Tatra but it is not known if he was offered work, though by that stage in the war there was a growing need for experienced engineering workers.

News of the German defeats on the Russian front spread through the Czech population and German official reports from 1944 speak of the growing expectation of German defeat. Whether many Czechs were able to hear the BBC broadcasts (*Volá Londýn* – London Calling) it is impossible to know today, but the Germans certainly believed that news was reaching the Czechs. The Czechs had more time than the Germans to meet and share news, since they were not allowed to join official Nazi organisations. In 1942 a German report spoke enviously of the way young Czechs could sit in cafés.[35] However, there were growing shortages of food and a number of *Beamte* were still without homes, three and a half years after Hitler had 'freed' the Sudetenland. However, there was one part of the Czech population which suffered very badly: the Jews.

The Jews[36]

In March 1939 when the Protectorate was established, many Jews were integrated into Czechoslovak life. Some regarded themselves as German, others as Czech or Slovak. When part of the puppet Slovak state had been given to Hungary in 1938, the Hungarians put German-trained anti-Semitic teachers in the schools. These created an anti-Semitic atmosphere.[37] Those Jews who considered themselves orthodox and wanted to found a new state in Palestine, the Zionists, went to live there in the mid 1930s. These people realised after *Kristallnacht* that they were in danger and made every effort to get their children to safety. In late 1938 Britain agreed to take 10,000 and just over 9,000 reached England under the *Kindertransport* scheme that took Jewish children from Austria, Czechoslovakia and Germany. The best known part in this was Nicholas Winton's in Czechoslovakia, which brought 669 to England and continued until the beginning of the war.[38]

After the creation of the Protectorate, to begin with, the Jewish population of the Protectorate did not feel the full effect of the Nuremberg laws, unlike those in Germany. But there had already been some examples of anti-Semitic government policy during the Second Republic. Jews had been dismissed from government posts. In Neurath's Jewish policy, as in other aspects of his administration, he tried to be 'firm but fair' but Frank, who was in charge of administration, introduced a series of measures that gradually restricted the freedom of Jews. This was often in petty ways such as forbidding them entry to sports grounds, restricting the times when they could go to shops, limiting their freedom to stay at resorts and stopping them fishing.[39] Soon after the Germans seized power they carried out a census that established a record of the population and seized synagogue records. Heydrich introduced a harsher policy in November 1941, when he transformed Terezín (Therienstadt) from a garrison town into a Jewish ghetto. As a further check to establish who was a Jew, all Jews were ordered to obtain an identity card. This ensured that they would be registered. In January 1942 the first Jews arrived at Terezín from Prague and Brno and when others were sent as well, the town became hopelessly overcrowded. In 1942 almost 40,000 Jews were sent from the Protectorate and 37,000 from Germany and Austria. This was compared to the town's previous population of 7,000.

In name it was a self-governing community, but it was under German control. It became a staging post in the transfer of Jews to concentration camps or East European ghettos. Responsibility for choosing who to send was the duty of the Jewish administration. Life in Terezín was extremely harsh and rations were barely enough to keep the inmates alive. Those in the so-called 'old people's home' died of exhaustion. They included Dr Ludwig Czech, former Chairman of the German Social Democratic Party of Czechoslovakia and a minister. There were Czech guards whose job was to check each person on arrival, but they often used their power to seize the few possessions that Jews had brought with them. There was also bitter rivalry between the Czech and German Jews as well as a great deal of petty thieving and corruption. The official heads of the community, Jakob Edelstein, Paul Eppstein and Benjamin Murmelstein can also be criticised for their failure to do more to protect their fellow Jews. They failed to inform the International Red Cross on their two visits in 1944 and 1945 of the true state of life in Terezín. The reality was that between 24 November 1941 and 31 August 1944, 32,647 Jews died in the town, 6,534 of 'senile disorder' (malnutrition).[40] Taking into account the final stage of the war, the total deaths amounted to 35,000, which includes those sent there in 1945 and who died of typhus. Of the 150,000 children who passed through, only 150 survived. One who did and subsequently wrote an account of it was Jana Friesová, who was sent to Terezín with her family in 1941 when she was 14, and spent the rest of the war in a girls' home there.[41] The effect of the Holocaust on towns was dramatic and heartbreaking. In Olomouc, for example, of the pre-war Jewish population of 2,500, only 12 survived.[42] The position in Brno was similar: there were about

12,000 Jews in 1938. They were taken to Terezín in 1943 and 1944. These included 820 children over the age of 14.[43]

There remains one aspect of Jewish–Czechoslovak history that has not been reported. It is best described by the example of a Jewish family in Ostrava and was recounted by Zuzana Skacelová. Her family had originally come from Poland, partly to look for work in this large mining and steel-producing city and partly to escape anti-Semitism. They kept their Polish passports and identity, perhaps because it was difficult to obtain Czechoslovak citizenship or possibly because they were not able to because of Polish–Czech tension. The father was a leather worker. Until the late 1930s he was able to continue his trade unhindered. During the Sudeten crisis however, as tension mounted again between Poles and Czechs, he was arrested by Czech police and ordered to go to Poland. He refused, well aware of Polish anti-Semitism. As a result he was taken to Prague, brought before a court and imprisoned for a year. His wife and family followed, probably finding shelter and support among the large Jewish community. On his release, he was expelled to Poland but heard of work camps that had been set up by Jewish organisations in Slovakia. By this point, Jews were losing their jobs and Jewish organisations saw an opportunity to provide some form of accommodation and livelihood in Slovakia, away from the Czech authorities. The father went there and was followed by the rest of his family.

At this point Slovakia separated from the rest of the Czechoslovak state and the camps came under the control of Slovak fascist guards. The Jews were able to remain there until Hitler ordered the Slovaks to begin sending them to Auschwitz and Majdanek concentration camps. Several members of the Skacel family were transported there. All of them died. However, in 1944 in the Slovak Uprising partisans released the remaining inmates. This family escaped, though the father was suffering from dysentery. They managed to reach a house on a hillside, some distance from their camp.[44] The family living there took them in and sheltered them in what Zuzana describes as a hole in the ground. In reality it was probably a room or rooms cut into the hillside behind the house, where the family stored wine, vegetables and farming implements. It was a wine-growing area, where the vineyards were laid out on the hillside and houses were situated nearby. This saved their lives. As soon as the Slovak revolt began, German troops entered Slovakia to crush it and any Jews they found were shot on sight. Zuzana and her family were sheltered at considerable risk until the Russian troops arrived and liberated them. She too became a Communist after the war in gratitude to the Russians. Later, she married Josef Skacel, whose father had been forced to go into hiding after the assassination of Heydrich and was similarly liberated by the Soviet forces and also became a Communist.

Other concentration camp victims

Not all those who were sent to concentration camps were Jews. Anyone whom the German authorities considered posed a serious threat to their psychological control of the Protectorate could be sent there. One example was the group of Czech university students in Prague who protested publicly in November 1939. Fortunately for them they were released on the insistence of Neurath. The Okresní museum in Most has collected the accounts of a number of victims of fascism who were imprisoned in concentration camps and survived the war.[45] These moving descriptions of life in the camps and in some of the underground factories are a stark reminder that Jews were not the only victims of the Germans' murderous policy. A map at the front of this museum's book shows that each of the camps had its own subsidiaries. This greatly increased the number of inmates. These accounts include one by František Baňka, a pilot in the Czechoslovak air force, who was arrested by the Germans when he tried to escape into Poland in 1939. He was sent to Sachsenhausen and later Flossenbürg and was liberated at the end of the war. Another victim was Jaroslav Benaš, who wanted to join the French Foreign Legion but delayed his attempt to escape for too long. Germany's defeat of Poland blocked that route and he next tried to reach Switzerland but was arrested and sent to a series of concentration camps: Flossenbürg, Ravensbrück, Dachau, Groß-Rosen, Mauthausen and Sachsenhausen, where he was finally liberated. Václav Lavička was another survivor. He had organised an anti-fascist youth group, was arrested in 1938 and sent to Buchenwald. From there he was forced to work in the notorious underground Dora factory.

The ones who got away

Others were more fortunate and escaped to fight in the Royal Air Force or Czech units in the British army. Each had a similar account. František Fajtl was a young pilot in the Czechoslovak air force when the Germans invaded Bohemia and Moravia in March 1939.[46] By chance he was awake during the night and heard the broadcast announcing the invasion, which ordered all military personnel to take no action against the German forces. He was forced to accept the humiliation of being part of the handover of the Olomouc airfield and was only slightly encouraged by the subsequent action of the Germans, who treated the Czechs with courtesy. He, like many others, managed to escape into Poland, posing as a tourist and joined the French Foreign Legion. In the early part of the war he fought in the French air force but escaped to Britain after the defeat of France and served with Bomber Command in Wellington bombers. After the war he returned to Czechoslovakia but was arrested after the Communists seized power in 1948 and was imprisoned as an enemy of the new state. The normal sentence seems to have been 20 years, but there was an amnesty in 1960.[47] This was the fate of many who had served in the RAF and a recent film 'Tmavo modrý svět' (Dark blue world) tells an almost identical story. Not all who had served with Allied forces and returned to Czechoslovakia were arrested. Some managed to escape. One former bomber pilot with the RAF managed to get his wife and child back to Britain as the arrests began and then stole an aircraft in the middle of the night with a few trusted companions and flew it to England. He returned to Czechoslovakia after the fall of Communism and, with others in a similar position, was given an official reception. Their numbers were relatively small, but it should be remembered that it was a Czech, serving in the Polish 606 squadron in the RAF, who was the top-scoring pilot in the Battle of Britain and that roughly 10 per cent of the RAF fighter pilots were Polish, Czech and Free French. Accounts of soldiers are often similar. But not all.

Some tried to establish an anti-German organisation of former soldiers under Vladimír Štěrba in Brno. This was the Polsko-československé mafie (PČSM), part of the illegal FFMU organisation at Brno, but they soon realised that this was an impossible aim.[48] They were unlikely to get any help from abroad and the power of the new Nazi state from March 1939 was too great. The much larger and better organised Obrana národa (ON) and Politické ústředí (PÚ) were decimated by mass arrests. The only hope of Beneš and his companions was to escape and continue the struggle abroad. They were able first to escape to Poland and in Krakow registered at the Czechoslovak consulate. From Poland they went first to Sweden, then to London and finally reached Paris. The intention was to form a Czech legion in France. There were difficulties, however, and they joined the French Foreign Legion as a way of continuing the struggle against Germany. They remained in the Foreign Legion until the surrender of France in June 1940 and were then demobilised at Agde. After receiving new identity cards at the Czechoslovak consulate at Marseilles, Beneš and the others decided to try and reach Gibraltar via Spain and Portugal. However, in Spain they were arrested and imprisoned, first at Figueras and later at Cervera. Their fear was that they would be handed over to the Germans, but instead the Czechs were sent to a concentration camp at Miranda der Ebro. Beneš' first plan was to try and get his release by writing to the German embassy in Madrid and to his family, but realised that he was likely to be arrested by the Gestapo on his return. Finally he was able to leave with the help of the Polish consulate in Madrid. He travelled via Portugal to Gibraltar and thence to England, which he finally reached in 1943. He joined the RAF and trained as a pilot, returning to Czechoslovakia after the war. Although Beneš does not refer to being imprisoned after the Communist coup in 1948, it is certain that he was, like others who had fought for the RAF. He was rehabilitated in 1990 after the fall of Communism, promoted to colonel and awarded a Czechoslovak decoration.

These were men who fled westwards and joined the French and British armies and air force. Others went east and joined Czechoslovak units in the Red Army. Among these were Slovaks who served initially with the Slovak army on the southern front in Russia but towards the end of the war, when the Slovak Uprising broke out, changed sides and fought against the Germans. Others such as Gustáf Donoval and Ludovik Kubo joined the Red Army. Finally, there was an important group that formed the team for operation KOZINA, who parachuted into Slovakia in 1943 to join and strengthen the partisan forces.

One of the bizarre aspects of the war was that people who had no more than a single German parent or grandparent could claim German nationality. Many did so because they either believed in an ultimate German victory, accepted the German racial theories or simply wanted to gain a more privileged position in a state that had reverted, as before 1918, to German control. Many of these were living in the Sudetenland, which was less racially pure than the Germans liked to admit. One result was that many people who were only partly German were enrolled in the German armed forces.[49] However, when they got the chance, they changed sides. One example is Otmar Malíř from the village of Prostřední Suché near Těšín.[50] He was registered on the *Volkslist* as *Volksdeutsch* and was called up in September 1942. In March 1943 he was with Rommel's Afrika Corps in North Africa, which by May had withdrawn to Tunis. There he deserted with seven friends, all from the Těšín area and was followed by another 24. He then enlisted in the British army and served in the Pioneer Corps. After six months he was sent to England and took part in the Normandy landings. After the war he returned home and, like others who fought on the British side, was imprisoned after the Communist seizure of power in 1948.

Not all those opposed to Germany were able to change sides. Štěpán V. was the radio operator for an anti-German group. As *Volksdeutsch* he had been forced to become a member of the Hitler Youth and in May 1942 was called up for the Wehrmacht. He made contact with a Czech opposition group in Pardubice in May 1943 but then was sent as interpreter on the eastern front and was in the forces besieging Sevastopol. When the Germans were forced to retreat because they were in danger of being surrounded, he escaped with others on a motor torpedo boat. He was transferred to the western front, where he fought in the battle of the Ardennes, but again escaped capture. At the end of the war he was in the Austrian Alps and finally returned home in his German uniform but with a Czechoslovak badge on his

lapel. Others included Karel P., who as a young man was a supporter
of Soviet Russia but became a bomber pilot in the Luftwaffe and lost
his illusions about both Russia and Germany. Václav P. was recruited
into the Waffen SS and took part in the invasion of Crete, Jan K.
served in a grenadier regiment and Gerhard B. was in the German
navy. Others included Gregor E. who was captured by the Russians
and ended the war in a prisoner of war camp. In many ways the period
from the Munich Conference to the liberation of Czechoslovakia bears
all the hallmarks of Hitler's desire to destroy the Czechs. He was
helped by the many Sudeten Germans who wanted to reverse what
they saw as the disgrace of the creation of the First Czechoslovak
Republic, when they had lost power. Even the initial treatment of the
Czechs by Neurath, the first *Reichsprotektor*, was marked by a strong
sense of German superiority over Czechs as Slavs. Neurath did not go
as far as Hitler would have liked in his punishment of anti-German
activity in the summer and autumn of 1939, but there can be no
doubt about the intention of what he did. He was determined to create stability so that the Czech resources could be used efficiently by
the Wehrmacht. Heydrich's appointment as his replacement marked
a new stage. His preparations for the imprisonment of Jews in Terezín
was only the first, tentative step towards destroying them. By the
summer of 1942, when German and Austrian Jews were also sent
there, the whole Jewish population was crammed into a town originally designed for 7,000 and were fed at a starvation level. It was only
a matter of time before large numbers would die. To put the town
under Jewish administration only made matters worse. Successive
governors were forced to choose who would be sacrificed and there
was also bitter rivalry between Czech and German Jews.

The accounts of those who managed to escape and fight in France
and then in the RAF and Czech units in the British army show another
aspect of their determination, to help defeat Nazi power even after their
betrayal at Munich. The decision by the Beneš government in exile to
assassinate Heydrich was one of the most terrible events of the war in
terms of its effect on the Czech population. The number murdered in
cold blood from cities, towns and villages across the Protectorate certainly achieved Beneš' purpose in poisoning Czech–German relations

and making the expulsion of the Sudeten Germans after the war much easier. Finally, forced labour by virtually a complete generation of young Czechs of both sexes under terrible conditions in Germany, Austria and in the Protectorate was another shameful aspect of German policy. The decision to rule the Protectorate by fear instead of a more lenient policy denied Hitler many of the advantages of using the large number of well-educated men and women in a more effective way.

CHAPTER 5

RESOURCES

Even before Hitler had gained the Sudetenland and seized the rest of Bohemia and Moravia, German military leaders had a good idea of the resources they would gain. The army had made more than one survey of Czech industrial assets and German firms were interested in investing in Czechoslovak companies. German penetration of Czechoslovak industry had begun before the First World War and continued during the First Republic, led by companies such as Mannesmann. After the Protectorate was created in March 1939 the army made another, brief, survey of Czech raw materials.[1] Germany soon took the first steps towards exploiting these important Czechoslovak resources but the full use of them only developed gradually and came to a climax after 1942 in the period of Speer's Total War. What these resources were and how they were developed to contribute to Germany's attempt to resist Russian forces forms the theme of this chapter.

Coal, iron and steel

As early as 1926 the German army had recognised the potential value of Czechoslovak industry and resources. A secret report in the German military archives gives a detailed analysis of mining and industry and where the different types of factory were situated.[2] It is comprehensive and even includes the number of workers employed and production totals. Later, in 1936–8, as the Munich crisis deepened, German military and industrial leaders reading this report will have realised that little had altered since 1926. The industrial landscape had not changed. Only the production totals and the number of workers had altered. But in some ways, the seizure of Bohemia and Moravia, though adding considerably to the industrial capacity, would only reach its full potential if the coalfields and iron and steel works in southern Poland were also seized. This helps to explain Hitler's long-term strategy, which was not merely to gain additional living space but also the industrial resources to take on and defeat the USSR as the ultimate goal.

To understand the significance of this it is necessary to see the geographical structure of Bohemia, Moravia and southern Poland. The main resources were coal and iron ore, often found in close proximity, but there were varieties in the type and quality of each in different areas. In West Bohemia, in the area of Most, there are large deposits of brown coal. Its high sulphur content made it less useful for smelting iron but, provided the moisture level was low, it could be used for the hydrogenation process of turning coal into oil and different types of fuel. The other important coal resources were in northern Moravia. These formed part of a large coalfield that continued into southern Poland.[3] This was black coal, most of it useful for coking and therefore better for smelting iron and steel. At the end of the First World War it was known as the Upper Silesian coalfield. Czech–Polish–German rivalry led to long-lasting disputes over where the new international postwar frontiers between the countries – and thus of ownership of the coalmines – should be. This dispute was never solved in a way that Czechs and Poles could accept and this permanently soured relationships between them in the interwar years. The frontier was finally agreed after a plebiscite in 1921 and much of the southern part of the coalfield was given to Czechoslovakia. It did not end the bitter rivalry between the two countries, because a great many Poles were left in the new Czechoslovakia. The coalfield awarded to Czechoslovakia was particularly important for the Czech iron and steel industry. The coalfield of the Ostrava-Karviná area supplied the iron and steel works of Vítkovice (in Ostrava) and Třinec further east. If this coalfield had become part of Poland, these important iron and steel foundries would have had to import the coal they needed, with significant political as well as economic consequences.

This new frontier also changed the nature of industry. Of the 22 German major mining and metallurgical companies in the disputed area before 1918, only five remained in Germany. Also, of the 2,800 square kilometres that Germany had possessed before 1918, only about 600 square kilometres remained German. In addition, estimated reserves of German coal were reduced from about 57.8 billion tons to about 8.7. German losses of coking coal were even more severe.[4] Czechoslovakia had between 35 and 40 mines in north Moravia including the Čéšký Těšín area. Some were west of Ostrava, the remainder were between Ostrava and Karviná and south of Karviná. One mine was state-owned, the others were in the hands of private companies. Two of the latter were owned by iron and steel works: the Báňská a Hutní Společnost and the Vítkovické Horní a Hutní Rěžířstvo.[5] They had the most important coal mines, with 16 pits. These produced more than half of the north Moravian coal and two-thirds of the coke. It was one of the main Czechoslovak industrial areas, producing about three-quarters of Czechoslovak coal and almost all its coke. Some was also used in the Bohemian blast furnaces, the rest was exported to Austria, Poland and Hungary.

There was also an attempt to export coal, wood and iron (including manufactures) to Romania, using the Société de Commission Tchecho-Roumaine I.L. in Bucharest.[6] Some of the iron ore for the Vítkovice steel works came from mines in northern Sweden owned by Vítkovice, though transport costs were high. The rest came from Slovakia and Hungary.[7] Vítkovice was one of the most efficient iron producers in Central Europe. The other iron works at Třinec had its own coal mines and iron ore mines in Slovakia, besides coke ovens. In addition to the blast furnaces and steel works, the Třinec firm also had a rolling mill and steel construction works at Karlová Huta, a wire-drawing mill at Bohumin and a chain works at Malá Moravska. The area as a whole produced about two-thirds of Czechoslovak pig iron and a slightly smaller proportion of steel, though it relied heavily on imported supplies of scrap metal. There were also important lead and zinc industries in north Moravia, though Polish production of zinc was higher.

When German troops invaded Bohemia and Moravia in March 1939, coal mining and iron and steel production had recovered from the Depression and were working at full capacity.

The transfer of the Sudetenland was the first step in capturing these assets. The next step, after the creation of the Protectorate, was for the Verband der Stahlwerke in Düsseldorf, the umbrella organisation for the German steel industry, to create a working arrangement with the Protectorate industry in Prague. While the details were being worked out, the Germans decided to import 30,000 tons of forgings a month for five months, of which one-third would be from the Sudetenland.[8] This would lead to the incorporation of the Protectorate's iron and steel industry into an international organisation. It relied on a supply of good coking coal. The exploitation of the north Moravian coalfield based on Ostrava suffered from the transfer of land to Poland in 1938.[9] When Poland forced Czechoslovakia to cede the formerly disputed territory there, Czechoslovak exports of coal fell. The area did not come under German control again until Germany's invasion of Poland in September 1939. Hermann Göring wanted to control heavy industry in Czechoslovakia, as he did in Germany through the Reichswerke. Deprived of part of the important north Moravian coalfields, he extended his influence to consolidate over half of all brown coal (lignite) mines in the West Bohemian part of the Sudetenland into a single body under VIAG and the new Reichswerke-Sudetenländische Bergbau A. G., Brüx (Most).[10] The share capital was increased from 50 million to 140 million Reichsmarks and the Reichswerke share increased to 78 per cent. The invasion of the remaining part of Bohemia and Moravia in March 1939 gave Göring the chance of extending his power into Czech heavy industry: Škoda, the Poldi steel works at Kladno, Vítkovice, and the Pražská železářská Společnost (the Prague iron company), which was already under Mannesmann control.[11] The development of the lignite mines at Most led to the building of a large hydrogenation plant in October 1939 for turning brown coal into oil, also under Reichswerke control. Before long the Reichswerke also controlled the rest of Czechoslovak heavy industry.

Companies were organised into associations in a similar way to those in Germany. The Vítkovice company archives contain a list of seven

Wirtschaftsgruppen for industry and mining, a Marktvereinigung for forestry and wood and a Zentralverband of industry in Bohemia and Moravia. The Wirtschaftsgruppen were subdivided into specialist Fachgruppen (there were eight for the iron industry). There were also three iron and steel cartels, two Treuhand and Prüfungsgesellschaften, associated industries abroad and six Vorprüfungstellen.[12] These were used to channel resources to companies to meet orders from the Wehrmacht. The German Military Archives contain an incomplete list of all the mines and iron works in September 1942, which includes four gold and silver mines in Slovakia.[13] Until 1943 the Protectorate acted independently of the German state planning system and the Reichswehrschaftministerium and Rüstungsamt decided the quotas of iron and steel that should be given to each company based on a quota system of 2.75 million tons per month.[14] In 1943, as Speer organised the total transformation of the economy of the area under German control, this earlier system was abolished and the Protectorate was brought into Speer's own planning system. To bridge the initial gap while the two parts were amalgamated, supplies of essential materials were provided by Germany to Protectorate companies.

Göring, after establishing his control over the Protectorate's heavy industry through the Reichswerke, continued to extend his power. He ordered Hans Kehrl of the Four Year Plan and Karl Rasche of the Dresdner Bank to buy the Česká eskomptní banka úvěrní ústav (Bohemian Discount Bank and Credit Society), one of the ten Czechoslovak banks. This was important because it held major shareholdings in large firms: 37.6 per cent of the První brněnská strojírenska společnost (the First Brno Engineering Company), 35 per cent of the Poldi steel works (that supplied steel to Škoda), 49 per cent of Zbrojovka (the main weapons manufacturer, which under Göring became part of the Waffenwerke A. G. with Škoda) and some shares in Škoda and mining and metallurgical companies. Later, acquisitions of shares by Göring gave him control of Škoda and Zbrojovka as well as some Slovak industry. He also gained indirect control of other coal mining and railway companies through the Four Year Plan. Only Vítkovice resisted him for a time. It had originally been owned by the Vienna branch of the Rothschild family and Gutmann Brothers, and was therefore Jewish, but ownership was officially transferred in 1939 to Alliance Insurance in London (another Rothschild company). When Göring tried to seize it as Jewish property he was told that it was now British and he had to wait until the outbreak of war with Britain to seize it as an enemy company.

This gradual extension of German economic control of Czech and Slovak industry through the purchase of banks and industrial shares led to the creation of the Reichswerke 'Montanblock'.[15] This controlled the coal, iron and steel production of the former Czechoslovakia and supplied the materials for weapons and armaments. Its development during the war is illustrated by the figures in Table 5.1.

Originally it was believed that this Reichswerke activity was limited to the Protectorate. But documents in the Vítkovice company archives show that in December 1942 the firm was trying to get a licence to export iron to Romania. It had exported steel before the war and continued to do so. In January 1943 Vítkovice had 21,150 tons of mostly ferromanganese iron waiting to be sent to firms in Germany and Austria, for which it would need 40–50 railway wagons a day.[16] To show the significance of these Czechoslovak industries for the wartime German economy, a comparison with Germany is given in Tables 5.2–5.

The more detailed figures in Tables 5.3, 5.4 and 5.5 show how production varied from one month to another in the first six months of 1944. This was when German forces were being forced to retreat and

Table 5.1 Sales by the Reichswerke 'Montanblock' 1941–4
Reichsmarks

	1941	1942	1943	1944
Silesian Group	242,267	306,923	348,382	344,292
Vítkovice	230,950	235,857	253,917	267,804
Nordbahn Prague	45,594	59,416	63,907	55,224
Poldi Steel Works	98,360	101,140	117,828	140,364
Sudeten Oil	1,999	33,687	139,708	89,736
Sudeten Coal	106,485	121,427	148,814	145,056
Total	*725,655*	*858,450*	*1,072,556*	*1,042,476*

Source: R. J. Overy, *War and economy in the Third Reich* (1944), p. 170.

Table 5.2 Reichswerke output, 1941–4
Million tons

	1941	1942	1943	1944
Iron ore				
Pre-war Germany	58.1	59.1	59.9	60.1
Slovakia	–	3.4	3.8	–
Pig iron				
Pre-war Germany	24.8	26.8	27.4	31.7
Czech	24.4	21.2	18.9	20.7
Crude steel				
Pre-war Germany	17.1	22.1	21.4	26.8
Czech	33.6	27.8	26.0	28.6
Rolling mill				
Pre-war Germany	20.3	23.8	19.2	25.2
Czech	32.1	27.8	28.1	31.6
Bituminous coal				
Pre-war Germany	25.7	22.0	20.3	19.3
Czech	17.3	17.4	19.4	19.2
Lignite				
Pre-war Germany	20.7	19.8	18.2	18.0
Czech	68.9	70.6	73.0	72.8

Source: ibid, p. 172.

Table 5.3 Steel ingot production 1943 and February–June 1944
000 tons

	1943	February	March	April	May	June
Silesia	2,821	233	249	229	247	240
Protectorate	1,732	146	154	136	143	142
Total German	30,603	2,484	2,674	2,494	2,478	2,516
Total	*35,156*	*2,863*	*3,077*	*2,859*	*2,868*	*2,898*

maximum steel output was required to build tanks and armoured vehicles.

These figures give a good idea of the scale of the Czech output of iron and steel at different times in the war. It does not include the Slovak iron and steel production, which was under Mannesmann control from 1940, but this was relatively small.[17] In terms of the total German production, the Protectorate's output was comparatively unimportant.

Table 5.4 Pig iron production 1943 and April–July 1944
000 tons

	1943	April	May	June	July
Silesia	1,324	105	110	107	106
Protectorate	1,200	97	99	101	95
Total German	24,234	1,951	1,875	1,888	1,949
Total	*26,758*	*2,153*	*2,084*	*2,096*	*2,150*

Table 5.5 Production of hot rolling mills March–June 1944
000 metric tons

	March	April	May	June
Silesia	111	108	108	106
Protectorate	93	81	94	91
Total German	1,460	1,325	1,282	1,326
Total	*1,664*	*1,514*	*1,484*	*1,523*

Source: British Library, Wetherby, CIOS 21, *Production statistics for the German steel industry 1943 and 1944,* pp. 4,9,14.

But the amounts, in terms of what they could be made into, are of course significant. It is surprising that in 1943, when Speer was driving the whole German and German-controlled European economy to ever-greater efforts, output in the Protectorate actually fell. In 1944, a critical period of the war for Germany, there was considerable variation in monthly output of different types of iron and steel. This was due to the effect of Allied bombing on rail communications, which limited supplies of raw materials to the steel works.[18]

Efficient rail transport was crucial to every aspect of the war, as Hitler noted in 1942, whether it was transporting men and supplies to the front line or goods, coal and raw materials between factories and foundries.[19] What Hitler was referring to at that time was a logjam of wagons in the East. This was caused by the transport of huge quantities of supplies to the armies fighting there. However, many Soviet lines were single track and a different gauge, and it was impossible to bring the wagons back. To meet the shortage of wagons in Germany, many had to be taken from France, Holland and Belgium.[20] The huge volume of rail transport was very difficult to organise. In June 1942, 14,535 wagons were being used, on average, each day and in July there were daily requests for 9,000. The bombing raids not only slowed the carriage of goods from place to place. Damage to railway lines also kept large numbers of wagons in areas where they were not necessarily needed. To try and bring this under control, there were stringent regulations about all forms of transport.[21] But these were not necessarily effective. Air raids, which began in Germany in 1943 and the Protectorate the following year, damaged railway lines, marshalling yards and steel works. The result was that dislocation of industry extended far beyond the area that was bombed. These uncertainties about rail transport explain why large steel castings such as tank turrets were carried by inland waterways rather than by rail. They moved more slowly but they were relatively safe from bombing and once loaded into barges were unlikely to be delayed.[22]

Important as these figures undoubtedly are, they do not show how this huge, German-controlled output was turned into weapons, tanks, armoured cars, military vehicles and all the other items that Czech companies contributed to the German war effort. To produce these items, steel works needed not only supplies of basic ores but also a range of other mineral ores to make special alloys for armour plate. Before the war, firms had stockpiled as much of these as they could, since most had to be imported.[23] The most significant for armaments production are shown in Table 5.6.

In the 1930s Germany had been well aware of the importance of these for the coming war and had stockpiled large quantities wherever possible. As a result, the country already held a significant proportion of the world's supply of some of these ores. This helps to explain German wartime strategy. The figures in Table 5.7 also show that the needs of the Protectorate armaments industry could be met either by direct trade or, where necessary, from Germany.

What Table 5.7 shows is the relatively large quantities of potentially vital raw materials that Germany either had within the country or had gained control of by 1941 when the atlas was produced. It excludes copper, which was produced in the Czech lands and Slovakia.[24] The list also shows the great attraction of the USSR, not merely for additional

Table 5.6 Minerals used in steel production

Mineral	Properties
Manganese	Cleansing agent, removes oxygen and sulphur from iron (ferrous sulphite and ferrous oxide). Increases tensile strength and resistance to abrasion.
Chromium	Makes steel stainless, stronger and more wear resistant.
Nickel	Vital for manufacture of artillery and ammunition.
Tungsten	Used in armour-piercing projectiles. Also heat resistant (has the highest melting point of all metals).
Tungsten carbide	Used in tank production.
Molybdenum	Used as a substitute for tungsten.
Cobalt	Used in an alloy with chromium, tungsten and molybdenum and to make cobalt steel.
Antimony	Used in an alloy with lead, tin and copper for making ammunition.
Bauxite	Used for aluminium for aircraft production.

Source. Oswald Hall, *A Geography of production* (London, 1971), pp. 83–92.

living space, but as a source of so many valuable metals. In fact in German eyes the amounts available must have seemed virtually inexhaustible. As far as the Protectorate was concerned, it was in a good position to gain adequate supplies for its own armament production either by direct trade or by allocation from German supplies through the industrial groups. However, so great were the demands of the armaments industry for these raw materials during the war that supplies were never more than adequate and great care was taken to use them economically. This also highlights the importance of the Protectorate's trade with countries such as Turkey and Bulgaria – not listed in the table – and reveals the importance of such innocuous items as those sold by Kotva and even Baťa's shoes, since these provided a way for the Protectorate to buy valuable mineral ores. Germany, by comparison, paid for Bulgarian manganese with agricultural machinery.[25]

Bulgaria was also an important source of chrome, which, like other imports from Eastern Europe and Turkey, was taken by barge up the Danube.[26] The figures also help to explain Germany's decision to include the Protectorate as part of Germany in commercial treaties with Turkey and Switzerland. This enabled Germany to obtain chrome ore,

Table 5.7 World output of raw materials 1941

Country	Reserves	Annual production	% of world production
	tons	tons	
Iron ore			
Germany	375 million	11.7 million	6.4
Austria		1,024,000	0.6
France		33,183,000	19
French Africa, Algeria, Tunisia		2,612,000	1.5
Britain		12,910,000	7.5
Luxemburg		4,896,000	3.8
Norway		847,000	0.5
Poland		469,000	0.3
Russia	8.7 billion	27,900,000	16.0
Sweden		11,245,000	6.5
Spain		2,633,000	1.9
USA		50,527,000	29.0
Manganese			
Egypt		135,000	2.5
Germany		232,000	4.0
Brazil		166,000	3.0
Russia		3,040,000	57.0
Czechoslovakia		93,000	1.5
Chrome			
Greece		48,000	5.0
Yugoslavia	12 million	54,000	5.0
Russia	6 million	219,000	21.0
Turkey	0.5 million	164,000	16.0
Molybdenum			
Norway		703,000	5.0
USA		7,795,000	85.0
Wolfram			
Portugal		1,380,000	6.0
Sweden		65,000	0.4
Spain		45,000	0.3
Nickel			
Greece		1,110,000	1.2
Norway		1,270,000	1.5
Russia		2,000,000	2.0
Canada		64,000,000	86.6

Source: German Military Archives, Freiburg, RH 8/I/5641, *Rohstoff Atlas* (Berlin 1941, Gedruckt im Oberkommando des Heeres), pp. 2–9.

of which Turkey was the main world producer, for Czech and German industry. Turkey's initial decision to forbid exports of chrome ore reflects its strategic importance and the need to observe international agreements on the duties of neutral states for fear of Allied reprisals. It was only when Germany in turn blocked the export of cartridges from the Protectorate, leaving Turkey's army defenceless against a possible Soviet attack, that Turkey relented and allowed chrome to be exported to the Protectorate.[27] It seemed at one time that it might be necessary to disguise the exports and send them, officially, to the Balkans. But this proved unnecessary and was abandoned. Chrome from Turkey remained an important element throughout the war. In 1943, as war production was increased, Germany assumed that it would import large quantities of Turkish ore: 45,000 tons by the end of March, followed by 135,000 tons, of which 45,000 would be by the end of 1943 and the remaining 90,000 the following year.[28]

Not all raw materials came from European countries. So great was the need for natural rubber (German artificial rubber – *buna* – did not have the same characteristics) that supplies were sent from the Far East first via the USSR and later, early in 1943, by blockade runners. Not all reached Germany. In March it was reported that two steamers had been captured with 3,000 tons of rubber. In spite of this setback Germany planned to try and import much larger quantities of rubber and wolfram in this way: 15,000 tons of rubber and 5,000 tons of wolfram.[29] Another commodity that Germany desperately needed was aluminium. The ore to make it – bauxite – was available in southern France but it needed a great deal of electrical power to smelt it. Switzerland, which generated a great deal of electricity from water power, seems to have been producing aluminium for the aircraft firms in the Protectorate and Germany.[30] Attempts to produce aluminium in the Protectorate were never very successful.

The main Czech and German companies all worked to a common standard. There was little difference between, for example, Škoda and the main German firms Bochumer Verein, Krupp, Ruhrstahl and other members of the Reichswerke.[31] All used electric arc furnaces for castings up to ten tons, and open-hearth furnaces for the larger castings. Electric arc furnaces made higher quality steel.[32] German steel makers used the same technology as American and British – the result of the interchange of ideas and information in the 1920s and 1930s. Research continued in Germany – though not in the Protectorate – during the war as firms developed new forms of high-speed steel and tried to cope with shortages and the substandard quality of some raw materials.[33] Supplies of Swedish iron ore continued to reach the Protectorate and Germany and, after the invasion of the USSR, large quantities of manganese ore were taken from the Nikopol mines in the Crimea.[34] Most of this was reserved for high-speed steel for tools; molybdenum steel had been virtually eliminated at the start of the war. The Czech Poldi company was one of only five that supplied virtually all the tool steel needed by Germany.[35] Poldi produced high-speed steel, cemented carbides (used as projectile cores), many types of tool steel, magnetic steels, heat- and corrosion-resisting steels as well as all forms of structural steel alloys.[36] Tungsten, mainly from France, Spain and Portugal, was available for tool steel and was used later in armour piercing projectiles. There was little cobalt. In general, because alloys were in short supply throughout the war, all companies in the Protectorate and Germany had to exercise very careful control over production. One result was that higher-carbon steels were used, which required more careful heat treatment and less drastic drenching to avoid cracking. High heat-resistant steels were often substandard. Because of Škoda's prestige and experience, it was left to decide the chemical composition and manufacturing methods of the steels that it used. German inspectors were concerned only with the final quality. But as the war continued and the standard of raw materials declined, they had to make important concessions to meet production targets.

The steel industry in the Protectorate and Germany had to cope with unexpected problems during the war. To begin with, Hitler expected to defeat the USSR by the end of 1941. The army was therefore not equipped to fight under the extreme cold of the Russian winter. Nor had much thought been given to designing and building tanks and military vehicles that would have to be used at temperatures that could fall to -30°C or below. Another problem was that the Germans were soon faced by a much more powerful tank than they had expected. The first Russian T34s were in action in the early winter of 1941 and the Germans realised that they needed a new tank that was better armed, had thicker armour plate and was faster. The Czech tanks (Škoda t35s and ČKD t38s) had initially proved a useful addition to the German Mark I, II and III and had been comparable, or better than, these equivalent German vehicles. One advantage of the Czech tanks was that their armour did not crack in the extreme cold, because the plates were bolted to the frame. German tank manufacturers preferred to weld the plates, believing that this was stronger and therefore better in combat.[37] But the welds cracked in the extreme Soviet winter. This weakened the tank's armour, making it vulnerable to tank and artillery fire. A military report of February 1942 put the problem very clearly: '... the welded joints on the front armour of German tanks are cracking to such an extent that the whole front plate is being pushed into the interior of the hulls under heavy enemy attack'.[38]

This posed a considerable technical problem. Welding different types of armour plate needed different types of electrode, because of variations in the chemical composition of the plates. The electrodes themselves were also made from scarce metals and the Germans tried to make new types using materials that were more freely available. As a result of these experiments, no specification for electrodes was drawn up until December 1944.[39] By then the situation was critical. Another problem was that in the beginning tank manufacturers often lacked experience in making armour plate. In 1936–41, tanks and tank manufacture were comparatively new. But the army wanted to have as many tanks as possible and many of the contracts for turrets and armour plating had been given to firms without experience of this work. Nor were they given any guidance in how to do the work. As a result, many of the early tanks were substandard from the beginning. To try and counter the weakness of welded joints, German firms coated them to create a hard surface. But the problem remained of great variations in the quality of the armour. This also became important in the Protectorate when the German army decided to use the hull of the Czech t38 as the base for a tank destroyer, the *Marder.* In place of the revolving turret, it had a low, fixed turret and a much larger and more powerful gun. This transformed it from a medium tank into a self-propelled anti-tank gun. Škoda and ČKD were given the task of making it. Neither firm had any experience of welding the plates to make the turret, because their method of manufacture of Czech tanks had been to bolt the armour plates to the tank frame. But neither company was allowed to do any research to try and solve the problem. Both were forced to rely on their own earlier experience of tank manufacture.

Underpinning the iron and steel industry were the coal mines, many of which were situated close to the coke ovens and blast furnaces. To try and ensure the most efficient use of all coal resources, a rationalisation of the industry was carried out in 1942 and by the end of the war this had developed into the Upper Silesia coal syndicate. Records of sales of coal from the Karviná mines at the end of the war show the scope of this. By then this important coalfield was sending coal to firms in Germany, Austria and Italy as well as the Protectorate, and it had unpaid debts of 9 million Reichsmarks.[40] There were also well-established links with mines in the Balkans that supplied the ores for steel alloys. Coal mining in north Moravia and southern Poland – the Upper Silesian coalfield – was fully integrated. In West Bohemia the lignite mines were supplying coal to the hydrogenation plant which produced oil and fuel. The whole of this formed an important part of Speer's industrial and commercial empire that was struggling to meet the needs of the German armed forces as they were being steadily driven back on all fronts towards Germany.

Oil

Speer, Germany's armaments minister from 1943 to the end of the Second World War, recognised that there were two crucial items in Germany's wartime economic strategy: oil and steel. If the supply of either had been halted, Germany would have lost the war very quickly. Yet in planning for war before 1939, neither Hitler nor any of his advisers could have had any clear idea of the exact quantities of oil and steel that would be needed. It is not enough to explain this by saying that because Hitler planned to launch a series of short, lightning wars of great intensity, the amounts needed would be far less than for a long, conventional war. The reality was more complicated. What German planners had to do was calculate the anticipated quantities of different types of fuel needed by the air force, navy and army, by estimating the number of aircraft, ships and vehicles of all types, together with their fuel capacity, probable distance travelled in a battle and the number that would be used. Military exercises provided a guide to the likely requirements. German planners next had to decide what resources were likely to be available and see how far these could be developed to meet anticipated as well as unexpected needs.

This met the requirements of the initial *Blitzkrieg* campaigns in Poland and north-west Europe. But the war in the USSR was different. After the initial success, German forces had to use ever-lengthening supply lines. What made matters worse from the German point of view was that their forces failed to capture the Russian oilfields in the Caucasus. The severe weather made fighting ever more difficult and the supply of oil was crucial in the great battles, especially Kursk. The next section tells the story of Germany's search for dependable supplies of oil, both crude and synthetic. Czechoslovakia played an important part in supplying this. Germany nearly ran out of fuel in the summer of 1944 and Speer reported to Hitler that he thought Germany would soon lose the war because of a lack of mobility. Although this did not happen, the fuel shortage hampered the Luftwaffe to such an extent that new types of aircraft, such as the jet-engined Heinkel He- 162, which might have made a difference towards the end of the war, were left standing idle on airfields.[41] They could not be used because of a lack of aviation fuel. The next section will explain how Germany gained control of these Czechoslovak resources, how they fitted into the overall German war economy and how they came under increasing attack from October 1943 as the range of British and American heavy bombers was extended from Britain and airfields in southern Italy, which had been captured by the Allies.

Germany's search for oil

Although before 1939 the German military planners could not know how much oil would be needed for Hitler's wars, they did know that

Germany had little oil of its own. An atlas of world output of raw materials in 1941 showed that over half of world oil production was American (61 per cent).[42] Next was the USSR with 10.3 per cent, followed by Romania with 3.5 per cent. Much of the exploitation of the latter oilfield and oil exports was in foreign hands, principally Royal Dutch Shell and Steana Romana. Britain held approximately a one-quarter of the shares in each.[43] Germany and Poland produced a small amount – 0.2 per cent of world output – and there was a much smaller quantity in Czechoslovakia and Hungary.[44] Although the quantity produced in Europe was steadily decreasing, there was still a surprisingly large amount available at the end of the war.[45] Germany's treaty with the USSR in 1939 was signed partly to get access to Soviet oil and raw materials. Hitler knew that he needed to stockpile huge quantities of this oil if his plans for victory in Europe and eastward expansion later were to succeed. He said that unless he could control Maykop and Grozny (the main refineries in the Caucasus), he would lose the war.

An attack on the USSR was inevitable at some time if Hitler was to get the eastern *Lebensraum* he believed Germany needed. He planned to defeat the West and East with lightning campaigns, but this new form of mechanised warfare used very large quantities of fuel. Even the troops supporting the main tank attack had to be moved by lorry. The *panzer* units were completely mechanised and consisted of large numbers of all types of vehicles, including tanks, lorries, scout cars, motor cycles, and command, staff and radio vehicles. To this was added air support. So it was hardly surprising that the *Blitzkrieg* used so much fuel. If this was to be successful, Germany had not only to get foreign oil but also become as far as possible self-sufficient, regardless of expense. Germany thus had to develop new ways of making synthetic fuel that could be used to supplement its own oil supplies.

Fortunately for German military planners, a method of producing fuel from brown coal had been developed. This was the Fischer Tropsch process, part of a system of making oil from brown coal (lignite) known as hydrogenation. Synthetic oil production had begun in 1922 at Leuna near Leipzig.[46] Initial output was 300,000 tons a year, which was increased to 500,000 tons. The intention was to meet half of Germany's needs by 1934–5 and further plants were built at Böhlen,

Magdeburg, Schwarzheide and Zeitz, all within the same area, which was also the centre of Germany's chemical industry. To begin with the main source of brown coal was the Ruhr. The Union Rheinische Braunkohlen Kraftstoff A. G. built a plant at Wesseling on the west bank of the Rhine, eight miles south of Cologne for drying brown coal and making it into briquettes.[47] By 1940 they were producing 4.3 million tons. The briquettes were used to make oil. This formed the synthetic oil programme.[48]

By using this process and importing oil from the USSR, Germany had built up large stocks of fuel by the summer of 1939. When war broke out in September, it was initially fought, as planned, as a series of short, intense battles: first in Poland in September 1939 and in Western Europe the following summer. Then, a year later, came the brief war with Greece and finally the attack on the USSR, driven, in Speer's view, by the need to get control of Soviet oil, especially since Romania was unable to meet Germany's needs.[49] Göring believed, like Hitler, that the war would be successful. He consulted Speer and Krauch, head of research and development in the Four Year Plan, on the advantages of converting German hydrogenation plants from using brown coal to refining (Russian) crude oil. But the expected victory in the USSR did not materialise and the plan was dropped. After the initial success the German forces gradually met increased resistance and were defeated at Stalingrad in January 1943. This changed the whole conduct of the war. From this point Germany was fighting against much larger Soviet forces and the demand for all forms of war materiel rose to an unprecedented level. This is where Czech resources – and those of other defeated and neutral European states – became crucial. The year 1943 is also when Speer took command of wartime production, and output rose. At the same time it marks the start of the Allied bombing campaign of factories and communications.

German development of synthetic fuel

It is against this background that the increase in the output of synthetic fuel needs to be seen. An example is the Wesserling plant that made brown coal briquettes – an essential ingredient in the production of synthetic fuel. In 1940, to meet the anticipated needs of the war in Western Europe, annual output had been at 4.3 million tons. In 1943, under the urgent need to expand production, it almost doubled to 7.1 million tons. In that year 430,000 tons of fuel was being produced, but at a price. The cost of making fuel – benzine, diesel and fuel oil – by this process was 20 per cent higher than refining crude oil. This was to some extent because of the cost of drying the brown coal and turning it into briquettes, partly the cost of transporting coal from the Ruhr to eastern Germany and also the higher production cost. To try and reduce this, the plants began to use similar coal from the Upper Silesian coalfield. A syndicate of Silesian coal-mine owners, in part financed by the government, set up a plant at Blechhammer, south of Erfurt. This continued in production until May 1944, when it was partly destroyed by a bombing raid; the anti-aircraft defences, here as elsewhere, proved inadequate to defend it.[50] By then total output from all the plants had been reduced by damage to the railway system, though this was more easily and quickly repaired.

A further problem for Germany at that stage of the war was the increasingly desperate need for fuel and muddled priorities of where it could best be used. By then the plants were using brown coal from the Ruhr, central Germany and the Sudetenland, which placed a heavy demand on the rail system. The hydrogenation process also required small quantities of coal tar, pitch, tar oils, coke, coke oven gas, hydrogen, various gases produced as by-products of the hydrogenation process and metals, including tin. Output was mainly of different types of fuel: high-octane aviation, oil, propane and butane for motor fuel. There were also by-products for iso-octane manufacture, including synthetic rubber. One of the other important products was ethylene synthetic oil that froze at a much lower temperature than normal lubricating oil. Until this was developed, many tanks – especially the Mark III – were immobilised by the extreme Russian winter because their engines and equipment froze at night.[51] When the Russians realised this, they began their attacks at dawn. This accounts for a large part of the German tank losses. There was also a shortage of diesel oil in 1941–2 when refineries were concentrating on producing high-test aviation fuel. The German army tried using petrol but this caused overheating. I. G. Farben made experiments at the Leuna plant using a mixture of 50:50 diesel fuel and fuel made by the hydrogenation process, with an octane rating of 35. The only disadvantages were a slight loss of power in small engines and vapour lock in the larger, low-speed diesels.[52]

Improved engine efficiency

The chemistry of fuel design, seen in the production of this synthetic lubricating oil, played an important part in the war. Initially, it seemed that all the ways of improving engine performance by mechanical means had already been tried. In the early days of motoring, engine designers had experimented with ways of increasing power by varying the size of pistons, adding more pistons in various configurations, moving valves from the side to the top of cylinders and increasing engine speed. In the 1930s designers were looking for new ways of increasing aircraft speed and making engines more powerful, economical and reliable. The initial impetus for this had come from the competition for the Coupe d'Aviation Maritime Jacques Schneider, known as the Schneider Trophy, for the fastest seaplane. This had emphasised the advantages of improved aerodynamic efficiency and greater engine power. In 1931 Britain had won the trophy for the third time with an aircraft that became the model for the Supermarine Spitfire. This British success, and experiments with improving the speed of racing cars, showed that future improvements could come through the development of more sophisticated fuels. Basic engine designs might not change but improvements could be made to engine accessories such as superchargers, carburettors and fuel injection.[53] These provided more air (oxygen) and measured the air–fuel supply more accurately, raising the engine efficiency and increasing power. Fuel injection was also important because it countered the effects of gravity (G force) when an aircraft went into a dive. Conventional carburettors could not maintain a fuel supply under these conditions.[54] At the same time, research into the physics of fuel combustion played an important role by showing the theoretical limits which engines could be made to achieve. All this had a part to play in the plans for fuel production in war.

Romanian oil

An important part of this preparation was the German need to gain access to Romanian oil, since this was the main source of crude oil in Europe. The main obstacle to German plans was British investment in the Romanian oil industry. Germany's first step was to try and exploit the Romanian need to sell agricultural products during the economic crisis of the 1930s. Romania had to repay French loans, but France refused to accept agricultural produce as payment. Germany, however, was prepared to do this, paid more than the world values and sold machinery at subsidised prices in return. This provided food for the German population and disposed of surplus machinery and consumer products. The trade suited both sides and Germany gradually expanded its share of Romania's commerce until, by the end of the 1930s, it had become the main trading partner. A further advantage for Germany was that it helped to increase its foreign currency reserves. It also made Romania politically dependent on Germany. Germany could put pressure on the pro-British Romanian administration to sell Germany oil. It was also possible to get Romanian oil by seizing Austria and Czechoslovakia, which were already buying it. The oil was carried by barge up the Danube and discharged at the river ports at Bratislava and Vienna where it was refined. In 1939 Bratislava was by far the more important: 90 per cent was imported there and only 10 per cent in Vienna.[55] This was because oil was being used as part payment for substantial quantities of Czech weapons, worth 557 million crowns in January 1937.[56]

Czechoslovak imports of Romanian oil

Czechoslovak imports of Romanian oil were valued at 12 million crowns a year. Of this, about 5 million crowns were returned to Romania in the form of aviation fuel. Other items that Germany was interested in were the refineries in Czechoslovakia, all but one of which were foreign-owned. The exception was the Czechoslovak Apollo company, which had a refinery and distribution network. This is what attracted I. G. Farben, which bought Apollo in the summer of 1939. Transport of crude oil from Romania to the Bratislava refinery was in the hands of a separate company, the Československá akciová plavební společnost dunajská of Bratislava, which owned a fleet of barges.[57] The cost of carrying this oil to Bratislava was met by the Romanian government. In a confidential protocol dated 31 March 1938, it had agreed to repay part of an earlier Czechoslovak debt in the form of oil which would be supplied to this company for use in its boats on the Danube. Besides these concessions on oil deliveries, there was some Czechoslovak investment in the Romanian oil industry. The Czechoslovak arms manufacturer Zbrojovka invested 47.5 million lei in the Standard oil refinery in Ploesti, using money earned by arms sales. But there was no official Czechoslovak government investment.[58]

The outbreak of war in September 1939 brought major changes to the Romanian oil sales. The price of oil began to rise because it was tied to an international gold standard and by October this was causing concern in the Protectorate.[59] The Czech companies were buying oil as members of a cartel. The cartel prices were rising but sales, presumably to Germany, were made under a system of parity of supply. This reduced the amount paid to the Czech companies, as shown by the prices in Table 5.8.

These prices only tell part of the story, however. The real extent of the price rise was much greater because the cartel price included a rebate of 2.50 crowns per kg and a proportional tax of 0.84 crowns

Table 5.8 Benzine prices September–October 1939

Date	Goldschillings light benzine Giurgiu	Cartel price benzine mixture Bratislava, crowns	Parity price crowns
30/9	81/	241.50	30.66
4/10	83/	241.50	32.27
7/10	88/	262.16	17.83
11/10	89.6	262.16	19.24
14/10	91/	270.34	11.74

Source: Moravský zemský archiv, Brno, Apollo company records, H127/11, Apollo-Mineralöl-Raffinerie, Pressburg to Dr Neumann, Pressburg, 16 Oct. 1939.

Table 5.9 Paraffin prices September–October 1939

Date	Goldschillings Giurgiu	Cartel price, Bratislava, crowns	Parity price crowns
30/9	55/	157	29.02
7/10	59/	157	34.01
14/10	60/	174	17.96

Source: ibid.

Table 5.10 *Gasöl* prices September–October 1939

Date	Goldschillings Giurgiu	Cartel Price Oderburg crowns	Parity Price crowns
30/9	53/6	158	28.73
7/10	56/	158	31.84
14/10	56/6	175.90	15.17

Source: ibid.

per kg. While this report was being written the price had increased by 28.84 crowns and the difference in real value had increased by 18.92 per cent per kg. It was a similar story with paraffin prices, as can be seen in Table 5.9. In the case of these, there was a rebate on the cartel price of 4.50 crowns per kg and a tax of 0.70 crowns per kg, so that the difference in real value had also fallen by 16.05 per cent per kg. The problem was repeated with *Gasöl* as shown in Table 5.10.

In this case the tax was at 0.60 crowns per kg, but the purchase price had risen by 17.9 crowns per kg, raising the difference in real value by 16.67 per cent per kg. Diesel fuel prices had risen by 18 October from 194 crowns to 211.90 crowns – an increase of 17.9 per cent per kg. However, the real price of machine lubricating oil had declined by around 30 crowns (118.13 crowns per kg). In October the cartel tried to raise the retail prices to increase their official profit from 70 to 80 hellers a litre. The fall in the real price of oil products had pushed this down to 60 hellers.

This increase in oil prices had two important results for Czech and Slovak refineries. The first was that it was proving impossible to recover

Table 5.11 Cartel-owned railway tankers October 1939

Benzine	254 wagons
Paraffin	55 wagons
Gasöl	61 wagons
Lubricating oil	9 wagons
Paraffin oil	20 wagons
Heating oil	1 wagon

Source: Moravský zemský archiv, Brno, Apollo company records, H127/10, Apollo Nafta to Dr Neumann, Pressburg, 16 Oct. 1939.

the full cost from Germany which was buying large quantities of oil. The problem was the unrealistic exchange rate. The second was that, under wartime conditions, trade between Romania and the Protectorate was becoming more difficult. The clearing system under which bills were paid was coming under strain.[60] In October Apollo-Nafta reported that it owed Internova in Bucharest 2 million crowns and the Vacuum Oil Company also owed a large amount. Part of the problem was that when Slovakia became independent, separate clearing systems had to be created for the Protectorate and Slovakia in their trade with Romania. The solution for Apollo-Nafta was to arrange for the Zbrojovka arms company, which was able to transfer funds directly to Romania, to send it on their own account. This payment of 5 million crowns had been arranged by one of the Apollo-Nafta directors, von Madeyski, early in September.[61] Of the 5 million crowns, 2 million were paid to Internova and 3 million to the Sanielevici refinery, both in Bucharest.

The outbreak of war had a further effect on the sale of petrol and diesel fuel in the Protectorate. Germany's needs were considered to be far more important than those of the Czech civilian population. Even factory managers had to have special permission to keep their cars for business purposes.[62] The emphasis on German needs is shown by the decision of Apollo-Nafta to close 13 petrol stations in Bohemia and 20 in Moravia – a move which was no doubt followed by other oil companies.[63] This drastic action reflected the urgency of Germany's need for Czech and Slovak oil. Until the outbreak of war the cartel had possessed sufficient ships and rail tankers to handle the imported oil. After the outbreak of war and the increased German demand, the cartel was faced with a shortage of rolling stock for carrying oil products. The stock in October 1939 is shown in Table 5.11.

It was difficult to see how the Czech and Slovak refineries could meet the increased German demands and two people from the Fanta refinery were sent to Bucharest to see if they could speed up the deliveries of refined fuel by boat.

Transport of oil on the Danube

However, it was one thing for Romania to agree to supply oil to the Protectorate. It was a very different matter to get it to Bratislava and elsewhere for refining. Delivery of the crude oil was normally by barge and the company possessed a large number of these, though navigation on the Danube was sometimes halted by ice in winter. There was also a rail link between Romania and Czechoslovakia, but it was not considered very reliable. For instance, in October 1938 there was a British Foreign Office report that a railway line from Czechoslovakia to Constanza via Poland had been torn up near the Polish frontier. In addition, the railway line was congested and comparatively few tank wagons were available.[64] Conditions had improved by November 1939, but serious problems remained.

Until the outbreak of war, only 36 per cent of Romanian exports to Germany had been sent by rail, 25 per cent had gone via the Danube and the remaining 39 per cent had travelled by sea.[65] After the outbreak of war, transport by sea was no longer practical. As to the railway, much of the Eastern European railway system was single track and there was a shortage of rolling stock. For transport on the Danube there were three shipping companies: Erste Donau Dampfschiffsfahrts Gesellschaft (DDSG) in Vienna, the Bayerische Lloyd (BL) in Regensburg and the Continentaler Motorschiffsfahrt A. G. (COMOS) in Amsterdam. Within Germany these formed the Schiffsfahrt Gruppe and the Dutch shares were owned by Germany. The Reichswerk Hermann Göring took control of the Erste Donau Dampfschiffsfahrts Ges. in December 1938.[66] There was also the Slowak Donau Schiffsfahrts A. G. in Bratislava which

Table 5.12 Danube shipping in the German *Schiffsfahrt* group, November 1939

Number of ships	Type	Total capacity tons	Power Hp
613	Small cargo vessels	439,260	
118	Tankvessels	92,123	
41	General freight vessels	23,948	18,130
14	Powered tankers	9,037	8,620
76	Tugs	–	47,910
862		558,368	74,660

Source: Moravský zemský archiv, Brno, Apollo company records, 9, report on Danube shipping.

was linked to the German group. On paper this appeared an impressive quantity of shipping, which should have been able to carry all the oil that Germany needed at the beginning of the Second World War. However, an analysis of the tonnage of the different types of vessels, shown in Table 5.12, reveals the serious problems of transporting oil.

Of this, the Erste Donau Dampfschiffsfahrts Gesellschaft owned 400 boats with a total of 250,000 tons, besides wharfs in Korneuburg and Budapest and warehouses and storage depots in Regensburg.[67] This shipping capacity was not enough to meet the wartime needs, as is shown in Table 5.13, the figures for peacetime average tonnage shipments.

The figures represent the actual tonnage of goods carried. There were, however, three programmes that called for much greater quantities to be transported: the 1938 *Reichsprogram*, the 1939 *Sofort Program* and the 1939 *grosse Bau Program*, which called for transport for an additional 6.75 million tons. Oil posed a particular difficulty. Capacity had to be doubled to 2 million tons to carry oil from Romania and the Caucasus that Germany was buying in November 1939 after the signing of the treaties with Romania and the USSR.

The problem for Germany was how to get the oil to the refineries. At the outbreak of war the British realised that if they could stop or slow down the deliveries of Romanian oil they could damage the German war effort. British interests in Romania therefore tried to hire or buy as many oil barges as they could. But this proved impossible because of the very large number. An alternative British plan was to cause an explosion and block the Iron Gates, where the Danube passes through a narrow gorge on the frontier between Romania and Yugoslavia. But this too failed; the plot was discovered and the people had to flee. The Germans were left undisturbed. Their plan was for the oil to be carried up the Danube beyond Vienna to Korneuburg. There it would be transferred from the Danube barges into rail tankers and would be taken by rail via Stockerau, Znojmo, Jihlava, Kolín to Mělnik, north of Prague. There, on the Elbe, it would be transferred to barges for shipment to Hamburg, Lübeck and through the Kaiser Wilhelm Canal to Kiel. It could also be taken along the Mittelland Canal which linked the Elbe to the Rhine and thence to almost anywhere in Germany.[68] Foreign containers from Sofia, Belgrade and Bucharest would be used to supplement the existing tankers. But this could only be a short-term solution, using the existing railway lines in the Protectorate. What was really needed was a railway that could carry very large quantities from the Danube to the Elbe. For this the report proposed building a double-track railway that would begin by running parallel to the Vienna–Gmünd railway (the Franz Josefs Bahn). Then it would go from the right bank of the Danube at Tulin (the Eisenbahndonaubrücke) to Sigmundsherberge, Allentsteig, Gmünd, Wittingau, across the frontier into the Protectorate, and thence via Tábor and Čerčany to Žláby south of Prague. The line could end there because that was the furthest limit for the 600–700 ton Elbe barges which would carry the oil to Germany. The total length of the proposed railway was 300 km, and would require an investment of 23 million Reichsmarks.

Germany's need for oil was so great that it overrode all other considerations about cost. There was a great difference between the price of transporting oil by water and by rail. Water transport cost 2.59 Reichsmarks per ton, rail 22.6 Reichsmarks per ton (presumably including the price of transferring oil from barges to rail tankers). But if water was cheaper, it was also much slower, mainly because from Romania the barges had to go upstream against a strong current at

Table 5.13 Average annual peacetime shipments on the Danube

1934–38 average	406,077 tons of grain
	295,480 tons of crude oil
	514,969 tons of goods in bulk
	535,409 tons of individual items
1939–40 average	1.7 million tons of grain
	1.5 million tons of crude oil
	540,000 tons of bulk
	commodities
Total for 1939–40	3,740,000 tons

Source: ibid

little more than walking pace. An average journey from the Romanian oil port of Giurgiu to Regensburg took 61 days and to Vienna 50 days. In addition, unloading generally took just over a month in summer and double that in winter, when there were often strong winds along the Danube. There was one more problem: seasonal differences in the depth of water in the river. When the water level was at its lowest, river navigation became impossible for all but shallow draught vessels. In 1943 there had been a fall in the water level that had reduced river traffic by 35 per cent.[69] There were also times when it was impossible to sail a fully loaded vessel up the river. These factors explain the large numbers of comparatively small vessels that were used on the Danube, as shown in Table 5.12. They could be used when there was insufficient depth of water for the larger and more efficient boats.

These elaborate and expensive proposals for transporting oil from Romania to Germany show how far Germany was prepared to go to obtain the oil that was needed for Hitler's plans. But, assuming that they were working from the best information available, it also shows that Hitler was reluctant or unable to plan very far in advance. For example, the proposal to build a double-track railway line across the Protectorate from the Danube to the Elbe was only practical if the supply of Russian oil could be guaranteed and there was enough time to build 300 km of railway lines. The plans were hardly practical if the supply of Russian oil would stop 19 months after the signing of the treaty (when Germany invaded the USSR) or if the railway lines would take longer than that to build. On the other hand, if the planners confidently expected Germany to win a war against the USSR within six months of opening hostilities, they were either extremely optimistic or extremely foolish. On paper, the plans seem to be another example of German wishful thinking.

German wartime planning

Much closer to reality was the way that Czechoslovak and other oil resources were integrated into wartime planning. Even before the outbreak of war in September 1939, all German companies had been integrated into national organisations which controlled the economy. In the case of the fuel group, there were 24 firms producing petroleum products, of which three were in Vienna.[70] The main German companies were Kontinental Oel A. G., Mineralöl Einfuhr Gesellschaft and Rumanien Mineralöl Einfuhr Gesellschaft. Oil was imported from the USSR, Galicia, Estonia, Latvia and Lithuania by the Mineralöl Gesellschaft. Oil imports of crude oil, topped crude oil and finished products from Romania and Hungary were handled by the Rumanien Mineralöl Einfuhr Gesellschaft. Distribution of fuel was by the Zentralbüro für Mineralöl (ZB) and lubricants by the Arbeitsgemeinschaft Schmierstoff Verteilung (ASV). There were also Czech companies which came under German control. This relatively large number of firms had to be brought under centralised planning if they were to be used effectively. It was fortunate for Germany that as the war in the USSR began to enter a critical stage after the defeat at Stalingrad, Speer replaced Todt as the minister responsible for armaments production. Speer was a much better organiser and his reforms included creating a mineral oil group: the Wirtschaftsgruppe Kraftstoff Industrie. Part of this was consultative: the Arbeitsgemeinschaft Erdölgewinnung und Verarbeitung, which was responsible for planning future output and reporting on production.

As the war progressed, planning became increasingly complicated. Each refinery was capable of producing a wide range of petroleum products. But at the same time, research into engine efficiency and power output was demanding a wider variety of types of fuels. For example, the Luftwaffe used three main types.[71] One 80 octane type contained about 30 per cent ethyl alcohol and was used in training aircraft. The second was 89 octane and was the normal grade of fuel for operational aircraft. The third was 95 octane for aircraft with heavy-duty engines. At the beginning of the war, fuel synthesis was based on hydrogenation from brown coal because this would allow an adequate production of good-quality 87-octane aviation fuel. This contained paraffins, iso paraffins, naphthenes and a small quantity of aromatics. In all there were 21 different components. It was essential to blend these accurately to ensure maximum engine efficiency. There was also the important aspect of research into engine design, which could require special fuels: new formulae for increasing engine power.

At the beginning of the war, the ingredients for diesel fuel were sent to secret locations designated by a number, and refiners were not told how they would be used. Separate organisations had the task of blending the fuel, though they were not told how it would be used.[72] The fuel experts for army supplies were in the Zentral Büro für Mineralöl in Berlin and for the Luftwaffe were in the Oberkommand der Luftwaffe. Research was under the control of the Wirtschaftliche Forschung Gesellschaft (WIFO), assisted by the Reichs Amt für Wirtschafts Ausbau. This took care of storage, blending and distribution of fuels at strategic sites in Europe. As the war progressed and the demand for fuel grew, to save time companies refined fuels according to agreed formulae and sent them directly to fuel depots. This technical complexity for aviation fuels did not always apply to the army or navy. But the severe Russian winter did reveal a major problem for the army. No research had been done on oil to see if it was suitable for the extreme Russian winter temperatures. The army was issued with 'universal oil' but, as noted already, this froze and immobilised the tanks. As a result 40-50 were lost each day until a synthetic oil was developed.[73] Research into problems like this was always carried out in Germany and not in the Protectorate or any of the other occupied countries.

Table 5.14 Oil companies in Czechoslovakia in the mid 1930s

Name	Annual capacity Tons
Pardubice (Tanto Werke A. G.)	185,000
Kolín (Vacuum Oil Co.)	100,000
Oderberg (Odra Mineralölindustrie A. G.)	90,000
Kralup (Kralupoda Raffinerie Lederer & Co.)	30,000
Oderfurt (Prevozer Oderfurter Mineralöl Werke A. G.)	30,000
Weitersdorf bei Schomberg (Apollo) Mineralöl Raffinerie A. G.	25,000
Bat'a , Batov for own works	Not known

Source: British Library, Wetherby, CIOS CXXVI-13, *Reich Minister of Armaments and War Production. Interrogation of Speer, Sauer, Mommsen and Bosch*, pp. 7–8.

Czechoslovak oil refineries

Refineries in the Protectorate were used principally to meet German and not Czech or Slovak needs. This had been planned well in advance. As early as the mid 1930s, the German army was collecting information about the Czechoslovak refineries. In an undated report, probably written in 1934 or 1935, the refineries, shown in Table 5.14, were listed with their capacities:

These estimates appear to be fairly accurate and provided a good basis for the German planners, as the following brief accounts of three Czechoslovak companies demonstrate.

Oderfurt Mineralöl Werke A. G.[74]

Information from the records of the Oderfurt company from 1941, shown in Table 5.15, reveal how production was increased under German control to meet wartime needs. These were the figures for the production of base stocks of benzine and paraffin. Table 5.16 shows the figures for 1940, when the Germans were firmly in control and show how this was translated into refined products.

This analysis of the refineries' output was followed by the familiar refrain that the plant needed to be modernised. Until then the refineries' products had been sold to wholesalers including a subsidiary,

Table 5.15 Oderfurt Mineralöl Werke, Moravian Ostrava 1936–40

tons

Year	Crude oil	Basic benzine	Basic paraffin
1936	c17,300	16,900	5,000
1937	c2,000	19,500	5,300
1938	c20,000	19,000	1,500
1939	c18,500	11,000	800
1940	c20,800	11,000	2,300

Source: Národni archiv, 3128, Bericht über die Untersuchung der Verarbeitungskosten der Oderfurter Mineralölwerke Akt. Ges. in Prag, Mineralölraffinerie in Mährisch-Ostrau-Oderfurt, Berlin, 23 May 1941, p. 1

Table 5.16 Refinery production 1940

tons

Product	From crude oil	From basic benzine	From basic paraffin
Benzine	4,058	10,116	–
Petroleum	6,539	443	2,383
Diesel fuel	1,187	19	3
Petroleum ether	2,675	95	–
Machine oil, distilled	1,756	–	–
Machine oil, refined	1,445	–	–
Paraffin	53	–	–
Asphalt	2,514	–	–
Petrolkoks	387	–	–
Total	21,314	10,673	2,386

Source: ibid.

the Ostranaft Mineralöl-Vertriebe A. G. A further analysis, shown in Table 5.17, reveals how the production had been divided in terms of quantity and value in Protectorate crowns.

The figures show that the company's main products, both in terms of output and in value, were benzine and paraffin. These indicate that Oderfurt's main function was to produce basic chemicals for the petroleum industry, rather than fuels that could be sold directly to the motoring trade. There are no figures for petrol, presumably because the company did not make any. This would have required blending

Table 5.17 Types of fuel produced

Product	Output kg	Value (excluding motor fuel and waste crowns
Benzine	13,145,577	49,255,430
Paraffin	9,315,979	27,399,710
Gasöl	5,626,370	–
Blauöl	254,063	13,013,460 (*Gasöl* and *Blauöl*)
Heating oil	61,120	136,520
Vulkanöl	20,774	87,890
Lubricating oil	1,450,069	5,841,900
Paraffin oil	734,159	4,805,540
Asphalt	432,558	505,750
Petrolkoks	320,000	198,810
Petroldestillat	31,360	72,950
Spindelöldestillat	1,247,680	3,417,810
Total	32,639,709	104,735,670

Source, ibid.

of different ingredients. The company did sell diesel fuel, however, which was a basic product of the refining process, though this formed a comparatively small part of the total output. It was sold to the distribution company Ostranaft (Ostrava Nafta – Ostrava diesel fuel). Like Apollo, Oderfurt was profitable from 1936, but probably not before. The figures for this period 1936–9 shown in Table 5.18 also reflect the political uncertainties.

These figures show how dependent the company was on its links with other refineries in the chain of petrol and oil production. Apart from sales of diesel fuel that were sold to Ostranaft, its other products were bought by companies who took the refining process a stage further. Oderfurt had built up its links with these since the founding of the First Republic. Most of the sales of petrol and motor oil had developed in the 1920s and the company had built its success on this. When the Sudetenland was transferred to Germany, Oderfurt lost many of its customers. Those that remained were also hit by their own loss of customers in the motoring community. This explains why Oderfurt's turnover and profits fell by over 2.6 million crowns in

Table 5.18 Oderfurt production and tax 1936–9

Year	Production crowns	Tax crowns	Percentage
1936	57,938,000	1,973,400	3.406
1937	80,945,000	2,532,300	3.128
1938	78,336,000	2,903,800	3.707
1939	71,156,000	1,513,000	2.126

Source

1938 and a further 7.2 million in 1939. A further problem the re-finery faced was that before the crisis over the Sudetenland, it was re-fining crude oil from Galicia, the USSR and USA. After the outbreak of war it relied entirely on Romanian oil. Whether the price of this oil was the same as for other oil is impossible to establish. Included in the price of Romanian oil were a number of items: commission, freight, customs, storage, insurance, hire of tankers, freight charges for returning empty tankers, water and sludge content and pumping. The different system of calculating costs that were introduced by the Protectorate also made it impossible to compare figures for 1939 with those of 1940.

Apollo Nafta

The importance of Czechoslovak oil companies for the German cam-paigns in the USSR is underlined by the record of the Apollo Nafta company. Like other firms, Apollo Nafta had made a succession of losses during the economic crisis but had begun to recover in 1936. As Table 5.19 shows, after 1937 its profits climbed steadily and the progress reflects the tempo of German planning before and during the attack on the USSR.

A steady rise is evident to 1940. There was no problem about obtaining supplies of Romanian oil, which the Apollo Nafta re-finery in Bratislava had been using for a long time. The company was not affected by the political crisis over the Sudetenland. Its distribution network was principally in the Czech area, but it suf-fered from the loss of territory to Poland from September 1939. It

Table 5.19 Apollo Nafta profits 1938–44

Year	Profit crowns
1938	2,230,690
1939	2,721,727
1940	1,030,400
1941	996,912
1942	7,217,964
1943	6,600,388
1944	7,248,599

Source, Moravský zemský archiv, Brno, Apollo Nafta company records, H 127/1, Bilanční deník, 1925–45.

is unlikely that Germany relied on supplies from Apollo Nafta for building up its fuel stocks before the war in Western Europe. The decline in 1940–1 reflects the fall in demand, partly because of the loss of territory to Poland and also because Czechs found it difficult to use their cars. Many of these were commandeered by the German forces. However, once it became clear that the USSR would not be defeated in 1941, as Hitler had confidently assumed, Apollo Nafta played its part in the increase in refining fuel for Germany. The sudden rise from under 1 million crowns in 1941 to over 7.2 million crowns in 1942 shows how oil production increased dramatically. The slight fall in 1943 reflects the influence of bombing, though the decline is due more to raids on the Romanian oil field at Ploesti and the dislocation of transport than any direct bombing of the Bratislava refinery. The return to profits of more than 7.2 million crowns in the last full year of the war reflects the final, desperate effort to produce fuel.

Control of the company by I. G. Farben had begun to take effect in September 1939. In a report dated the 7th it was stated that seven of the directors had been removed from the board. Four lived in Prague, two in Paris and one in Bratislava. They were replaced by two Slovaks and a Czech, all of whom had to sign a statement that they were not Jewish. There was no need to add more Germans from I. G. Farben to the board, which could be relied on to follow instructions from

Germany. A new member was added in 1940, von Madeyski, who was allotted 600 shares from the 6,300 held at the Živnostenska bank which were transferred to the Bratislava branch. A commissioner, Dr Struck, a member of the Gestapo, was also appointed with responsibility for the company. The next step was to reassess the value of the company's capital. The value of the plant was estimated at 2.1 million crowns and shares at 2 million. There was also some discussion of the way that the refinery had financed Apollo Nafta and the credit terms of 6–8 weeks on deliveries of petrol and diesel fuel to customers. This had been considered normal under peacetime conditions but in war it had led to outstanding debts of 5 million crowns.

The separation of the Protectorate from Slovakia (which the report seems to have assumed would happen) made it essential for I. G. Farben to come to an understanding with the Bratislava refinery. There was also a question of the current value of the shares, which had earlier been at 150 per cent of their book value. Looking ahead to the end of the war, the report claimed that a reckoning would have to be made on the assumption that the shares had declined in value. I. G. Farben had paid 2.6 million crowns for the company but the capital value in February 1941 was only 1.2 million. In addition, the value of the refinery was divided 60 per cent to Bratislava and 40 per cent to I. G. Farben. Faced with a decline in the share value, I. G. Farben decided to use part of its shares to buy control of Dynamit-Nobel A. G. in Bratislava. This complemented I. G. Farben's interests as well as providing an investment in another company which might play an important part in the war.

Apollo Nafta had one other advantage that had attracted I. G. Farben. Oil had been discovered at Göding in south Moravia and though this was not a large quantity, it suggested that there might be more substantial amounts there if they could be found.[75] As a result there was an extensive programme of drilling that had begun in 1919. At first the ouput had been small, but this had gradually risen to a peak production in the mid 1920s and had fluctuated thereafter. But by 1939 output was in decline. Drilling had continued – over 70,000 metres between 1919 and 1939 – but without finding any significant amounts of oil.

In March 1940 came the first serious difficulty for Apollo Nafta. Czech companies which were manufacturing items for Germany were trying to get motor oil. These companies included Vítkovice, Brünner Waffen (formerly Zbrojovka), Prager Eisen, Poldi, Škoda and Pilsner Urquell and were among the most important in the Protectorate. Apollo Nafta had tried to get motor oil from Hamburg or Holland but had been unsuccessful. Attempts to get it from Switzerland had failed because of shortage of time and there was no prospect of importing it via Genoa or Trieste because of the risk of it being captured. Nor had it been possible to obtain it from a motor wholesaler in Dubová because of uncertainty over quality. However, it was possible to get the different-sized containers that were needed to transport oil for an order from Motapol by buying them from Luft in Tetschen, Sphinx in Turn-Teplitz and Meva in Prague, though import duty had to be paid. Nevertheless, at the end of December the company held stocks worth almost 4 million crowns, principally of paraffin (620,000 crowns) and motor oil (537,000 crowns). German demand for oil had eased by February 1941 and it was possible for Apollo Nafta to look for other markets. One was the possible export of oil to Hungary and it seemed at the end of February that a trade agreement might be possible. But it seems likely that the problems that emerged in discussions of establishing a standard measure for deliveries, and the complexity of making payments through the clearing system at the national bank, proved too much.

To regulate this market, wholesale oil companies in the Protectorate were organised into trade associations (*Wirtschaftsgruppe*) in June 1940. There were four: wholesale and export firms, individual, commission agents and travelling salesmen. Within each association firms were divided into subgroups for each trade and Apollo Nafta was controlled by the *Fachgruppe Mineralöl* in Prague, which had a permanent senior administrative staff of three. Apollo Nafta came under the authority of this group in all its dealings with Germany. The problem of customs duties emerged again in 1941 over the payment of customs dues on shipments of oil to Germany. It had been hoped that customs duties on trade between Germany and the Protectorate and Slovakia would be abolished at the beginning of October 1940. But this did not happen and had an adverse effect on Apollo Nafta's profits.

The temporary pause in German demand for oil in the spring of 1941 also gave the company an opportunity to reassess its own position. Table 5.20 gives a comparison of turnover from 1937 (before the Sudeten crisis) to the winter of 1939–40 and for the whole of 1940, which shows how the situation had changed. This indicates the effect of the transfer of the Sudetenland on one of the oil companies in terms of lost revenue on sales of fuel. It does not include the loss of capital (buildings, oil storage tanks etc). But in spite of this the company remained profitable. The invasion of the USSR in the summer of 1941 marks the turning point.

As the time for the invasion approached, Apollo Nafta's relationship with Romania became more important and every effort was made to maintain a steady supply of oil. There had been problems over settling debts in the past but in April, shortly before the invasion of the USSR was due to begin, the office of the *Reichsprotektor* in Prague wrote to Apollo Nafta to tell the company that it would be paid for Romanian oil on a foreign account. This ensured that the company had suitable foreign currency to pay for the oil and avoided possible delays in payment and settlement of any debt because of delays in the clearing system. This was also one of the consequences of Slovakia becoming part of the Gross Deutsches Reich, a matter reported by the Treuhand und Revisions G.m.b.H. in Prague in May. For economic reasons, the company was made a member of the Zentralverband der Industrie für Böhmen und Mähren in Prague. It also became a member of the Zentralverband für Gerichtssachverständigen im Protektorat Böhmen und Mähren which, as a legal body, demanded the political reliability of all employees. These measures indicate the gradual process of regulating the trade in Romanian oil, but it did not end the problem of rising prices. The main reason for this was that the price was fixed in gold dollars, and Germany tried to control the increase in May by ending this system of calculating prices.

The remaining part of the war is a story of rising production against a background of increasing bureaucratic control, bombing raids and increasing pressure on workers. In March 1942 the working week was increased to 48 hours (five-and-a-half days) and later apprentices were used as fully trained workers.[76] This was a modest increase by

Table 5.20 Comparison of turnover (sales) 1937–40

	kg	kg	
Turnover, 1937		14,075,014	
Turnover in Sudetenland	4,588,284		
Turnover in Slovakia	5,212,737	9,801,021	
Balance in Protectorate		4,273,993	
Turnover, 1/10/30–30/4/40			
In Protectorate		5,707,797	
Proportion for 7 months in 1937		2,493,162	
Consisting of			
a) petrol stations, 71.30%		2,292,034	Loss in kg = 39.60% Loss in crowns = 907,645
b) storage depots, 19.87%		638,747	Loss in kg = 20.80% Loss in crowns = 132,859
c) main storage, 8.83%		No loss	
Turnover 1/5/40–31/12/40			
In Protectorate	4.895,528		
Proportion for 8 months in 1937	2,849,328		
Including increase in turnover	2,045,200		
Consisting of			
a) petrol stations, 71.30%		1,485,940	Loss in kg = 56,849% Loss in crowns = 829,393
b) storage depots, 19.87%		406,597	Loss in kg = 33.170% Loss in crowns = 134,862
c) main storage, 8.83%		No loss	
			Total loss = 2,004,760 crowns

Source: Moravský zemský archiv, Brno, Apollo company records, H127/6, Abrechnung, Prague, 19 March 1941.

comparison with workers in many factories in the Protectorate later in the war. By then many, especially where there was a shortage of skilled men, were working up to 70–72 hours a week in 10–12 hour shifts and had one day off per fortnight.[77] The working week at Apollo Nafta was related to the supply of oil reaching the refinery. As the Romanian oil refineries came within the range of Allied bombers from airfields in the Foggia region of south-east Italy, Romanian refineries were attacked. Problems emerged at Apollo Nafta that included the inability of the VOC Company to import part-refined products from Romania.[78] This led to increased bureaucratic efforts to limit civilian use of motor fuel still further.[79] In October a circular was issued forbidding price competition in petrol sales – due to falling demand – because this was reducing the income of oil companies.[80] The same month regulations were issued restricting supplies of fuel for agricultural and forestry use.[81] In November came an order stating that future deliveries of fuel would only be made when used oil was returned; a circular of February 1943 gave details of 22 depots to which the oil could be taken. At the end of December deliveries to retailers were restricted to 50 litres each for the first quarter of the following year.[82] Those who could prove they had a greater need would be given two deliveries, one in each half year. Wholesalers were similarly restricted about the amounts they could be given. The interruption of oil supplies led to a decline in production and a circular issued in March called on all producers to increase their output. Companies which had suffered financial loss could claim some state compensation and Apollo Nafta appears to have qualified for this in 1943. This, together with the demand for greater production, explains why the company increased its capital by selling a block of 72,128 new Apollo Mineralöl-Raffinerie shares at a price of 260 crowns each through the Deutsche Länderbank.[83]

Also in 1943 Speer became the minister for war production and reorganised the oil industry. In April there was an announcement that all refiners of artificial and crude oil would be united into a single group, the Wirtschaftsgruppe Kraftstoff Industrie, of which the Arbeitsgemeinschaft Erdölgewinnung und Verarbeitung was a consultative part.[84] This included the Kontinental Oel A. G., Mineralöl Einfuhr Gesellschaft and the Rumanien Mineralöl Einfuhr Gesellschaft.

Speer also set up a body to plan and report on production, the Arbeitsgemeinschaft Erdölgewinnung und Verarbeitung (AEV). This replaced the pre-war Zentralbüro für Mineralöl (ZB) which had handled the distribution and the Arbeitsgemeinschaft Schmierstoff Verteilung (ASV) for distributing lubricants. This new organisation combined the refineries producing synthetic oil, those making crude oil and the oil distribution companies – a total of 21 firms. Speer also recognised that part of the problem of supply had been that companies were not being paid, could not pay their own debts and were being denied further supplies. But there was a serious shortage of money and Speer had to resort to force to guarantee supplies. Circular No. 2 in July 1943 stated that the army (including the SS and similar bodies), state and town organisations and public utilities would receive deliveries of fuel on credit.

Major companies working for the German war economy such as Škoda, ČKD and Baťa would also be supplied with fuel in the same way. Further reorganisation took place in September, when petrol retailers and suppliers were also amalgamated into a single body. This did not solve the general problem of supply, however. The difficulty that emerged in October was a general shortage of tankers. The reason was that a large number were reserved for the Wehrmacht, and many of the others were being kept by different institutions (including the Gestapo, fire brigade, customs offices, post and telegraph) to guarantee their own supplies. Each jealously guarded its own tankers, which effectively took them out of general use. At the same time, Apollo Nafta was trying to supply machine oil to companies such as the Brünn-Königsfelder Maschinenfabrik in Brno, which was a particularly important customer, the Waffenwerke A. G. in Brno and the Berg und Hüttenwerke in Prague. The following year was the crucial one for the German army and air force, partly because of the loss of Romanian oil and partly because of heavy bombing raids on refineries in Germany and the Protectorate. In August the drastic measure was taken to restrict road traffic by instituting a plan for sharing vehicles within a 10 km zone covering the centre and outskirts of Prague and a 20 km zone in Brno.[85] This applied both to state organisations such as the Waffen SS, NSDAP, police and Wehrmacht as well as private and agricultural users.

Table 5.21 Profits 1943

Product	Turnover kg	Selling price crowns	Cost crowns	Profit crowns
1/7–31/12/1943				
Vergaserkraftstoffe	11,530,128	14,607,854	7,006,846	7,601,208
Diesel fuel	5,926,842	2,220,570	1,475,033	745,477
Paraffin	18,220,236	8,269,438	2,391,571	4,587,967
Technical benzine	2,068,380	423,097	196,344	244,863
Heating oil	84,097	17,877	7,046	10,831
Total	*31,838,520*	*24,226,836*	*11,078,600*	*13,150,236*
1/1–30/6/1944				
Vergaserkraftstoff	9,936,460	11,431,196	5,228,365	6,204,831
Diesel fuel	5,037,800	1,931,667	1,201,490	730,187
Paraffin	10,446,530	5,971,294	1,759,279	4,212,005
Technical benzine	2,270,012	476,812	117,312	358,500
Heating oil	35,400	5,830	3,321	2,509
Total	*27,726,202*	*19,816,789*	*8,307,757*	*11,506,032*

Source: ibid, Vorläufige Netto Gewinn Aufteurung auf Produkte, Prague, 24 Nov. 1944.

Table 5.21 shows that these problems were reflected in the fall in Apollo Nafta production and profits from the end of 1943 to the following summer and: how the turnover of the refinery had fallen by 4.1 million kg in the first six months of 1944 – the effect of air raids – which contributed to the general shortage of fuel in Germany. The fall in production of diesel fuel of almost 1 million kg was particularly significant. Hitler had shown a preference for diesel over petrol engines. In the 1930s there had been considerable debate about the merits of Otto (petrol) and diesel engines. This had not been easily resolved because the petrol engines were generally smaller and much more research had been done on these than on diesel. Manufacturers were making many more petrol than diesel engines and did not want the high cost of re-tooling to manufacture different engines.[86] Some new diesel engines were designed to satisfy Hitler but it was not until the outbreak of war that the army finally stated that diesel engines were superior for armoured vehicles. Also, at that time the army did not expect to have a definite answer to the question of which was superior in general. This had implications for fuel-refining policy. The fall in diesel oil production early in the war had been caused by uncertainty about the actual needs of the army. From the summer of 1944, when many more diesel engines were being used in lorries as well as armoured vehicles, it was therefore of crucial importance. Germany was fighting a bitter rearguard action in which heavy tanks, which used large amounts of fuel, played an important part.

As the end of the war approached, it became more difficult to find the money to pay for deliveries of oil – a problem that hit not only Apollo Nafta but also other firms in the Protectorate. To this was added difficulties in finding metal tanks for transporting fuel – there was a shortage of over 19,000 in April 1945. Air raids in the period October 1944 to March 1945 added to the problem, as can be seen in Table 5.22.

Table 5.22 Fuel losses from air raids October 1944 – March 1945

Date of air raid	Target	Damage crowns
24/8/44	MVG depot 429 at Pardubice	421,486
1/11/44	MVG depot 503 at Kolín	68,376
28/12/44	MVG depot 429, Pardubice	36,008
15/3/45	MVG depot 503, Kolín	4,909
22/3/45	MVG depot 102, Kralup a. d. Main	110,283
25/3/45	MVG depot 510, Prague-Wissotschen	13,540 (Naphta Co.)
25/3/45	MVG depot 106, Prague-Wissotschen	127,994 (Fanta Co.)

Source: ibid.

The result of these raids was a loss of over 65,000 kg of diesel and other forms of fuel, as well as destruction of metal storage tanks, valued at over 782,000 crowns. More important, however, was the destruction of fuel storage facilities that could not easily be replaced. This was the position in the closing stages of the war: shortage of crude oil and increasing difficulties in production as refineries and railways came under attack. Finally, the town of Bratislava was captured by Russian forces and the war ended as far as Apollo Nafta was concerned.

Both the companies described briefly above were already established when the Protectorate was created. All the German authorities had to do was buy them (as shown by I. G. Farben's purchase of Apollo Nafta) or seize them as enemy property in September once war had broken out.

Sudetenländische Treibstoffwerke A. G., Hydriewerk[87]

In the third example, the refinery for synthetic fuel in West Bohemia at Brüx (Czech Most), the factory was built only after the area had been seized by Germany. Very quickly after the German occupation the Reichswerke gained control of all the leading parts of Czech heavy industry. Lignite mining was incorporated into the Sudetenländische Bergbau A.G. (SUBAG) Brüx, which was controlled by the Reichswerke and VIAG.[88] The army was well aware that the area contained large quantities of brown coal that could be used for making synthetic fuel. The success of the Wesserling plant had shown that the process was feasible from a technical point of view. It was also possible to integrate it into the group of refineries which would help produce the fuel needed for the coming war. Soon after the German troops entered Brüx (Most), geological tests were made to assess the prospects for building a huge chemical factory in the town. The aim was to build a refinery that would produce 660,000 tons of fuel from 6.6 million tons of brown coal, in cooperation with the Leuna Werke, a modern refinery which already had an annual output of 400,000 tons. This would make Most the largest of all the synthetic oil refineries. The order to begin work on building the refinery was given on 28 March 1939 and the work was to be supervised by the specialist company Mineralöl Baugesellschaft A. G. By the end of April a suitable site had been chosen near Most at Záluží u Most and plans were also prepared for modernising the existing lignite mine. It was meant to be part of the Four Year Plan and run by the Mineralölbau G.m.b.H. but instead it came under the Reichswerke as a trustee for Germany in October 1939. If the production plans had been fully realised, the Most refinery would have become the major producer of synthetic fuel for the German armed forces, surpassing even Leuna.

The outbreak of war in September emphasised the need for a new source of fuel. The air force had stocks of aviation fuel for four-and-a-half months, the army had petrol for about the same and diesel fuel for three. The aim was to win a decisive victory in as short a time as possible, and the existing stocks were considered adequate. The first war, against Poland, lasted only a few weeks. But the next stage might take longer and require much larger quantities of petrol. The official foundation of the company was on 9 October, when it was named the Sudetenländische Treibstoffwerke A. G. It formed part of the Hermann Göring Werke, which owned 98 per cent of the company and was linked to Sudetenländische Bergbau A. G., the mine that would supply the lignite for the refinery. Finally, it came under the control of the Reichsministerium für Rüstung und Kriegsproduktion, since the entire output would be used by the military forces.

To begin with, the construction work was carried out by 2,000 Polish prisoners of war. But after the defeat of France 3,000 more French, Belgian and Dutch prisoners arrived. As noted above, these could be put to work under the Geneva Convention, provided the work was not of strategic importance. In this case, as in others, the terms of the Geneva Convention were ignored. As already noted, non-commissioned officers could be used as supervisors, though there is no evidence of the rank of the prisoners.[89] There were also civilians from the Protectorate and from countries allied to Germany including Bulgarians, Slovaks and Italians. These were only part of a very large workforce. By the second half of 1940 there were 14,000, who now included Norwegians, Danes and British from the Channel Islands. They were housed in wooden barracks. As the building work continued, more were drafted in to work in the growing refinery and coal mines. These included Czechs who were sent for labour service. There were also Russian prisoners of war and more workers from occupied countries. They were fed on a diet of 50 grams of meat every other day and a weekly ration of 29 grams of fat, 300 grams of bread, 2 grams of tea and 15 grams of sugar. They also got a watery soup made from rotten vegetables. Many Russian soldiers were ill with typhus and around 800 died. Work discipline was enforced by members of the Werkschutz, a form of factory police dressed in military uniforms.

The refinery finally started producing fuel in December 1942. The delay in production had been due no doubt to the use of underfed, unskilled labour, which finally included concentration camp prisoners. Another factor was the original decision to build a huge plant that would inevitably take much longer to complete, especially during wartime when materials were in short supply. The refinery was run by Eric Ericson, a man who had been born in Brooklyn in 1891 but had gone to Stockholm as a young man to study fuel technology. He became an expert, established his own business and became attracted to Nazism after the defeat of Poland. He was approached by a member of the SD and at the end of 1939 went to Germany, where he studied the most modern methods of fuel production. As an expert with managerial experience, Ericson was put in charge of the refinery and escaped at the end of the war

To begin with, the refinery was only protected from bombing by a barrage balloon. There was no serious threat of bombing raids. Earlier in the war, in October and November 1940 and November 1941, there had been three raids on the Škoda factory in Plzeň, but the Whitley bombers had been operating at the limit of their range, and had failed to find and hit their target.[90] This had lulled the Germans into a false sense of the security of Sudeten and Protectorate factories. But in 1942 the Avro Lancaster entered service. This had more powerful engines, could carry a much larger bomb load and had a longer range. Bombing raids also became more effective through the use of De Havilland Mosquitoes to locate and mark targets with flares. The refinery now needed full protection and was given searchlights and a variety of anti-aircraft guns – a sign of the refinery's importance, since these were only provided to factories and refineries at greatest risk.[91]

By the end of 1942 a total of 1,705 tons of petrol and 4,968 tons of diesel fuel had been produced, which was sent to the WIFO refinery in Vienna.[92] Output at the refinery, now named Hydriewerk, increased rapidly. In June the refinery had an annual output of a 1,000 barrels of motor fuel and almost twice that amount of diesel fuel. This formed an important part of large-scale synthetic fuel production which in 1944 included 21 refineries and was capable of producing 7.1 million tons of mineral oil (2 million tons in 1939, 5.7 million tons in 1943).[93]

Bombing raids had interrupted production in May and June, but the raids had concentrated on refineries producing aviation spirit. Until then the Luftwaffe's needs had been met. In April it had used 165,000 tons of the total output of 175,000 tons.[94] Thereafter daily production, which had been 5,850 tons, fell, though there was a recovery at the end of the month. In July 1944 the position became serious and arrangements were begun to establish refineries underground.[95] Production of carburettor fuel had fallen from 125,000 tons in April to 58,000 tons. Diesel fuel output had declined from 88,900 tons to 62,000 tons. Table 5.23 gives the figures for daily production in July, showing the effect of bombing raids on Most and other refineries, and revealing how important the Royal Air Force considered these synthetic oil refineries to be and the part that Most played in oil production.

But the figures given in the table were only for aviation fuel. The general fuel situation in July was so serious that production tables were drawn up for Speer, showing what had been expected following the raids and what had actually been achieved. The table for July 1944 shows that the highest anticipated output was at Leuna, where production of synthetic fuel had begun in 1922.[96] In July 1944 anticipated daily output was 1,024 tons, by far the highest of all refineries. It is worth remembering, however, that if the original plans for the Most refinery had been carried out, daily production there would have been 1,800 tons – higher than Leuna achieved. But Leuna, better known to the Allied powers, was the main target for bombing raids, as the figures for the month show: for the first six days in July output ranged from 1,100 to 1,800 tons. Then production fell to 600 tons on the 7th and there was a gap in output until the 12th, when production began again with 800 tons. Within two days it was back at 1,400 tons and continued at a high level until the 20th (with one day of low output on the 19th of 700 tons). Then there was another break until the 24th, when output was resumed with 400 tons, rising to 1,400 on the 26th, interrupted by another bombing raid on the 27th which again stopped production. These figures show that output at this very important plant was being pushed to its limit (i.e. the foreign workers were being pushed to their limit) and at its highest was far exceeding the scale of anticipated production. What is also striking is the speed with which

Table 5.23 Daily output of aviation fuel, July 1944

Date	Air raid target	Output Tons
1		1,043
2		1,086
3		954
4	Scholven	1,065
5	Scholven	1,393
6	Scholven	1,645
7	Scholven, Leuna, Luetzerndorf, Boehlen, Heydebreck	916
8	Scholven	600
9	Scholven	870
10	Scholven	961
11		751
12 (Production resumed at Leuna)		1,133
13		1,278
14		1,271
15 (Increased production at Leuna)		1,714
16 (Switch-over to special fuel production at Leuna)		1,588
17		No data
18		1,378
19	Wesseling, Scholven	856
20	Leuna	970
21	Wehlheim, Most	120
22		140
23		140
24 (Resumption at Leuna)		600
25		417

Source: Imperial War Museum Archives, Duxford, Speer Papers, Report on oil production, July 1944.

full production was resumed after a bombing raid – again, a reflection of the way the workers were being treated.

No other plant matched Leuna. Others were Scholven (planned daily production 481 tons), Wehlheim (432 tons), Wesseling (484 tons), Blechhammer (277 tons) and Ludwigshafen (129 tons). Most were in the east, using the brown coal produced by the mines near Magdeburg and Leipzig. Only Wesseling and Ludwigshafen were in the west, using coal from the Ruhr. Of the others, Scholven and Wesseling were in production until 17 July, Wehlheim until 19 July, Blechhammer 2nd to the 7th, 18th to the 2th and from the 24th to the end of the month. Pölitz was producing 900 tons on the 25th and smaller quantities from the 27th to the end of the month. Most had already been severely damaged by raids in May and June and in July had an anticipated daily production of only 35 tons. An attempt to hide the plant was made at the end of June, using a complex network of apparatus around the factory and mine that produced smoke.[97] It is significant that the refinery was given this elaborate system of defence, since there was a shortage of sulphuric acid that was used for it. The Luftwaffe introduced a system of priorities in late 1944 to try and offer some protection to staff and workers. Bunkers were built of various sizes to protect at least the more important staff, who had bunker passes and metal identity discs. No oil was made at Most until the 15th and total production for the month was only 600 tons, produced in four days. Of the others, 12 were expected to produce only small quantities and in fact made no oil. Put another way, daily production had fallen from 3,700 tons (slightly above the anticipated 3,433 tons) at the beginning of the month to 540 tons at the end. Furthermore, on three days, 21–23 July, output had been only 100, 200 and 100 tons. The result for the month was that instead of the anticipated production of 106,420 tons of oil, only 58,460 tons were made – approximately half.

Those were the bleak results for July 1944. Bombing raids continued. Most and its coal mines were hit again in August and September. These raids were directed against other plants as well and were made by groups of between 88 and 185 British and American aircraft (Lancasters, Liberators and Flying Fortresses). Most was hit by a force of Flying Fortresses on 24 September that dropped a total of 310.9 tons of bombs. After these raids, another table for output in November 1944 shows that fuel production had fallen at Leuna to 14,740 tons (22,100 tons in July), Pölitz made 17,450 tons (2,800 in July), Most was again in production (9,760 tons) and Blechhammer 1,940 tons (5,000 tons in July). This, together with smaller quantities from other plants, made a total for the month of 71,300 tons (106,420 tons in

July). During this month there were only three days when output rose above 3,000 tons and 18 when it was above 2,000 tons. This helped to raise the year's production to 71,300 tons (58,460 tons in July). The figures for December show that production had stopped at Leuna and only two other refineries had exceeded 10,000 tons for the month: Böhlen, 10,770 tons and Pölitz 15,380 tons. Output at Most was 8,200 tons in the first half of the month. Elsewhere the results were modest: almost 30,000 tons below the anticipated 88,190 tons, a total that had been revised in view of the bombing raids. It is small wonder that German aircraft had no fuel.

The July 1944 crisis shows the importance of fuel for the German armed forces. They were fighting wars on several fronts, of which the eastern was by far the most demanding. Oil production had progressed a long way from the initial production of synthetic fuel at Leuna in 1922. The refinery at Most, planned as one of the largest in Europe, escaped many of the early bombing raids because it attracted less interest than the German refineries. But when it and a German plant were attacked in July there was a dramatic fall in output. Production at this huge plant was more important than many Allied planners realised. In the same way, Apollo Nafta's refinery for Romanian crude oil was very important for helping to transform the main supply of crude oil into fuel for military use while output of Romanian crude oil still reached Bratislava. Without these and other Czech refineries, Germany's position, especially in the later stages of the war, would have been very much worse. As Speer's account shows, Germany was only able to continue fighting after July 1944 by getting the refineries back into production in a remarkably short time. The part played by Czechoslovak resources in Germany's struggle is therefore highly significant.

Chemicals

The centre of the Czechoslovak chemical industry was in Ústí nad Labem (Aussig) in the Sudetenland. The main Czechoslovak company was the Aussiger Verein, the Association for Chemical and Metallurgical Production, Aussig.[98] This was the fourth largest in Europe, with many subsidiaries in Czechoslovakia and abroad and combined profits of 1.78 million Reichsmarks in 1938. Sole Czechoslovak control, established under nostrification, was lost in 1929 when the majority of the shares were sold to the Belgian Solvay & Cie (15.4 per cent) and the Živnostenska bank (49 per cent). To exclude I. G. Farben from the Czech explosives industry, the Verein cooperated with Imperial Chemical Industries, but had to compensate the German firm with cartel privileges in Czech and South European markets. Within Czechoslovakia, I. G. Farben owned Dynamit A. G. of Bratislava, three sales companies and held shares in three other small firms. After 1934 both I. G. Farben and Aussiger Verein tried to expand sales in Eastern Europe, but the German company avoided a direct confrontation, fearing that it would lose its cartel arrangements and aware that the Verein was supported by large British, French and Belgian companies. As a result, it was only in early 1937, when it looked as if the Imperial Chemical Industry would sell its shares in the Verein, that I. G. Farben and its subsidiary Dynamit A. G. made any attempt to invest in it.[99]

The rise of Sudeten nationalism, encouraged by Henlein's Karlsbad demands in April 1937, led the Aussiger Verein to move its headquarters to Prague. It looked as if the Sudetenland would come under German control. Since the Verein, now called the Prager Verein, could not move its chemical plants at Aussig and Falkenau, the company decided to reach an understanding with I. G. Farben. The Verein's director general, Antonin Basch, suggested to I. G. Farben that a number of Verein shares might be exchanged for Dynamit shares. Although attractive to the German company, the proposal had a number of disadvantages. It was possible that the whole of the company's assets in the Sudetenland would pass to I. G. Farben. In that case, considerable investment would be necessary to raise productivity once the firm had lost its tariff protection. But to raise the money for this, I. G. Farben would have to sell the plant or company shares and this would benefit I. G. Farben's competitors. The German company would either face a stronger rival or lose part of its share in the German market. The Verein produced large quantities of organic and inorganic chemicals and dyes, and the latter was the basis of I. G. Farben's prosperity. For this reason, I. G. Farben could not allow a competitor to get control of the Czechoslovak company.

As a preparation for taking control of the Verein, I. G. Farben dismissed all except two non-Aryans from its sales companies in Czechoslovakia and ended all contracts with non-Aryan firms. When Chamberlain made his first visit to Germany and it looked as if the Sudetenland would ultimately come under German control, I. G. Farben appointed four of its senior staff, terMeer, Schnitzler, Kühne and Ilgner to form a special committee for the Aussig and Falkenau plants. Two of these, terMeer and Schnitzler, visited the Reich Economic Ministry on 22 September to express the company's interest in the plants. They also nominated two people, Dr Wurster and Dr Kugler, as commissars to administer the factories pending a decision on their final status. This was partly successful. Kugler, appointed to Aussig, dismissed the Czech and Jewish employees to win Nazi support. Wurster, at Falkenau, was rejected by the Sudeten Nazis in favour of the Sudeten Nazi Dr Josef Brunner. This marks the end of what is known about the Czechoslovak chemical industry. Incorporated into I. G. Farben, its wartime activities were hidden within the business of the huge German company. There were other chemical companies in the Sudetenland and Protectorate, but they were relatively small and nothing is known about their wartime activity. What is certain is that, like the other, better known companies, they were fully exploited during the war.

CHAPTER 6

BENEŠ' GOVERNMENT IN EXILE, THE END OF THE WAR AND THE EXPULSION OF SUDETEN GERMANS

Beneš went into exile in October 1938. Within a year war had broken out in Europe and Beneš formed a government in exile in London. It was some time before this was officially recognised but once it was achieved Beneš was faced with three problems: how to reverse the Munich Agreement, how to unify the exiled Czech, Slovak and Sudeten German groups to form a unified government in postwar Europe and how to solve the Sudeten problem. None of these was easy to solve and Beneš needed the support of the major powers if he was to find a solution to them. This explains his considerable wartime political activity in the USSR, USA and Britain. Later, as the war was ending and a new government had been created, a new problem emerged: how to decide which Germans to expel and which could be allowed to remain in Czechoslovakia. He could not know immediately after the war whether expulsion of the Sudeten Germans would 'solve' the problem. Nor could he tell whether it would prevent any future minority issue as, for example, over the Poles in north Moravia or the Hungarians in Slovakia. Only time would tell.

Beneš began his exile in London with one great advantage. He had great prestige after working with Masaryk for so long. He had been foreign minister for many years and when Masaryk resigned, Beneš had been elected president in his place. His anti-appeasement policy had been proved to be correct and the appeasers wrong. Neither of the other important exiles – Milan Hodža, former prime minister or Štefan Osuský, envoy to Paris – could rival him. Beneš was the one man that the Czechs, Slovaks and the major powers recognised as the natural leader. To begin with he was a benevolent absolute ruler of his government in exile. He was not accountable to anyone and appointed the members of the three groups – cabinet, state council and judicial council – that, with the Presidency, formed the government. These bodies were advisory; they had no power. However, Beneš, though carrying out many different roles as the Czechoslovak leader, was always careful to consult with his colleagues before taking any action.

Reversing Munich

Beneš wanted above all to reverse the effects of Munich, so that at the end of the war Czechoslovakia could return to the boundaries of the First Republic. He made this clear in his *Memoirs*: 'Ever since September, 1938, I kept thinking of it literally day in and day out, I lived by it and suffered from it, and all of my political actions were directed toward it.'[1] Beneš wanted to avoid a similar situation occurring again. To try and achieve this he set himself five aims:

1. To form a Czechoslovak government in exile which would carry sufficient weight with the major powers.
2. To persuade Britain to repudiate the Munich Agreement and everything that had resulted from it.
3. To end the Sudeten German problem.
4. To ensure the safety of a postwar Czechoslovakia through alliances with the USSR and Poland and, at the same time, maintain friendly relations with the Western powers.
5. To come to an understanding with the Czechoslovak Communists in order to minimise the dangers of extremism in the chaos of postwar Europe after Germany had been defeated.

Beneš was by no means the only distinguished Czech or Slovak to flee from Czechoslovakia. There were also important generals, diplomats and politicians and it was impossible to offer them all important posts in his government. Those who were left out felt that their talents were not being recognised and were potential rivals. There was also the problem of the Sudeten German Social Democrats who had also fled. These were the largest group of anti-Nazi exiles but in 1939 were not prepared to join Beneš. They wanted their own areas to be able in the future to join a German confederation, much as others had hoped after the creation of the First Czechoslovak Republic in 1918. As a result, it was impossible for Beneš to achieve total unity among the Czechoslovak exiles. This delayed recognition by the major powers. There was a further difficulty: many of those responsible for Munich were still in positions of power in Britain and France in 1939 and 1940. In August 1939 Beneš was told not to mention Czechoslovakia in his first speech in Britain, which was to the Liberal summer school in Cambridge. He discussed democracy instead. In France the prime minister, Daladier, failed to reply to his telegram offering support after France declared war on Germany in September 1939. Later, although France signed an agreement with 'the provisional government of the Czechoslovak Republic' for a Czechoslovak army to be created in France, the French government later refused to give Beneš' government official recognition. All the French were prepared to do was recognise a Czechoslovak national committee. Britain followed suit in December. Beneš was thus the leader of an ill-defined group with no more than 'authority to represent the Czechoslovak people'.

Gradually those in France and Britain associated with Munich were forced to resign. Daladier was replaced by Reynaud in March 1940 and the following month Germany invaded Norway and Denmark, ending all chance of a compromise peace. One month later, Chamberlain also resigned. But when Beneš again tried to get Britain to recognise his government he was met with the demand that it should include all Czech and Slovak interests – i.e. including Osuský and Hodža. Britain finally recognised a larger national committee as the 'provisional Czechoslovak government' in July 1940. Beneš celebrated this by announcing it to the Czech people in a BBC broadcast on 24 July as 'the first great step towards victory'.[2] It was an improvement, but still left the Czechoslovak government in exile in a lower position than other exiled governments. Beneš raised the matter again in March 1941. By then the worst of the Blitz was over and it seemed less likely that Germany would invade Britain. But he found that difficulties remained. The British government had recognised the new Slovak government and Hácha claimed that his government was the true representative of the Czech people. There was also the difficulty of accommodating the exiled Sudeten Germans, whose leader Wenzel Jaksch refused to accept Beneš' leadership. Finally, not all the supporters of appeasement had fallen from power in the British Conservative Party and Jan Smuts, South Africa's leader, was also hostile to the idea of granting full recognition to Beneš.

A British change of heart came almost by chance. Winston Churchill paid a visit to a Czech military unit on 19 April 1941 and Beneš gave him a summary of the Czech arguments for full recognition. Churchill was already pleased with the spirit shown by the Czech soldiers and was moved to tears when they sang 'Rule Britannia' at the end of his visit. He was struck above all by their desire to serve Britain after being betrayed at Munich. A few days later Churchill gave Beneš' statement to Eden, who was already pro-Czech, with the remark: 'I do not understand why the Czechs could not have the same status as the other allies. They deserve it.'[3] The final official recognition was issued by Britain and the USSR on 18 July and by the USA on 31 July.

While Beneš was still the head of a provisional government in exile, he created the concept of Czechoslovak legal and political continuity. On this basis he claimed that everything that had followed the Munich Conference had been illegal and carried out by force, terror and violence. Therefore Beneš claimed:

1. The Czechoslovak Republic still existed as an International Legal Person.
2. The Slovak secession had no legal validity, and there could be no Slovak state.
3. The Munich Agreement was invalid.

4. Territory transferred to other states was still legally part of Czechoslovakia.
5. His own resignation as president was the result of force and therefore invalid. Therefore he remained the legal Czechoslovak president.

On one point he gained rapid support. After Hitler had invaded the Czech lands in March 1939, Britain and France had protested and stated that they regarded this as a flagrant violation of the Munich Agreement and made it invalid. But there remained opponents of this. Halifax, one of the earlier appeasers and pro-German, made it clear on 18 July that the British government did not accept Beneš' claim either to legal continuity or to the restoration of territory. Even when Halifax was replaced by Eden, Beneš failed to get the support he needed and at one point threatened to state publicly that everything that had happened since Munich was not the fault of the Czechs but of the British government: 'Every Englishman must realise that Munich continues to stand between our nation and England, and that it will not be forgotten until it is undone. I am afraid that you Englishmen with your lack of political foresight do not realise what could be the consequences of your attitude in post-war Central European and overall European politics.'[4] Beneš finally got British official support in August in a statement that since Germany had violated the terms of the Munich Agreement, Britain no longer recognised it. This gave Beneš most of what he wanted. France, represented by General de Gaulle, supported him entirely and stated on 29 September 1942 that the whole Munich Agreement had been illegal. The USSR and USA had already given their support.

Sudeten Germans

Having persuaded the Allies to reject the Munich Agreement and the transfer of the Sudetenland to Germany, Beneš turned to the Sudeten German question. In December he made his position regarding the Germans clear to Jaksch: 'The small Czechoslovak nation cannot live with a German revolver permanently against its breast.'[5] But what Beneš had in mind to begin with was not the expulsion of all of them. His initial intention was to reduce the number of Germans in Czechoslovakia by the transfer of predominantly German territory to a German state. In January 1943 he said that he was prepared to cede to Germany parts of West Bohemia: Chebsko (Egerland), Liberec (Reichenberg) and Krnov (Jägerndorf). His aim was to win the support of the Allies in this way and then remove the rest of the Sudeten German population by transferring them elsewhere. He proceeded cautiously, suggesting at first that 300,000 to 400,000 Sudeten Germans would leave as refugees at the end of the war because they would be afraid of reprisals by the Czechs for German atrocities. An additional 1.2 to 1.4 million could then be transferred to Germany. An exchange of some frontier districts would remove another 600,000 to 700,000, leaving only about 600,000 to 1 million in Czechoslovakia. Britain agreed to these proposals and Beneš gained American support in June 1943. The USSR was initially more cautious, claiming that the Sudeten matter was an internal Czechoslovak issue, but gave its support in June 1943. The only problem that remained was that the Sudeten Social Democrats in London refused to accept the proposal, even though Beneš offered them citizenship in the new Czechoslovak state.

Czechoslovak search for security

It would not be enough to remove the Sudeten German threat from postwar Czechoslovakia. The new state would also need the support of Poland and the USSR if Germany in the future renewed its policy of *Drang nach Osten* (eastwards expansion). Initially, while the USSR was an ally of Germany from 1939 to 1941, Beneš had not been able to hope for Soviet support. He therefore worked towards Czech–Polish understanding. Initial discussions in 1940 with General Sikorsky were favourable and in January 1942 agreement was reached on the principles of a future Czech–Polish confederation. These would include common policy on all major internal and external matters as well as a customs union. To take this policy further it was necessary to get the support of the USSR. In 1941, after the German invasion, the prospects appeared good. The USSR opened relations with the Polish government in exile. But, at about the time that Beneš reached his agreement with Sikorski over the principles for future Czech–Polish relations, it became clear that Stalin had changed his mind. By the summer of 1942 the USSR had rejected the idea of a Czech–Polish confederation. Beneš faced the unenviable task of choosing between the two: the USSR or Poland, since any alliance with one would anger the other. He chose the USSR partly because of the long-standing Soviet support for Czechoslovakia and partly because he continued to hope that Poland might be included in the alliance with the USSR at some point. The most he achieved was a protocol to the December 1943 alliance allowing another country to be included. But this apparent goodwill Soviet gesture proved an illusion.

Search for an understanding with Czechoslovak Communists

The third potential problem that a postwar Czechoslovakia would face was the threat of internal disorder and of a Communist seizure of power. Beneš realised that the Communists would try to exploit postwar anarchy. The Czech and Slovak Communists would have the support of the Soviet army, which by then would have liberated the country. The USSR had in any case been popular with most Czechs and Slovaks for a long time. This was another reason for Beneš to improve Czech–Slovak relations.

He therefore did all he could to maintain good relations with the USSR, believing that this would hinder Communist attempts to undermine his authority. He signed the treaty with the USSR as soon as he could and allowed the USSR to block the Czech–Polish confederation. He also agreed, very unwillingly, to the Soviet demand for Ruthenia to be transferred to the Ukraine, on the specious claim that this represented the wishes of its people. Beneš also tried to reach an understanding with the Czech and Slovak Communists by inviting them to join his government in London. He hoped that this would limit their power to cause trouble. The result was the inclusion of several Czechoslovak Communists who were in London in the Czechoslovak government in exile. When he was in Moscow in 1943, he even offered to give Communist leaders two seats in his cabinet but the offer was rejected. Beneš also agreed to Communist demands that the existing system of local government be changed to a network of people's committees similar to that in the USSR. Finally, in March 1945 he agreed to give Communists important positions in his postwar cabinet.

The end of the war

While Beneš was preparing to lead a postwar Czechoslovak government, resistance to the Germans was beginning in Czechoslovakia.[6] Resistance groups were gradually formed and in 1944 were amalgamated into associations headed by the Council of Three (R3). This was associated with the Communist National Revolutionary Council, (Přípravný národné revoluční výbor – PNVR) and the illegal trade union movement (ROH). These followed a Communist programme, calling for an end to the old political parties, large-scale social and economic reforms and close association with the USSR. The R3, like the Communist group, anticipated an armed struggle and planned for it. In February 1944 Soviet forces entered Slovakia and Beneš called for a national uprising. Britain sent parachute groups to improve communications between the Czech groups and the SOE (Special Operations Executive) in England. However, many Czech partisans were arrested and the Communist youth movement Vanguard (Předvoj) also suffered heavy losses. Some managed to evade arrest, including escaped Russian prisoners of war, who provided training and leadership for the partisans.

The Slovak Uprising broke out in the summer of 1944 and the Germans immediately sent troops to crush it. A special force on the Protectorate–Slovak frontier stopped Slovak partisans entering the Protectorate. But this took German troops away from the central area of the Protectorate, weakening German control, and Soviet parachute groups landed there at the beginning of October. They joined the main resistance group R3 and on the 26th a combined force captured the gendarmerie post at Přibyslav. It rapidly became clear that the Gestapo, SD and other Nazi Party organisations were unable to fight the partisans effectively. German troops were more successful and the uprising became a guerrilla war. The partisan units, now part of the Red Army, were directed from partisan headquarters on the Ukrainian front. To help them, more parachutists were sent from airfields at Brindisi in southern Italy. Progress was also made on the political front. Czech exiles in London and Moscow, who held widely differing views about postwar plans, seemed to be moving towards a compromise. This also encouraged similar progress between Communist and non-Communist resistance groups in the Protectorate and Slovakia, but progress was hampered by the arrest or death of their leaders. In 1945 left-wing and Communist groups formed the Czech National Council (Česká národní rada – ČNR). The Council officials were mainly party members rather than active resistance fighters. Alex (a military group) and the conservative Central National Committee were excluded from the Council. As a result, the main political resistance movement ignored the Council's call to prepare for an armed revolt.

Although both the Allies and the USSR sent small numbers of troops to help the resistance, they did not supply many weapons and the groups were only able to conduct small-scale guerrilla warfare. In western Moravia and eastern Bohemia these groups were able to disrupt German communications and when supplies of weapons were sent in April 1945 the groups were able to mount more effective raids. These began on 1 May when Přerov was seized. The revolt spread. Towns were captured, Germans were disarmed, all traces of the German occupation were removed and Czech flags appeared on public buildings. The Germans fought back, trying to safeguard their own communications. Villages were destroyed and their inhabitants were shot. On 4 May, an uprising began in Prague.[7] On the 5th the military group Alex seized Prague Radio and broadcast urgent appeals for help.

General Karel Kutlvašr, the leader of Alex, took control of the uprising. Armed Czechs and Protectorate police seized public buildings and the Czech National Council assumed political responsibility. On the night of 5/6 May 1,600 barricades were erected. The German army and SS only held small parts of the city, but they outnumbered Czechs and were well armed. There followed three days of fighting between 30,000 armed Czech civilians and 37,000 to 40,000 German troops supported by tanks and artillery. The American forces, which had liberated Plzeň, made no attempt to help the Czechs; Eisenhower had agreed that Soviet troops should liberate Prague. But Soviet forces south of the city under General Bělov made no attempt to help the Czechs and the new Košice government also ignored the uprising.[8] Fighting ended on 8 May when the German forces surrendered. Two thousand Czechs had been killed. The next day the first Soviet troops entered the city and received a great welcome. On 10 May the new government entered Prague and the resistance fighters handed over control. None of their leaders was included in the new government, which was predominantly left-wing and in which the Communists played a leading part. As soon as the war ended, the new government nationalised the assets of all Germans and Czech collaborators. Initially the government faced an almost impossible task: how to provide a new administration quickly that was untainted by the past six years of Nazi control?

Czech revenge

Beneš had always assumed that large numbers of Sudeten Germans would flee westwards to escape from the advancing Soviet forces. Part of his postwar strategy of dealing with the Sudeten problem was based on an assumption that many would do so. What he and others failed to foresee was the scale and ferocity of Czech revenge on the Germans who did not escape. Unpopular senior Germans in companies were seized and killed. All Germans had to wear arm bands that distinguished them from Czechs and Slovaks and this made them more vulnerable to random attacks. Successful, middle-class Germans living in Prague suffered the least. They were forced to work on clearing the barricades left from the uprising and conducting menial tasks in the city. There was no wholesale slaughter and after a time they were moved to camps while the Czech authorities decided what to do with them. In the countryside many Germans were killed indiscriminately. There was a total breakdown of law and order. The new government was unable to exercise any control. Into this vacuum came groups of vigilantes, who seized German property and possessions and ill-treated and killed their owners. Sudeten Germans claimed that these groups were composed of criminals and prostitutes and there can be no doubt that criminal elements seized the opportunity to enrich themselves in the absence of any normal police presence.

This anarchy was on a scale that was much worse than in any other country that had been under German control and there is considerable debate about the causes of it. It would be easy to explain this period as a mixture of revenge and criminal activity in the absence of any form of police control. But any explanation needs to go beyond this. German administration of the Protectorate had been based on a belief that Czechs were not comparable to Germans and should not be treated like normal human beings. This was in stark contrast to the Czechs' own sense of being integrated into Western, liberal traditions. The Nazi administration had taken steps to try and destroy the basis of Czech culture, banning any celebration of Masaryk's life, removing all pictures of Masaryk from public buildings and even destroying memorials. Czech universities had been closed and it was clear that Germans wanted to destroy the basis of Czech education, even to the point of limiting the number of Czech teachers in schools. Attempts had also been made to conduct all business in German, relegating Czech to the countryside. Czech Jews, many of whom had assimilated to Czech society to the point of losing their original Jewish identity, had been arrested, taken to Terezín and thence to concentration camps, where they were killed. There was no history of anti-Semitism in Czech culture, although some anti-Semitic measures had been taken by the government of the Second Republic.

The Germans had intended to destroy the Czech culture and sense of national identity. To this should be added the regulations about forced labour, including work in German factories and elsewhere for the Todt Organisation, where Czechs were very badly treated and paid low wages. As the war progressed, much of the work became harder and more dangerous, as it included work repairing railway lines, removing rubble from bomb-damaged buildings and finally digging anti-tank ditches. Many Czechs had also been sent to concentration camps and others were held in German prisons.

To this was added the regime of terror. Ordinary life had been threatened by the presence of the Sicherheitsdienst (SD) in factories – many of whom were anonymous – and the Gestapo. Even Czech police were under German control and were feared. Finally, the mass arrests and executions that followed the assassination of Heydrich had struck at areas of the Protectorate that had previously escaped the full brutality of the German occupation. The destruction of two villages and their inhabitants was also designed to strike terror into Czech hearts. Add to this the conscious German decision to use the assassination of Heydrich as a chance to destroy the Czech elite – especially in education – and the Czech reaction to the end of German rule comes as no surprise. In the aftermath of war, there was little to distinguish one German from another in Czech eyes.

The situation in May 1945 was that Czechoslovakia claimed that 250,000 had died in the war and over 100,000 had suffered permanent injury. Damage to homes, factories and other material assets was calculated at 1,284.5 billion crowns.[9] This reflected the intense anti-German feeling in the country, emphasised by the fact that many Germans seemed unrepentant and 'sullen and dangerous.'[10] Some continued to fight after the formal surrender. The final stage of the war also witnessed SS brutality in the armed struggle between partisans and the German forces. In addition to the SS units there were also other armed groups (Werewolf, Guttenberg, Zeppelin, Vernichtungsbrigade Egerland etc.), which delayed the reintroduction of normal Czechoslovak administration.[11] The Czechs celebrated the end of the war by taking revenge on all the Germans they could find – *Reichsdeutsch* as well as Sudetens. In many towns groups of revolutionary guards established courts which provided summary justice to any whom they believed were enemies. In Brno, for example, young National Guards expelled the German population of about 25,000 on 30 May 1945 and drove them south towards the Austrian border.[12] This was the so-called Brno death march, which has roused fierce controversy. Sudeten German sources tried to equate it to the death march by concentration camp prisoners who were taken westwards at the end of the war. They claimed that it caused the death of a great many innocent civilians, largely because of Czech brutality. Until recently there has been no attempt on the Czech side to counter this with any degree of accuracy. Although it is now impossible to establish the truth, a clearer picture of events has emerged, largely as a result of cooperation between German and Czech historians.[13]

The Land National Committee in Brno issued a decree on 29 May 1945 stating that all German women, children and men younger than 14 and older than 60, together with men unable to work, would be taken out of the city. They would be allowed to take as many of their possessions as they could carry, except for bank books and jewellery. All other Germans would be put in an internment camp and would work at clearing the city of debris left by the war. When that was finished they too would be taken away. No invalids, pregnant women, mothers who had recently given birth, Germans from mixed marriages registered as Czechs, German Jews or anti-fascists were to be included in either group. The official figure for those who were taken was 19,000–19,500. The Sudeten Germans claimed that there could have been as many as 30,000. But there is no official record to provide any proof for either.

The likely explanation for the action is that the Czech committee planned to send the Germans to the area of Rajhrad and Pohořelice to do agricultural work. For several days after 30 May groups under armed escort went to Pohořelice, but no preparation had been made to receive them. At this point, those forming the armed escort seem to have taken matters into their own hands and continued to take the Germans towards the Austrian frontier. Their intention was apparently to escort them over the frontier and hand them over to the Austrian authorities. The Germans undoubtedly suffered a great deal during the march, but there is nothing to support the Sudeten German claim that there were mass graves, ditches filled with the dead, sadistic Czech guards and a total loss of life of up to 10,000. Those who remained in a camp at Pohořelice also suffered. Conditions in the camp were very bad and dysentery broke out, causing many deaths. More recent estimates were, on the German side: 1,950 dead on the Brno–Pohořelice march, 2,000 dead at the camp, and other deaths, making a total of about 5,200. On the Czech side the official estimate was 3 on the march and 455 at the camp. In 1997, in the new spirit of academic freedom given by the fall of Communism, further research in the Brno Magistrate's Office revealed a total of 1,700 deaths on the march, which included those who died of exhaustion, hunger and disease in Austria. However, although this is the best recent estimate, the final figure can never be known. The episode remains one of the most serious consequences of the end of the war.

The rest of the Sudeten Germans also suffered. Their food rations were reduced and all German schools were closed, though Beneš urged caution and patience, hoping to limit Czech revenge. In some cases the treatment of Germans was relatively mild, but humiliating. In Prague they had swastikas painted on their backs – later replaced by badges and they were made to clear the barricades.[14] Elsewhere, Germans were arrested by Czech partisans and put in punishment camps or interned in barracks.[15] Women and girls were raped by drunken Russian soldiers. The general picture, in other words, was similar to that experienced elsewhere in the area liberated by the Russians. From the Czech point of view, it was a chance of getting revenge for all that had been done to Czechs and the Second Republic since the Munich Conference as well as during the war. All signs of the German occupation were quickly removed. Unpopular Sudeten Germans were seized and killed. In the Škoda factory, for example, one man who was universally loathed was Dr Rudolf Schicketanz. He was an ardent Nazi and was regarded as particularly dangerous. He was hanged.[16]

There were also German refugees in the Protectorate who had fled from the advancing Soviet forces. They knew about the atrocities committed by Germans during the advance into the USSR in the summer and autumn of 1941 and were terrified of Soviet revenge. Some of these ended the war in hospital, ill and exhausted, and many died there. These were elderly and had suffered very badly during their forced march. At Příbram for example they included Max Hassmann, aged 75 from Mokrarata, Renate Breitkopf from Birkenberg, Augusta Kaiser, aged 72 from Dresden and Heinrich Szibat aged 69 from Dudenwalde in East Prussia. All died from lack of food, physical exhaustion and shock. But not all were old. The dead included a young woman, Marta Grabowski, a widow aged 30 from Unter Ehebit, which shows how severe the conditions were.[17] The eyewitness accounts collected by Sudeten Germans and published in the early 1950s provide a picture of Czech brutality, apparently mindless revenge and German humiliation. The accounts include some by people in Prague: a physicist known only as K. F., German women and various professional people, all of whom claimed to be opposed to Hitler.[18] It was as bad as the Czechs experienced after the German seizure of the Sudetenland. The invasion in March 1939 had also been conducted in an apparently legal manner, but Czechs had been humiliated. The incorporation of the Sudetenland into Germany and the appearance of the Gestapo, SS and SD there and in the Protectorate had led to a rule of terror, which was infinitely worse than anything the Czechs or Sudeten Germans had experienced before.

Retribution courts and the Great Decree

The new Czechoslovak government was faced with two problems. How should they deal with the members of the terror organisations (Gestapo, SS and SD) who had committed criminal acts, and should other Sudeten Germans be punished for less serious offences committed during the Sudeten crisis and the war? It was necessary to halt the revenge killing of individuals and replace this with a proper system of justice which everyone would accept. A court could also demand equal punishment for all those who were guilty according to a generally accepted scale that had been worked out by the government in exile during the war. The model was the interrogation and trial of German war criminals at Nuremberg, using a system of international law based on the principles of universal human rights. On 4 June the government passed the retribution decree no. 16/1945 known as the Great Decree. This was for the punishment of 'Nazi war criminals, traitors and their accomplices'. This was followed on 19 June by Decree no. 17/1945 which established the National Court in Prague. The Great Decree established a system of 24 Extraordinary People's Courts (*retribuční soud*) to try Hácha and the Protectorate government as well as those accused of crimes against the state, property, people and for the crime of 'Denunciation'.[19] The panel of judges for each court was composed of lay members as well as those with legal training. They could hand down punishments of prison sentences (of a minimum of five years), fines, the death penalty and 'loss of civic honour', which in effect made it extremely difficult for a person to find work. Many of these crimes concerned matters which until then had been legal and the courts, for political reasons, acted retrospectively in a way that denied normal legal principles. But in spite of this, there could be no appeal against conviction and sentence. Another feature of the court was that when it imposed the death penalty – and many of the early trials resulted in this – the convicted person was executed within two, or occasionally three, hours.

The National Court was finally created on 2 October 1945 and the first judges were sworn in on 12 December.[20] The beginning was not auspicious; the first chief justice, Ferdinand Richter, resigned suddenly. Richter had a distinguished war record with the resistance but he was compromised in the eyes of the justice minister, Prokop Drtina, by a letter he had written to Hitler pleading for mercy. Richter's replacement, František Tržick, was equally distinguished. He had been a judge, a district attorney and chairman of the Social Democratic judges. During the war, he had been arrested by the Nazis. But in December he alienated many people by suggesting that a number of defendants should be released while they were awaiting trial. Cabinet ministers disagreed. This led to bitter disputes in the government between Communists and non-Communists about which of the accused should be released when it became clear that there was little evidence to support charges against some of them. These disputes delayed the start of trials by at least six months. Finally, the first to be tried were three former generals, Otto Bláha, Robert Rychtrmoc and Gustav Mohapl. All had distinguished pre-war records but during the Protectorate had supported the Germans. The first two were condemned to death and executed, but the cremation of their corpses at the national crematorium caused more controversy. The Communists claimed that this had posthumously honoured the men. In the following spring members of Czech fascist organisations were tried. In this early part of the retribution, the majority of those who were tried were found guilty and executed.

It was not until 29 April 1946 that the court finally began the trial of members of the Protectorate government. Many of these had played an important part in pre-war politics and there was still public sympathy for them. But they were not the principal figures, three of which were already dead. Hácha, reviled by the government as the leading collaborator, was considered neither a Nazi nor a traitor by the pre-war US ambassador George Kennan. But Hácha died before he could be brought for trial. Emanuel Moravec, Education Minister and noted collaborator, had committed suicide. František Chvalkovský, the pro-Nazi pre-war Foreign Minister, had been killed in Berlin in a bombing raid. Those who were left were, by comparison, comparatively minor figures. There were five who were tried: Jaroslav Krejčí (former Premier), Richard Bienert (former Minister of the Interior), Jindřich Kamenický (former Railway Minister), Josef Kalfus (former Finance Minister) and Adolf Hrubý (former Agriculture and Forestry Minister). They faced the charge that they had supported the Nazi and fascist movement in the media and in public and defended German illegal acts. The trial turned into a struggle between the Communists led by Gomułka, who wanted the three leaders sentenced to death, and the remainder who wanted a less severe punishment. Much of the early evidence supported the defendants. The final outcome, on 31 July 1946, was that none was given a death sentence. Hrubý was given life imprisonment, Krejčí 25 years, Kamenický 10 years, Bienert 3 years, and Kalfus was found guilty but not punished because he had supported the resistance. The Communists reacted against these sentences by sending delegations and petitions from works committees in Communist towns: Ostrava, Kladno and elsewhere. These achieved nothing, since it was realised that the only important complaints came from the Communist working-class organisations.

After these leading figures had been tried, it was the turn of those who had served in the Nazi administration at a lower level. Known members of the Nazi terror organisations, whose names appeared in the organisations' own correspondence, were easily identified and arrested. They were held in camps which originally had been built to hold Czechs either as workers or for punishment. Other Sudeten Germans, who were members of the SA, Henlein's SdP or the Nazi Party and who had taken a less active political role, were also taken into custody. The latter group were by far the more numerous and represented the large numbers of Sudeten Germans who had acted illegally during the crisis of 1938 and supported the German regime during the war. It was claimed, for instance, that two-thirds of the Sudeten Germans had supported Henlein.[21] But there was no attempt to conduct all the trials quickly. It took time to establish the courts and collect evidence, partly because of a lack of suitable judges and partly because of shortages of materials and office equipment to keep records. Those responsible for conducting the trials were initially understandably uncertain about how they were supposed to work, in an atmosphere of heightened tension. In fact, in the case of the court at Cheb (Eger) in West Bohemia, the trials did not start until the expulsion of Sudeten Germans was beginning. After the initial desire to exact justice on the most serious criminals, most of whom were executed, the courts began to slow down the legal procedures and gradually reduced not only the number of executions but also the severity of the punishment.[22] One result was that many of the Sudeten Germans were released from prison so that they could join the groups that were being expelled. This meant that as time went on, most of those who were brought before the courts were Czech.

Those arrested were in general held for at least 18 months before being brought to trial. This had the advantage that the courts had time to collect and assess the evidence against the very large number of Sudeten Germans and others that were arrested. The records of the court at Cheb are particularly useful because the town was in a Sudeten German area where there were few Czechs. It provides a cross-section not only of the Sudeten German population, which supported Henlein, but also of those Czechs who found themselves in a minority when the territory had been transferred to Germany. The German population were virtually all members of one or other of the Nazi organisations that were the subject of the Great Decree. A study of the decisions by the retribution court at Cheb shows how the system worked. Almost 2,000 (1,767) men and women were brought before the court between 1946 and 1948 from districts in West Bohemia: Aš, Cheb, Karlovy Vary, Loket, Mariánské Lázně, Nejdek, Planá u Mariánské Lázně, Sokolov, Teplá and Tachov. Of these, 242 were proved innocent, 37 were sentenced to life imprisonment and 15 were condemned to death.

Most of the remainder received sentences of between one and thirty years; some had lesser sentences of several months. The court's first priority had been to arrest all those who had been part of the Nazi system of terror: the Gestapo, the SS and the SD. It is through these organisations that the population had been kept in a state of constant fear of arrest and being sent to almost certain death in the concentration camps. This applied as much in the former Sudetenland – part of the Reich from September 1938 – as in the Protectorate. In some ways it was relatively straightforward to establish from administrative records who was a member of these organisations. With the restoration of Czechoslovak frontiers at the end of the war, the Sudetenland was reintegrated into Czechoslovakia and these records fell into Czech hands. The evidence of the Cheb courts shows that, for instance, some members of the Gestapo were *Reichsdeutsch* and others were Sudeten. In the Protectorate, as in other countries under German control, the number of *Reichsdeutsch* Germans in the administration was relatively small and members of the local German population were added when the organisations grew.

In the case of the Gestapo, the organisation had the reputation of being so evil that all members were considered equally bad. The evidence of the Cheb trials, however, shows that this was not true. Josef Bäuml, Jindřich Brockmann, Ludvig Griesinger, Richard Langhammer, Vojtech Müller, Martin Wagner and Otomar Wettengel were all members of the Gestapo, but their sentences ranged from 18 months' imprisonment to death. Brockmann, born in 1900, was *Reichsdeutsch*. He had been sent to the Protectorate to help the SS deal with criminal activity. He rose to the rank of Oberscharführer and at the end of the war fled with the retreating German forces. He was arrested by the British and interned in June 1945 in the Neuengamme concentration camp near Hamburg. He was extradited to Prague to face trial and as an old Nazi (he had joined the party in 1932 and was a member of the Gestapo from 1936) was given a sentence of 10 years. Müller was a Sudeten German. He had joined Henlein's SdP in 1935, fled to Germany during the crisis of 1938 and later joined the Gestapo. But he never played a leading role in it and was perhaps lucky to be given a sentence of only 18 months.[23] The court considered that he had been on the administrative staff and not involved directly in persecuting Czechs.

Richard Langhammer was a very different person.[24] Born at Bublavy in 1906, he joined the SdP in 1938. He was then in his early 30s, ambitious and efficient. He was appointed an official in the Karlovy Vary Gestapo office in 1939, joined the SS and became a Hauptscharführer. In the course of his career he arrested a group of Czechs and accused them of sabotage – a capital offence. Three later died in concentration camps and for that Langhammer received the death sentence. Of the other two, Martin Wagner was a German, born in 1907. He was sent from Nuremberg to the Protectorate to run a training school. At the end of the war he was arrested by the Americans, taken to Plzeň and later interned in the Herzbruck internment camp. As an administrator he received a comparatively light sentence of 40 months. Finally, Otomar Wettengel, born in 1912 at Vejprty, served in the Czechoslovak army in 1933–4 and then joined the police in Vejprty.[25] He continued to serve in the police until 1943, when he joined the Gestapo and later became a member of the SD. At the end of the war he was captured by the Americans and interned in the Moosberg camp before being sent back to Czechoslovakia to face trial. He was given a prison sentence of five years.

The SS and SD were also organs of state terror. Evidence from investigations by British intelligence officers after the war show how they had controlled Czech business. Both were elitist Nazi organisations and seem to have been composed entirely of *Reichsdeutch* Germans. The SS had originally been formed to provide protection for Hitler and had replaced the SA when the latter was destroyed in the putsch of June 1933. As a prestigious organisation within the Nazi Party it attracted many able businessmen, who saw membership in it as a path to high office within companies. The example from Škoda shows how this worked. Dr Krust, a chemist at Škoda, was a member of the SS and Dr Zurtayk, appointed to Škoda as a new German director in 1944, was rumoured to be connected with it.[26] The SD was different. This had been formed by Himmler in 1932 as the intelligence section of the SS and put under the control of Heydrich. Its original role was to watch over members of the Nazi Party and report any activity it considered suspicious to the Gestapo. From this it developed into an organisation that was used to control and report on business. In this role it attracted many professional and business people.

During the war the SD was used to direct industry in the Protectorate. Its members were put in senior positions within organisations and used this power to control the companies. The evidence from British visits to Škoda immediately after the war shows that membership was restricted to Germans. This also helped to attract experienced and capable businessmen who, as in the case of the SS, saw this as a path to senior positions in companies. Sudeten Germans were apparently not invited or allowed to become members. In Škoda the heads of factories at Brno and Povadska Bystrica, Wolf and Dr Witt, were members of the SD. Both fled with the retreating German forces and disappeared at the end of the war.[27] There was also a medical student, Wolfgang Böhm, born in 1920 and who lived in the village of Bublava.[28] During the war he first studied medicine at the German university in Prague and then joined the army as a doctor in Poland and the USSR. He rose to the rank of Feldwebel and was a member of the SA. It is his membership of the SA and his activities as an energetic young man in a provincial village that resulted in his five-year prison sentence. Politically active, professional people of this type were as much a danger to Czech society, as similar Czechs had been to German.

In identifying these criminals, the Czech authorities also searched for Czech collaborators. If it became clear that Czechs had done no more than carry out German orders, they were given a certificate that showed that they had been examined and found to be trustworthy. Among these was Dr Staller of Škoda, who was deputy managing director during the war and was subsequently cleared of all suspicion. He was given a certificate by the Czech General Headquarters.[29]

The members of the Gestapo, SS and SD were the most serious criminals in Czech eyes. There were others who had committed very serious crimes but without being members of these terror organisations. One example is the German Jindřich Hechtfischer. He is described in the court records as a managing director (ředitel) of a factory, a position that would not normally have been a serious crime. Hechtfischer, born in Bavaria, had worked in the Rosenthal porcelain factory since 1922 and in 1938 was, or became, the technical director of a similar Bohemia company. When aryanisation began to drive Jews out of business, Hechtfischer, by then a member of the SA, gained the assets of the Jewish Petschka family and used them to buy the shares of the Bohemia firm. During the war he used concentration camp prisoners as workers in his factory. To the end of 1942 these were from Nové Roli and later were from Flossenburg and Ravensbrück. Like other firms that used these people, the Bohemia company was under the control of the SS and the working conditions were appalling. Hechtfischer was implicated in this and the retribution court sentenced him to death.

These were the more serious cases. But the problem of guilt extended throughout Sudeten society because so many young men and women had been conditioned by their experience in the Hitler Youth and the BDM to obey Hitler without question. They supported German policy because of their anti-Czech cultural attitude. The older Sudeten Germans were also deeply prejudiced against Czechs, as the example of Professor Pfitzner shows. Before the war he had been a history professor at the German university in Prague, but he had political ambitions. He had hoped to be appointed *Gauleiter* of the Protectorate but instead became mayor of Prague. In a memo of 8 September 1938 he had complained that German firms in Prague were not allowed to use their own language but only Czech. This was untrue, as the records of German companies show.[30] In the same vein he complained that German culture was being suppressed by what he clearly felt were the inferior Czechs.[31] This changed with the creation of the Protectorate and the gradual suppression of Czech nationalism. The result was that by March 1942 German had replaced Czech as the language of administration and business.[32]

The effect of political indoctrination on German youth was another matter. The example of Henry Mittelmann is one that applies equally to Sudeten German teenagers. Born Heinrich Mittelmann in Altona, near Hamburg, he became an enthusiastic young Nazi through the influence of his Hitler Youth training, even though he had a devout Christian mother and a left-wing trade unionist father, who worked in the Hamburg docks.[33] Neither parent dared to speak openly of their anti-Nazi views for fear of being inadvertently betrayed to the Gestapo. It was only as a tank commander on the eastern front, experiencing defeat and being able to communicate with Russian prisoners (he had learnt some Russian) that he realised the extent of his indoctrination and the value of his parents' ideals. He was lucky enough to be transferred to Normandy, where he was taken prisoner in June 1944. By then he had become anti-Nazi and remained in Britain after the war. Similar experiences of young Sudeten Germans made it essential at the end of the war for the Czech retribution courts to decide the extent of indoctrination and to root out and punish those who were guilty.

Judgement of Sudeten Germans was complicated by their indoctrination in Hitler's ideas on race. This sense of German racial superiority had persuaded many children of mixed German–Czech marriages to regard themselves, and be classified as, German. This posed a problem for Czech authorities after the war, when they had the chance to reverse this decision and reclassify them as Czech, especially if the people had made it clear that they had changed their outlook and now regarded themselves as Czech. Initially the prospect of joining the 'master race' had been attractive. It had opened prospects for greater opportunities but it had also meant that the people had to join German organisations, some political, others social and some connected with control through terror. In the same way, from 1942, when the German military losses mounted, anyone except Czechs were encouraged to join the SS and the army and fight the Russians.[34] In theory, entry into the army was strictly controlled, as the call-up papers indicated.

But reality was sometimes different. Examples in Czech archives show how this worked. Each recruit had to bring with him documents that established his German nationality, immersion in German culture and showed that he had taken part in the appropriate German Nazi activities. To prove that he was Aryan, the recruit had to show the following documents where appropriate:

1. His birth certificate or a certificate authorised by a vicar.
2. Proof of the right to vote (*Ahnenpass*).

3. Educational and trade documents that showed he had completed an apprenticeship.
4. His work record (*Arbeitsbuch*) that showed he had fulfilled his labour duty.
5. Documents showing he had been a member of the Hitler Youth (which included army, navy and air force sections), together with any certificates for specialist training.[35]

These demonstrated that the recruit had the correct racial and cultural background. The army also needed to know whether the recruit had been given any special training that would make him suitable for the navy or air force or had shown sporting ability. In every case the youth courses had been arranged by a Nazi organisation – the call-up document refers to 11 groups – and these issued certificates. The complexity of this structure of state organisations shows that it was impossible for young German men and women to escape Nazi influence. It covered every aspect of life. This made most if not all of them ready to obey Hitler's commands as they were passed down through the party and state system. It also made them potential enemies of Czechs and ready to take part in anti-Czech activities.

This was all taken into account by the judges in the retribution courts. They knew that Henlein's SdP Party, like the Nazi Party that replaced it, attracted many young lower-middle-class men, but often these had done little during the war that could be punished severely. The list of those brought before the court reads like a cross-section of Sudeten society. In the case of the Cheb court, most were in their 30s and 40s; a few were retired. Every occupation was included, from coachmen to peasant farmers, teachers, gamekeepers, skilled artisans and industrial workers of all types, besides bakers, butchers, postmen, stone masons and many others.[36] This was to be expected in view of the general appeal of the Nazi ideals. Their crimes were not generally held to be severe and they received sentences ranging from eight months to eight years. Those who had committed more serious crimes against Czech people, as in the case of the members of the Gestapo, SS and SD received appropriate punishment. But there were also examples of well-educated people who received light sentences, which probably reflected the desire of the courts in time to be more lenient. Their sentences equalled the time they had already spent in prison and they were immediately released. Adolf Hegenbarth at Karlovy Vary, born in 1892, was a professor of architecture. His sentence was 18 months. František Heinzl of Pernick, born in 1900, was a headmaster of a town school, ten months. Ludvík Kasseckert of Nové Metternich, born 1914, was a professor of a commercial college, sentenced to five years' imprisonment.[37] These were the exceptions. The experience of these retribution courts is that justice was carried out on the same principles as at Nuremberg, though at a much lower social and political level. Since the expulsion of the Sudeten Germans, the Sudeten German Party has never criticised these courts or their decisions, which it would certainly have done if it had only represented Czech revenge or been politically motivated.

The Small Decree and offences against national honour

The Great Decree had been intended to form the basis for punishing all those who, in the eyes of the Czechs, were war criminals. The decree was therefore framed to include all who could be considered 'enemies of the state'. No one initially knew how many would have to be tried or how long the preparation and trials would take. To ensure that no one who might be considered a criminal could escape, many Czechs as well as Germans were arrested. In an attempt to minimise the damage to society and 'cleanse' it quickly, a time limit was set. The trials were to end in June 1946, one year after the Great Decree had become law. As this approached, great efforts were made to clear the very large number of remaining cases. Courts discovered that many of those who had been arrested had been the victims of hearsay evidence of merely personal rivalry and vindictiveness. These were released. But there remained many who were considered by the Communists – a major force in the government – to be guilty of crimes against the people. The Communists also considered that at least some of those who had already been tried and either found not guilty or had been given light sentences were in fact serious criminals. Their crimes, if crimes they were, were ideological rather than criminal. The Communist leader,

Klement Gottwald, demanded that a new crime of 'offence against national honour' should be created. The result was that after much argument and discussion in parliament, the decree on national honour (no. 138/1945) – the Small Decree – was passed.[38] The definition of this crime was extraordinarily broad, for it covered all 'unbecoming behaviour insulting to the national sentiments of the Czech or Slovak people'. In practice this was interpreted as any attempt by people of mixed Hungarian-Slovak or Czech-German race to get Hungarian or German nationality. It also included any form of support, written or spoken, for the Nazis, and any attempt to gain favour with them or seek personal advancement. Finally it covered anyone who had terrorised Czechs or Slovaks in support of the occupying powers. This wide-ranging and vindictive decree judged people against a totally unrealistic standard, especially in a state where mixed marriages had been common.

The best example of a victim of this is perhaps František Holík, a retired police captain in Litoměřice in the Sudetenland.[39] After the transfer of the town to Germany in 1938, he quickly realised that he would either have to leave and join the Czech and German refugees or face a very uncertain future as part of a despised minority under a harsh Nazi regime. Aged 63, it was hard for him to move. He would lose everything and as a pensioner he could not hope to start again and make a new life. In any case, he probably considered that as a pensioner he could live quietly and unobtrusively. He therefore opted for German nationality. His case came before the court as a person who had offended national honour. But although he was found guilty, his punishment of public censure was mild, though this carried the additional disadvantage of being considered 'unreliable' and reduced him to the status of a second-class citizen. For those of working age, this was a serious penalty, for it made it virtually impossible for the person to get employment.

Zikmund Hess, a Polish railway worker from Český Těšín, was accused of working for the German railways and taking German nationality.[40] As a Pole, Hess was a member of an unpopular minority in the Ostrava-Karviná area. He may even have attempted to gain Czechoslovak citizenship during the First Republic and been refused.

There had been years of Czech–Polish rivalry and Poland had finally been able to seize the disputed territory north of Ostrava in 1938. Taking German nationality seemed a sensible decision to avoid the stigma of being Polish. The court found him guilty and he had to pay a fine of 12,000 crowns. But this was not the end of the matter because, as his wife said in a letter to the president, she and her husband faced destitution because he had no 'certificate of national reliability'. This threat of being found guilty by the courts – even when people had already been tried and declared innocent – hung over them until the end of April 1946, when the decree officially ended. In retrospect, both the Great and Small Decrees were, in strict legal terms, unjust in that they punished people for crimes that only existed after the war had ended. The Beneš government's Great Decree was an attempt to punish those who had taken the German and Hungarian side and helped terrorise their own compatriots. The Small Decree was a Communist attempt to punish all those whom the party considered in some way 'enemies of the people'. Both delayed attempts to form a more normal peacetime government and administration.

The expulsion of the Sudeten Germans

The decision to expel Sudeten Germans had been taken by Beneš' government in exile in London during the war and had received the support of the Allies. This had been followed in 1944 by a statement that 1.6 million Germans would be expelled from Czechoslovakia and about 800,000 reliable Germans would be allowed to stay.[41] This was not the total Sudeten German population; Beneš had claimed that about 250,000 would be killed during the war and another 500,000 would flee before the end of it. The proposal was submitted to the Allies, who considered that although regrettable, the expulsion was necessary to ensure future peace and would lead to a better balance in Central Europe.

With regard to the Germans who would be allowed to stay, the new Košice government stated, in its programme of April 1945, that Germans would be allowed to remain if they had actively fought against Nazism.[42] Others would be assessed on an individual basis and, if their application was rejected, they would be stripped of their Czechoslovak nationality and expelled with no right of return. It was therefore inevitable that this should have been done once the new government had been able to separate the guilty Sudeten Germans who were to be imprisoned or expelled from those who were pro-Czech who could be allowed to remain. Part of the problem was that prisoners of war captured by the Russians were returned to Czechoslovakia. Many of these were of mixed Czech-German parents and by no means all were supporters of Hitler. The retribution courts formed an essential part of this process of identifying the guilty. Even before then the Czech government had decided that Germans should be rounded up and held in custody while the courts collected evidence. Surveys were made of Sudeten Germans, which formed the basis for arrangements for their transfer under Red Cross supervision.[43] But this applied only to those who were considered likely to be expelled, most of whom were from towns.

In the countryside the Sudeten Germans were left to work on their farms, although the ownership had passed to Czechs and Slovaks, some at least of whom were inexperienced and needed Sudeten German help.[44] Much of the land in the frontier areas inhabited by these people was hilly and of poor quality and needed a great deal of hard work and experience to be cultivated. The Czechs and Slovaks who arrived to take over these farms initially lacked this. The arrest and detention of thousands of Sudeten Germans was, in its own way, a terrifying ordeal for many of them. The eye-witness accounts collected by the Sudeten German Party speak of people being arrested, their possessions seized and of them being held in some cases under appalling conditions. It is important to remember, however, that the camps which were used for this had been created originally by Germans to hold Czechs, Jews, Gypsies and others considered undesirable or merely economic assets to be set to work under inhuman conditions. One Sudeten who was arrested was a lawyer from Friedland, Dr Bermann, who was imprisoned at Terezín.[45] Others, like Ursula Hübler, were sent to internment camps such as the one at Kutná Hora (Kuttenberg), an old hospital that had been used as a military field-dressing station. In April 1946 she was finally sent to Germany.[46]

The original estimate of the total number of Sudeten Germans to be expelled was 747,335.[47] The first proposal was for 12 trains to be sent each day from 1 April: six from the American zone and six from the Soviet. These would carry a total of 1,200 people. By 13 April 172,800 people would have been transported to the American and Soviet zones. However, in addition to these it was claimed that a further 734,617 people independently reached the American zone and 185,518 the Soviet, making a further total of 920,135. The transfer began on 25 January 1946 with one train each day.[48] From February this was increased to two per day and from April this rose to four. On 15 July the number of daily trains was reduced. Transport to the Soviet zone finished on 20 September but continued to the American zone until 10 November.

In addition to these Sudeten Germans there were approximately 130,000 Carpathian Germans in Slovakia.[49] These had played a smaller part in the war than the Sudeten Germans, but they had tried to exert a strong influence on Tusa's wartime government. They were also expelled. The final official result was that by 30 September 608,353 had been transferred by official trains to the Soviet zone and 1,076,873 to the American, making a total of 1,685,226. Whether these figures are accurate is another matter. A more recent estimate is 265,000–270,000 and a German estimate of 300,000–400,000, but these are apparently of economically active people, which excludes women, children and pensioners.[50] It is also at odds with the pre-war total, which was probably reasonably accurate. The estimate of the number of Sudeten Germans who remained in Czechoslovakia is probably better: 134,143 in 1961, which declined to 39,106 in 2001. An additional 30,000 had left Czechoslovakia voluntarily by June 1949. By January 1949, 7,568 former prisoners of war had been sent to Germany and in October 1949 a further 20,000 were allowed into Germany in an attempt to reunite families that had become separated.

The Sudeten German view

The most painful part of this history for the Sudeten Germans is that they believed that Germans had lived in the Sudetenland for at least

800 years and therefore had the right to remain there.[51] They considered that it was their ancestors who had cleared the forests and begun to cultivate what they believed had been 'a virtually uninhabited wasteland'.[52] They considered the expulsion grossly unfair and they frequently claimed that they were opposed to Hitler. They also tended to believe that the German regime in the Protectorate during the war had been relatively benign, as the following statement shows:

> The Czechs were exempted from military service. The food was not worse, perhaps even better than in Germany. As a result of the transfer of numerous armaments factories and other industries and the establishment of vast depots, Bohemia and Moravia became a sort of storeroom for Hitler's war industry. The yield required of these industries as well as of agriculture was, in general, not inferior to the German yield. As in Germany, the Gestapo in Bohemia and Moravia interned the obvious opponents of the Hitler regime in German concentration camps. A part of the Czechs was called up for service in the German war industries. No active resistance to the German armies of occupation, as in Poland, was ever observed, not even in the last weeks of the war. The attempt on Heydrich's life was planned and organised from abroad. The bloody retaliatory measures for this attempt however, especially the destruction of the village of Lidiče and of all its male inhabitants, did raise the spirit of Czech resistance to some extent. These events of course were highly welcome to the Czech propaganda in London. The facts that the Sudeten Germans, as a national group, had no share in the happenings and that only a small group of National Socialist leaders could be responsible for the retaliatory measures for the attempt on Heydrich's life was concealed; and, as in 1938, the Germans were represented as collectively guilty.[53]

However, the Potsdam Conference of August 1945 ignored this view. It returned the Sudetenland to Czechoslovakia and agreed to the expulsion of the Sudeten Germans. In the turmoil that followed the end of hostilities it is believed that 250,000 Germans were killed and most of the rest were sent to Germany. In Sudeten German eyes this amounted to deportation – a crime against humanity and a war crime. This left the members of the political party representing the Sudeten Germans in Germany with a feeling that a serious crime had been committed against them and that they deserved restitution. This was the view publicly expressed first in the early 1950s and repeated in 1984.

The Czech view

In the immediate aftermath of the war the views expressed above were rejected out of hand by Czechs who had experienced or witnessed at first hand the events of the crisis of 1938, the subsequent treatment of Czech minorities in the Sudetenland and the wartime occupation of the Protectorate, especially the persecution following the assassination of Heydrich. Above all, Czechs resented the unspoken claim that the Germans represented a superior culture and level of industrial achievement. The Sudeten Germans' sorrow at leaving their traditional homeland was at odds with Beneš' claim that it was a relatively straightforward matter of no great significance. Those Czechs with a German parent would have seen matters in a different light, because they would have been more aware of the contribution that each had made to the economic, cultural and political success of the First Czechoslovak Republic. They would have been aware, as many were not, of the freedom of Czechs and Germans to intermarry, a freedom that was not confined to an intellectual elite who stood above racial divisions. They, like the more enlightened Sudeten Germans, would have been aware of the Czech domination of the First Republic, which had done little to check the Sudeten resentment. To some extent it was inevitable that in the economic crisis the small firms serving the consumer market should have suffered most. It was unfortunate, from a political as well as a social point of view, that these should have been concentrated in the Sudeten area, which had already suffered serious economic disruption when the new political state boundaries were established after 1918. Masaryk claimed that he was founding a federal state that would in time resemble

Switzerland. Economic distress and the resentment that resulted from it destroyed that hope, though there was probably a greater tolerance by both sides than either the Sudeten Germans or Czechs would have admitted after the war.

After 1945 there were Czech organisations that kept alive the memory of the expulsion of Czechs from their homes in the Sudetenland.[54] These included *Kruh občanů ČR vyhnaných v roce 1938* [Circle of Czech citizens expelled from the border areas in 1938)] and the more radical *Klub českého pohraničí* [Club of the Czech border areas]. There were discussions in London between Czech ex-servicemen and representatives of the Sudeten German community. But both sides were entrenched in their views; the memories of the war were too vivid. The views of Czech exiles were expressed in Jaroslav Stránský, *Odsun Němců z ČSR z hlediska národního a mezinárodního* (The transfer of the Germans from the Czechoslovak Republic from a national and international perspective) (Prague, 1953) and Jaromír Smutný, *Němci v Československu a jejich odsun z republiky* (Germans in Czechoslovakia and their transfer from the Republic) (Prague, 1956). This was followed in 1964 by the publication in London of the first expert historical study by a Czech, Milan Hübl: *The transfer of the Sudeten Germans.* In 1967, the lifting of restrictions on research and writing led to the publication of Jan Křen, *Odsun Němců ve světle nových pramenů* (The transfer of the Germans in the light of new material). This was the first piece of research based on Czech and foreign writing. It placed the transfer in the context of conditions at the end of the war and showed that it was part of a wider international process of European reorganisation. This was followed by further discussion and research but publication was stopped by the Soviet occupation of Czechoslovakia in 1968 and the subsequent 'normalisation' (repression). For 20 years official policy was to restate the earlier, ideologically based view of events, though exiled Czech historians continued to publish in the exiles' Paris magazine *Svědtvi.* After the fall of Communism, Staněk produced a major monograph *Odsun Němců z Československa* (The transfer of Germans from Czechoslovakia) (Prague, 1996) which is now the standard work on the subject. Further research on aspects of the transfer have been encouraged by the Czechoslovak-German Commission of Historians, which has resulted in important work by both young German historians including Volker Zimmermann and Ralph Gabel, as well as Czech historians.

Jewish survivors

Hitler failed to destroy the European Jews completely, but he left only a small remnant. The story of their life in the concentration camps has often been told, but what is less well known is the reaction to the survivors who returned home. Zuzanna Skacelová's family survived in Slovakia but found on their return that it was difficult for her father and the family to get Czechoslovak citizenship. They were still officially Polish as they had been before the war – a situation that had led to her father's arrest and imprisonment when he refused to go to live in Poland. Other situations are recorded by Lyn Smith in her *Forgotten voices of the Holocaust.* For example, when Jan Hartman returned to Prague:

> We got to Prague on a street car, still wearing our striped caps. We got out near our home to find out if our parents had survived. As we got out of the street car in our caps which made it very obvious that we had just come out of a concentration camp, we met a very nice person on the corner of the street who lived in one of our houses.
>
> We asked him 'Could you tell us whether our parents are back?' He said, 'No, but it's wonderful to see you, there is a leak in my ceiling'. That was our return home.[55]

Jan Hartman was luckier than most. Anna Bergman and Josef Perl had worse experiences. When Anna arrived back in Prague she was initially put up in a hotel. Then she was able to stay with a cousin. When the summer came she went to the family home in Trebechovice to reclaim it but found that it had been allocated to other Czechs. She was allocated a room in her sister's house, with no facilities, but friends managed to find and return all the family's valuable jewellery, china and silver cutlery.[56] Josef Perl had a worse experience. When he returned to his house in Veliky Bochkov he was confronted by a man whom he knew, who was carrying a shotgun. 'What!' he said. '*You* are still alive! Get off this property!' I said, 'But this is mine.' 'No more, this is all mine now.' Although Josef also had a gun, he decided that he wasn't going to lose his life over a house. He left, wept and then went to Budapest where he had been told he could get help.[57]

The postwar experience of many survivors of the Holocaust is that often the other members of their families had been killed. As a result, at family celebrations such as *barmitzvahs* and weddings there are no family relatives, whereas before the war there had been 50 or 60. The survivors are those who escaped on the *Kindertransporte*, or were hidden, taken in and brought up by Christian families as their own or survived the concentration camps and the subsequent death marches.

Post-Communist attempts at reconciliation

The Communist regime that governed Czechoslovakia from 1948 to 1989 deliberately fostered the view that West Germany was still a fascist state that wanted to conquer Central Europe. Seen from this perspective the role of the USSR was to protect the states under its control. This allowed no room for any consideration of justice in the Sudeten German claims or of a possible Czech response. At a human level, Sudeten Germans continued to show an interest in the areas where they and their parents had lived. They still do so, visiting former Sudeten German villages, restoring graves and tracing family histories.[58] Ursula Hübler's account of her return to Prague in 1962 shows this only too clearly.[59] The fall of Communism in 1989 provided an opportunity for both Czechs and Germans to try and begin some form of reconciliation. In 1997 both Václav Havel and Franz Niebauer expressed regret for all that had happened during and after the war.[60] The declaration was criticised by a specialist in international law, Otto Kimminich, for four reasons:

1. The resolution of the Council of the League of Nations on 10 January 1939 recognised Germans who had fled from the Sudetenland (most of whom were German Jews, Social Democrats and Communists) as refugees.

2. According to the terms of the German–Czechoslovak Citizenship Treaty of 20 November 1938 the Sudeten Germans were foreign citizens.

3. That international law banned confiscation of foreign property without compensation.

4. The Hungarian Foreign Minister, János Gyöngyösi, had protested successfully early in 1947 against an article justifying expulsion in the Paris Peace Treaty.[61]

This was followed by Petr Pithart, the Czech prime minister, who spoke of the two sides of a common history of Bohemia and Moravia. These statements recognised the moral obligation of both sides to seek reconciliation; but national sentiment among the Czechs was unchanged.[62] This did not end the resentment on both sides. Bavarian politicians, with a large Sudeten German political presence in Munich, continue to court these votes and in the Czech Republic (which separated from Slovakia in 1992) there was a similar hostile reaction to continued Sudeten German claims. In 1998 right-wing Austrian politicians began to voice political complaints. The result was that the assembly of Upper Austria openly criticised the Beneš Decrees that had formed the basis for the expulsion. After similar demands had been made by other Austrian political bodies, the new coalition of the conservative People's Party and the Freedom Party included this in their programme in February 2002. They demanded compensation for the ill treatment of Sudeten Germans along the lines agreed by the German government for forced labourers and surviving Jewish victims of National Socialism. Strong feelings were again voiced in 2002, when the Czech Prime Minister Miloš Zeman made uncomplimentary remarks about Sudeten Germans.[63] On the German side, the building of a *Zentrum gegen Vertreibung* (Centre against expulsion) in Berlin, concerned with recording the expulsion of all ethnic Germans in 1945, was the result of action by Erika Steinbach, the leader of the German Expellees' Association. Tension was further raised in June by Edmund Stoiber, a candidate in the election for Federal Chancellor, who claimed that the Czech Republic must abolish all decrees inconsistent with European values and legal order. In the long term,

Czechs have been unwilling to reject the Beneš decrees because they are afraid that this will open the door to German claims for compensation and also for patriotic nationalistic reasons. At the time of writing, the matter has not been resolved and it is unlikely that it will be in the foreseeable future. It is too closely linked with Czech memories of German treatment during the war and on the German and Austrian side by a belief that they have a legal claim to some form of compensation – victims of Nazi treatment were awarded $500 million by the German government.

But there have also been more encouraging signs that both sides have accepted that wrongs had been done by both sides and that these do not have to be forgotten. Ursula Hübler's account of her treatment at the end of the war ends with a chapter about her return to Prague and meeting Czech former colleagues. She sees this as a step towards a new and more positive future. Stephan Aust and Stephan Burgdorff, in cataloguing the plight of all Germans who were forced to flee to Germany at the end of the war, are careful to point to signs of political reconciliation between Germans and Czechs at the highest political level. The freedom to describe Sudeten–Czech relations in the 1920s and the wartime experience of Czechs in the Allied, Soviet and German armies is also a hopeful sign of moves towards a less biased view of a common history.

There are also other, comparatively minor though significant signs of a practical nature. For example, in the town of Lenora, in Šumova in the south-west of the Czech Republic, the war memorial to the dead of the First World War has inscriptions in both German and Czech. These refer to 'husbands, brothers and sons' who were killed. This is significant for two reasons. It is a conscious effort to reconcile those from the town who fought on opposite sides. Normally, war memorials in the Czech Republic are to Czechs, usually showing soldiers in French or Italian uniforms as members of the Allied forces. Occasionally, as in Český Těšín (the Czech part of what was originally the German town of Teschen), there is a memorial to those who died fighting in the Austro-Hungarian army. In this case the soldier is dressed in an Austrian uniform. There are also two examples of practical help given by both sides in restoring aspects of their common cultural heritage. One is the restoration of the Schwarzenberg Canal in southern Šumava by Czech and German organisations. The other is the rebuilding of a chapel and altars forming a calvary at Borova Lada in south Šumava built in 1860 by Germans, destroyed by the Communists in 1956 and restored by individual Czechs and former inhabitants of the nearby Sudeten German village now named Nový Svět.

In conclusion, the linking of Sudeten German resentment to Hitler's aims at German eastward expansion (*Drang nach Osten*) had disastrous consequences for the Sudeten Germans. They undoubtedly suffered severe economic hardship and some measure of discrimination during the First Republic. It is also clear that many of them were caught up in the nationalistic fervour that accompanied Henlein's bid for power with his SdP Party. Many took an active part in the 1938 Sudeten crisis, when Czechs living in the Sudeten area felt threatened and it appeared for some time that a German invasion from Austria was imminent. After the transfer of the Sudetenland to Germany in September 1938 many began to realise that they had exchanged one set of problems for another, as the Gestapo, SS and SD began to make their presence felt. During the war young Sudeten Germans had to serve in the German armed forces and many fought on the eastern front. Those who survived felt, at least until the defeat at Stalingrad, that they had become members of a master race that was sweeping from victory to victory across Europe. This reinforced any preconceived ideas about their racial superiority over the Czechs with whom they had coexisted for hundreds of years. But, as in the case of Metelmann, successive defeats removed all belief in German superiority, though by the end of the war, many were not prepared to return to the status of second-class citizens in a renewed Czech-dominated Czechoslovakia. The reaction of Czechs to the harsh treatment they had received from March 1939 was inevitable, as was their ill treatment of many Sudeten Germans at the end of the war and in the months that followed. The retribution courts were an attempt to exact just retribution in accordance with international law along the lines of the Nuremberg Trials. The post-Communist re-examination of the expulsion of these Germans has been an attempt to justify the punishment of criminal acts and make amends for similar Czech actions. This has met with some success. But time is needed for both sides to accept their own mistakes as well as those of their former enemies. In the early twenty-first century the matter remains important and unresolved in many people's minds.

NOTES

Introduction

1. Zdeněk Kárník, *České země v éře první republiky (1918–1938); díl první; vznik, budování a zlatá léta republiky (1918–1929)* [The Czech homeland in the period of the First Republic (1918–1938); part 1, the rise, growth and golden summer of the republic (1918–1929)] (Prague, 3 vols, 2000, 2002, 2003), p. 41.

2. Charlotte Natmeßnig, 'The establishment of the Anglo-Czechoslovak Bank: conflicting interests' in Alice Teichova, Terry Gourvish and Agnes Pogány (eds), *Universal banking in the twentieth century; finance, industry and the state in North and Central Europe* (Aldershot, 1994), p. 105.

3. Jan Hájek, 'Origins of the banking system in interwar Czechoslovakia' in ibid, pp. 29–30.

4. For an account of the negotiations between the Bank of England and the Czechoslovak Finance Ministry, see Natmeßnig, 'Establishment of the Anglo-Czechoslovak Bank' in ibid, pp. 96–115.

5. Alice Teichova, *An economic background to Munich; international business and Czechoslovakia 1918–1938* (Cambridge, 1974), pp. 2–3.

6. Ibid, p. 63.

7. Ibid, p. 195.

8. The company records are in the Moravské zemský archiv, Brno.

9. Ibid, pp. 76–9.

10. This led to bitter disputes over the position of the frontier – and thus of control of the coal mines – that caused major Czech–Polish tension throughout the period of the First Republic. Czechs seized the area after the First World War, there was at least one major skirmish between Czech and Polish troops

and Poland demanded, and got, the area after the Munich Conference. If the area had been given to Poland earlier, it would have separated the major Czech iron and steel producers in North Bohemia from their coal mines and severed the Czech rail link to Slovakia.

11. Teichova, *Background to Munich,* pp. 96–103.

12. The company records are in the company's archive at Plzeň. There is also a history of the company: Vladimir Karlický, Petr Hofman, František Janáček and Vlastislav Krátký, *Svět okřidleného šipu; Koncern Škoda Plzeň 1918–1945* [the world of the flying arrow; the Škoda company 1918–1945 (Plzeň, 1999).

13. Ibid, pp. 126, 113.

14. For a history of Tomáš Bat'a see Anthony Cekota, *Entrepreneur extraordinary; the biography of Tomas Bata* (Rome, 1968). The company archives are in the Moravské zemský archiv in Zlín.

15. For a more detailed account of the following see Patrick Crowhurst, 'The Sudeten German problem and the rise and fall of the Sudeten Nazi Party', *Kosmas; Czechoslovak and Central European Journal,* 22 (2008), No. 1, pp. 50–71.

16. *Documents on German Foreign Policy, Ser. DII* (London, 1950), pp. 208–9.

17. Ibid, p. 209.

18. This is the view of Henderson B. Braddick, *Germany, Czechoslovakia and the 'Grand Alliance' in the May Crisis, 1938* (University of Denver Monograph No. 2, 1968–9), pp. 15–126.

Chapter 1 Deepening crisis, the Munich conference and refugees

1. This is discussed at length in Boris Celovsky, *Germanisierung und Genozid; Hitlers Endlösung der tschechischen Frage. Deutsche Dokumente 1933–1945* (Dresden and Brno, 2005), passim.

2. Harry Hanak, 'Great Britain and Czechoslovakia,' in Rechcigl (ed), *Czechoslovakia,* p. 793.

3. J. V. Polišenský, *Britain and Czechoslovakia* (Prague, 1966), pp. 71–5. Seton-Watson is widely known and respected in the Czech Republic and Slovakia; there is a statue of him in Žilina in Slovakia.

4. Stephen Borsody, 'Czechoslovakia and Hungary' in Rechcigl (ed), *Czechoslovakia,* p. 670.

5. Lásló Kontler, *A history of Hungary* (2002), p. 371.

6. Herbert Michaelis and Ernst Schraepler (eds), *Ursachen und Folgen vom deutschen Zusammenbruch 1918 und 1945 bis zur staatlichen Neuordnung Deutschlands in der Gegenwart. Eine Urkunden und Dokumentensammlung zur Zeitgeschichte; vol.*

12, *Das dritte Reich; Das sudetendeutsche Problem; Das Abkommen von München und die Haltung der Großmächte* (Berlin, no publication date), (hereafter referred to as *Das Dritte Reich*), discussion between Ribbentrop, Imrédy and Kánya, 23 August 1938, pp. 273–4.

7. University of Birmingham, Eden Papers, 13/1/68G, Captain Liddell Hart to Eden, 10 June 1938.

8. National Archives, Foreign Office, FO371/21782.

9. E. L. Woodward and Rohan Butler (eds), *Documents on British Foreign Policy 1919–1939; 3rd ser., vol. III 1938–9* (1950), p. 1.

10. Ibid, pp. 1–2.

11. Ibid.

12. A. J. P. Taylor, *The origins of the Second World War* (1964), p.217.

13. Eric W. Pasold, *Ladybird, ladybird* (Manchester 1977), pp. 483–4.

14. Ibid, p. 3.

15. For Hungarian policy, see Kontler, *History of Hungary*, pp. 371–2. The Hungarian army received Austrian weapons when the Austrian army was re-equipped with German, Sir Ralph Glyn to the Foreign Office, Budapest, undated, Eden Papers, 13/1/68E

16. The older part of the town, north of the river, was already Polish. The river at that point forms the frontier. The river is not very wide and normally shallow. It could easily be crossed at any point.

17. Ivo Vondrovský, *Pevnosti; opevnění z let 1936–1938* [Forts; defensive works from the years 1936–1938], (Varnsdorf, Czech Republic, 1993), pp. 53–4, 56.

18. *Documents on British Foreign Policy,* pp. 8–9.

19. University of Birmingham, Eden Papers, 13/1/66Z, Masaryk to Halifax, 12 November 1938.

20. University of Birmingham, Eden Papers, 13/1/66C, Colin R. Coote to Eden, 20 September 1938.

21. Mark Slouka, *The visible world* (2008), p. 79.

22. Ibid, p. 21.

23. *Documents on British Foreign Policy*, Kennard to Halifax, Warsaw, 23 Sept. 1938, Ibid, pp. 24–5, 27, 35.

24. Knox to Halifax, Budapest, 26 Sept. 1938, ibid, p. 37.

25. For a description of the Czech gun see Chris McNab, *Twentieth-century small arms*, p. 149.

26. National Archives, Foreign Office, FO 371/21581, f. 87.

27. Ibid, f. 80.

28. Ibid, ff. 113–14

29. *Documents on German Foreign Policy 1918–1945; Ser. D.,* (1951), p. 1.

30. Ibid, pp. 4–5.

31. Étienne Mantoux, *The Carthaginian Peace or the economic consequences of Mr. Keynes* (London, 1946), p. 18.

32. Ibid. p. 5.

33. *Documents on British Foreign Policy*, Kennard to Halifax, Warsaw, 27 Sept. 1938, ibid, p. 41.

34. Ibid, Newton to Halifax, Prague, 1 Oct. 1938, ibid, p. 62.

35. Ibid, Kennard to Halifax, Warsaw, 1 Oct. 1938, ibid, p. 93.

36. National Archives, Foreign Office, FO 371/21581, ff. 133–4.

37. *Documents on British Foreign Policy*, Halifax to British Delegation, Foreign Office, 29 Sept. 1938, ibid, pp. 48–9.

38. See for example the copy of the transfer moratorium in the Tatra company archives, Kopřivnice, Böhmische Escompte Bank to Dr Hans Ringhoffer, Prague 3 Sept. 1938.

39. Minutes of the Third Meeting of the International Commission, Berlin, 1 Oct. 1938, *Documents on German Foreign Policy*, p. 12.

40. František Kavka, *An outline of Czechoslovak history* (Prague, 1960), p. 5.

41. *Documents on British Foreign Policy*, Newton to Halifax, Prague, 1 Oct. 1938, p. 67.

42. Ibid, p. 77, Note by Roberts, Foreign Office, 2 Oct. 1938.

43. Ibid, pp. 15–16, Memorandum by Foreign Ministry official, Berlin, 2 Oct. 1938.

44. There was considerable rivalry between Germans and Czechs from the second half of the nineteenth century. For details see Karel Jiřík, 'Vítkovice – nejvice germanizovaná obec v Předlitavsku' [Vítkovice – the most Germanised area in pre-Lithuania], *Ostrava*, 16, (1991), pp. 162–95.

45. University of Birmingham, Eden Papers, 13/1/66P, Sir Roger Lumley to Eden, 2 October 1938

46. One example is the town of Žatec in north-west Bohemia shown in Peter Glotz, *Vyhnání; České země jako poučný případ* [Exile; the example of the Czech lands], (Prague, Litomyšl, 2006), p. 99.

47. Ibid, p. 102.

48. Pasold, *Ladybird*, p. 486.

49. The following is from Herbert Michaelis and Ernst Schraepler (eds), *Ursachen und Folgen; Vom deutschen Zusammenbruch 1918 und 1945 bis zur staatlichen Neuordnung Deutschlands in der Gegenwart; Part 12, Das Dritte Reich; Das sudetendeutsche Problem; Das Abkommen von München und das Haltung der Grossmächte* (Berlin, no date), pp. 481–2.

50. German military archives, Freiburg, RH64/18, Kriegstagebuch des H. Gru. Kdo. 3, 3 Oct. 1938

51. Ibid.

52. Michaelis and Schraepler (eds), *Das Dritte Reich,* pp. 489–90, Telegram from Henke, Prague, 4 Oct. 1938, *Documents on German Foreign Policy,* Memorandum of State Secretary, 4 Oct. 1938, p. 30.

53. Ibid, pp. 32–3, Protocol signed by German Foreign Minister and British, French and Italian ambassadors, Berlin, 5 Oct. 1938.

54. Memorandum by State Secretary, Berlin, 5 Oct. 1938, ibid, pp. 33–4.

55. The following is based on Ivo K. Feierabend, 'The Second Czech Republic, September 1938 – March 1939' in Miloslav Rechcigl, Jr., (ed), *Czechoslovakia past and present, vol. 1; International, social and economic aspects* (Hague, 1968), pp. 65–75.

56. Memorandum by the Director of the Political Department, Berlin, 7 Oct. 1938, ibid, pp. 46–9.

57. Jan Gebhart and Jan Kuklík, *Druhá republika 1938–1939; svár demokracie a totality v politickém, společenském a kulturním životě* [The Second Republic 1938–1939; the quarrel between democracy and totalitanianism in political, economic and cultural life] (Prague, 2004), p. 163.

58. Beneš et al, *Facing History,* p. 117.

59. Oldřich Svoboda, *Češi v Opavě a na Opavsku, 1938–1945; vzpomínky III* [Czechs in and around Opava, 1938–1945; recollections III] (Prague, 2003), p.16. The book contains the recollections of Czechs living there and who witnessed the events.

60. Radan Lášek, *Jednotka určení SOS* [SOS; determined forces] (SOS was the frontier defence force) (Prague, 2006), pp. 92–3.

61. German Military Archives, Freiburg, RH2/298, Lagebericht No. 1, Berlin, 19 March 1939.

62. Jan Kouřil, Jan Bortoš and Jaroslava Čajová, *Zapomenuté pohraničí; Šumvald u Uničova 1938–1945* [Oblivion across the frontier, Šumvald u Uničova 1938–1945] (Prague, 1999), passim.

63. Nikolaus Wachsmann, *Hitler's prisons; legal terror in Nazi Germany* (New Haven & London, 2004), p. 200.

64. Keitel to the Foreign Ministry, Berlin, 10 Oct. 1939, *Documents on German Foreign Policy,* p. 53.

65. Pasold, *Ladybird,* pp. 486–7.

66. Volker Zimmermann, *Die Sudetendeutshe im NS-Staat* (Essen 1999), p. 189–90.

67. Harold James, *The Deutsche Bank and the Nazi economic war against the Jews* (Cambridge, 2001), pp 148–9.

68. National Archives, Foreign Office, FO 371/21581, ff 70, 1189.

69. The text is in Michaelis and Schraepeler (eds), *Das Drite Reich,* pp. 505–6.

70. The passage in Hitler's speech was:: 'It only needs that in England, instead of Chamberlain, Mr Duff Cooper or Mr Eden or Mr Churchill should come to

power, and then we know quite well that it would be the aim of these men immediately to begin a new World War'.

71. *Documents on German Foreign Policy,* pp. 305–6.

72. Weizsäcker to Ott, Berlin, 11 Oct. 1938, ibid, pp. 681–2.

73. Oderberg (Czech Bohumin) was an important railway junction between the Vienna–Warsaw line and the Prague–Slovakia line. It was also an industrial town with chemical and other factories.

74. For details of these bunkers that were similar in design to the Czech, see Ivo Vondrovský, *Pevnosti; Opevnění z let 1936–1938 na Slovensku* (Varnsdorf, 1993), passim.

75. Circular from State Secretary, Berlin, 31 Oct. 1938, *Documents on German Foreign Policy,* p. 117.

76. Hitler's directive to the Wehrmacht, Berlin, 21 Oct. 1938, ibid, pp. 99–100. It is also in *Das Dritte Reich,* pp.534–5.

77. Pasold, *Ladybird,* p. 487.

78. For details of the German terror campaign against Czechs, see Volker Zimmermann, *Die Sudetendeutschen im NS-Staat* (Essen, 1999), pp. 98–100.

79. This and subsequent statements are in the Archiv města, Plzeň, Příloha a prohlašení, 18 Nov. 1938, č. 887.

80. Ibid, 16 Nov. 1938.

81. Ibid, 12 Nov. 1938.

82. Ibid, 17 Nov. 1938.

83. German Military Archives, Freiburg, RH2/298, Lagebericht No. 1, Berlin 19 March 1939, Lagebericht No. 2, 25 March 1939.

84. Evans, *Third Reich in power,* p. 685.

85. Vítkovice company archives, Ostrava, VHHT/10, Hlášení zabykání v Kotsbasích, 1938–9.

86. The following is based on the Státní okresní archiv, Ústí nad Labem, archives of the Landrat 1938–1945, karton 1.

87. The following is based on Ladislav Deák, *Viedenská arbitráž; 2 November 1938; Dokumenty II, okupácia (2 November 1938–14 marec 1939)* [The Vienna Arbitration, 2 November 1938; Documents II; occupation (2 November 1938 – 14 March 1939)] (Martin, 2003), passim.

88. Report of 9 November 1938, ibid, pp. 39–40.

89. Report of 12 November 1938, ibid, p. 50.

90. Report of 14 November 1938, ibid, pp. 55–6.

91. Report of 16 November 1938, ibid, p. 39.

92. Report of 16 November 1938, ibid, p. 72.

93. Report of 20 November 1938, ibid, p. 82.

94. Report of 21 November, ibid, p. 89.
95. Špiesz, *Dejiny Slovenska*, p. 205
96. Deák, *Viedenská Arbitráž*, Report of 27 November 1938, ibid, p. 101.
97. Report of 3 December 1938, ibid, p. 130.

Chapter 2 The destruction of Czechoslovakia

1. *Documents on German Foreign Policy 1918–1945, Ser. D, vol. IV* (London, 1951), pp. 99–100, Hereafter referred to as DGFP.
2. Ibid, pp. 133–4.
3. Pasold, *Ladybird,* p. 487. The exchange rate valued the Czechoslovak crown at 37½ to the German Reichsmark. This was higher than before Munich, but factory production costs increased by a similar amount.
4. *DGFP, Ser. D, vol. IV,* pp. 135–6.
5. Ibid, pp. 138–9.
6. Ibid, p. 139.
7. Ibid, p. 140.
8. *DGFP, Ser. D., Vol. IV,* p. 151, fn. 4.
9. Ibid, p. 144.
10. The same could be said of the decision by the West German government to unite the two parts of Germany after the fall of Communism. This placed a very heavy economic burden on the former Western part of the country.
11. *DGFP, Ser. D., vol. IV,* pp. 149–50.
12. Milan Kučera and Zdeněk Pavlík, 'Czech and Slovak demography' in Jiři Musil (ed), *The end of Czechoslovakia* (Budapest, 1995), p. 15
13. *DGFP, Ser. D., vol. IV,* p. 562.
14. Ibid, pp. 155–6.
15. Ibid, pp. 156–7.
16. Ibid, pp. 163–4.
17. Ibid, p. 167, Memorandum by Woermann, Berlin, 23 November 1938.
18. Ibid, p. 168.
19. Beneš et al, *Facing history*, p. 116.
20. *DGFP, Ser. D., vol. IV,* p. 178.
21. Ibid, p.p. 179–81.
22. Ibid, p.p. 185–6.
23. Ibid, p. 187.
24. Jan Gebhart and Jan Kuklík, *Druhá republika,1938–1939; svár demokracie a totality v Poliitickém, společenském a kulturním životě* [the Second Republic, 1938–1939 the fate of democracy in political economic and cultural life] (Prague, 2004), pp. 163–71.

25. Bundesarchiv, Berlin, R2/13526, Bankwesen in Böhmen und Mähren.

26. Ibid, Deutsches Konsulat, Pressburg to the Auswärtiges Amt, Berlin, 26.10.1938.

27. Škoda archive, Plzeň, K2979, Gř535, Extract from *Neue Wiener Tagblatt, 21 Jan. 1939*.

28. Ctbor Necas, *Vítkovické Železárny v době národní nesvobody 1938–1945* [The Vítkovice steelworks in the time of national captivity 1938–1945] (Ostrava, 1970), p. 18. The transfer had taken place on 8 May 1937.

29. Details of the loan are in the Bank of England archives, TP51, OV6/23–157/4; Czechoslovakia, assets and liabilities.

30. Gebhart and Kuklík, *Druhá republika*, p. 174.

31. Ibid p. 175.

32. The German view was that the Hungarian–Czech frontier discussions should continue as before, *DGFP, Ser. D, .vol. IV*, pp. 206-7.

33. *DGFP, Ser. D., vol. IV*, pp. 209-15.

34. Ibid, p. 215.

35. Ibid, p. 242. Britain reluctantly agreed to the transfer.

36. For general accounts of this meeting from the Slovak point of view see Anton, Špiesz, *Ilustrované dejiny Slovenska na ceste k sebauvedomeniu* (Bratislava, 2002), p. 212 and Dušan Kováč, *Dejiny Slovenska*, (Prague, 1998), pp. 215-16.

37. Ibid, pp. 36–8.

38. *DGFP, Ser. D., vol. IV*, p. 260.

39. Ibid, p. 261.

40. Ibid, p. 270.

41. The following is based on František Fajtl, *Dva Údery pod pás* (Two blows below the belt), (Prague, 1993), passim. This was one of the first accounts by pilots to appear after the fall of Communism. There have been many others since. There is also a film *Tmavo modrý svět* [Dark blue world] which tells the story of two who escaped in this way, subsequently fought in the RAF and the fate of the survivor who returned and was imprisoned after the Communist seizure of power in 1948.

42. Mark Slouka, *The visible world* (London, 2008), pp. 79-80

43. *DGFP, Ser. D., vol. IV*, pp. 273-4.

44. Ibid, pp. 274-5.

45. Quoted in Josef F. Polišensky, *Britain and Czechoslovakia; a study in contacts* (Prague, 1966), p. 76.

46. The text is in Ján Gronský, *Komenované dokumenty k ústivním dějinám Česckoslovenska, I, 1914-1945* (Annotated documents on the history of the development of Czechoslovakia, I, 1914-1945) (Prague, 2005), pp. 341-44.

47. The following is based on Victor S. Mamatey and R. Luža (eds), *A history of the Czechoslovak Republic 1918-1948* (Princeton, 1973), pp. 299 ff.

48. The following is based on Josef Beneš, *Život v odboji; autentické svědectví o osudech čs. vojaká za druhú světově vájky* (Service in wartime; authentic accounts of Czechoslovak soldiers during the Second World war) (Olomouc, 1999), passim.

49. Their accounts are in Jiří Šolc, *Osudná rozhodnutí; kapitoly z historie československého odboje v letech 1939-1945* (Fatal decisions; chapters from the history of the Czechoslovak struggle in the years 1939-1945) (Prague, 2006], passim.

50. National Archives, Foreign Office, FO371/21581, D. Morton to Major Gen. Ismay, 1 Oct. 1938.

51. Evans *The Third Reich in power*, p. 685.

52. German Military Archive Freiburg, ZA1/2022, Verwendung von Beutematerial im Zweiten Weltkrieg.

53. In the light of Rheinhardt's comments, Evans is surely wrong in claiming that 'All of this ... amounted to only a tiny fraction of Germany's military requirements', Evans, *Third Reich*, p. 685.

54. Fajtl, *Dva Údery pod pás*, pp. 13-5.

55. German Military Archive Freiburg, RH2/298, Report on Czechoslovak military stores sent to Berlin, 2 March 1939.

56. Ibid, Lagebericht No. 3, 22 April 1939.

57. Peter Chamberlain and Hilary Doyle, *Encyclopedia of German tanks of World War Two* (London, 2004), p. 42.

58. A British War Office team examined one but considered it too cramped.

59. Ibid, p. 43, David Miller, *Tanks of the world from World War I to the present day* (London, 2004), p. 39, B. T. White, *Tanks and other AFVs of the Blitzkrieg era 1939-1941* (Poole, 1972), pp. 108-9.

60. Ivana Smolka and Jaroslav Folta, (eds) *Studie o technice v českých zemích V; 1918-1945, 1*, [[Studies of Czech technology in the Czech lands] Prague, 1995], p. 520.

61. Mike Spick, *The illustrated directory of fighters* (2004), pp. 24-5, Zbyněk Válka, *Stíhací letedla 1939-45/ Itálie, Francie, SSSR, Československo, Polsko, Holandsko, Švédsko, Austrálie*, (Olomouc, 1999), pp. 77-81.

62. Bundesarchiv, Berlin, R25/50, I. G. Farben to Reichsstelle für Wirtschaftsaufbau, Berlin, 26.10.1938. Negotiations between I. G. Farben and the Aussiger Verein for the purchase of the company and its coal mines did not go smoothly. The Czechs at first demanded a price in currency that could be freely negotiated (Freie Divisen), but German refusals, backed by implied threats, forced the Czechs to accept a relatively low price in German marks.

63. Bundesarchiv, Berlin, R7/997, Tochtergesellschaften der Österreichisch-Alpine Montangesellschaft – Wien, undated. The company also had sales offices in Austria, Prague, Budapest and Milan.

64. Státní oblastní archiv, Plzeň, 359, Prodejna sdruženýz Plzně a okoli v Plzní, 1938-1945.

65. Gronský, *Komentované dokumenty*, pp. 355-9.

66. Škoda archives Plzeň, L29279, Gř535, Steyr to Voss, 11 April 1939.

Chapter 3 The protectorate government

1. G. Hirschfeld, *Nazi rule and Dutch collaboration: the Netherlands under German occupation* (Oxford, 1988), p. 194, quoted in Mark Mazower, *Hitler's empire; Nazi rule in occupied Europe* (2008) p. 270.

2. Ján Gronský, *Komentované dokumenty k ústavním dějinám československa, I, 1914-1945* [Annotated documents on the history of the development of Czechoslovakia] (Prague, 1945), pp. 341-4.

3. *Trial of the major war criminals before the international military tribunal, Nuremberg, 14 Nov. 1945 – 1 Oct. 1946* (Nuremberg, 1949), VIII, 2. henceforth referred to as *Nuremberg Trial*.

4. Anthony Read, *The devil's disciples; the lives and times of Hitler's inner circle* (London, 2004), p. 540.

5. Gronský, *Komentované dokumenty*, pp. 345-6.

6. The background to Neurath's rule as *Reichsprotektor* is given in the *Nuremberg Trial*, vols. XII and XVII, passim.

7. Archiv města, Ostrava, IIB/1186, Deutsche Bücherleien Ausgaben 1942.

8. Archiv města, Ústí nad Labem, Landrat, karton 11, Aussig 31.8.1939.

9. Vojtech Mastny, *The Czechs under Nazi rule; the failure of national resistance* (New York, 1971), p. 65.

10. Ibid, p. 69.

11. Národní archiv, Prague, Alois Berger to Ministerialrat Dr Černak, Prague, 1 April 1939.

12. Zemský archiv, Opava, 2621 I-16 Familienunterstüzung.

13. Státní oblastní archiv, Plzeň, SBR Jachymov, 54/126/27, Betriebsordnung für die Gruben von St Joachnistaler Begbau.

14. Zemský archiv, Opava, archives of the Regierungs Präsident, Inv. č. 1840 contains the correspondence between Röder and the Regierungs Präsident and the latter with the Landräte in Jan. 1939.

15. A description of a German Beamte Aryan card is given in the Archiv města, Plzeň, karton 835, Personalausweise der Beamten des Amtes des Reichsprotektors, 11.9.1939.

16. Mastny, *Czechs under Nazi rule*, pp. 76-7.

17. See, for example, the example of Jan Hartman, who lived in Prague. Both his parents were Jewish but were liberal, upper middle class who did not

practise their religion. They and their son Jan did not think of themselves as Jewish until the German occupation; Lyn Smith, *Forgotten voices of the Holocaust; a new history in the words of the men and women who survived* (London, 2005), p. 9.

18. Mamatey and Luža (eds), *History of the Czech Republic*, p. 300.

19. Státní okresní archiv, Plzeň, Betrachtungen zu dem Probleme der Beschäftigung von Tschechen im Reichsgebiet und insbesondere in der Rüstungsindustrie, Lübeck, 2 Feb. 1940.

20. Statní okresní archiv, Přibram, OÚ, inv. č. 251, úřad práce v Přibami, 29.1.1940.

21. On Czech fascism see Tomáš Pasák, *Český fašismus 1922–1945 a kolaborace 1939–1945* [Czech fascism 1922-1945 and collaboration 1939–1945] (Prague, 1999), Chapters 7 and 8 and pp. 456–7. Emanuel Moravec, *V úloze mouřenmína* [In a dark room] (Pardubice, 2004), an autobiography by a well-known Czech fascist collaborator during the Second World War, ends at Munich.

22. Statní okresní archiv, Přibram, OÚ, Karton 28, Inv. č. 895, documents concerning the prosecution of Vlajka members, June 1940.

23. Jiří Hochman, *Historical dictionary of the Czech state* (London, 1998), p. 132.

24. Zemský archiv, Opava, Kart. 487, Bekanntmachen, Prague, 17 Nov. 1939.

25. Archiv města, Ostrava, kart. 487, inv. č. 3258.

26. German Military Archives, Freiburg, RW 22/1, Kriegstagebuch der RüIn, Prague, 26.8–31.12.1939.

27. Škoda company archives, Plzeň, record card of Ju Dr Josef Fried.

28. Statní okresní archiv, Přibram, OÚ, inv. č. 468.

29. *Nuremberg trials*, XVII, 9.

30. Alena Míšková and Vojtěch Šustek (ed), *Josef Pfitzner a protektorátní Praha v letech 1939–1945* [Josef Pfitzner and the Prague Protectorate in the years 1939–1945] (2 vols, Prague, 2000–1), I, 286.

31. Bohumil Hrabal, *I served the King of England* contains a parody of this. The central figure collaborates with Germans and marries one after a medical examination.

32. Statní okresní archiv, Přbram, inv. č. 362, Oberlandrat, Tábor, 2.4.1941, inv. č. 122. Registration of retired and former Legionnaires.

33. Zemský archiv, Opava, Regierungspräsident, Kundmachung, 7 Aug. 1940.

34. Statní okresní archiv, Přibram, inv. č. 218.

35. Archiv města, Ústi nad Labem, karton 286, Gebietsbefehl, Reichberg, 27.10.1941.

36. Henry Metelmann (born Heinrich Metelmann) became a committed Nazi through membership of the Hitler Youth. His father was a Communist

dockworker in Hamburg and his mother was a committed Christian. Both opposed his views but it was only the experience of fighting on the Russian front that made him change his mind; Henry Metelmann, *Through hell for Hitler* (Staplehurst, 2003), passim. A copy of the Hitler oath for all Germans in the Protectorate is in the Archiv města, Přibram OÚ, inv. č. 473, Gelöbnis, Mar. 1940.

37. Zemský archiv, Opava, Regierungspräsident, 729, dissolution of Young Catholic group, 21.2.1940.

38. Statní okresní archiv, Přibram, inv. č. 62, Bestimmung der Qualification für das Jahr 1940, inv. č. 444; it is clear that the 1940 order was not fully carried out. It was repeated a year later.

39. Statní okresní archiv, Karviná, AO Darkov, inv. č. 23, census returns, undated, but probably 1939.

40. Statní okresní archiv, Přibram, inv.č. 276, Präsidium, 23.2.1940.

41. Ibid, OÚ, inv. č. 729, 735, forbidden books.

42. Archiv města, Ostrava, IIB/1439, Lichtspiel Theatre, 1939, 1942.

43. Statní okresní archiv, Přibram, inv.č. 12, closure of Junák.

44. Beneš et al (eds), *Facing history*, p. 178. The detailed report on the Czech opposition is in Kárný et al (eds), *Protektorátní politika Reinharda Heydricha*, pp. 168–72.

45. Miroslav Kárný, Jaroslava Milotavá and Margita Kárna (eds), *Protektorátní politika Reinhardarda Heydricha* [The policy of Reinhard Heydrich as Reichsprotektor] (Prague, 1991), pp. 124–5.

46. Klaus P. Fisher, *Nazi Germany* (London, 1995), p. 332.

47. Kárný et al (eds), *Protektorátní politika Reinharda Heydricha*, pp. 113–15.

48. Wachsmann, *Hitler's prisons*, p. 200.

49. Beneš et al (eds), *Facing history*, p. 178.

50. Kárný et al (eds), *Protektorátní politika Reinharda Heydricha*, pp. 125–6.

51. Jiří Hochman, *Historical dictionary of the Czech state* (London, 1998), p. 79.

52. M. R. D. Foot, *Resistance* (London, 1979), p. 205.

53. Heydrich never normally travelled without an armed escort but that morning he had been delayed at home and told his escort not to wait. He felt secure because no attack had been made in Prague. In the assassination, Gabčík tried to shoot Heydrich, but his sten gun jammed. Heydrich ordered his driver, Klein, to stop and tried to shoot back. Then another agent, Kubiš, threw a hand grenade which injured Heydrich and Kubiš, who then jumped on a bicycle and escaped with blood streaming down his face. Gabčík then pulled out a second gun and shot Heydrich. Gabčík escaped, disabling Heydrich's driver, Klein, by shooting him in the legs when he tried to follow.

54. The following is based on Zděnek Plachý, *Černé dny naší historie; Protektorát proti Londýnu – 38 dní heydrichiády* [Black days of our history; the Protectorate against London – 38 days of Heydrich revenge] (Nové Sedlo u Lokte, Czech Republic, 2006), passim.

55. Boris Celovsky, *Germanisierung und Genozid. Hitlers Endlösung der tschechischen Frage; Deutsche Dokumente 1933–1945* (Dresden, undated), pp. 327–9.

56. Hochman, *Historical dictionary of the Czech state*, p. 81.

57. His reminiscence is in Magda Hettnerová, Kateřina Hlatká, Jitka Holešínská, Veronika Podušková, Lucie Truhelková, Martin Divíek, Honza Fait, Petr Husička, *Kniha živých; hovory s pamětníky 2. světové války* [The book of life; conversations about the memories of the second world war] (Kostelní Vydří, Czech Republic, 2005), pp. 40–55.

58. The work of the foundation is described in Andreas Wiedemann, *The Reinhard Heydrich Stiftung in Prag 1942–1945* (Dresden, 2003), Czech translation *Nadace Reinharda Heydricha v Praze 1942–1945* (Prague, 2003).

59. Quoted in Wachsmann, *Hitler's prisons*, p. 315.

60. Quoted in Celovsky, *Germanisierung und Genozid*, p. 210.

61. German Military Archives, Freiburg, RW 22/12, Kriegstagebuch der WiRü zu Prag, 1/6–30/9/1942.

62. Plachý, *Protektorát proti Londýnu*, p. 34.

63. For a description of events in Olomouc, see Zbyněk Válka, *Olomouc pod hákovým křížem* [Olomouc under the swastika] (Olomouc, 2001), pp. 83–8.

64. For details of their imprisonment, see Nikolaus Wachsmann, *Hitler's prisons; legal terror in Nazi Germany* (New Haven, 2004), pp. 286, 296, 324.

65. For details of CARBON, IRIDIUM, IRON and the other operations, see Jiří Šolc, *Osudná rozhodnutí; kapitoly z historie československého odboje v letech 1939–1945* [The fatal decision, chapters from the history of the Czechoslovak resistance in the years 1939–1945] (Prague, 2006), pp. 9–42.

Chapter 4   Forced labour

1. There was a sharp public reaction in Britain to the transfer of the Sudetenland to Germany and the subsequent influx of Czech refugees to the remains of Czechoslovakia. This resulted in a large British loan of £10 million to provide money for refugees to emigrate and receive financial help; £4 million of the £10 million was a gift. This was in addition to an appeal by the Lord Mayor of London, which raised a great deal of money. It appears from correspondence in the Bank of England archives that money from the loan reached the Czechoslovak government in time for it to be spent on

helping refugees, including providing work at work camps; Bank of England archives, OV6/23-157/4, correspondence regarding Czechoslovak assets and liabilities January–March 1939, passim.

2. Národní archiv, Prague, Arbeitsamt, Reichsarbeiterminister to Reichsprotektor, Berlin, 15 May 1939.

3. Bernard P. Bellon, *Mercedes in peace and war; automobile workers, 1903–1945* (New York, 1990), p. 252. Others at Mercedes were from France (over 1,600), Holland, Italy, Armenia, Poland and Belgium.

4. Herbert Ulrich, *Fremdarbeiter, politik und praxis des "Ausländer-Einsätzes" in der Kriegswirtshaft des Dritten Reichs* (Berlin, 1985), p. 112.

5. Zemský archiv, Opava, Inv. č. 2109, Landrat.

6. Martin Chalmers (ed), *To the bitter end; the diaries of Victor Klemperer 1942–45* (London, 1999), pp. 6–9.

7. Statní okresní archiv, Příbram, OÚ, Inv. č. 251, úřad práce, Příbram, 29 Feb. 1940.

8. Zemský archiv, Opava, Českomoravské company archives, Verzeichnis der durch das Arbeitsamt abgozogenenen Facharbeiter, Charlottenhütte, 13 Nov. 1943.

9. Havlíková et al, *Museli pracovat*, p. 24.

10. Zemský archiv, Opava, Reich company records, Dr Schreck, der Hauptgeschäftsführer der Wirtschaftsgruppe Glasindustrie zu Wirtschsgruppe Glasindustrie der Zentralverband der Industrie für Böhmen und Mähren, Prague, 30 Mar. 1943.

11. German Military Archives, Freiburg, RW 22/12, Kriegstagebuch der WiRü zu Prag 1/6–30/9/1942.

12. Zemský archiv, Opava, Českomoravské company records, Böhmisch-Mährische Glasfabrik A. G., vorm. S. Reich & Com. to Ředitelství Prague, Krásna, 19 Jan. 1943.

13. Národní archiv, Prague, Arbeitsamt, Leiter der Sektion A to (Arbeits) minister, Prague 11 Sept. 1943.

14. One Czech who had been working for the Todt organisation in Cherbourg escaped after the Allied invasion and tried to get back to the Protectorate. He was arrested by British soldiers and treated as a prisoner of war; Norman Kirby, *1100 miles with Monty; security and intelligence at TAC HQ* (London, 2003), p. 40.

15. F. W. Siedler, 'L'organistion Todt', *Revue d'histoire de la deuxième guerre mondiale et des conflits contemporains,* 134 (London, 1984), p. 55.

16. Achiv města, Ústí nad Labem, Landrat, K2, Aufrufung zum Kriegseinsatz, *Aussiger Tagblatt,* 8 Feb. 1943.

17. German Military Archives, Freiburg, RW 22/52 RüKDo, Prag II, Kriegstagebuch 1.1–31.3.1944.

18. Zemský archiv, Opava, Českomoravské company archives, BMM to Ministerium für Wirtschaft und Arbeit/durch die Wirtschaftsgruppe Glasindustrie, Prague, 17 Apr. 1944.

19. Several letters asking for leave in 1943 are in the Reich company archive. They are from workers in the German railways and the Maschinenfabrik A.G. Plauen und Vogt in Plauen to the director of Reich. The writers evidently hoped that he would be able to get permission for them.

20. Her story is in Stanislava Zvěřinová, *Devatenáct nám bylo pryč.* [At eighteen I was old enough.] (Prague, 2001), passim.

21. For examples of badges at Zeiss, see Walter Rolf, *Zeiss 1905–1945* (Cologne, Weimar, Vienna 2000), p. 279.

22. For examples of some from North Moravia, who served in the German army and navy, see František Emmert, *Češi ve Wehrmacht;* [Czechs in the Wehrmacht] (Prague, 2005).

23. Miroslav Eisenhammer, 'Nasazení studentů středních škol v rámci organizace technische nothilfe', in Zdeňka Kokošková, Jaroslav Pažout (eds), *Museli pracovat pro Říši* (Prague, 2004), pp. 63–73.

24. Sdružený archiv, Vítkovice, Ostrava, Berg und Hüttenwerks Gesellschaft, Draht und Kettenfabrik, Wamberg, Böhmen, 2 Nov. 1944.

25. Statní okresní archiv, Příbram (Sedlčany), Inv. č. 1251, escape of Stanislav Šimak of Petrovice, 17 Oct. 1939.

26. Hettnerová et al, *Kniha živých*, pp. 9–21.

27. Miroslava Langhamerová, 'Otrocká práce vězňů v Litoměřichích' [Slave labourers at Litoměřicích] in Kokošková (ed), *Museli pracovat*, pp. 148–54.

28. A picture of the anti-tank ditch at Olomouc is in Válka, *Olomouc* p. 80, IV and for Brno is in Válka, *Brno*, p. 106.

29. German Military Archives, Freiburg, RW20/8/20, Lagebericht der Rüstunsinspektion, VIII, Heft 4, 15.8.1940–13.3.1941, RüIn VIII, 14.8.1940 Bericht der Werkschutzleiters der Tatra Werke in Nesseldorf.

30. The slogan is shown in a photograph in the Škoda car company archives; there are also photographs of decorated floats in the Vítkovice archives.

31. Sdruenžý archiv, Vítkovice, Ostrava, company to Polizeidirektion, Prague, 1 Dec. 1943 and Steindörfer, Rüstungsobmann in Prague to Rüstungobmann at Vítkovice, 17 Dec. 1943.

32. Imperial War Museum Archive, Duxford, Speer papers, Box 56, Der Arbeiteinsatz im Deutschen Reich, 20 Nov. 1942.

33. Statní oblastní archiv, Plzeň Jachymov company records, 54/126/23 report on prisoners of war 1942–5.

34. Archiv města, Ústí nad Labem, Landrat, Marktordnung für die Wochenmärkte und Jahrmärkte in Aussig, undated.

35. Zemský archiv, Opava, Landrat, Inv. č. 730 report 2 Mar. 1942.

36. The background to Jewish history in the First Republic is in Kateřina Čapková, *Češi, Němci, Židů? Národní identita Židů v Čechách 1918-1938* [Czech, German or Jewish? The national identity of Jews in the Czech lands, 1918-1938] (Prague, 2005).

37. Smith, *Forgotten voices*, pp. 48-9.

38. Nicholas Winton is better known in the Czech Republic than in England. A train ran on 1 September 2009 from Prague to London, to commemorate the last of the Winton trains. This was caught in Berlin with Czech orphanage children on 1 September 1939 by the British declaration of war on Germany. Smith, *Forgotten voices*, p. 57. For an account by one who escaped on a Winton train, see Sylva Součková, *Psána osudem a politikou* [Writings of fate and politics] (Prague, 2002). A book is also be published: Věra Gissingová, *Perličky dětství.*[Small pearls of childhood].

39. Statní okresní archiv, Příbram, OÚ, Inv. č. 1284, Politische Expositur im Doberschisch, Kundemachen, 2.7.1940.

40. E. Lewinsohn, 'Aspects of Jewish leadership in Terezín' (Leicester University M. Phil. 2001), pp. 106, 112.

41. Jana René Friesová, *Pevnost mého mládí* [The fortress of my youth] (Prague, 2005).

42. Zbyněk Válka, *Olomouc pod hákovým křížem* [Olomouc under the swastika] (Olomouc, 2001), p. 26.

43. Zbyněk Válka, *Brno pod hákovým křížem* [Brno under the swastika] (Olomouc, 2004), p. 56.

44. The camp was in a village near Lučenec, close to the Hungarian frontier.

45. *V zaje ísmrti; vybrané vzpomínky členů OV ČSBS okresu Most, bývalých vězňů koncentračních táborů nacistické Německa* [Deadly captivity; selected accounts of members of OV ČSBS of the Most district, formerly the site of concentration camps of Nazi Germany] (Most, 1995), passim.

46. František Fajtl, *Dva údery pod pás* [Two blows below the belt] (Prague, 1993). A similar account is given by Honza Fait, in Hettnerová et al, *Kniha živých*, pp. 56-71.

47. Jiří Navrátil was a law student at the Charles University in Prague and was sentenced to 20 years' imprisonment in 1949 for anti-state activity. He was released under an amnesty in 1960; Hettnerová et al, *Kniha živých*, pp. 72-85.

48. Josef Beneš, *Život v odboji; autentické svědectví o osudech čs. vojáků za druhé světové války* [Life in the resistance; authentic witnesses to the fate of Czechoslovak soldiers in the Second World War] (Olomouc, 1999), pp. 11-28.

49. Karlheinz Filipp has tried to explain the progress of his own family from Austrian to Czechoslovak to Sudeten German in *Malí lidé ve velkých dějinách;*

od vlastenecké fronty československé k sudetoněmecké [Little people in a greater historical context; from the Czechoslovak national front to Sudeten German] (Prague, 2005), translated from the German *Misericordia Bohemia* (Dresden, 2003).

50. František Emmert, *Češi v wehrmachtu* [Czechs in the Wehrmacht] (Prague, 2005), pp. 17–33.

Chapter 5 Resources

1. German Military Archives, Freiburg, RH2/298, Einmarsch Tschechen vom 4 Okt 1938–22 April 1939.
2. Ibid, RH8/I/889, Die industrielle Bedeutung der Tschechoslovakei, 1926.
3. The following is based on Norman J. G. Pounds, *The Upper Silesian industrial region* (Indiana, 1958), Chapters VIII–X.
4. Ibid, p. 161.
5. Ibid, p. 182.
6. Bundesarchiv, Berlin, R2/13535. The financial arrangements during the war were handled by the Deutsche Union Bank, the Rumänischen Kreditbank, the Gewerbebank and the Böhmische Escompte Bank.
7. There were nine iron ore mines in Slovakia which produced 78,820 tons in August 1943. Slovakia's other principal output was of manganese (11,448 tons) and coal (66,529); German Military Archives, Freiburg, RW 29/5, Lageberichte der Gruppe Wehrwirtschaft beim Deutschen General beim Slowakischen Verteidigungsministerium, Bd 1, Sept. 1943–Mar. 1944.
8. Ibid, RW 19/66, Wirtschaftsbericht, 17.5.1939.
9. The Böhmische Union Kohlenhandelsgesellschaft m.b.H. in Moravian Ostrava reported a loss; Bundesarchiv, Berlin, R2/13535, Prague, 19.3.1941.
10. R. J. Overy, *War and economy in the Third Reich* (London, 1994), p. 151.
11. These were incorporated into the Reichswerke, although Göring was not able to get complete ownership of Vítkovice until the outbreak of war with Britain. For details of how he tried to achieve this, Overy, *Goering,* p. 113, R. J. Overy, *War and economy in the Third Reich* (London, 1994), pp. 151–2.
12. Vítkovice company archives, Dienstellen: a list of organisations and banks in the Protectorate.
13. German Military Archives, Freiburg, RW 19, Anhang 1/1006, 2.3/2.9.1942, Die wichtigsten Firmen der Tschechoslovakei.
14. Imperial War Museum Archives, Duxford, Speer Papers, Box 6, vol. 175, 5/5/43, iron quotas.
15. Another German bank which gained an important share in the ownership of Czech iron and steel companies was the Deutsche Union Bank. The records

are in the Bundesarchiv in Berlin, R2/13535. I am grateful to Professor Philip Cottrell for this information.

16. Vítkovice company archives, Verkaufstelle vereinigte Eisenwerke, Prague to Witkowitzer Bergbau- und Eisenhütten-Gewerkschaft, Prague, 7 Dec. 1942; letter to Transportbeauftragten der Rüstungskommando, Brno, 15 Jan. 1943.

17. Bundesarchiv, Berlin, R2/13535. The company was Max Graber & Sohn in Bratislava. The Deutsche Bank held shares in Mannesmann.

18. For an example of a complaint about delays in deliveries of raw materials, see Tatra company archives, Hauptausschuss Kraftfahrzeuge beim Reichminister für Rüstung und Kriegsproduktion to Generaldirektor Ringhoffer, Berlin, 9.5.1944.

19. Ibid, President des Reichsbahn-Zentralamts, Berlin to Betriebsführer der Firma Ringhoffer-Tatra-Werke, Berlin, 18.2.1942.

20. German Military Archives, Freiburg, RW 22/12, Kriegstagebuch der Wi. Rü. Zu Prag, 1/6–30/9/1942.

21. Tatra company archives, Hauptgruppe Kraftfahrzeuge, Berlin, 21 Dec. 1944.

22. There was an extensive network of canals and navigable rivers in Central and Northern Europe that included the Rhine, Danube, and Oder Rivers and their tributaries.

23. Imperial War Museum Archives, Duxford, FIAT 755, *Highlights of German iron and steel production technology*, p. 31.

24. Copper and silver were often found together and Czech and Slovak firms were frequently linked, as for example the Kupferwerke Böhmen at Pömmerle in the Sudetenland and the Sandvik Silber und Metallwaren Fabrik at Dolny Hamry in Slovakia, Bundesarchiv, Berlin, R2/13535, Prague 21.3.1941.

25. Germany imported more manganese ore from Romania than Bulgaria in 1944. The prices were different, though this may have reflected quality. Imperial War Museum Archives, Duxford, Speer Papers, Box 343, FD 3046/49, Stichwortartiger Kurzauszug aus dem Bericht der Herren Bergassessor ... vom 3.3–4.4.1944.

26. German Military Archives, Freiburg, RW 29/46a Einzelne Angelegenheiten – Bulgaria, 1941-3.

27. The correspondence is in the Statní narodní archiv, Turkey, Reichswirtschaftsminister to Reichsprotektor, Berlin, 30 Jan. 1940 and ff.

28. Imperial War Museum Archives, Duxford, Box 6, vol. 151, 20.11.1942.

29. Ibid, Speer Papers, Box 6, vol. 157, 1.2.1943.

30. The armed forces' share of aluminium production rose from 52 per cent to 67 per cent by the end of 1943. This seems to have had the result that Swiss

cheese was wrapped with thinner sheets of aluminium to prevent it decaying. This prompted the following dialogue between Milsch and Mueller-Zimmermann on one of Speer's committees: Milsch, 'Can't the cheese be wrapped differently? Each time I eat cheese I get annoyed at the aluminium getting stuck between my teeth.' Mueller-Zimmermann, 'There's nothing to be done; otherwise the cheese would decay.'; Imperial War Museum Archives, Duxford, Speer Papers, Box 6, vol. 187, 21.11.1943.

31. Ibid, BIOS, *German steel foundry methods*, p. 3.

32. There were problems when the Germans tried to introduce the Siemens Martin process at Kladno in September 1942. Three of the leading Czech engineers were taken to Germany and given a course; Ibid, Speer Papers, Box 308, Peine to Reichsministerium für Bewaffnung und Munition, 19. 9. 1942.

33. Škoda, for example, had a very well-equipped laboratory from before the war, but did no research, Ibid, BIOS 43, *Skoda works, Pilsen, Czechoslovakia*, p. 5.

34. *German steel foundry methods*, p. 7.

35. The others were Deutsche Edelstähle (Krefeld), Krupp (Essen), Röchling (Wetzlar) and Bohler Werkseng Stahle at Kopfenberg in Austria, ibid, FIAT 755, *Highlights of German iron and steel production technology*, p. 54; CIOS 31/1001, *German tool and special steel industry*, p. 1.

36. Ibid, p. 6. For information on the importance of hard-cemented carbide projectiles, see Imperial War Museum archives, Duxford, FIAT 772, *German powder metallurgy*, p. 3.

37. The first welded hulls and turrets were apparently made in 1923 for police light armoured cars. But little was known about the thermal effects which may cause cracking in alloy steels during welding. Austenic welding was developed at Woolwich in Britain in 1929 and in Germany in 1933; British Library, Wetherby, CIOS XXXIII, *German research and development in tank armour welding*, pp. 2–3.

38. Ibid, pp. 7–8.

39. Ibid, BIOS 258, *Tests and specifications for the services*. The standard test for welding was that the joints should be able to withstand a pressure of 65 kg/mm^2. There was no crack reliability test for economical electrodes.

40. Vítkovice company archives, Oberschlesisches Steinkohlen-Syndikat; Verkaufsvereingung der Karwiner Steinkohlen Gruben in Teschen, Teschen, 14.4.1945.

41. For details of this aircraft see John Batchelor and Malcolm V. Lowe, *The complete encyclopedia of Flight, 1939–1945* (Lisse, Netherlands, 2004), pp. 278–9. Its top speed of 522 mph was very much faster than any piston-engined aircraft.

42. German Military Archives, Freiburg, RH8/I/5641; Rohstoff Atlas (Berlin, 1941). Although the atlas dates from 1941 it is unlikely the proportion of

output of each country would have changed significantly since the outbreak of war. The data on which the figures were based may in any case have been from 1940 or earlier, since it is unlikely that any new information would have been available after the outbreak of war.

43. German Military Archives, Freiburg, RW 19, I/1243, Deutsches Institut für Bankwissenschaft und Bankwesen, 23.7.1940. There were 16 companies. Britain held shares in all of them, ranging from total control to one-third of the shares.

44. Hitler ordered a winter offensive in Hungary to try and protect the oil-fields there; British Library, Wetherby, CIOS XXXVI–14, *Reich Ministry of Armaments and War Production. Interrogation of Speer – Reich Minister, Saur – Head of Technical Office, Mommsen – Technical Office, Bosch Planning Office; Part III, Summary of Economic and General Manufacturing*, p. 8.

45. Ibid, *German diesel fuels* (US Technical Mission in Europe), p. 4.

46. The following is based on the interrogation of Dr Bütefisch in BIOS report 1697, ibid.

47. Ibid, BIOS 82, *Inspection of Hydrogenation and Fischer-Tropsch plants in West Germany during September 1945*, pp. 2–3, 6–7.

48. In 1938, it was intended that this would be completed in 1946; R. J. Overy, *Goering, the iron man* (London, 1984), p. 83.

49. Ibid, p. 216, Romania was also unwilling to send all its oil to Germany; British Library, Wetherby, CIOS XXVI-14, *Reich Ministry of Armaments and War Production. Interrogation of Speer, Sauer, Mommsen and Bosch. Pt. III*, p. 5.

50. Imperial War Museum Archives, Duxford, Speer Papers, Box 8, vol. 216, Report of 30 June 1944.

51. The Mark III suffered very heavy losses in Russia and North Africa in the first year of the war. 1,900 were lost; Peter Chamberlain and Hilary Doyle, *Encyclopedia of German tanks of World War Two* (London, 2004), p. 66.

52. British Library, Wetherby, *German diesel fuels* (US Technical Mission in Europe), p. 8.

53. For example, the Messerschmitt Bf-109, the most important German fighter during the war, initially had a 635 hp Jumo 201D engine. By the outbreak of war in September 1939 this had been replaced twice, first with the fuel-injected 730 hp Jumo 210 G and later with the fuel-injected 1,100 hp Daimler Benz DB 601A. In January 1941 there was a new version with a 1,300 hp DB 601E and later versions had even more powerful engines, giving greater speed. But by the end of the war the aircraft became extremely difficult to fly, especially at take-off and landing, because of other changes; Mike Spick, *The illustrated directory of fighters* (London, 2004), pp. 264–70.

54. The Messerschmitt Bf-109 had fuel injection before the Spitfire. Rolls Royce engineers and designers continued to believe for some time that a carburettor was more efficient.

55. German Military Archives, Freiburg, Report of 14.6.1939.

56. Národní banka archiv, Prague, protocole 31 Jan. 1937.

57. Ibid, protocole finale confidentiel annexe à l'accord de paiement, 31 March 1938.

58. German Military Archives, Freiburg, RW19/1582, OKW report, 11 Oct. 1938.

59. Moravský zemský archiv, Brno, Apollo company records, H127/11, Apollo-Mineralöl-Raffinerie A. G. to Dr Neumann, Pressburg, 16 Oct. 1939.

60. Ibid, 16 Oct. 1939.

61. Ibid, H127/6, Apollo Nafta to Dr Fischer, director of I. G. Farben, Berlin, 6 September 1939.

62. Vítkovice archives, letter from EFBE Werke, Franz Brauner, Freudenthal, to the Industrie und Handelskammer in Troppau, 3 Apr. 1940.

63. Ibid, Seznam zevřených stanic, 12 Sept. 1939.

64. National Archives, FO371/21581, W. Hough to Viscount Halifax, Prague, 11 Oct. 1938.

65. German Military Archives, Freiburg, RW19/2327, Donau Denkschrift, 8 Nov. 1939.

66. Ibid, RW 19/49, WO1-8/278, 16.12.1938.

67. The company also owned coalfields and the Mohacs-Fünf Kirchen Railway in Hungary and a Bulgarian shipping company, ibid.

68. For details of the extensive system of waterways, see Vítkovice archives, Oberkommando des Heeres to Daimler Benz, Berlin, 2 May 1943.

69. German Military Archives, Freiburg, RW 29/5, Lageberichte der Gruppe Wehrwirtschaft beim Deutschen General beim Slowakischen Verteidigungsministerium, Bd 1, Sept. 1943-Mar. 1944.

70. British Library, Wetherby, BIOS 513, *Notes on the organisation of the German Petroleum Industry during the War.*

71. Ibid, BIOS 119, *Deutsche Versuchsanstalt für Luftfahrt (DVL) Institut für Betriebstoff Forschung.*

72. Ibid, *German diesel fuels* (US Technical Mission in Europe), pp. 4–5.

73. Ibid, CIOS CXXVI-13, pp. 7–8, *Reich Minister of Armaments and War Production. Interrogation of Speer, Sauer, Mommsen and Bosch.*

74. Narodni archiv, Prague, 3128, Bericht über die Untersuchung der Verarbeitungskosten der Oderfurter Mineralölwerke Akt. Ges. In Prag, Mineralölraffinerie in Mährisch-Ostrau – Oderfurt.

75. Ibid, Apollo Nafta to Arbeitsministerium in Prague, 20 June 1940.

76. Ibid H127/10, Rundschreiben 31 Mar. 1942 and H127/11, Zentralverband des Handels für Böhmen und Mähren, 15 Mar. 1943.

77. British Library, Wetherby, BIOS *Report on visit to Czechoslovakia 16th November to 9th October*, p. 10.

78. Denis Richards and Hilary St George Saunders, *The fight avails, vol. 2* (London, 1975), p. 348.

79. Moravský zemský archiv, Brno, Apollo Nafta company records, H127/1, Bilančno denik, Bericht über die Zeit vom 1. bis 15. Mai 1942.

80. Ibid, H127/9, Rundschreiben Nr. 18 der Benzinabteilung. Nr. 15/42, Prague, 15 Oct. 1942.

81. Ibid, Prague, 31 Dec. 1942.

82. Ibid, Prague, 29 Dec. 1942.

83. Ibid, H127/6, Deutsche Länderbank to Apollo Nafta Handels A. G., Berlin, 19 May 1943.

84. Ibid, H127/6, Gesellschaftsvertrag der Arbeitsgemeinschaft Schmierstoff-Verteilung/ASV/, Hamburg, 19 Apr. 1943, British Library, Wetherby, *BIOS Report, Notes on the organisation of the German petroleum industry during the war*, passim.

85. Ibid, Abschrift from *Der neue Tag*, 5 Aug. 1944.

86. The following is based on Wetherby, FIAT 667, *Summary report on German automotive engines*, passim.

87. The following is based on Radovan Helt, *Mostecký benzín hoří! Úvod k historii letecké války nad Mostem 1939–1945 pohledem svědků ze země* [Most petrol is on fire! Introduction to the history of the war in the air at Most 1939–1945; a study of the evidence in the country] (Cheb, 2005), passim.

88. Overy, *War and economy in the Third Reich*, p. 151.

89. Captured soldiers were asked what work they had done as civilians. Those wanting to avoid work said they had been deep-sea divers or some other unlikely work, but all were found work of some kind. Stories of life in prison camps and escapes from them were all told by officers.

90. For details of the Armstrong Whitworth Whitley see Batchelor and Lowe, *The complete encyclopedia of Flight*, pp. 60–1, for the raids, see James Wyllie, *The warlord and the renegade; the story of Hermann and Albert Goering* (Stroud, 2006), p. 147.

91. British Library, Wetherby, CIOS 28, *Interrogation of Speer and others*, p. 21.

92. Helt, *Mostecký benzín hoří*, p. 47.

93. British Library, Wetherby, CIOS 28, *Interrogation of Speer and others*, p. 15.

94. Imperial War Museum archives, Duxford, Speer Papers, Report on oil production.

95. Ibid.

96. Ibid.

97. Helt, *Mostecký benzín hoří*, pp. 114–19.
98. The following is based on Peter Hayes, *Industry and ideology; I. G. Farben in the Nazi era* (Cambridge, 1987), pp. 232–43.
99. Dynamit A. G. wanted to buy 15.3 per cent of the shares in Explosia of Prague, a subsidiary of the Aussiger Verein. In this way it would have regained its share of the Czech explosive industry that had passed to Imperial Chemical Industries; ibid, p. 233.

Chapter 6 Beneš' government in exile, the end of the war and the expulsion of Sudeten Germans

1. Quoted in Edward Taborsky, 'Politics in exile, 1939–1945' in Mamatey and Luža (eds), *History of the Czechoslovak Republic*, p. 323.
2. Ibid, p. 327.
3. Ibid, p. 328.
4. Ibid, p. 333.
5. Quoted in ibid, p. 334.
6. The following is based on ibid, pp. 354–61.
7. The events are recorded in Jan B. Uhlíř and Jan Kaplan, *Praha ve stínu hákového kříže* [Prague in the grip of the swastika] (Prague, 2005), pp. 152–73, Rudolf Ströbinger, *Poker o Prahu; posledních 100 dní protektorátu* [Playing, poker for Prague; the last 100 days of the Protectorate] (Olomouc, 1997), pp. 69–77.
8. Ströbinger, *Poker o Prahu*, p. 134.
9. Ludvík Němec, 'Solution of the minorities problem' in Mamatey and Luža (eds), *A history of the Czechoslovak Republic*, p. 416.
10. Mazower, *Dark continent; Europe's twentieth century*, p. 220.
11. Beneš et al (eds), *Facing History*, p. 256.
12. Mazower, *Dark continent*, pp. 220–1.
13. The following is based on Brněnský pochod smrti 1945; mýty a skutečnost' [The Brno death march: myth and reality] in Hynek Fajmon and Kateřina Hloušková (eds), *Konec soužití Čechů a Němců v Československu* [Interpretations of World War II and asymmetric relations between Czechs and Germans in Europe] (Brno, 2005), pp. 63–79.
14. Stefan Aust and Stephan Burgdorff, *Die Flucht. Über die Vetreibung des Deutschen aus dem Osten* (Munich, 2005), p. 120 ff.
15. Ursula Hübler, *Meine Vertreibung aus Prag; Erinnerung an den Prager Aufsand 1945 und seine Folgen* (Munich, 1991), pp. 47–69.
16. Imperial War Museum Archives, Duxford, BIOS, *Report of a visit to Czechoslovakia, 16th November to 9th December 1945*, p. 73.

17. Státní okresní archív, Příbram, Karton 78, Inv. č. 1061, deaths at the hospital.

18. Wilhelm K. Turnwald (ed), *Documents on the expulsion of the Sudeten Germans* (Munich, 1953), passim.

19. Benjamin Frommer, *National cleansing; retribution against Nazi collaborators in postwar Czechoslovakia* (Cambridge, 2005), pp. 77–93.

20. Ibid, pp. 268–93.

21. Hübler, *Vertreibung aus Prag*, p. 7.

22. A greater proportion of those sentenced to death were executed – 91 per cent (686 of 723 sentenced) – than in any other occupied country; Frommer, *National cleansing*, p. 91. The next largest was Norway, 88 per cent, of a much smaller number (22 out of 25).

23. Ibid, pp. 108, 129, 659.

24. Ibid, pp 97, 113–14, 479, 653.

25. Ibid, pp. 57–8, 84, 90, 124, 681.

26. Imperial War Museum Archives, Duxford, CIOS 143, *Skoda works, Pilsen, Czechoslovakia*, pp. 7, 11.

27. Ibid, p. 74.

28. Václav Jiřík, *Nedaleko od Norimberku; z dějin retribučních soudů v západních Čechách* [Not far from Nuremberg; from the history of the retribution courts in western Bohemia] (Cheb, 2000) pp. 479, 491, 629.

29. Imperial War Museum Archives, Duxford, *Skoda works, Pilsen*, p. 27.

30. Alena Míšková, Vojtěch Šustek (eds), *Josef Pfitzner a protektorátní Praha v letech 1939–1945* [Josef Pfitzner and the Prague Protectorate 1939–1945] (2 vols, Prague, 2000, 2001), I, 289.

31. He was tried and executed after the war, though some Czechs considered this excessive. Frommer, *National cleansing*, pp. 98–9.

32. Ibid, pp. 408–10.

33. During the war he fought as a tank commander on the eastern front and gradually realised the myth of Hitler's power. By the end of the war he had been transferred to the West and was taken prisoner. He stayed in Britain and changed his name; Henry Metelmann, *Through hell for Hitler. A dramatic first-hand account of fighting on the Eastern Front with the Wehrmacht* (Staplehurst, 2003), passim.

34. German Military Archives, Freiburg, RH 21/1422 Oberkommando des Heeres/Generalstab des Heeres. Recruitment of Freiwillige units to fight the Russians. Those allowed to join the SS were Finns, Estonians, Latvians, Cossacks, Ukrainians, Ruthenes, Indians, Romanians, Bulgarians, Norwegians, Dutch, Belgians and French. There was also a unit of 'East Turks' named Hasan al Raschid. There were similar regulations

about those allowed to join the army: *Ostvölker* (except Cossacks), Poles, Hungarians, Italians, Spaniards, Slovaks, Croatians, Lithuanians and Arabs.

35. Archiv město, Ústí nad Labem, Landrat, Bekanntmachung über die Erfassung der Dienstpflichtigen des Jahrganges 1925.
36. Jiřík, *Nedaleko od Norimberku*, pp. 626–85.
37. Ibid, pp, 187–8, 641–2, 647.
38. Frommer, *National cleansing*, pp. 187–227.
39. Ibid, p. 226.
40. Ibid, pp. 209–10
41. Ludvík Němec, 'Solution of the minorities problem', in Mamatey and Luža (eds), *History of the Czechoslovak Republic*, pp. 416–22.
42. The new Czechoslovak government had been formed in the eastern Slovak town of Košice by the Russians. It was broadly left-wing , but the Communist members followed a moderate policy. Beneš returned to Czechoslovakia once the fighting had stopped.
43. For a description of how this was done in České Budějovice, Jiří Petráš, 'Odsun Němců z Českých Budějovic' [Departure of Germans from Český Budějovice] in Zdeňka Kokošková, Jiří Kocián and Stanislav Kokoška (eds), *Československo na rozhraní dvou epoch nesvobody*, [Czechoslovakia at the boundary between two evil states] (Prague, 2005), pp. 242–7.
44. Wilhelm K. Turnwald, *Documents on the expulsion of the Sudeten Germans*, (Munich, 1983), pp. 128–30.
45. Ibid, p. 139.
46. Hübler, *Vertreibung aus Prag*, pp. 70–130.
47. Král, *Deutschen in der Tschechoslovakei 1933–1947*, pp. 596–8.
48. Němec, Solution of the minorities problem', in Mamatey and Luža, (eds), *History of the Czechoslovak Republic*, p. 421.
49. Valdis O. Lumans, 'The ethnic German minority of Slovakia and the Third Reich' *Central European history*, 3: (1982), pp. 266–96.
50. Lukáš Novotný, 'Německá menšina a česko-německé vztahy' [The German minority and Czech–German relations] in Kokošková, Kocian and Kokoška (eds), *Československo na rozhraní dvou epoch nesvobody*, pp. 233–9.
51. Turnwald claims the Germans had lived in Bohemia for a thousand years and built cities in Central Bohemia as well as the borderlands; Turnwald (ed), *Expulsion of the Sudeten Germans*, p. ix.
52. Fritz Peter Habel, *The Sudeten question; brief exposition and documentation*, (Munich, 1984), p. 3.
53. Turnwald, *Expulsion of the Sudeten Germans*, p. xix.
54. The following is based on Beneš et al (eds), *Facing History*, pp. 276–9.

55. Ibid, p. 298.
56. Ibid, pp. 299–300.
57. Ibid, p. 300.
58. Sudeten Germans and their descendants are the main visitors to record offices in Opava and Plzeň which contain the main Sudeten family records.
59. Hübler, *Vertreibung aus Prag*, pp. 137–47.
60. Aust and Burgdorf (eds) *Die Flucht*, p. 116.
61. Arnold Suppan, 'Austrians, Czechs and Sudeten Germans as a Community of Conflict in the Twentieth Century' (Working paper 06–1, Center for Austrian Studies, University of Minnesota), pp. 3–4.
62. Oldřich Tůma, 'Češi a Němci, vyhnání/odsun: nač se ještě ptát?' [Czechs and Germans, expulsion/transfer: are there any more questions to ask?] in Hynek Fajmon, Kateřina Hloušková (eds), *Konec soužití Čechů a Němců v Československu* [Interpretations of World War II and asymmetric relations between Czechs and Germans in Europe] (Brno, 2005), p. 17.
63. Piotr M. Majewski, 'Comparing attitudes of the Czech and Polish representations to the issue of post-war settlement' in ibid, pp. 111–13.

BIBLIOGRAPHY

Primary Sources

Czech Republic

Brno, Moravský zemský archiv (Moravian provincial archive)
Company records of Apollo
Karlovy Vary, Státní okresní archiv (regional archive)
Das Sudetenbuch. Handbuch für den Reichsgau Sudetenland (1940)
Landrat, records of the regional council
Osobní věci zaměstnanců, population records
Karviná, Státní okresní archiv (regional archive)
Gau Schlesien, Einwohnerzahl, Bevölkerung nach Bekenntnissen und
    Muttersprache, census records
Kopřivnice
Company records of Tatra a.s.
Mladá Boleslav, Škoda Auto Museum archiv
Company records of Škoda Auto a.s.
Olomouc, Státní okresní archiv (regional archive)
Company records of Moravia a.s.
Opava, Zemský archiv (provincial archive)
Company records of Báňská a hutní společnost-Železárny, Třinec
Company records of Baňská a hutní železárnská společnost, Třinec
Company records of Bohumínské chemické závody a.s.
Company records of Branecké železárny akciová spol., Branka v Opavě
Company records of Českomoravské sklárny a.s. (Reich a spol.)
Company records of Optimit
Company records of the Berghütte Berg- und Hüttenwerkgesellschaft,
    Teschen O/S

Landrat, records of the regional council
NSDAP, Nazi Party records
Oberpräsident, Troppau, Treuhandbetriebe, records of companies under the control of the Treuhand
Policejní ředitelství v Mor. Ostravě, records of police in Moravian Ostrava
Regierungspräsident, records of the Reich Protectektor
Reichsbund für Deutschen Beamten, records of the Deutsche Beamte
Reichsstatthalter, Personalstand, Familienunterstützung, records of economic support for families
Steuerabzugsbuch, tax correspondence
Vrchní finanční president, Opava (Oberfinanzpräsident) 1938–45, financial records
Ostrava, Archiv města (town archive)
Hauptspiel Theater M. O. Hruschau, theatre records, Hruschau
Landrat, IIB/1186 Deutsche Büchlerien Ausgabe 1942, regional council records of banned books
Registrace uprchlíků podle pracovních záznamů, employment records
Ostrava, Sdružený archiv (group archive)
Vítkovice company archive
Prague, Archiv České národní banky (archive of the Czech national bank)
Records of the Zivnostenska banka for Českomoravské-Kolben Daněk and Škoda
Prague, Národní knihovna (national library)
Prague, Státní ústřední archiv (central archive)
Exportní ústav československý, Czechoslovak export records
Prague, Statní oblastní archiv (national archives)
Hospodářsko-finanční styky: Romania, economic relations
Hospodářsko-finanční styky: Switzerland, economic relations
Hospodářsko-finanční styky: Turkey, economic relations
Úřad říšského protektoraty, Prague, records of the Reich Protector
Příbram, Státní okresní archiv (regional archive)
Manipulační období, administrative records
Okresní Úřad, Příbram, district records, Přibram
Okresní Úřad, Sedlčany, " " Sedlčani
Státní báňské ředitelstvi, Jáchymov , mining records, Jachymov
Úřad práce, employment office records
Plzeň, Archiv města (town archive)
Landrat, records of the regional council
Okresní úřad, records of the district office
Policejní úřady a expository, police records
Plzeň, Škoda company archive
Plzeň, Státní oblastní archiv (regional archive)
Company records of Nejdecká česárna vlny a přádelna na česanou přízi, Nejdek
Company records of N. Urbánek a spol., továrna na hračky, Hartmanovice

Company records of Optimit, optický průmysl Heydegger a spol. v Chomutově
Company records of Státních Dráh v Plzni
Company records of St Joachimsthaler Bergbau Ges.
Ústí nad Labem, Archiv města (town archive)
Company records of Baťa
Landrat, regional council records
Zlín, Moravský zemský archiv (district archive of the Moravian archive in Brno)
Baťa company archives

Germany

Bundesarchiv, Berlin
R2/13526 Bank records
R7/997 Subsidiaries of the Austrian Alpine Montangesellschaft
R25/50, I. G. Farben
German Military Archives, Freiburg im Breisgau
RH2/298 Report on Czechoslovak military stores, 1939
RH2 Reports to General Staff HQ and Economics Ministry
RH5 Military economic-geographic records
RH8/4551 Report on a visit to Škoda, March 1945
RH21 Recruitment of *Freiwillige* units to fight on the Eastern Front
RH31 Reports by German military mission to Romania
RW19 Monthly armaments production reports
RW20 Lageberichte des Rüstungsinspektion
RW22 Kriegstagebüche
RW29 Lageberichte der Gruppe Wirtschaft in Slovakia
RW46 Report on the inspection of Czech industry
ZA1/2022 Building materials in World War II

Britain

Bank of England Archives
TP51 OV2/23–157/4, Czechoslovakia, assets and liabilities
British War Office reports in the Imperial War Museum Archives, Duxford and the British Library, Wetherby (most reports held in both centres)
AL946, Dr Rolf Wagenfuhr, *Rise and fall of the German war economy*
BIOS 34, *Report on interrogation of Dipl.-Ing. Ernest Kniekamp*
BIOS 44 *Report on the visit to Czechoslovakia 16th to 9th November 1945*
BIOS 82 *Inspection of hydrogenation and Fischer-Tropsch plants in West Germany during September 1945*
BIOS 119 *Deutsche Veranstalt für Luftfahrt (DVL) Institut für Betriebstoff Forschung* (German diesel fuels)

BIOS 258 *Tests and specifications for the services*

BIOS 273 *Symposium of interrogation reports on German methods of statistical reporting*

BIOS 313 *Report on visit to Czechoslovakia by Armament Design Department*

BIOS 320 *German aero industry*

BIOS 513 *Notes on the organisation of the German petroleum industry during the war*

BIOS 861 *The Stratton Report on the mission to Germany*

BIOS 922 *Tatra car type 87, v-8 air-cooled engine at rear. By Vauxhall Motors*

BIOS 1378 *Investigation of diesel engines made by Klockner-Humboldt-deutz AG, Cologne, with a view to setting up the manufacture of these engines in this country*

BIOS 1874 *Investigation into the inspection organisation of the German armaments industry*

BIOS C2/273 *German armament development techniques*

BIOS F403 *Interrogation of Dr Rolf Wagenfuhr by Mr John Selwyn at Bau Neuheim, August 4 and 5 1945*

CIOS 18 *History of German tank development, development of the German Waffenträger (Weapons Carrier)*

CIOS 18/2 and 19/7 *Interrogation of Dr Stiele von Heydekampf, President of the Panzer Kommission*

CIOS 25, *Spare parts and provisioning for the German Air Force*

CIOS 69 *Report on a visit to Junkers Werke, Dassau (Jumo and JFA plants)*

CIOS XXIX-44 *Welding of German armoured vehicles*

CIOS XXIX-46 *Armament design and development at the Skoda Works, Pilsen*

CIOS XXVII *Tovarna na nabojky a kovove zbozi, Rokycany, Czechoslovakia*

CIOS XXXI-69 *Spare parts and provisioning in the G. A. F.* [German Air Force]

CIOS XXXI-70 *Skoda works, Pilsen, Czecho-slovakia* and *Skoda Works, Czechoslovakia* (two reports)

CIOS XXXIII *German research and development in tank armour welding*

CIOS XXXVI-14 *Reich Ministry of Armaments and War Production. Interrogation of Speer – Reich Minister, Saar – Head of Technical Services, Mommsen – Technical Office, Bosch – Planning Office; Summary of Economic and General Manufacturing*

CIOS 113 *Automotive target in 12th Army Group area*

CIOS 143 *Skoda Works, Pilsen*

CIOS 323 *Interrogation of General Director K. Frydag and Professor Dr E. Heinkel. Some aspects of German aircraft production during the war*

FIAT 667 *Summary report on German automotive engines*

FIAT 824 *The miscellaneous glass industry of Central Europe*

Imperial War Museum Archives, Duxford

Speer Papers

National Archives, London

FO371/21581, Correspondence on British war preparations

Printed primary sources

Das deutsche Vereinwesen in Böhmen und Mähren (Prague, 1942)

Das Sudetenbuch 1940; Handbuch für den Reichsgau Sudetenland (Teplitz-Schönau, 1940)

Documents on British Foreign Policy 1919–1939, 2nd ser., Vol. XVIII (1980), *3rd ser., vols. 1, 3* (London 1949, 1950)

Documents on German Foreign Policy 1918–1945; Series C (6 vols, London, 1957–83), *Series D, vols I, II, IV, VII* (London, 1950–6)

Geschäftsordnung für die Behörde des Reichstatthalters in Sudetengau in Reichenberg (Liberec, 1941)

Král, Václav (ed), *Die Deutschen in der Tschechoslovakei 1933–1947* (Prague, 1964)

Sudetendeutsches Jahrbuch (Augsburg, Eger and Böhmische Leipa, 1920–1937)

Trial of the major war criminals before the International Military Tribunal, Nuremberg, 14 November 1945–1 October 1946 (Nuremberg, 1949)

Von deutscher Kultur in der Tschechoslovakei; aus Anlaß der Ausstellung für zeitgenössische Kultur in Brünn 1928 (Kassel-Wilhelmshöhe, no date)

Secondary sources

Adler, H. G., *Theresienstadt 1941–1945* (Munich, 1955)

Ailsby, Christopher, *Barbarossa; the German invasion of Russia 1941* (London, 2001)

Albrecht, Catherine, 'Economic nationalism among German Bohemians', *Nationalities Papers,* vol. 24, 1, March 1996, pp. 17–30

Anon, *Státní hospodářství za války a po revoluci* (Prague, 1946)

Arndt, Veronika, *Die Fahne von Saaz; Konrad Henlein in seiner Zeit* (Magdeburg, 1998)

Aust, Stefan and Burgdorff, Stephan (eds), *Die Flucht; über die Vertreibung der Deutschen aus dem Osten* (Munich, 2005)

Barth, Boris, Faltus, Josef, Křen, Jan and Kuba, Eduard (eds), *Konkurence i partnerství; Německé a československé hospodářství v letech 1918–1945* (Prague, 1999)

Batchelor, John and Lowe, Malcolm V., *The complete encyclopedia of flight 1939–1945; a comprehensive guide to aviation* (Lisse, Netherlands, 2004)

Bellon, Bernard P., *Mercedes in peace and war; German automobile workers, 1903–1945,* (New York, 1990)

Beneš, Josef, *Život v odboji; autentické svědectví o osudech čs. vojáků za druhé světové války* (Olomouc, 1999)

Beneš, Zdeněk and Kural, Václav (eds), *Facing history; the evolution of Czech–German relations in the Czech provinces, 1848–1948* (Prague, 2002)

Berend, Iván T. and Ránki, György, *Economic development in East-Central Europe in the 19th and 20th centuries* (London, 1974)

Bergier, Jean-François, *Die Wirtschaftsgeschichte der Schweiz; von den Anfängen bis zur Gegenwart* (Zürich, 1983)

Biman, Stanislav, *Der Fall Grün und das Münchener Abkommen* (Berlin, 1983)

Birkenfeld, Wolfgang (ed), *Georg Thomas. Geschichte der deutschen Wehr- und Rüstungswirtschaft (1918–1943/45)* (Koblenz, 1966)

Boelcke, Willi A., *Deutschlands Rüstung im Zweiten Weltkrieg; Hitlers Konferenzen mit Albert Speer, 1942–1945* (Frankfurt am Main, 1969)

Bohemicus, *Czechoslovakia and the Sudeten Germans* (Prague, 1938)

Bonjour, Edgar, *Geschichte der schweizerischen Neutralität; Kurzfassung* (Basel & Stuttgart, 1978)

Bonjour, Edgar, *Histoire de la neutralité Suisse; quatre siècles de politique extérieure fédérale, vols. IV-VI* (Neuchâtel, 1970)

Boog, Horst, Förster, Jürgen, Hoffmann, Joachim, Klink, Ernst, Müller, Rolf-Dieter and Ueberschär, Gerd R., *Das deutsches Reich und der Zweiten Weltkrieg; Band 4, Der Angriff auf die Sowjetunion* (Stuttgart, 1983)

Borák, Mečislav, *Spravedlnost podle dekretu: Retribuční soudnictví v ČSR a Mimořádný lidový soud v Ostravě (1945–1948)* (Ostrava, 1998)

Boross, Elizabeth A., *Inflation and industry in Hungary* (Berlin, 1995)

Bourgeois, Daniel, 'Les relations économiques Germano-Suisse 1939–1945,' *Revue d'histoire de la deuxième guerre mondiale,* 121 (1981)

Braddick, Henderson B., *Germany, Czechoslovakia and the 'Grand Alliance' in the May Crisis 1938* (University of Denver, 1968–9)

Brandes, Detlev, *Der Weg zur Vertreibung 1938–1945; Pläne und Entscheidungen zum "Transfer" der Deutschen aus der Tschechoslovakei und aus Polen* (Munich, 2001)

Brandes, Detlev, Ivaničková, Edita and Pešek, Jiří, *Erzwungene Trennung: Vertreibung und Aussiedlung in und aus der Tschechoslovakei 1938–1939 im Vergleich mit Polen, Ungarn und Jugoslawien* (Essen, 1999)

Brandes, Detlev, *Die Tschechen unter deutschem Protektorat: Besatzungpolitik, Kollaboration und Widerstand im Protektorat Böhmen und Mähren* (2 vols., Munich, 1969, 1975)

Breznitz, Schlomo, *Memory fields; the legacy of a wartime childhood in Czechoslovakia* (New York, 2001)

Brügel, Johann Wolfgang, *Tschechen und Deutsche 1939–1946* (Munich, 1974)

Bruegel, Johann Wolfgang, *Czechoslovakia before Munich; the German minority problem and British appeasement policy* (Cambridge, 1973)

Bryant, Chad, *Nazi rule and Czech nationalism* (Cambridge, Mass, 2007)

Bullock, Alan, *Hitler: a study in tyranny* (London, 1974)

Calafeteanu, Ion, 'Les relations économiques Germano-Roumaines de 1933 à 1944' *Revue d'histoire de la deuxième guerre mondiale et des conflits contemporains,* 140 (1985), pp. 23–36

Campbell, F. Gregory, *Confrontation in Central Europe; Weimar Germany and Czechoslovakia* (Chicago, 1975)

Čapková, Kateřina, *Češi, Němci, Židi? Národní identita Židů v Čechách 1918–1938* (Prague, 2003)

Carsten, F. L., *Fascist movements in Austria* (London, 1977)

Carsten, F. L., *The First Austrian Republic 1918–1938* (London, 1986)

Cekota, Anthony, *Entrepreneur extraordinary; the biography of Tomas Bata* (Rome, 1968)

Celovsky, Boris, *Germanisierung und Genozid; Hitlers Endlösung der tschechischen Frage. Deutsche Dokumente 1933-1945* (Dresden, no date)

Češi v Opavě a na Opavsku 1938-1945; vzpomínky III (Prague, 2003)

Chalmers, Martin (ed), *To the bitter end; the diaries of Victor Klemperer 1942-45* (London, 1999)

Chamberlain, Peter and Doyle, Hilary, *Encyclopedia of German tanks of World War Two* (London, 2004)

Clark, Alan, *Barbarossa; the Russian-German conflict 1941-1945* (London, 1965)

Cornwall, Mark, 'Dr Eduard Beneš and Czechoslovakia's German Minority 1918-1943' in Morrison, J. (ed), *The Czech and Slovak experience* (London, 1992), pp. 167-202

Cornwall, Mark and Evans, R. J. W. (eds), *Czechoslovakia in a nationalist and fascist Europe, 1918-1948* (Oxford, 2007)

Cottrell, P. L. (ed), *Rebuilding the financial system in Central and Eastern Europe 1918-1994* (Aldershot, 1997)

Crowhurst, Patrick, 'Czechoslovakia, Czech tanks and the Second World War; the Munich conference reconsidered' *Kosmas*, vol. 19, No. 2, pp. 94-111

Crowhurst, Patrick, 'The making of the first Czechoslovak Republic and the national control of companies: the nostrification policy and economic nationalism, 1918-38', *Journal of Industrial History*, 5, (2002), pp. 92-105

Crowhurst, Patrick, 'The Sudeten German problem and the rise and fall of the Sudeten Nazi Party' *Kosmas*, vol. 22, 1, 2008, pp. 50-71

Davies, Norman, *Europe at war 1939-1945; no simple victory* (London, 2006)

Deák, Ladislav, *Viedenská arbitráž; 2 November 1938; Dokumenty II, okupácia (2. November 1938-14. Marec 1939* (Martin, Slovakia, 2003)

Deutsche Gesellschaftsgeschichte, Vierter Band, Vom Beginn des Ersten Weltkriegs bis zur Gründung der beiden deutschen Staaten, 1914-1949 (Munich, 2003)

Das deutsche Vereinwesen in Böhmen und Mähren (Prague, 1942)

Doležal, Jiří and Křen, Jan, *Czechoslovakia's fight; documents on the Resistance Movement of the Czechoslovak People, 1938-1945* (Prague, 1964)

Durčák, Josef, *Opevnění Ostravska v letech 1935 až 1938* (Opava, Czech Republic, 2005)

Eberle, Henrik and Uhl, Matthias (eds), *The Hitler book; the secret report by his two closest aides* (London, 2005)

Eichholz, Dietrich, *Geschichte der deutschen Kriegswirtschaft 1939-1945; Band I: 1919-1941* (Berlin, 1969)

Emmert, František, *Češi ve wehrmachtu; zamlčované osudy* (Prague, 2005)

Epstein, Helen, *Where she came from; a daughter's search for her mother's history* (New York, 1997)

Ericson, John, *The road to Stalingrad, Stalin's war with Germany* (2 vols London, 1975, 1983)

Evans, Richard J., *The Third Reich in power 1933-1939* (London, 2005)

Fajmon, Hynek and Hloušková, Kateřina (eds), *Konec soužití Čechů a Němců v Československu; Sborník k 60. výročí ukončení II. Světové války* (Brno, 2005)

Fajtl, František, *Dva údery pod pás* (Prague, 1993)

Fest, Joachim C., *Hitler* (London, 1982)

Filipp, Karlheinz, *Malí lidé ve velkých dějinách; od vlastenecké fronty československé k sudetoněmecké* (Prague, 2003)

Foot, M. R. D., *Resistance* (London, 1978)

Forstmeier, Friedrich and Volkmann, Hans-Erich, *Wirtschaft und Rüstung am Vorabend des Zweiten Weltkrieges* (Düsseldorf, 1975)

Foud, Karel, Krátký, Vladislav and Vladař, Jan, *Poslední akce; operace amerického a britiského letectva nad územím Čech v dubnu a květnu 1945* (Plzeň, 1997)

Franzel, Emil, *Die Vertreibung Sudetenland 1945-1946* (Landshut, 1979)

Friesová, Jana Renée, *Pevnost mého mládí* (Prague, 2005)

Frommer, Benjamin, *National cleansing; retribution against Nazi collaborators in postwar Czechoslovakia* (Cambridge, 2005)

Gall, Lothar (ed), *Krupp im zwanzigsten Jahrhundert: die Geschichte des Unternehmens vom Ersten Weltkrieg bis zur Gründung der Stiftung* (Berlin, 2002)

Gebel, Ralf, *'Heim ins Reich!' Konrad Henlein und der Reichsgau Sudetenland 1938-1945* (Munich, 2000)

Gebhardt, Bruno, *Handbuch der Deutschen Geschichte; Band 4: Die Zeit der Weltkriege* (Stuttgart, 1960)

Gebhart, Jan and Kuklík, Jan, *Druhá republika 1938-1939; svár demokracie a totality v politickém, společenském a kulturním životě* (Prague, 2004)

Gillingham, John, *Belgian business in the Nazi New Order* (Ghent, 1977)

Glanz, David M., *Before Stalingrad; Barbarossa – Hitler's invasion of Russia 1941* (London, 2003)

Glassheim, E., 'National mythologies and ethnic cleansing; the expulsion of Czechoslovak Germans in 1945' *Central European History,* 33, 4 (2000), pp. 463-86

Glotz, Peter, *Die Vertreibung; Böhmen als Lehrstück* (Berlin, 2004)

Glotz, Peter, *Vyhnání; České země jako poučný případ* (Prague, Litomyšl, 2006)

Gomola, Miroslav, *Automobily Aero aneb cililink a jeho sestry* (Brno, no date)

Graml, Hermann, *Europa zwischen den Kriegen* (Munich, 1969)

Gregor, Neil, *Stern und Hakenkreuz; Daimler Benz im Dritten Reich* (Berlin, 1997)

Gronský, Ján, *Komentované dokumenty k ústavním dějinám Československa, I, 1914-1945* (Prague, 2005)

Grossmann, Kurt R., 'Die Exilsituation in der Tschechoslowakei' in Durzak, Manfred (ed), *Die deutsche Exilliteratur 1933-1945* (Stuttgart, 1973)

Gruber, Josef, *Czechoslovakia; a survey of economic and social conditions* (New York, 1924)

Habel, Fritz Peter, *The Sudeten question; brief exposition and documentation* (Munich, 1984)

Hahnová, Eva and Hahn, Hans Henning, *Sudetoněmecká vzpomínání a zapomínání* (Prague, 2002)

Havlíková, Jana, Hořák, Martin, Jakschová, Viola, Košková, Zdeňka, Kokoška, Stanislav, Koura, Petr, Pažout, Jaroslav and Sedláková, Monika, *Museli pracovat pro Říši; nucené pracovní nasazení českého obyvatelstva v letech 2. světové války* (Prague, 2004)

Hayes, Peter, *Industry and ideology; IG Farben in the Nazi era* (Cambridge 1987)

Heimann, Mary, *Czechoslovakia; the state that failed* (New Haven, Conn., 2011)

Heiss, Friedrich, *Das Böhmen und Mähren Buch; Volkskampf und Reichsraum* (Prague, 1943)

Helt, Radovan, *Mostecký benzín hoří; Úvod k historii letecké války nad Mostem 1939–1945; pohledem svědků ze země* (Cheb, Czech Republic, 2005)

Herbert, Ulrich, *Fremdarbeiter. Politik und Praxis des 'Ausländer-Einsätzes' in der Kriegswirtschaft des Dritten Reiches* (Berlin, 1985)

Hermann, A. H., *A history of the Czechs* (London, 1975)

Herz, Frederick, *The economic problems of the Danubian states; a study in economic nationalism* (London, 1947)

Hettnerová, Magda, Hlatká, Kateřina, Holešínská, Jitka, Podušková, Veronika, Truhelková, Lucie, Fait, Honza and Husička, Petr, *Kniha živých; hovory s pamětníky 2. světové války* (Kostelní Vydří, Czech Republic, 2005)

Hinsley, F. H., *British intelligence in the Second World War. Its influence on strategy and operations* (2 vols, London, 1981)

Hitchins, Keith, *Romania 1866–1947* (London, 1994)

Hochman, Jiří, *Historical dictionary of the Czech state* (London, 1998)

Homza, Edward L., *Foreign labor in Nazi Germany* (Princeton, 1967)

Hübler, Ursula, *Meine Vertreibung aus Prag* (Munich, 1991)

Hull, Oswald, *A geography of production* (London, 1971)

Iggers, Wilmer (ed), *Die Juden in Böhmen und Mähren; ein historisches Lesebuch* (Munich, 1986)

James, Harold, *The Deutsche Bank and the Nazi economic war against the Jews; the expropriation of Jewish-owned property* (Cambridge, 2001)

Jančík, Drahomír and Kubů, Eduard, *'Arizace' a arizátoři; drobný a střední židovský majetek v úvěrech Kreditanstalt der Deutschen (1939–45)* (Prague, 2005).

Jaworski, Rudolf, *Vorposten oder Minderheit? Der sudetendeutsche Volkstumkampf in den Beziehung zwischen Weimarer Republik und CSR* (Stuttgart, 1977)

Jelínek, Zdeněk, 'Nálety na Kolín za druhé světové války', in *Středočeský sborník historický*, 15 (1980), pp. 45–60

Jiráček, Milič, *Válečná generace* (Prague, 2005)

Jiřík, Karel, Klíma, Bohuslav, Myška, Milan, Pitronová, Blanka, and Steiner, Jan,*Dějiny Ostravy* (Ostrava, 1993)

Jiřík, Václav, *Nedaleko od Norimkerku; z dějin retribučních soudů v západních Čechách* (Plzeň, 2000)

Johnson, Owen V., *Slovakia 1918–1938; education and the making of a nation* (Boulder, Col., 1985)

Jung, Rudolf, *Die Tschechen; Tausend Jahre deutsch-tschechischer Kampf* (Berlin, 1937)

Karlický, Vladimír, Hofman, Petr, Janáček, František, Klimek, Antonín and Krátký, Vladislav, *Svět okřídleného šípu; Koncern Škoda Plzeň 1918–1945* (Plzeň, 1999)

Kárník, Zdeněk, *České země v éře První republiky* (3 vols, Prague, 2000, 2002, 2003)

Kárný, Miroslav, Milotová, Jaroslava and Kárná, Margita (eds), *Protektorátní politika Reinharda Heydricha* (Prague, 1991)

Kárný, Miroslav, 'Flossenbürgské komando v Panenských Břežanech,'*Středočeský sborník historický*, 17 (1990), pp. 148–56

Kay, Anthony, *Junkers aircraft and engines, 1913–1945* (London, 2004)

Kershaw, Ian, *Hitler 1936–1945: Nemesis* (London, 2000)

Kieser, R. and Spillmann, K. R. (eds), *The new Switzerland; problems and policies* (Palo Alto, Cal, 1990)

Kirschbaum, Stanislav J., *A history of Slovakia; the struggle for survival* (New York, 1995)

Kliment, Charles K and Nakládal, Břetislav, *Slovenská armáda 1939–1945* (Prague, 2006)

Kokošková, Zděnka, Kocián, Jiří and Kokoška, Stanislav (eds), *Československo na rozhraní dvou epoch nesvobody; sborník z konference k 60. výročí konce druhé světové války* (Prague, 2005)

Kokošková, Zdeňka, Kokoška, Stanislav and Pažout, Stanislav (eds), *Museli pracovat pro Říši; nucené pracovní nasazení českého obyvatelstva v letech 2. světové války* (Prague, 2004)

Kokošková, Zdeňka, Kocian, Jiří and Kokoška, Stanislav (eds), *Československo na rozhraní dvou epoch nesvobody* (Prague, 2005)

Kontler, Lásló, *A history of Hungary* (London, 2002)

Kopecek, Herman, 'Zusammen Arbeit and Spolüprace': Sudeten German-Czech cooperation in interwar Czechoslovakia' *Nationalities Papers*, vol. 24, 1, March 1996, pp. 63–78

Korbel, Josef, *Twentieth century Czechoslovakia; the meaning of its history* (New York, 1977)

Koukolík, Václav and Kvapilová, Alena (eds) *V zajetí smrti; vybrané vzpomínky členů OV ČSBS okresu Most, bývalých vězňů koncentračních táborů nacistického Německa* (Most, Czech Republic, 1995)

Kouřil, Jan, Bartoš, Josef and Čajová, Jaroslava, *Zapomenuté pohraničí; Šumvald u Uničova 1938–1945* (Prague, 1999)

Kováč, Dušan, *Dějiny Slovenska* (Prague, 1998)

Kreis, Georg (ed), *Switzerland and the Second World War* (London, 2000)

Krejčí, Jaroslav and Machonin, Pavel, *Czechoslovakia 1918–1992; a laboratory for social change* (London, 1996)

Krofta, Kamil, *Das Deutschtum in der tschechoslovakischen Geschichte; Zwei Vorträge gehalten in der Prager Urania am 16. April und 16. Mai 1934* (Prague, 1936)

Krůta, Václav, 'Rakovnické keramické závody za druhé světové války (Výroba zboží a jeho realizace)', *Středočeský sborník historický*, 11 (1976), pp. 43-52.

Krůta, Václav, 'Economický vývoj rakovnických keramických závodů v letech 1883-1945', in *Středočeský sborník historícký*, 15 (1980), pp. 79-95

Kučera, Milan and Pavlík, Zdeněk, 'Czech and Slovak demography', in Musil, Jiři (ed), *The end of Czechoslovakia* (Budapest, 1995)

Kudzbel, Marek, *Bata the business miracle; the story of an extraordinary entrepreneur* (Marianka, Slovakia, 2006)

Lášek, Radan, *Jednotka určení* (Prague, 2006)

Lewinsohn, E., 'Aspects of Jewish leadership in Terezin', (Leicester University M. Phil., 2001)

Luh, Andreas, *Der Deutsche Turnverhand in der Ersten Tschechoslowakischen Republik* (Munich, 1988)

Lumans, Valdis O., 'The ethnic German minority of Slovakia and the Third Reich, 1938-1945', *Central European History*, XV, 3 (1982), pp. 266-96

Luža, Radomir, *The transfer of the Sudeten Germans; a study of Czech–German relations, 1933-1962* (New York, 1964)

Macdonald, Callum, Kaplan, Jan, *Prague in the shadow of the swastika: a history of the German occupation, 1939-1945* (Vienna, 2001)

Macoun, Jiří, *Československé pevnosti* (Brno, 2005)

Mamatey, Victor S. and Luža, R. (eds), *A history of the Czechoslovak Republic 1918-1948* (Princeton, 1973)

Manning, Olivia, *The great fortune* (London, 2002)

Mastný, Vojtěch, *Protektorát a osud českého odboje* (Prague, 2003)

Mastný, Vojtěch, *The Czechs under Nazi rule; the failure of national resistance* (New York, 1971)

Mazower, Mark, *Hitler's empire; Nazi rule in occupied Europe* (London, 2008)

Mazower, Mark, *Dark continent: Europe's twentieth century* (London, 1999)

McNab, Chris, *Twentieth-century small arms* (London, 2005)

Meier, Heinz K., 'Les relations de la Suisse avec la Grande-Bretagne et les États-Unis', *Revue d'histoire de la deuxième guerre mondiale*, 121 (1981)

Metelmann, Henry, *Through hell for Hitler; a dramatic first-hand account of fighting on the Eastern Front with the Wehrmacht* (Staplehurst, 2003)

Michel, Bernard, *La mémoire de Prague* (Paris, 1986)

Miller, David, *The illustrated directory of tanks of the world from World War I to the present day* (London, 2004)

Míšková, Alena and Šustek, Vojtěch (eds), *Josef Pfitzner a protektorátní Praha v letech 1939-1945* (2 vols, Prague, 2000, 2001)

Moïsuc, Viorica, 'L'écroulement des alliance de la Roumanie à la veille de la deuxième guerre mondiale,' *Revue d'histoire de la deuxième guerre mondiale et des conflits contemporains*, 140 (1985), pp. 1-22

Moravec, Emanuel, *V úloze mouřenína* (Pardubice, 2004)

Morgenheimer, Heinz, *Hitler's war; Germany's key strategic decisions 1940-1945* (London, 1998)

Morrison, J. (ed), *The Czech and Slovak experience* (London, 1992)

Musil, Jiří, (ed), *The end of Czechoslovakia* (Budapest, 1995)

Nečas, Ctibor, *Vítkovické železárny v době národní nesvobody 1938–1945* (Ostrava, 1970)

Němeček, Jan a kolektiv, *Cesta k dekretům a odsunu Němců* (Prague, 2002)

Nohovcová, Ladislava, Mazný, Petr and Krátký, Vladislav, *Škodovka v historických fotografiích* (Plzeň, 2004)

Orzoff, Andrea, *Battle for the Castle; the myth of Czechoslovakia in Europe, 1914–1948* (Oxford, 2009)

Overy, R. J, *War and economy in the Third Reich* (London, 1994)

Overy, R. J., *Goering, the iron man* (London, 1984)

Overy, Richard, *Interrogations; the Nazi elite in Allied hands, 1945* (London, 2001)

Pajer, Miloslav, 'K vývoji a výrobě raketových zbraní v Příbrami v letech druhé světové války', *Podbrdský, XIII* (2006), pp. 155–171

Parker, J. and Smith, C., *Modern Turkey* (London, 1942)

Pasák, Tomáš, *Český fašismus 1922–1945 a kolaborace 1939–1945* (Prague, 1999)

Pasold, Eric W., *Ladybird, ladybird* (Manchester 1977)

Pavlica, Tomáš, 'Obrněná vozidla z Tatrovky', in Rozenkranz, Karel and Kozlovský, Jan, (eds), *K dějinám Tatry Kopřivnice; sborník příspěvků IV* (Kopřivnice, 1990) pp. 31–50

Paxton, Robert O., *The anatomy of Fascism* (London, 2005)

Plachý, Zdeněk, *Protektorát proti Londýnu – 38 dní heydrichiády* (Nové Sedlo u Lokte, Czech Republic, 2006)

Polišenský, Josef F., *Britain and Czechoslovakia; a study in contacts* (Prague, 1966)

Pollack, Martin, *The dead man in the bunker; discovering my father* (London, 2006)

Pounds, Norman J. G., *The Upper Silesian industrial region* (Indiana, 1958)

Procházka, Theodor, *The Second Republic; the disintegration of post-Munich Czechoslovakia (October 1938-March 1939)* (Boulder, Col., 1981)

Quinlan, Paul D., *Clash over Romania; British and American policies towards Romania: 1938-1947* (Los Angeles, 1977)

Rabl, Kurt, *Staatsbürgerliche Loyalität im Nationalitätenstaat; Dargestellt an den Verhaltnissen in der böhmischen Ländern zwischen 1914 und 1938* (Munich, 1959)

Radvanovský, Zdeněk (ed), *Historie okupovaného pohraničí 1938–1945, 7,* (Ústí nad Labem, 2003), pp. 9–46

Read, Anthony, *The devil's disciples; the lives and times of Hitler's inner circle* (London, 2003)

Rechcigl, Miloslav, Jr (ed), *Czechoslovakia past and present* (The Hague and Paris, 1968)

Rees, Philip, *Biographical dictionary of the extreme right since 1890* (London, 1990)

Rich, Norman, *Hitler's war aims; ideology, the Nazi state and the course of expansion* (London, 1973)

Richards, Denis and Sanders, Hilary St George, *The fight avails* (London, 1975)

Robbins, Keith, *Munich 1938* (London, 1968)

Roden, Rudolf, *Paměť naruby* (Prague, 2003)

Rosenkranz, Karel, *Tatra passenger cars; 100 years* (Prague, no date)

Rosenkranz, Karel, *Tatra trucks; 100 years* (Prague, no date)

Rosenkranz, Karel and Jan Kozlovský, *K dějinám Tatry Kopřivnice; sborník příspěvků IV* (Kopřivnice, Czech Republic, 1990)

Ruffieux, R., *La Suisse de l'entre-deux-guerres* (Lausanne, 1974)

Sajer, Guy, *The forgotten soldier* (London, 1999)

Salis, J. R. de, *Switzerland and Europe; essays and reflections* (Abama, 1971)

Schacht, Hjalmar, *Account settled* (London, 1949)

Schacht, Hjalmar, *My first seventy-six years* (London, 1955)

Schlesinger, Rudolf, *Federalism in Central and Eastern Europe* (London, 1945)

Schramm, Percy Ernst, *Hitler; the man and the military leader* (London, 1972)

Serena, Gitta, *Albert Speer; his battle with truth* (London, 1996)

Shirer, William L., *The rise and fall of the Third Reich; a history of Nazi Germany* (London, 1998)

Sieberka, Paul, *Die tschechische Gefahr* (Munich, 1938)

Siedler, F. W., 'L'organisation Todt', *Revue d'histoire de la deuxième guerre mondiale et des conflits contemporains,* 134 (1984), pp. 33–58

Slouka, Mark, *The visible world* (London, 2008)

Smelser, Ronald M., 'The expulsion of the Sudeten Germans', *Nationalities Papers,* vol. 24, No. 1, March 1996, pp. 79–92

Smith, Lyn, *Forgotten voices of the Holocaust; a new history in the words of the men and women who survived* (London, 2005)

Smolky, Ivana and Folta, Jaroslav (eds), *Studie o technice v Českých zemích; 1918–1945* (Prague, 1995)

Šolc, Jiří, *Osudná rozhodnutí, kapitoly z historie československého odboje v letech 1939– 1945* (Prague, 2006)

Součková, Sylva, *Psáno osudem a politikou* (Prague, 2002)

Später, Jörg, *Britische Debatten über Deutsche und Nazis 1902–1945* (Göttingen, 2003)

Spick, Mike, *The illustrated directory of fighters* (London, 2004)

Špiesz, Anton, *Ilustrované dejiny Slovenska na ceste k sebeuvedomeniu* (Bratislava, 2002)

Stone, Norman and Strouhal, Edouard (eds), *Czechoslovakia; crossroads and crises 1918–1988* (London, 1989)

Stransky, Jan, *East wind over Prague* (Westport, Conn., 1979)

Ströbinger, Rudolf, *Poker o Prahu; posledních 100 dní protektorátu* (Olomouc, 1997)

Suppan, Arnold, 'Austrian, Czechs and Sudeten Germans as a community of conflict in the Twentieth Century, (Working Paper 06–1, Centre for Austrian Studies, University of Minneapolis, October 2006)

Svoboda, Oldřich, *Češi v Opavě a na Opavsku 1938–1945; vzpomínky III* (Prague, 2003).

Taborsky, Edward, *President Eduard Beneš between East and West 1938–1948* (Stanford, Cal, 1981)

Talpes, Ioan, 'La politique militaire de la Roumanie (1938–1940)', *Revue d'histoire de la deuxième guerre mondiale et des conflits contemporains*, 140 (1985), pp. 37–52

Teich, M. (ed), *Bohemia in History* (Cambridge, 1998)

Teichova, Alice, *An economic background to Munich; international business and Czechoslovakia 1918–1938* (Cambridge, 1974)

Teichova, Alice, *The Czechoslovak economy 1918–1989* (London, 1988)

Teichova, Alice and Cottrell, P. L. (eds), *International business and Central Europe, 1918–1939* (Leicester, 1983)

Teichova, Alice, Gourvish, Terry and Pogány, Agnes (eds), *Universal banking in the twentieth century; finance, industry and the state in North and Central Europe* (Aldershot, 1994)

Tesař, Jan, *Traktát o 'Záchraně národa'; texty z let 1967–1969 o začátku německé okupace* (Prague, 2006)

Thompson, S. Harrison, *Czechoslovakia in European history* (Hamden, Conn., 1965)

Tooze, Adam, *The wages of destruction; the making and breaking of the Nazi economy* (London, 2007)

Turkey, vol. 2 (Geographical Handbook Series, Naval Intelligence, Mar. 1943)

Turnock, David, *The economy of East Central Europe, 1815–1989; Stages of transformation in a peripheral region* (London, 2006)

Turnock, David, *The Romanian economy in the twentieth century* (Beckenham, 1986)

Turnwald, Wilhelm K. (ed), *Documents on the expulsion of the Sudeten Germans* (Munich, 1953)

Uhlíř, Jan B. and Kaplan, Jan, *Praha ve stínu hákového kříže* (Prague, 2005)

Ulrich, Herbert, *Fremdarbeiter, politik und praxis des 'Ausländer-Einsätzes' in der Kriegswirthschaft des Dritten Reichs* (Berlin, 1985)

Urner, Klaus, 'La Suisse pendant la guerre. Économie et neutralité. Neutralité et politique commerciale pendant la seconde guerre mondiale', *Revue d'histoire de la deuxième guerre mondiale* 121 (1981)

V zajetí smrtu (Most, Czech Republic, 1995)

Válka, Zbyněk, *Brno pod hákovým křížem* (Olomouc, 2004)

Válka, Zbyněk, *Olomouc pod hákovým křížem* (Olomouc, 2001)

Válka, Zbyněk, *Stíhací letadla 1939–45/Itálie, Francie, SSSR, Československo, Polsko, Holandsko, Švédsko, Austrálie* (Olomouc, 1999)

Vaněk, Miroslav, *Diana; továrna na smrt 1944–1945; z historie železniční trait Brno-Havlíčkův Brod* (Brno, 2003)

Vaňourek, Martin, *Hraničáři od Hlučína* (Mohelnic, Czech Republic, 2000)

Verrier, Anthony, *The bomber offensive* (London, 1974)

Vital, David, 'Czechoslovakia and the Powers, September 1938' *Contemporary History*, 1, 4 (1966), pp. 37–68.

Vondrovský, Ivo, *Pevnosti; architectura militaris; opevnění z let 1936–1938 na Slovanska* (Varnsdorf, Czech Republic, 1993)

Vrba, Jan, *Sebrané spisy Jana Vrby, LXXI; chodský černý týden* (Prague, 2001)

Wachsmann, Nicolaus, *Hitler's prisons, legal terror in Nazi Germany* (New Haven and London, 2004)

Walter, Rolf, *Zeiss 1905-1945* (Cologne, 2000)

Wheeler-Bennett, Sir John W., *Munich, prologue to tragedy* (London, 1948)

White, B. T., *Tanks and other AFVs of the Blitzkrieg era* (Poole, 1972)

Wiedemann, Andreas, *Die Reinhard Heydrich Stiftung in Prag 1942-1945* (Dresden, 2000)

Wiskemann, Elizabeth, *Czechs and Germans* (London, 1938)

Wiskemann, Elizabeth *Undeclared war* (London, 1967)

Wolf, Jacques, 'Le financement de la deuxième guerre mondiale; un essai de présentation', *Revue d'histoire de la deuxième guerre mondiale et des conflits contemporains* 144 (1986), pp. 1-18

Wylie, Neville, *Britain and Switzerland in the Second World War* (London, 2003).

Wyllie, James, *The warlord and the renegade; the story of Hermann and Albert Goering* (Stroud, 2006)

Young, Edgar P., *Czechoslovakia: keystone of peace and democracy* (London, 1938)

Zaharia, Gheorghe, 'La vie politique en Roumanie (1940–1944)' *Revue d'histoire de la deuxième guerre mondiale et des conflits contemporains*, 140 (1985), pp. 53-68

Zeman, Zbyněk, 'Czechoslovakia between the Wars: democracy on trial', in Morrison, J. (ed), *The Czech and Slovak experience* (London, 1992), pp. 163–6

Zgorniak, Marian, 'Forces armies allemandes et tchéchoslovaques en 1938', *Revue d'histoire de la deuxième guerre mondiale*, 122 (1981), pp. 61-72

Zimmermann, Volker, *Sudetští Němci v nacistickém státě; politika a nálada obyvatelstva v říšské župě uděty (1938-1945)* (Prague, 2001) [a Czech translation of Zimmermann, Volker, *Die Sudetendeutschen im NS-Staat* (Essen, 1999)]

Zvěřinová, Stanislava, *Devatenáct nám bylo pryč...* (Prague, 2001)

INDEX